MW00851111

"Beachhead Don"

"Beachhead Don"

REPORTING THE WAR
FROM THE EUROPEAN THEATER,
1942−1945

Don Whitehead

Edited by John B. Romeiser

FORDHAM UNIVERSITY PRESS

NEW YORK 2004

Copyright © 2004 John B. Romeiser

All rights reserved. No part of this publication may be reproduced, stored in a
retrieval system, or transmitted in any form or by any means—electronic,
mechanical, photocopy, recording, or any other—except for brief quotations
in printed reviews, without the prior permission of the publisher.

World War II: The Global, Human, and Ethical Dimension, No. 3
ISSN 1541-0293

Library of Congress Cataloging-in-Publication Data
Whitehead, Don, 1908–
"Beachhead Don" : reporting the war from the European Theater, 1942–1945
/ Don Whitehead ; edited by John B. Romeiser.— 1st ed.
p. cm. — (World War II—the global, human, and ethical dimension ; no. 3)
Collection of articles originally published in various American newspapers.
Includes index.
ISBN 0-8232-2412-0
1. World War, 1939–1945—Campaigns—Western Front. I. Romeiser,
John Beals, 1948– II. Title. III. Series. IV. World War II—
the global, human, and ethical dimension ; 3.
D756.W43 2004   940.54'21—dc22
2004019063

Printed in the United States of America
08 07 06 05 04   5 4 3 2 1
First edition

All reprinted material in this volume, including photographs and artwork,
is used with permission of the Associated Press.

*In fond and lasting memory of two extraordinary men
who served their country with distinction during the Second World War,
my father, George Clement Romeiser (U.S. Army, 1939–47),
and my father-in-law, Ronald Wesley Cornwall (U.S. Navy, 1941–81).*

GEORGE CLEMENT ROMEISER RONALD WESLEY CORNWALL
1917–1974 1922–1991

Contents

Foreword

W ARS have always attracted writers and journalists. Some writers pack off to the front lines simply because they want to be close to the action of the moment, while others yearn to be at the battlefront of history as it rises over the horizon.

One of the finest reporter-writers in World War II, who covered the action from the deserts of North Africa to the beaches of Normandy and beyond, was Don Whitehead, a war correspondent for the Associated Press.

After World War II, Whitehead covered the Korean War, for which he won a Pulitzer prize. In 1952 he earned his second Pulitzer for a story he wrote on President Dwight D. Eisenhower's trip to Korea after the presidential election. At that time, only seven other journalists in the history of the award had won two Pulitzers.

In 1959, Whitehead, born in 1908 in Inman, Virginia, became a columnist for the *Knoxville News-Sentinel* until he retired in 1978. He came out of retirement in 1980 to write once more for the *News-Sentinel*, and then died one year later.

During his fifty-year career, Whitehead, who called himself a "hillbilly at heart," wrote close to 12 million words, which included not only his newspaper columns and war stories, but also five books. *The FBI Story* became a best seller.

But it was his World War II coverage that earned him widespread notoriety, not only among his readers back home, but among peers in the trenches with him and also the boys on the front lines, because that's where he could be found.

Like his buddy, Scripps Howard's Ernie Pyle, Whitehead went with the troops, and he lived in the foxholes and tents to see for himself what war was all about. Writing in an inimitable style, he relayed those dreadful scenes in vivid and precise detail and with the color and horror that combat produces.

Whitehead once said that the Invasion of Normandy, when he landed at Omaha Beach with First Infantry Division, the "Big Red One," was one of the most exciting moments in his career. "Our boys had to fight it out at the water's edge. One of every three was killed or wounded. You just don't live through something like that without a little excitement," he once said.

The war took him to Cairo, Libya, Palermo, Sicily, Anzio, and Normandy.

He wrote stories about General George Patton's Seventh Army in the invasion of Sicily. He wrote of being behind German lines in Italy, of being surrounded by German forces at Brolo, Italy, and at Anzio, where he waded ashore with the troops. Later, he said that Anzio was "a nightmare and a bloody graveyard."

After Anzio, the AP sent Whitehead to England for some deserved rest. He promptly sought out General Omar N. Bradley, commander of the First Army. In talking to Bradley, Whitehead learned that the Normandy Invasion would come in three phases: the landing, the buildup of war supplies on the beachheads, and then the breakout into France to push the Germans back to Berlin.

Later reflecting on the war, Whitehead wrote:

> None who saw it can ever forget the horror of that day on Omaha Beach. None can forget the suffering, the sacrifice or the heroism of the soldiers and sailors who died or were maimed as they fought their way ashore with the odds four to three against them.
>
> Wave after wave of troops hit the beach and then flung themselves into the gravel, which gave them little protection from the German fire. They lay shoulder to shoulder as far as I could see in either direction. And each time a shell landed someone was killed or wounded.

And now with this book, Beachhead Don comes alive once more for many readers who were not born when World War II began, but are the grandsons and granddaughters of those who fought so long ago on those distant beaches.

Here, through John Romeiser's painstaking work in the University of Tennessee Hoskins Special Collections Library, which received all of Whitehead's papers and memorabilia from the family, you can read Whitehead's war stories as they appeared in the nation's major newspapers of the time.

This book, bound to become a text for future generations of war correspondents, begins in 1942, retaining Whitehead's datelines as they appeared, and moving on through to the war's end.

You are with Beachhead Don in all the dramatic North Africa and European landings, and especially in Normandy. He carries you along through the breakout in St-Lô and into Paris, and then on the Rhine with the First

Army. He crosses the Rhine and then is with U.S. soldiers when they meet the Russians on the Elbe River in a dramatic linkup of the two great armies of World War II.

The stories come to life as they did more than sixty years ago and are as wonderful to read now as then. They are just as important to this generation as they were to the Greatest Generation who fought the battles that Beachhead Don wrote about so eloquently. Thank goodness for John Romeiser's digging out these stories and taking us along on this journey with Beachhead Don, one of the best at the business of war writing.

Whitehead survived and went on to other battles and other wars when they called. As a journalist and as a writer, he had to go. And the nation is better for having had him there, telling us the story of war like no other war correspondent before or since.

These are masterful stories for any generation.

FRED BROWN

Acknowledgments

T HE genesis of this book came from a conversation with Fred Brown, senior writer for the *News Sentinel* in Knoxville, Tennessee, while he and I were traveling the lush, narrow lanes of the Norman countryside in June 2001. Fred was in France to write a series of articles on D-Day and on the University of Tennessee's Normandy Scholars program, which I was codirecting with my colleague Karen Levy. We had been talking about wartime journalism and our shared interest in how it evolved and came of age during World War II. It was then that Don Whitehead's name first surfaced. Fred said that I should investigate the Whitehead archives at the Hoskins Library Special Collections on our campus.

Upon my return from Europe, I immediately went to the Whitehead collection and discovered a treasure trove of letters, press clippings, scrapbooks, taped conversations, and photographs. A whole compelling life and distinguished journalistic career lay in wait on the dusty shelves of the Hoskins Library. It was evident that few people had looked at this material since Whitehead died January 12, 1981, and since his daughter, Ruth Whitehead Graham, had donated her father's memorabilia to the collection that same year. I knew that something needed to be done to bring to the attention of the public Whitehead's contributions as a journalist and eyewitness to some of the most significant events of the twentieth century. I decided to focus first on his voluminous World War II dispatches for the Associated Press. With the support and encouragement of Carolyn Hodges, my department head in Modern Foreign Languages and Literatures, I began to transcribe several hundred yellowed press clippings in three oversized scrapbooks. I was aided in this process by a graduate student, Claryce Caviness, who toiled with quiet efficiency and constant good humor. This book would never have seen the light of day without her careful reading of the original stories and diligent keyboarding skills. At the beginning of this process, I was also fortunate to receive technical guidance and assistance from Lesli Rowan, a 1999 Normandy Scholar and now a library research coordinator. In addition to her regular duties, Lesli devoted countless hours to scanning over a hundred Whitehead articles, as well as many photographs, and digitizing them for preservation and ease of access.

The Whitehead World War II stories themselves had originally been published in a variety of large-circulation U.S. newspapers, such as the *New York Herald Tribune, Chicago Tribune, Kansas City Times, Detroit News,* and smaller outlets such as the *Knoxville News-Sentinel* and *Charlotte Observer.* The transcriptions that follow are taken directly from the clippings and not from the original Associated Press wire stories. Consequently, it is essential to realize that the articles as printed in this book may not correspond word for word with the original wire service versions. It was the practice of copy editors to add or delete a few lines, and at other times rearrange the sequencing of the story, in order to meet certain layout and space constraints. This phenomenon will also help explain why some of the stories overlap in parts (e.g., see the articles from Part 4, June 18, and Part 5, August 26). Also, there is some variation in spelling and punctuation between the articles. It would, of course, have been preferable to use the original wire service reports, which I would have had to consult at the AP archives in New York. Time and finances would not permit such a venture. It is my fervent hope that readers of this book will agree that having access to the printed story that hit American newsstands and front porches during the war will compensate for this omission.

It was a special privilege to have the opportunity to meet two of Don Whitehead's family members—his daughter, Ruth Whitehead Graham, and granddaughter, Marie Weidus—during a visit to their home in Tulsa, Oklahoma. Both were generous in sharing their time and precious information about Don Whitehead. Ruth pointed me in the direction of her father's war diary, spanning the seven months he covered the campaigns in Egypt and North Africa with the British Eighth Army. Sadly, Ruth W. Graham has since passed away. My profound regret is that I was not able to spend more time with her, so that I could have learned more about Don Whitehead's intriguing life. Her offer of his meticulously kept war diary will, I hope, provide grist for another study of Whitehead, this one focusing on his life and career as a journalist and author. I thank Marie Weidus for allowing me to quote from the diary.

I would also like to express my appreciation to the many colleagues and friends who have guided me and provided invaluable assistance with this project: University of Tennessee librarians Anne Bridges and James Lloyd; David Lee, professor of German and my departmental colleague; Kurt Piehler, director of the University's Center for the Study of War and Society, who has also been my associate in the Normandy Scholars program;

Harriet and David Thomas, my sister and brother-in-law, for serving as my important Tulsa connection with the Whitehead family; and, of course, my eternally supportive wife, Carole, who has indulged my World War II "pastimes" for over a decade.

I would like to conclude with a special note of thanks and friendship for Command Sergeant Major Ben Franklin (First Infantry Division, Sixteenth Regiment), with whom I have enjoyed many hours of stimulating conversation about his World War II experiences. Walking along Omaha Beach on two occasions with Ben, and hearing him tell of how his landing boat was blown up at H-Hour on June 6, 1944, forcing him to swim ashore without equipment and start fighting the Germans yet again, after tough combat in North Africa and Sicily, have been truly unforgettable moments.

Introduction

JOURNALIST Don Whitehead hit the hostile shores of Sicily, Italy, and Normandy with U.S. invasion forces during World War II, yet his writings are little known. One of the preeminent reporters of America's mid-century, Whitehead developed a unique style of reporting that many journalists compare favorably with Ernie Pyle. Some say that his dispatches even surpassed Pyle's both in terms of their eloquence and intrinsic human interest. Whitehead's nickname was "Beachhead Don," recognizing him for having covered more Allied amphibious landings in the European theater than any other reporter. He later earned two Pulitzer prizes for his reporting of the Korean conflict. Despite many years of globe-trotting and working in world capitals, Whitehead remained close to his Appalachian roots, finishing out his career in Knoxville, Tennessee, where he and his wife, Marie, could return to the mountains they loved and be nearer to their relatives in Kentucky.

Born in Inman, Virginia, on April 8, 1908, newsman and author Don Whitehead became city editor of the *Harlan Daily Enterprise* in 1929 and covered the labor wars of the early 1930s in Harlan County, Kentucky. Whitehead's affiliation with the Associated Press began when he joined the wire service in 1935 as night editor in Memphis, Tennessee, and then became an AP correspondent in Knoxville from 1937 to 1940. In early 1941, Whitehead was transferred to New York as a feature writer. His salary increased from $65 to $85 per week, but only after he informed his boss in New York that he could not make ends meet on his Knoxville salary.

After the attack on Pearl Harbor in December 1941, Whitehead increasingly saw his assignments shift as he began to cover the preparations for war stateside, including the Lend-Lease shipments of bombers to England via Newfoundland and military maneuvers in the Carolinas, where recruits trained with logs on wheels in place of artillery and shouldered pieces of wood instead of rifles. He, like many, knew that the U.S. Army had a long way to go before it would be ready to tackle the disciplined, well-equipped troops of Nazi Germany and Imperial Japan. In August 1942, he was notified that he would be going overseas, and he began the process of being accredited as a war correspondent. In September of the same year, he was sent to Egypt, where he was assigned to the British Eighth Army as it began its campaign against General Erwin Rommel's Africa Corps. Whitehead's selection as a foreign correspondent came as a surprise to him, although he had been desperately wanting to write about more substantial topics than Manhattan "glitterati." As he once commented, "I wanted to be with the fighting men." In the first entry in his war diary, dated September 9, 1942, he wrote:

> Actually, I don't believe I ever thought I'd be chosen as a war correspondent for the A.P. It was one of those vague and incredible jobs, about which you read with a great deal of envy for those who were helping write the history of World War II. When I read the stories of Bob St. John and Larry Allen and Quentin Reynolds and Drew Middleton, I felt so restless and dissatisfied that my work became a burden of trivia. It seemed slightly absurd to be writing of movie stars, Harlem and front page celebrities when there was a war to write about—the raw material of death and agony and heroism.
>
> More and more I knew I could never be happy until I had a chance to report this war from a sideline seat. There would have been a gnawing frustration that would have poisoned me for years to come.[1]

After Rommel's defeat, Whitehead joined the U.S. Army in Algeria. He went on the invasion of Sicily with the First Infantry Division, landing at Gela, Italy, and then joined the U.S. Navy for the invasion of Italy at Salerno, before returning to the army to cover the Italian campaign. He landed at Anzio with assault forces in January 1944. Whitehead was then transferred from the Italian front to London to join AP's staff preparing for the invasion of France. He was able to return briefly to the States to see his family after seventeen months on assignment in North Africa. Once he arrived in London to cover the upcoming invasion of France, he joined the largest team of correspondents ever assembled to cover an event. The period of waiting and anticipation—not knowing where or when the assault would occur—was interrupted by some good news for Don Whitehead and for his close buddy Ernie Pyle. Whitehead learned that he had been selected to lead the AP invasion press team in Europe, and early on the morning of May 28 he got the call to report to join "Danger Forward," the code name for the First Infantry. From that moment, he knew that he would be going in on one of the early waves. In terms of Pyle's own success, Whitehead was standing in the AP office in London in early May when the story that Pyle had been awarded the Pulitzer came across the teletype. He immediately called the stunned

Pyle at the Dorchester Hotel with the good news, then went over to celebrate: "We tapped a bottle and had a little celebration there in his room." Pyle asked Whitehead if he was kidding about the Pulitzer, and Whitehead reassured him that he was not. Pyle then groaned and said he had lost a $100 bet with his boss, who had wagered that Pyle would win it.

The night of June 5, Whitehead was on board the *USS Samuel Chase*, the headquarters ship for the Sixteenth Regiment, as they prepared to head out into the English Channel. He remembered that the correspondents spent a lot of time studying the beach maps and that he was "nervous and scared like everyone else." Around 6 a.m., June 6, he climbed over the side of the *Chase* into a landing boat. The rough seas made him and the soldiers sick as dogs. He scrambled ashore on Omaha Beach at 8 a.m., with a small cadre of other correspondents, and headed for a German bunker that had been firing on them a short time before, until a navy destroyer silenced its 88-millimeter gun with three shots. He wrote his first story on the invasion, then learned that the radio jeep he and other reporters had counted on to transmit the dispatches had been knocked out. All he could count on initially was giving his stories to sailors headed back to London. Exhausted, with no real rest in almost forty-eight hours, Whitehead decided to take a sleeping pill and went to sleep in a foxhole, where Ernie Pyle eventually found him, later inspiring a famous story that appeared in Whitehead's hometown newspaper in Harlan, Kentucky. The headline, "Harlan Boy Speaks from Foxhole," was a classic and led to much kidding in the months to come. On a potentially more somber note, someone reported that he had seen Whitehead shot and go down on the beach and had shared the news with the AP office in New York. A well-intentioned colleague then called Marie to tell her the news before she heard it on the airwaves where it would have been a "spot of color." Once the truth was known, he and Marie joked that he would have been just a "spot of color" if he had been killed at Omaha Beach.

Whitehead then covered the fierce hedgerow fighting in Normandy, the fall of Cherbourg, the breakout at St-Lô, and the sweep across France. Stories were now getting out a lot faster ever since civilians had arrived with a press wireless unit. With the five-hour time difference on their side, he and other correspondents could go to the front, return to hammer out the story, and then transmit almost instantaneously to New York at a rate of 300 words a minute. "We were covering the war in Normandy as you would cover a story in Washington or New York," he remembered. Whitehead also got the first story through censorship on the liberation of Paris on August 25. Subsequently, he covered the drive of the U.S. First Army into Belgium and Germany.

In early December 1944, Whitehead returned to the United States for a well-deserved rest and reunion with his family, whom he had not seen in almost nine months. Unfortunately, he missed reporting the Battle of the Bulge, assuming "nothing much was going to happen," which was what he had been told by a trusted military confidant. During the years he had been away, his wife, Marie, had taken seriously the call for women to move into traditionally male roles and had become an airplane mechanic on Long Island where she, Don, and their daughter Ruth lived. But her "Rosie the Riveter" career was cut short after a disagreement with her foreman, who wanted to slow down a production line. She had told him to pick up the pace. She then went to work with an advertising agency for the remainder of the war.

Whitehead's first stop on his Christmas leave from the war zone was the home office of the Associated Press in New York, where he briefed the editorial staff. The interview, which humorously mentions the "Purple Heart" he should have won for gashing his hand opening a bottle of champagne to celebrate his arrival in New York ("I earned my Purple Heart after I got home. I damn near cut my thumb off"), raises the issue of continued heavy casualties before the war would end and the challenges faced by war correspondents: "You lose all contact with the home front and don't know when your stories are getting there unless the home office tells you." Pointing out that for press service correspondents the whole war had changed with the inception of improved communication facilities, he went on to add: "In the desert and in Sicily there was only one courier a day. We would spend plenty of time writing our stories. Sometimes I'd even rewrite mine and dress them up."[2] Anticipating the instantaneous global communications that war correspondents enjoy today, Whitehead remarked, "Now we have a flash-bulletin war. We're actually filing flash bulletins from the front. The campaign on the Western front has become the toughest in history to cover. I've never seen correspondents work so hard or under such pressure."

Whitehead was back on the line in late February 1945 to cover the crossing of the Roer and Rhine Rivers, the capture of the Remagen Bridge, the liberation of Buchenwald, and the meeting of American and Russian troops on the Elbe River just as the war ended in Europe. He tried to reach Berlin to report its fall, but failed this time, unlike his Paris venture. After the war ended, Whitehead was one of sixteen correspondents awarded the Medal of Freedom by President Harry S. Truman. During the 1950s, Whitehead served as Washington bureau chief for the *New York Herald Tribune* and wrote the first of five books, the best-selling *The FBI Story*, later made into a popular movie starring James Stewart. Whitehead returned to Knoxville in 1959 to begin writing thrice-weekly columns for the *News Sentinel*, a pleasant change from the grueling pace of war reporting and working in Washington, D.C. Whitehead died in Knoxville on January 12, 1981, at age seventy-two. His research notes, letters, press clippings, photographs, and taped interviews now belong to the University of Tennessee's Hoskins Library Special Collections, where they can be consulted by researchers and the general public.

Whitehead's biggest scoop was his eyewitness account of the liberation of Paris, the first such story to clear the censors and reach U.S. newspapers. Fellow AP journalist and friend Hal Boyle recorded the following sequence of events in a article dated August 25, 1944, from Rambouillet, France, thirty miles southwest of Paris:

A tiny, dust-covered jeep whirled into the driveway of the Hôtel Grand Veneur early this afternoon while scores of war correspondents milled about waiting for word when Allied troops would move into Paris.

Tall Don Whitehead, chief of the Associated Press staff in France, unlimbered his six-feet-one-and-a-half-inches and climbed stiffly out of the jeep. His face was dusty and streaked with perspiration from the broiling August sun as he ambled unhurriedly toward the hotel's lounge, converted into a press room.

"Where've you been, Don?" asked one correspondent sitting leisurely on a bench.

"Paris," said Whitehead.

Immediately he was surrounded by a surging crowd of correspondents all excitedly asking questions. Whitehead answered as many as he could in a few seconds and then sat down to his typewriter.

In exactly 45 minutes, he pounded out a 1,600-word account of the capture of Paris. It was the first eye-witness story of one of the most dramatic days of the war.

His spectacular accomplishment made ludicrous an opposition claim of a beat of an hour and a half on the first story out of Paris. This was evidently based on the fact that one of its correspondents grabbed the microphone of the Paris radio in violation of military censorship and got out a few words for which he was suspended by the SHAEF [Supreme Headquarters Allied Expeditionary Force].

Whitehead observed his signed pledge to clear his story through censorship and came out with the first real story, a complete and beautiful job.[3]

But his proudest accomplishment as a journalist was his reporting of the D-Day landings in Normandy, France, in June 1944. "It was one hell of a story," he recounted, "and you wanted to be there and see it and report it." Joining the First Infantry Division as they went ashore at Omaha Beach at H-Hour during the early dawn, Whitehead vividly recalled being pinned down on the beach by a German infantry division they did not expect to be there. "We didn't get off the beach for four hours," he recalled. "Then things began to move." He further described the horror of those agonizing initial minutes on "Bloody Omaha." Evoking a scene that might have inspired the graphic opening minutes of *Saving Private Ryan* over fifty years later, Whitehead reminisced:

> I remember the youth with one leg blown off who whimpered, "Please for God's sake, get me back to a ship." A medic gave him a shot of morphine and tried to stop the bleeding, but that's all he could do. Wounded boys lay shivering on the rocks with cold waves lapping over their legs, only their eyes appealing for help. But we couldn't help them. I remember troops digging into the gravel with their bare hands until blood dripped from their fingers—trying to get some cover from the mortar and machine guns and eighty-eights.

In that kind of chaos, when individual soldiers had to muster all they had to move forward, the voice of a commanding officer seemed heaven sent. Whitehead remembered one such miraculous moment:

> And then Colonel George Taylor yelled to his men: "Gentlemen, we're being killed on the beaches, let's move inland and be killed." And they began to drive up that ridge.
> That's what your soldiers went through on D-Day to break into Hitler's Europe. Many of them never got beyond the beach, but they helped open the way for thousands of others. None should ever forget their sacrifice.

When one attempts to assess the significance of Whitehead's contributions to war reporting during World War II, it is inevitable that Ernie Pyle's name will be invoked. In fact, Pyle is as indissolubly associated with this aspect of America's involvement in the Second World War as are such military leaders as General Dwight D. Eisenhower, General George S. Patton, and General Douglas MacArthur. Interestingly, Pyle himself honored Whitehead for his unflagging commitment as a war correspondent. It is clear they knew one another quite well and were good friends. Pyle is even reported to have commented once to other war correspondents in North Africa, "You know, none of us is fit to carry Don's typewriter."[4] Whitehead later paid equal tribute to Pyle, stating that "Ernie brought the greatest name out of WWII." Physically, Whitehead's more than six-foot frame dwarfed that of the diminutive Pyle in photographs taken of them together. The level of affection and esteem that Pyle held for Whitehead becomes especially apparent in *Brave Men*, a 1944 compilation of his columns, in which he described the preparations for Operation Overlord and the subsequent landings on the beaches of Normandy. Speaking of the twenty-eight correspondents destined to be in the assault group, Pyle wrote, "about two-thirds had already seen action in various war theaters. The old-timers sort of gravitated together, people such as Bill Stoneman, Don Whitehead, Jack Thompson, Clark Lee, Tex O'Reilly and myself." Referring to Whitehead specifically, Pyle commented, "Men like Don Whitehead and Clark Lee who had been through the mill so long and so boldly, began to get nerves. Frankly, I was the worst of the lot and continued to be."[5] Whitehead himself reminisced about Ernie Pyle: "I never had the feeling that my number was up. But Ernie felt he wouldn't make it to the end of the war."

Pyle also lauded Whitehead in the section of *Brave Men* recounting the D-Day landings on June 6:

> Don Whitehead hit the beach with one regiment just an hour after H-hour. They were on the beaches for more than four hours under that hideous cloudburst of shells and bullets.
>
> Whitehead was still asleep when I went to his foxhole. I said, "Get up, you lazy so-and-so." He started grinning without even opening his eyes, for he knew who it was.
>
> It was hard for him to wake up. He had been unable to sleep from sheer exhaustion, and had taken a sleeping tablet.[6]

And a bit later, after reminding the reader that war is romantic only when you are far away from it, Pyle paid homage to Whitehead's accomplishments as master of the beach assault:

> Whitehead had probably been in more amphibious landings than any other correspondent over there. I know of six he made, four of them murderously tough. And he said, "I think I have gone on too many of these things. Not because of what might happen to me personally, but I've lost my perspective. It's like dreaming the same nightmare over and over again, and when you try to write you feel that you have written it all before. You can't think of any new or different words to say it with."
>
> I only knew too well what we meant.[7]

There has been speculation over the years as to the degree of Whitehead's influence on Pyle's wartime reports. One apocryphal scenario even had Whitehead writing the poignant account of the dead Captain Waskow in Italy ("This One Is Captain Waskow"), for which Pyle later received a Pulitzer, because he was too inebriated at the time to do the story. Retired Command Sergeant Major Ben Franklin recounts a lunch he once had with Whitehead in the early 1960s. They met at the Andrew Johnson Hotel dining room in Knoxville to discuss their war experiences. Whitehead had covered Franklin's Sixteenth Regiment during their landings at Omaha Beach. While talking about Normandy, Franklin said to Whitehead, "You must have won some prizes for your D-Day reporting," to which he replied, "Yes, but the first one I didn't get credit for." Whitehead then asked Franklin whether he was familiar with the Captain Waskow story later published in *Brave Men*. He went on to say, "Unfortunately, I can't reclaim that prize." Franklin then pressed Whitehead for more details. Whitehead remarked that Pyle was "off on a binge" and that there was pressure to do the story. Since Pyle was not around the press tent, Whitehead decided to "write the story on it."[8]

Whitehead provided a somewhat different account a decade later when interviewed about the Captain Waskow story. However, his version can be read on several levels. Calling the Waskow tribute "one of the great stories of the war," he remembered how Pyle came back from the front to the old Caserta palace outside Naples where the correspondents were billeted and based:

> He was absolutely whipped physically and mentally. I was with him in the room where he wrote the story. He asked me to read it, because he was afraid he had lost his touch. He said, "I don't think it's worth a damn. I've just lost my feeling." I read it and then told him, "My God, Ernie, if you've lost your touch writing that story, I hope I can lose mine!"

It was a beautiful story, Whitehead recalled, noting that he helped Pyle "get it back to New York where it deserved the play it got and the attention it deserved." All the same, it is intriguing to speculate what he had in mind when he said he helped Pyle "get" the story back to New York.

When one noted war correspondent pays a glowing tribute to another of his profession, that is the highest form of praise. Whitehead once received such commendation from Quentin Reynolds, a top-flight correspondent for *Collier's* magazine. Reynolds told of a gathering of correspondents at the Hotel Scribe press headquarters in Paris near the end of the war, at which the discussion turned to the correspondent who had done the best job of reporting. It was decided to take an informal vote among the twenty-three writers present. Twenty-one votes went to Don Whitehead. It was an accurate appraisal of a man who did not boast or engage in one-upsmanship, instead contenting himself by writing fairly, with razor-sharp clarity, of the events he had witnessed.

If Pyle has achieved everlasting fame as the war reporter of 1942–45, just as Bill Mauldin did for his Willie and Joe cartoons, it is, nonetheless, important to keep in mind that the type of wire service reporting that Whitehead was assigned to carry out departed significantly from that of Pyle and of many other World War II journalists. While human interest anecdotes often punctuate Whitehead's dispatches, the primary focus was on conveying clearly what was happening at the front lines to readers back home, so they could get a sense of how the war was progressing. He had to follow the official AP press creed, as expressed through the words of one of its own correspondents: "My business is to communicate facts; my instructions do not allow me to make any comment upon the facts. My dispatches are sent to papers of all manner of politics. I therefore confine myself to legitimate news and I try to be truthful and impartial."[9] Moreover, Whitehead, like most combat reporters, was fully cognizant of the respect and devotion that were owed to the frontline troops. He also expressed his fears while on the job—not so much of losing his life or of being wounded, but of getting the story right. "I was scared to death every story I went on," he once remarked, "and I stayed that way. Guess it was the Depression." Growing up during the lean years following the crash on Wall Street, Whitehead knew that his family's survival depended on his writing skillfully and efficiently.

However, Whitehead did recollect one time when he experienced fear as he had never known it before. It happened in December 1943, during the attack on the German positions in San Pietro, Italy. He had joined an infantry platoon for the assault and was watching the German troops in the distance through a pair of field glasses. There was a sudden "whoosh," and a mortar shell dropped so close that it knocked him off his feet. He reacted instinctively by clawing his way up the hill like an animal. Heart pounding, he finally regained control of himself. There, Whitehead stated, "I learned for the first time what it meant to be afraid. I understood that fear does not mean cowardice. It controls a man for a while then you shake it off." One way of dealing with the fear and pressure was to relax in whatever bars they could find or with stolen caches of wine and spirits left behind by the retreating Germans. As Whitehead recalled, "Those days we drank more than we should have."

Reporting the hard facts of battle and the progress in the war was central to Whitehead's task as a war correspondent. Unlike Pyle, and the countless authors and magazine writers who flocked to Europe and Asia to cover the most amazing story they would ever observe, Whitehead infrequently used first-person narration when reporting a battle or invasion. With few exceptions, each story would begin with a sentence or two situating the story geographically and describing what the weather conditions were like. In Italy, for example, the weather conditions were miserable for most of the months that Allied troops were slogging their way north toward Rome. Whitehead's technique, not unlike that of film, was to begin with an establishing shot to situate the story contextually. Next, he would add supporting detail through interviews with officers and enlisted men. Hometowns of the troops were always listed so that family and friends could establish a personal connection. Finally, he would often drop in a human interest anecdote dealing with either the soldiers or local inhabitants.

Whitehead got as close as he could to the actual fighting. In World War II, reporters were free to move around without significant restriction. He remembered that he had not gone that close to the front lines in the early weeks in Egypt, but then he met *Time* magazine correspondent Jack Belden, who was also with the British Eighth Army. Whitehead said that Belden would disappear from time to time, and the other correspondents wondered where he was and what was going on. One day Whitehead asked him where he had been, and Belden replied that he had been up front with the troops. Whitehead realized that he "had not been covering the war as it should have been covered." "From that time on," he recalled, "I decided I would use the Belden approach to reporting and get as close as I possibly could to the fighting," despite the dangers. Later, during the invasion at Salerno, Belden's leg was shattered by machine gun fire. Whitehead was concerned that he would lose the leg, but excellent medical care allowed him to keep it, although "he always walked with a limp after that."

Still another unique perspective that Whitehead provided in his war coverage was the view from the sea. While Pyle and most other correspondents trudged along the muddy roads and mountain trails with the infantry and armored regiments (which Whitehead did extensively as well), Don Whitehead also sought to portray the superlative contributions of the U.S. and Allied Navies in tackling Hitler's Fortress Europe. For one thing, he realized in Sicily for the first time that he could actually see shells from navy destroyers in flight. Here is an example of Whitehead's appreciation for naval contributions written in his characteristic, taut prose on board the *USS Biscayne* September 16, 1943:

Seven days after the first assault troops swarmed over the beaches to establish a bridgehead on Italian soil, the enemy still is blasting at our ships from the skies with hit and run attacks by small forces slipping through the Allied fighter protection. Five and six times each day the ship's loudspeaker crackles with the general quarters alarm. Sailors boil up from the lower decks to their battle stations. Portholes are closed, hatches are closed and the gunners point their weapons at the sky waiting for the attack.

And then the ship is tense with expectancy, shipboard life freezes into hard resistance. Small boats scurry away from the large ships. One moment there is the calm inaction of peace. The next moment the lid is blown off with a gush of anti-aircraft from hundreds of guns as enemy planes come within range, usually diving out of a bright sun. That's when your stomach turns into a hard knot and you crouch involuntarily, watching to see if a bomb is dropping your way, while the smaller ack-ack guns hammer away and the larger guns cause the ship to shudder.

Censorship both impeded and provided an incentive to Don Whitehead, as it did for many frontline journalists. On at least one occasion, he railed against the censors for preventing a "friendly fire" story from reaching the public during the operations in Gela, Sicily. Allied ships had mistakenly fired on their own planes carrying paratroopers to a drop zone near the German lines. Whitehead was ready to do the story, but he was told by military censors that sending the dispatch would have given "aid and comfort" to the enemy. In retrospect, he said, the story should have been told from the very first. As it turned out, the unplanned, scattered drop of paratroopers from planes trying to escape the friendly fire actually created tremendous confusion for the Germans and facilitated the assault.

On another occasion, Whitehead had uncovered what he knew could be a scoop of monumental proportions. He had interviewed an Italian officer who had made his way from Rome to the Salerno beachhead, where he informed Whitehead through an interpreter that Benito Mussolini had been arrested and thrown in prison, then later had been helped to escape by the Germans. Whitehead immediately pounded out the story with a dateline of September 9, 1943, knowing that it was front-page material. However, navy censorship held it up for a week, at which time official sources released the same information from Rome. By then, Whitehead recalled, the story "didn't do much good," since it was old news.

Another major scoop that did make it home in a timely way occurred after the Anzio landings January 22, 1944. After wading in to shore from an LST (landing ship, tank) at 2 a.m., his typewriter strapped to his back in a plastic bag, Whitehead found a quiet place to sit down and compose. He was astonished that there was not any significant German resistance, no guns flashing from the surrounding countryside. It was in eerie contrast to the unfriendly reception they had received at Gela and Salerno. In fact, as he remembered, the only German he saw on the beach was a soldier making love to an Italian girl. When the German started to run, "the poor guy was cut down by machine gun fire." Whitehead did not recall what happened to the girl, only that she must have "got home in a hurry, because her father was probably out looking for her."

After finishing his story—correspondents were limited by the censors to only 200 words for the Anzio landing—he ran to the truck that contained a radio for press transmissions. They had been told that their stories would be sent to Naples in the order of receipt by the censor. Unfortunately, Whitehead arrived about the same time as his chief opponent, UPI (United Press International) correspondent Reynolds Packard. "We had worked against each other for a long time," Whitehead recalled.

> Well, we had a big argument about whose dispatch was going to be sent first. I said that I was there first and that my story was going to go first and that if my story didn't go first, I was going to tear the radio off that truck barehanded. The argument was settled, and my story went first. No sooner had those 200 words cleared than the radio broke down. So for twenty-four hours, I had the only story off the beach. That was one of those times when you got credit for something you didn't deserve.

Not long after America joined the war against the Axis powers, E. B. White (*Harper's* magazine, April 1942) expressed his frustration with the war reporting he had witnessed so far:

> Quite apart from the emphasis, the newspaper reader finds it very difficult to get at the truth of any situation, through the great mass of conjecture and rumor and conflicting statements. Often, he feels completely baffled and defeated. This is not the fault of the press—it is just that the war is too big and moves too fast and the facts are not always available. The news is the privilege which the customer enjoys, but it is also the crossword puzzle which he alone must solve. One moment he experiences the full flush of victory, the next moment the chill of defeat. From two stories on the same page, sometimes from two paragraphs in the same story, he runs the whole gamut.[10]

As is clearly demonstrated in his reporting, Don Whitehead was not only an accomplished writer, he epitomized the consummate war correspondent. His accounts of the battles, while excelling in their accuracy and authority, are imbued with a human element that transforms them into compelling vignettes of battle. It is equally clear that Whitehead was respected by officers and enlisted men alike. Frequent quotations from high-ranking officers as well as privates and corporals indicate that he was trusted and well liked. Moreover, there are an unflagging optimism and hopefulness in Whitehead, a dramatic departure from the darkness exhibited in other war accounts. In his articles, it is crystal clear to him that the Allies will eventually win the war. American ingenuity and resolve will overcome German efficiency and fanaticism. In addition, though mounting U.S. casualties are mentioned, they are not underscored. The pathos—and there is a great deal of it in the poignant stories he tells—more often than not can be traced in the faces of the innocent victims of the war, especially the displaced civilian populations of the aged, women, and children.

Don Whitehead's reportorial voice, while not unique, was that of one of countless journalists who, like the men and women they wrote about, suffered the same hunger and cold, and likewise risked their lives in the prosecution of what we now call the Good War. Although this book does not set out to provide a biography of the man, aiming instead to let his eloquent dispatches speak for themselves, it does offer a glimpse into his character. Louis Menand has written that historical research tends to cut us off by a wall of print from the life we have set out to represent: "You can't observe historical events; you can't question historical actors; you can't even know most of what has been written about."[11] While all this may be true, it is nonetheless undeniable that Whitehead's war reporting captures the spirit of the time and provides stark snapshots of soldiers and civilians sucked into the vortex of merciless combat. And in doing so, it affords us a vision of his own personality and psyche.

For his last official dispatch from Europe after the war had drawn to a close, Whitehead fittingly returned to Normandy in early June 1945, just one year after the landings that had opened the road to Berlin and the toppling of the Nazi regime. It is perhaps the most poignant and moving report he wrote, blending his personal lyricism with an elegiac tribute to those who had paid the supreme sacrifice. Recalling the agonizing scenes from twelve months before, Whitehead observed:

Men were dying by the scores or their bodies were being torn by flying chunks of steel. Boats were sinking before they could get their human cargoes to the water's edge. Tanks, trucks and guns were being knocked out by enemy fire before they could get into action. Doughboys hugged their bodies against the shallow cover of a gravel embankment in a common misery of fear. . . .

But waves and shifting sands have covered most of the signs of the great invasion battle. Rusting skeletons of ships still are clutched in the brown sand as gaunt monuments to a monumental victory. They lie with broken backs or with gaping holes in their sides just as they died in battle.

High on the beaches are LCVP's [landing craft, vehicle, personnel], some of them with ramps lowered as they were when a shell hit them. They stand in an orderly row as though they just had raced in to put troops ashore.

Gearing back to peacetime came as a challenge to Don Whitehead, just as it did to scores of other correspondents and returning GIs. As he wrote in July 1945,

War reporting had become a way of life for most of us, with discomforts and danger a part of the job. We always knew where the story was—it was out there where doughboys were fighting. Then came the surrender and that assignment was finished except for mopping-up operations on stories that had not yet been told. Personally, I'll always remember the letdown that came with the war in Europe. There was a tremendous relief that the killing had ended, plus a sort of mental and physical lethargy. Nothing for a time seemed of much importance. It hardly seemed that peace had come.

He remembered that there were no celebrations by the combat troops, just general relief.

It would be another five years, when hostilities broke out on the Korean peninsula, before Don Whitehead could return to the war reporting that he loved so passionately and performed with such distinction. For his efforts, he received two Pulitzer prizes and recognition for journalistic excellence that was long overdue.

NOTES

1. Quoted from Don Whitehead's unpublished war diary covering September 19, 1942, to April 1, 1943.
2. This and many of the other anecdotes and quotations mentioned here came from a series of twenty-six taped conversations with Don Whitehead, recorded by the University of Tennessee Public Radio Services in the late 1970s. Their exact recording dates are unknown.
3. AP *Inter-Office* magazine, September 1944, pp. 9, 34.
4. This appeared in the *Harlan (KY) Daily Enterprise*. The exact date is unknown.

5. Ernie Pyle, *Brave Men*, Intro. by G. Kurt Piehler. Lincoln and London: University of Nebraska Press, 2001, p. 376.

6. *Brave Men*, p. 388.

7. *Brave Men*, p. 389.

8. Interview with Command Sergeant Major Ben Franklin, 14 February 2003.

9. AP *Inter-Office* magazine, November 1943

10. E. B. White, "Sugar-Coating the War News: February 1942," in *Reporting World War II, Part One: American Journalism 1938–1944*. New York: The Library of America, pp. 301–302.

11. *The New Yorker*, March 24, 2003, p. 80.

A Note to the Reader: Every effort has been made to verify the accuracy in spelling of place names and the names of individuals. However, due to the transmitted state of the wire dispatches and their subsequent distribution to hundreds of newspapers throughout the country, as well as variations in style practices from newspaper to newspaper, there may still be some inconsistency in spelling.

Although there may be some duplication of material from story to story, we have opted to include such articles, especially the accounts of the Paris liberation, because there is usually a fresh slant or the inclusion of new information.

One

PRELUDE, 1942

New York, January 3 — When the guns are spiked, the banners furled and the bombers are quiet again, there still will be a thrilling tale to tell of the courage and high adventures of the men who are writing the history of the war in the news. It's a crazy, incredible pattern in the scarlet fabric of a world at war, following the blitzkrieg across Europe, through the Balkans, over the frozen wastes of Soviet Russia, the parched sands of Libya and into the Pacific.

For two years the war correspondents for the Associated Press have stayed on the heels of the marching armies, or else have been just one jump ahead fighting a day and night battle to get the news to the United States. They've lived out of suitcases and rucksacks for weeks at a time while skipping from one strategic point to another in an exhausting, nerve-racking race with time and censors. But they came through with the news from the bomb-battered capitals and shell-pocked villages despite some fantastic brushes with death along the way. Two were wounded and narrowly escaped the tragedy of Edward J. Neil, the A.P. correspondent who was killed in the Spanish Civil War.

Up in the hills of Massachusetts near the little town of Methuen lies the grave of Eddie Neil. Eddie was a big, blond, laughing giant of a man with a lusty love for life and the things that make it tick. He was one of the best-known sports writers in the nation—but that wasn't enough for Eddie. He wanted to be a war correspondent. He went to Ethiopia to see Signor Mussolini's legions conquer the black tribes of the Lion of Judah. When the Spanish Civil War began he went to Spain. Wherever the action was heaviest, Eddie was likely to be there. On the last day of 1937, a shell exploded near his car. It was war's end for Eddie Neil—but the story he started in the desolate hills of Ethiopia is still being written.

The conflict caught up with others finally when the Axis powers declared war on the United States, and now they're fretting in Berlin, Rome, Shanghai and Tokyo waiting for release through an exchange of nationals among belligerent nations. But on the Allied side, their fight still goes on. The cables and wireless messages filed from the battle zones add new chapters to the story which already has become the unfinished saga of journalism.

Most of the war correspondents for the A.P. are small-town boys from places like Chickasha, Okla., Selma, Ala., Mount Savage, Md., or Mineola, Texas, although some come from the large cities. Probably none of them ever dreamed that one day he would be sitting on the rim of a man-made hell watching an epic struggle between the world's military giants.

Sometimes the vantage point is the deck of a mighty battleship blasting an enemy harbor or fighting off swarms of enemy bombers. Sometimes it's a sandy knoll overlooking a raging battle of tanks. It might be from a London rooftop as the incendiaries and explosives rain down or on the icy plains of Russia strewn with wreckage of the retreating Nazi armies. But wherever they might be, they're watching the greatest story of their lifetime unfold in an eruption of death and destruction on a scale of unbelievable proportions.

Life was pretty placid for a thirty-year-old Tom Yarbrough until the day two years ago he set sail for England to become a war correspondent. A native of Chickasha, Okla., he was graduated from the state university and served a hitch with the *Oklahoma City Times* before joining the A.P. in 1935. He worked in Kansas City, St. Louis and New York and grabbed at the chance to see this war for himself. He didn't wait long. One night in London the sirens screamed an air raid warning. The searchlights shot their beams into the skies seeking the Nazi planes dropping bombs on the city.

And then it was that Tom Yarbrough saw death dealt from a cold deck. The calm voice of an official said, "It is feared casualties may be heavier than recent nights." But Tom wasn't calm. "I saw rescue workers bring the still forms of a baby and five women from the basement of a flaming bomb-shattered home in northeastern London," he says . . . and that was during just one ambulance ride to gather up the dead and injured. "Then I watched a woman ambulance driver pump faint signs of life into two of the women victims while the bombs still thundered around us and anti-aircraft guns boomed in answer."

Tom rode through this carnage watching the rescue work, and as a gray dawn began to dispel the ghostly gloom, the woman ambulance driver said to him: "Thank God. There's always hope with the dawn." The A.P. decided to shift Yarbrough to Cairo. He was routed by way of Honolulu. His ship eased into the harbor one bright Sunday and Yarbrough had traveled halfway around the world in time to see the Japanese strike their surprise blow against America's Pacific outposts. He thought at first it was merely a big-scale war game until a bomb fell a few yards from the ship. Someone said this was the real McCoy. So Yarbrough pitched in to help report the battle of the Pacific.

Remember the "phony phase" of this war? This was way back in the early days of 1940 when the French and Germans eyed each other from the sup-posedly impregnable Maginot and Siegfried lines. But the Germans struck through the lowlands and one May day Drew Middleton sat in a dingy little bomb-shaken hotel somewhere in Belgium and wrote: "Allied troops, ready for a storm, found themselves in the path of a hurricane today . . . the hurri-cane rides on the wings of the German air force."

Confused, hopeless days followed as the French and British vainly tried to stem the first rush of the German assault that was to end at Dunkirk and Paris. Drew watched the terror mount among the people and this lad who once flunked an English course in college wrote some of the most moving stories to come out of the war. "There was two-way traffic on the roads," he said, "moving toward the distant sound of guns were British men, materials and munitions in trucks . . . moving painfully away from the guns was anoth-er army, the army of the homeless and stricken . . . .[T]heir voices haunt you."

Ordered with other correspondents to leave Belgium, Drew returned to London. But London wasn't refuge because the bombers followed. On one occasion Middleton watched the Germans pour tons of explosives on Croy-don airport, but even among this destruction he noted that "one mother herded her brood of seven before her like a scene from a Mother Goose book."

During one particularly savage air raid, G. H. P. Anderson, a reporter for the A.P. of Great Britain, watched on the rooftop while Middleton and the others worked below. "They're dropping a goodish bit of stuff," Anderson called down. A few minutes later a bomb fell on the A.P. building. Opera-tions were shifted to another previously prepared building and the work continued. The boys in the London bureau took a terrific pounding at the height of the assault on England. Bureau Chief Bob Brunelle, late of Asheville and Atlanta, was knocked out of bed by a bomb and each of his mates had similar experiences. Anderson later was transferred to the Libyan front and was captured by Axis forces. He is believed to be held in Rome. Middleton has transferred his operations to Iceland. He was on hand to get the first eyewitness story of the U-boat attack on the United States destroy-er *Kearney*. It's a lonely vigil, but things have a way of happening wherever Middleton may be.

In a London apartment a phonograph was blaring "Night and Day" and Eddy Gilmore was drumming out the rhythm with his fingers when the Luftwaffe paid one nocturnal call. Eddy grabbed a tin hat and ran out in time to see all hell break lose. He got his story and rushed back to write: "If my heart would just get out of my mouth for a few minutes, perhaps I could write this story." Eddy's a guy who finds something funny in everything, even a war. He's given this one a touch of the ridiculous. Fat and thirty-four, he hadn't been in England long before he reported that the R.A.F. pilots were making low altitude reconnaissance flights—over a nudist camp.

A Selma, Ala., product, Eddy became a war correspondent after newspaper experience in Selma, Atlanta and Washington. One day in London he listened respectfully to official warnings that a stranger wandering about England's blacked-out countryside was in danger from vigilant home guards, police and troops and other defenders of British soil. Eddy wasn't convinced. He had to see for himself. And one night he traveled 150 miles with a friend through England asking dozens of questions—and even visiting an anti-aircraft station—without getting a single challenge. Eddy's in Russia now where even a fat man can get cold, but the bets are that not even the sub-zero weather can freeze the Gilmore humor.

For two years thirty-three-year-old Larry Allen, of Mount Savage, Md., lived a charmed life riding the blue waters of the Mediterranean with the British fleet—but his luck almost played out a few days ago when he was wounded by a German bomb. Robert St. John, now an N.B.C. news commentator, was the first A.P. casualty in the current war. He was wounded by a machine gun bullet in Greece. They call Larry the "Darling of the Mediterranean Fleet" and when all the returns are in the story of Larry Allen will be a volume by itself, for no other single war correspondent has watched the naval warfare that Larry has seen.

He saw the British shell Tripoli. He was aboard a flagship when the fleet knocked a hole in Mussolini's sea power by sinking three Italian warships in a day-long battle. He rode with the British when they slipped past the heel of the Italian boot into the Adriatic and battered Valona in one of the most daring naval adventures of the war. Allen was on hand for the Bardia siege which lasted for eighteen days and he was aboard the *Illustrious* as she took a terrific battering from the Nazi and Italian bombers. Wherever the fleet went, Allen was there.

"This is the toughest Annapolis in the world," he once said, and told how it feels to watch a bombing attack on a battleship: "Now I lie flat on the deck and hope bombs won't come too close. I cannot imagine any greater hell on earth than when the thousand-pound bombs hit the warship. My heart is beating like a heavy pendulum. . . ."

And there are many others—J. Reilly O'Sullivan, who hails from Kansas City, seems to attract war like a magnet—he was in Amsterdam when the Germans invaded the lowlands—he went to Budapest in time to see the Balkans aflame—he ducked into Greece and helped write the story of Greece's fall—and now he's in Ankara, another trouble spot.

A Harvard vocational adviser told Henry C. Cassidy, thirty-two-year-old Bostonian, that he was "too bashful" to be a newspaper man and advised him to take up a teaching career—but Cassidy's the A.P. veteran covering the Russian campaign—he took the assignment after watching France fall.

But even in the midst of the grim business of war, there are scenes that might have been lifted from a comic opera . . . such as the time an A.P. correspondent quelled an Arab riot in Barce, Libya, with two rocks, a stout stick and an air of authority. Preston Grover of Farmington, Utah, who has been with the British forces battering across Libya, walked far ahead of a motor column recently during a lull in the fighting. When he entered the town of Barce, he found one hundred Italians cowed by a rioting mob of Arabs looting the place. Grover called on the English-speaking hotel manager.

"Tell these Arabs," he said, "that if looting and shooting are not stopped, the English will execute at least fifty when they enter the town." And then the undaunted Grover calmly went about organizing an Italian committee to receive the British armed forces.

On Christmas eve in Manila, big Clark Lee of Oakland, Cal., was tired and muddy and unshaven after four days in the wild country on the island of Luzon. But he had a great story—the first eyewitness account of the Japanese invasion along the Lingayen Gulf, of how American and native troops blasted at the waves of little brown men in an heroic defense that still continues. Lee started out in immaculate white, but he returned in a borrowed khaki shirt and denim trousers after dodging Japanese bombs, trudging mountain trails with native guides, and sleeping in a blacked-out native village in the headman's hut. Once he jumped behind a rock seeking shelter from shrapnel and hung over the edge of a 200-foot precipice. A few hours after he left a railway station, Japanese planes smashed it and left twenty-one dead.

One day last month a message came from Berlin over the A.P. printer in Bern, Switzerland, saying: "We're being jugged. Gotta go now. Good-bye." It meant that Louis Lochner, dean of the A.P.'s European staff, and his men were being taken into custody by the Germans pending an exchange of nationals. Those held with Lochner, who hails from Springfield, Ill., are Alvin J. Steinkopf, Minnesota farm boy, Edwin Shanke, of Milwaukee, Angus Thuermer, of Quincy, Ill., and Ernest G. Fischer, of Bartlett, Texas. The same thing had happened elsewhere. Richard G. Massock of Blue Mound, Ill., is held in Rome; Max Hill of Colorado Springs and Joseph Dynam of Chicago are held in Tokyo; Relman Morin, of Freeport, Ill., is a prisoner at Saigon; and Morris J. Harris of Columbia, Mo., and J. D. White, of Appleton, Mo., are interned by Japanese at Shanghai.   □

An Air Base Somewhere in Newfoundland, July 22 — We called our big bomber the "Flying Dutchman" when we saw the slim, dapper pilot who was to sit at the controls of the 3,000-mile flight from Canada to Britain. . . . For in his homeland Hans is listed officially as dead. He is only a ghost pilot. Hans is not his real name. It wouldn't be safe for the family he left in the Netherlands if the Germans knew he was still riding the skyways, piloting bombers to Britain.

Hans was in Rotterdam when the Germans struck at his country. He saw the bombers rip the city apart, leaving thousands dead in the smoldering rubble. And a hate was born that will never die. With four companions, he fought his way to Belgium and into France, and then escaped to England to join the British fleet air arm. A year ago he came with the Royal Air Force Ferry Command which is co-operating with Canadians and Americans in getting bombers across the oceans to the fighting fronts. He looked too slender to handle the big Consolidated Liberator but then his looks were deceiving.

There were twelve of us besides the crew of five who clambered up the hatchway into the belly of the bomber to crouch in the bomb bay. Later we could walk around and look the ship over, but the weight had to be forward for takeoff. Nine of the passengers were going all the way to Britain. Three of us—a uniformed young Newfoundland woman, Wide World photographer George Hill, of Boston, and myself—were stopping off at the ferry command airdrome somewhere in Newfoundland, a skyway stop through which the United States, Britain, and Canada are pouring planes and aircrew personnel to the fighting fronts.

Everyone was a little self-conscious, trying to appear unconcerned about the flight ahead. We fidgeted with the parachute harness, joked about our appearances, peered down at the pile of 'chute packs lying beside the hatchway, the only exit if a jump had to be made. A few hours before, a young R.A.F. flight lieutenant had told us how to use the oxygen masks in case the pilot climbed into the thin air over 14,000 feet. They were to be plugged into oxygen vents in the walls of the ship. "And by all means don't go to sleep," he warned. We had been fitted for a parachute harness by a grinning oldster named Charlie who found the whole procedure very amusing. He also gave us our parachute packs. "Listen," someone said, "if I have to jump and this thing doesn't open, I'm coming back to give you hell."

"Ain't nobody come back to complain yet," Charlie chuckled. He still was grinning when we climbed into the Flying Dutchman. Our "ghost pilot" taxied to the end of the long runway beside which dozens of bombers waited for crews to take them across, perhaps today, perhaps tomorrow.

Suddenly Hans swung the ship about. He had clearance orders. The four motors roared. The ship vibrated. Slowly it gathered speed, bumped slightly, lifted smoothly, and began its climb for the 1,000-mile flight to Newfoundland. The clouds below were a fairyland fantasy, fields of cotton out of which jutted fluffy mountains of spun sugar. Hans drove the ship on and an American pilot passenger shook his head approvingly: "The guy can really fly an airplane. You could feel it as soon as he began his run for the takeoff."

Most of the ferry captains taking bombers to Britain are like Hans, a strange breed of men who have flocked into Canada from all parts of the world. There are Canadians, Norwegians—but the majority of the civilian pilots are Americans. They are mature, experienced aviators with thousands of hours of flight-time in commercial aviation, air races, private flying and the old barnstorming days. Put wings on a bathtub and they could fly the thing. They'd laugh in your face if you called them daredevils. But there's no better way to describe them. Not so many years ago the Atlantic was a challenge and a death trap. The challenge still is there, but experience and the swift advance of aviation have cut down the hazards.

Sometimes the bombers disappear over the horizon and there is only silence. That isn't often. The safety record of the trans-Atlantic ferry is remarkable. Less than three per cent of the planes have been lost en route. Not a single ship has been shot down by the enemy before delivery to far-off places. And the far-off places seem very close when you are flying above the clouds in a bomber like our Flying Dutchman.

It didn't take Hans long to get into the clear, cold atmosphere. The plane climbed to 5,000 . . . 6,000 . . . 8,000 . . . and then leveled off at 9,500 feet. The motors beat steadily. You felt the surge of power running through the ship. The young Newfoundland woman's knuckles were white from gripping the seat edge. It was her first plane trip. One passenger read a book of Shakespeare—or pretended to. He didn't turn the pages very often. Some tried to sleep on piles of mattresses in the bomb bay. Ice began forming on the wings and antenna wire. Occasionally it broke loose and peppered against the side of the cabin with a sound like dried beans rattling.

Hans started climbing to get above the level of moisture. The altimeter climbed to 11,000 and we were above the ice. It was cold up there. The outside temperature was one degree below zero. Our cabin was as cold as a drafty refrigerator room. We huddled under blankets, coats and sweaters, shivering. No one had bothered to put on the heavy fleece-lined flying suits en route to Newfoundland because we hadn't expected to fly so high. They would be needed on the second leg of the flight when the plane might climb to 20,000 feet or more. The radio man gave his woolen mittens to the woman passenger.

The flight engineer, Vic Stack of Syracuse, poked his head into the aft cabin and asked for an oxygen mask. Stack has made forty Atlantic crossings. "Are we high enough to use oxygen masks?" someone asked. "No," Stack smiled. "There's a young chap aboard who went on a farewell party last night. He's already 20,000 feet high. The oxygen will make him feel better." I squirmed through the passage into the pilot's cabin. Hans smiled and gave us thumbs up. There was no sense of excitement, no tension. The crew—pilot, co-pilot, navigator, flight engineer and radio man—might have been doing a routine job instead of starting a trans-Atlantic crossing.

Back in the tail of the plane were heaps of luggage and gear. There were two rubber lifeboats to be inflated in case of a forced landing on the water and "Mae West" belts to be donned. One jerk of a cord and they would be inflated automatically. On the sides of the lifeboats were marine flares to lead rescue parties. Inching along the narrow catwalk to the end of the tail, you felt the bumps and the ship's vibrations more sharply. Through small side windows you could see the earth far below between cloud patches. And then we passed the eastern coast of Canada and headed across 400 miles of water, the Gulf of St. Lawrence.

The water rippled in the sun. Unconsciously you found yourself looking for a cigar-shaped shadow that would mean an enemy submarine. But there was nothing to be seen. Looking out of the glass panels from the rear gunner's position you wondered if you would have the nerve to make a parachute jump. Not that you thought that anything would go wrong—but you still wondered. Probably all the passengers were thinking the same thing at one time or another, even though no one ever mentioned it.

By this time we were getting hungry. There were individual lunch boxes containing two sandwiches, apple and two cookies. Thermos jugs were filled with hot coffee. We warmed our numb fingers on the cups.

Soon the Flying Dutchman crossed the Newfoundland coast and headed over the desolate, glacier-gouged marshlands and rocklands dotted with lakes. Patches of snow were on some of the hills. There was no place in those forests of scrub pine, birch and spruce or in the open places where a plane might land. It was too rough and wild. A lost plane might not be found down there for weeks.

As we neared the airdrome, Hans began dropping the Liberator slowly. The radio operator signaled the approach and gave identification. They take no chances on not being identified because of the anti-aircraft guns and machine guns ringing the field. Dead ahead was a magnificent airdrome carved from the wilderness, aviation's farthest eastern airport on this side of the Atlantic. There was a gentle bump and the Liberator came to a stop. It was only a short stop for Hans and the rest of his passengers. They climbed back into the plane, bundled in flying suits. Again the motor roared. Hans waved farewell. The Flying Dutchman roared into the sky and soon was a ghostly shadow on the horizon.

Next stop: England. ☐

Air Base in Newfoundland, [July] — The fighting pledge of the United Nations' forces stationed here is this:

"We'll get things done, we'll make things hum,

"We'll send your ships to Britain;

"And if these dam' things can't be done,

"We'll all be off to quittin'."

They're not quitting. They're sending ships to Britain through this wilderness station in great flocks. Five years ago this spot was a wild, desolate region of rock and scrub pine and spruce forest. Now it's one of the largest airports in the world. Some day this place may become an important stopping place for trans-Atlantic aviation. That was the purpose when the British started it. Now it's rendezvous for the bombers headed east.

Around the flying field, the hangers and administration buildings, new construction is under way. Runways are being lengthened greatly. New buildings are going up. Tractors are yanking stumps out of the thin, rocky soil. Anti-aircraft guns point their snouts into the sky from strategic locations. Machine gun nests ring the field. Canadian and American troops stand guard everywhere. To walk across the runways is forbidden; the guards shoot first and ask questions later.

Just before we arrived here, an R.A.F. lieutenant started across a runway at dusk. A sentry challenged him and then opened fire. The lieutenant complained to his commanding officer. "Did the shot hit you?" the officer asked. "No." Then, I shall see that the guard gets some additional target practice," was the curt reply.

The sun doesn't fall over the horizon until 11 p.m., and it's up again five hours later, so that the little airport city never seems to sleep. The several thousand British, Americans, Canadians and Newfoundlanders here have nowhere to go and nothing much to do except work. Time means little. While it seems so near the fighting fronts, news of the war is scarcely heard. Few newspapers arrive and commercial radio reception is poor due to atmospheric conditions.

Here the bombers get their final check and fueling for the long hop. As each ship lands from an airdrome somewhere in Canada, a crew of expert mechanics gives it final, thorough going over to make sure everything is in perfect condition. No ship leaves the ground until the chief maintenance engineer gives his okay. While the mechanics are at work and tanks are being filled with gasoline, the pilots and crews get the weather reports and map their flight plans on the basis of prevailing wind and cloud conditions.

No one ever orders a ferry pilot to take off at a given time or on a certain date. Each pilot makes his own decisions about when to leave, for he is considered the best judge of the range of his ship, the gas load, fuel consumption and other things with which he must contend once he gets over the Atlantic. This is an important factor in the low rate of ships lost by the Royal Air Force Ferry Command.

Usually, however, the fliers accept without question the forecast of the meteorologist here and at Montreal who have been studying Atlantic weather for years. But when the weather closes in and the flights are canceled, then the pilots gather at the inn or at the home of a friend and swap stories of their flights. Most of the civilian pilots with the R.A.F. Ferry Command are Americans, like Clyde Pangborn, Duke Schiller of Onawa, Iowa; Big Tom Smith of Atlanta, Ga.; serious Bob Leroy of Los Angeles; Jack Terry of Clarksdale, Miss.; Bob Coffman of Baton Rouge and Earl Ortman of Los Angeles.

The majority are married and live with their families in or near Montreal. They're the flying elite, since they draw $1,000 each month during the first year of service, $1,100 the second and $1,200 the third year. But some of them see the time coming when the civilian pilots will be replaced by Canadian and British service men. A great many already are being trained for the job.

Most of the civilian pilots are a dashing, care-free lot. There's Duke Schiller, for example. Duke's forty. He's considered too old for combat duty, but not for the ferry service. He's the type they want at the controls of a $500,000 investment in freedom. Duke has been flying for years in the United States and Canada. He married a Sault Ste. Marie girl and she flew with him wherever he went until he joined the ferry service eighteen months ago. Their eight-year-old daughter with golden pigtails, Barbara Jane, has been in the air more than one hundred hours. I visited them in Montreal. Fear? They don't know the meaning of the word or else they keep it to themselves. "I always feel Duke is as safe in the ferry game as any other," Mrs. Schiller said. "Besides, Duke wouldn't be happy if he wasn't flying."

While there is adventure for the pilots and their crews passing through here, the men at the base find their chief outlet in work and more work to dull the sense of loneliness and the boredom of a remote outpost in which there is only a handful of women. During the winter, the snows pile high and the little narrow-gauge railroad which is the lone overland link with the outside is sometimes snowbound for days. Then the only means of transport is by plane. The chief diversion is trying to get a short leave and plane ride to Montreal for a fling.

That doesn't mean the station is a crude spot itself. The workmen, soldiers and flying personnel are comfortably housed. A clean, modern little inn provides shelter for pilots, crews and the few civilians who get into this place. American movies are shown once a week. Sometimes there is a dance. And there are sports for the athletic. Salmon and trout abound in the nearby streams. Hunting is good.   □

Cairo, November 10 — Given bases along the entire coast of North Africa, United Nations air forces could control the Mediterranean and re-open shorter supply lines to Allied shipping, Air Chief Marshal Sir Arthur William Tedder, commander in chief of the R.A.F. Middle East command, said today. The air chief said land-based planes could throw a protective umbrella over shipping along the southern Mediterranean once bases were seized. And that day, it was indicated, may not be far distant. Sir Arthur paid tribute to the Americans fighting in the Middle East. "American bombers have an improved batting average," he chuckled. "I told them they would when they were more experienced."

He disclosed that the Allies did not have air superiority when the battle of Egypt reopened, but gained it with paralyzing blows beginning October 9, from which Field Marshal Rommel's air force never recovered. "The enemy was knocked off his stride at the very beginning," Tedder declared, adding that this was a major factor in the Eighth Army's victory, "since a land battle really depends on air superiority."

Rommel was not given a chance to recover, although apparently he made a desperate effort to strengthen his air force by bringing planes from Russia. The Allied air forces also played an important role in smashing Rommel's supply convoys on sea and land and in hunting down enemy shipping in Italian, Greek, and North African ports. "What really mattered," Tedder declared, "was the snapping of the enemy's life blood and stopping his ability to live." Indications were that the Germans left many planes on their fields for lack of fuel, since there was no other apparent reason for abandoning them.   □

En Route to the Western Desert Front, Libya, November 17 — I have seen the graveyard of Rommel's hopes to conquer North Africa and it is a terrible sight to see. Even this scene of death and destruction on the desert, however, is not as awesome as that of Britain's victorious Eighth Army giving chase to the retreating enemy who is not many miles ahead.

The roads to Poland, Belgium, France and Greece must have looked like those I saw today—except that this time it was the Germans who were on the run and the British who were advancing. The Italian radio said this morning that the Axis armies in North Africa were "advancing" to new positions. It was not funny; it was a rather pathetic thing to hear after seeing the tremendous number of British troops, tanks, guns and supplies moving up to the front in a line unbroken for miles and miles. Transports moving along the coast road looked like a great brown snake writhing across the desert floor through the littered wreckage of twisted, burned enemy tanks, planes, and trucks. As far as I could see dust swirled and billowed over the army on the move. The sight made you feel warm inside with the knowledge that this time the Allies were going for the knockout and that there was stuff going up to do the job.

I came into the desert looking for the advance R.A.F. unit to which I am to report. But as yet, I am unable to catch up with it. It is always just ahead. Planes move into airdromes right behind the enemy withdrawal. That is how fast this advance is going right now. I left Cairo yesterday with only a vague idea of where I was headed. In fact, no one could say definitely where the advance units were. They had moved since the last reports.

The plane that brought me up was a Blenheim with a glass-enclosed front and so I had a grandstand seat over the battle area where Rommel's defense was broken. We were flying about an hour when the pilot turned the nose of the Blenheim down. I thought we were going to plow into the sand. Then we leveled off and skimmed over the desert in a ride I will remember as long as I live. We were not more than five feet off the ground at times, hurtling along at almost 200 miles an hour. I could almost have reached out and scooped up a handful of sand.

And then I saw why Pete had brought us down so low. Ahead were the gaunt, fire-blackened skeletons of what once had been Rommel's tanks. They littered the desert over an area known as "the Hill of Evil Men." Many of them must have been funeral pyres for their crews. Many were knocked out by American-made Sherman tanks which broke through the minefields behind the nighttime bayonet attacks of the infantry.

Sometimes it seemed that we were going to crash into a wrecked tank, but Pete would touch the controls, hop over, then grin like a devil. There was plenty of evidence that the Germans and Italians had dug in to hold the El Alamein line. Trenches, gun emplacements, dugouts and the remains of fortified positions were thick. I could almost identify abandoned articles of clothing and small equipment, we were flying so low. Pete is a marvel at this sort of flying which, I was told, is the safest way for a slow plane to escape detection by the enemy. He learned it doing low-level bombing over enemy-occupied channel ports. Although Pete is only twenty, he has been flying almost three years with the R.A.F.

Over to the right of us were the blue Mediterranean and the coast road along which we were streaming transports. There were truck-borne Sherman tanks, guns of all kinds and hundreds and hundreds of vehicles rolling along without even a sign of interference from Jerry. On either side of the road were destroyed trucks and vehicles shot up by the R.A.F. and American fliers as the enemy fled in panic westward.

A few minutes after passing the tank battleground we roared low over the airport of El Daba, which a short while ago was one of Rommel's major advance bases. Here the scene was almost the same as the one we had left except that the sand was strewn with wrecked planes instead of tanks. It looked almost like one hundred on that field alone. Skimming the dunes and dipping into depressions, we roared over the pens of German and Italian prisoners. Some of them instinctively started to run. Others stared. They did not shake their fists or wave. They just stared, then ducked before we passed. We were so near I could see their tired, drawn, sun-blackened faces.

Once Pete climbed to 500 feet and then a couple of Hurricanes patrolling the road moved in to look us over. They were like a couple of hawks diving on a fat goose—but they saw our markings and veered off to keep watch over the brown column which had no end.

It was shortly after noon when Pete landed on an airfield pitted with bomb craters, cluttered with wrecked German and Italian planes and dozens of fifty- and 250-pound bombs the Germans left behind in their haste. I left the plane at this field. My outfit was supposed to be there but it was not. So I hitched a ride on a truck. We merged with a transport column in a choking cloud of dust. At one point we passed a large space filled with British trucks. A sign on the roadside said: "parken verboten"—"no parking." We drove for ninety minutes, then turned off into the desert where headquarters was supposed to be. But my R.A.F. had just moved on.

Perhaps tomorrow I will be able to catch up with this war.   □

Editor's Note: Don Whitehead was assigned to follow the British Eighth Army during the remainder of the North African campaign. He continued to file stories for the Associated Press on the various encounters with Rommel. These dispatches are not included here. After the conquest of Tunisia in May 1943, he joined General Mark Clark's headquarters in Oujda, Morocco, as preparations were made for the invasion of Sicily. In July 1943 he was in Algiers harbor on board the Chase, *as part of the invasion convoy. The convoy steamed first toward Tripoli and then turned toward Sicily on July 9. As he wrote later, "Like pieces of a puzzle, the convoys were falling into pattern for invasion." The next part, "Sicily, Salerno, and the Advance On Rome, 1943," chronicles the harrowing campaigns to pry the Germans out of their Fascist ally's homeland.*

Two
———

SICILY, SALERNO, AND THE
ADVANCE ON ROME, 1943

With the Allied Expeditionary Force at Troina, August 6 — It was dark when we reached the top of the ridge and found the battalion's advance command post preparing for the final American drive to break the enemy's strong positions before Troina. One attack from the northwest had failed to shake the enemy loose from its hold on the strategic crossroads city, and now a pincer movement was under way to envelop him and smash his pockets of resistance on the ridges and in the valleys before us. This battalion, under Maj. Charles (Chuck) Horner, Doylestown, Pa., was to drive straight to Troina. Another was swinging in from our right and a third from the left to cut roads leading out of the city to the east. This was August 4. Below us in the wheat stubble Pvt. Christopher Finley, High Splint, Ky., and Sgt. Benjamin Fiarowich of New York City, are sweeping for mines. "The Germans are booby-trapping their mines," Finley said, "but they are not using as many as they did in Tunisia."

The command post was in a road culvert. Lieut. Melvin Groves of Lawrence, Kan., entered the post grunting as he sat down. "What's the matter?" someone asked. "Hell, I went through all that shooting this morning and then sprained my back in a fall," Groves said.

"How are things going?"

"The dirty bastards won't let me get our wounded off the field," Groves said. "If you go out after the wounded they shoot at you. If a wounded man wiggles they shoot him again."

Up the hill came a pack train of mules carrying ammunition, food and water. The Army requisitioned the long-eared transports from Sicilian farmers to carry supplies up ridges where jeeps are unable to travel. "These are smart mules," Groves said. "On that last ridge we were bringing up mortar ammunition when a mortar shell burst nearby. One of the mules fell down. We thought he was killed, but pretty soon we went back and found him grazing on the hillside. That mule just naturally took cover whenever there was a shell blast near him."

Capt. Alan Moorehouse of Providence, R.I., came along the ridge road with his company, going into position for attack. Other companies were turning off the road below us and dark forms walked silently through the night. We didn't have to wait long to know the enemy still was on the ridge ahead. There was the crackle of machine gun fire. German flares illuminated the sky. Behind Troina a great fire blazed. Our artillery had connected with something, probably a fuel dump.

The battalion was unable to make any progress. We wrapped ourselves in blankets and lay down by the roadside to wait for dawn. Tracer bullets from machine gunners below us raked the enemy positions. Figures dashed out of hiding and ran over behind the ridge. "Get McCarthy up here," Horner said. "He's the best damned mortar man in this man's army. He'll get 'em off there." He was referring to Second Lieut. John E. McCarthy of New York City. "With six mortars," Horner said, "that guy can get sixty shots in the air before the first shell lands. He can drop them in a rain barrel."

"There's a tank or halftrack shooting at our man over there," someone said.

No sooner were the words spoken than a shell screamed into the hill twenty yards from us, and shrapnel buzzed over our heads. The enemy gunner had seen us on the road. We ran for cover and circled around the hill. Another shell whistled through a gap and exploded down the slope. Glancing up as we passed a little stone shelter, I saw a soldier who seemed to be praying. He was kneeling with his hands outstretched. Then I saw a bullet had stopped his hands as they reached for a weapon. He was a German machine gunner.

When we reached the observation point McCarthy was at work. Mortar bursts were raining on the ridgetop. "Look at them running out of that house," exclaimed Lieut. Everett Booth, East Chicago. Booth was right. The Germans, demoralized by heavy mortar and machine gun fire, were running toward our lines, hands in the air. Sixteen came dashing across the field shouting surrender. Then the Yanks who had been pinned down by a machine gun fire during the night advanced to the ridgetop and engaged a pocket of the enemy on the other side. His defenses are beginning to crack.

It is 8 a.m. now, and overhead a formation of American bombers roars on a mission behind the enemy lines. It is the beginning of an all-day shuttle of bombers.   □

Brolo, Sicily, August 12 — A desperate German counter-attack at 5 o'clock yesterday afternoon swept away the beach defenses and left our grim and weary battalion trapped on Mt. Brolo with no sign of relief. We couldn't get even the scum-covered water from a filthy hillside pool because the water point was under machine gun fire and none of us could leave our slit trenches anyway with 88-millimeter guns slamming shells against the crest and shrapnel buzzing viciously over our heads.

Our beach defenses had begun to collapse with the loss of communications. Machine gun fire and shelling had fired the dry brush and weeds on the mountainside, and the fires burned through the telephone wire strung from the hilltop to the beach. The only communication left was by runners working their way under heavy enemy fire, through the flames and down the cliff-like face of the mountain. All during the day we had been unable to get fire support from destroyers and cruisers lying offshore. With communications cut, all that Lieut. Col. Lyle Bernard of Highland Falls, N.Y., commander of the battalion, knew was what he saw and what news could be brought by runners. He had sent company F to the beach to support company G to hold Mt. Brolo. He leaned back in a foxhole, smiling and puffing at his red pipe as though he hadn't a care in the world. We hadn't heard from the regiments attacking from the coast road and from the southwest to relieve us. We could only hope that they were near, for our situation was desperate.

A young soldier edged up. "Excuse me, sir, have you heard anything from the other regiments?" "Sure," smiled the colonel. "Sure. See that ridge over there? One of them is in that valley and they'll be here before long. We have nothing to worry about." Even as he was talking, bucking up the spirit of his troops, German Mark IV tanks moved in to engage our guns covering the road. With two quick shots one tank knocked out the road guns before our artillery smashed it.

"We both fired at the same time," said First Lieut. John L. Packman of 1139 Highland Avenue, Los Angeles. "He hit and we missed. We tried to get the guns up, but the tanks were in on us, shelling the artillery. We knocked out three tanks, but they got three of our guns." But the tanks broke through to the beach and shelled the ammunition dump boxes and cases of ammunition. Some of it, on dead mules, was strung all the way from the beach up the slopes of Mt. Brolo.

Then planes roared in from the sea. They strafed in from the sea. They strafed and bombed in the flats and came roaring toward our ridge. I dodged into a slit trench as the first bomb whistled down. The ear-splitting crash made the earth shudder. Smoke, dirt and the acrid fumes of burnt powder rolled over. Behind the first came another whistle . . . another blast . . . and the screams of the wounded as the motors faded. A soldier had jumped into the trench on top of me. I could feel his heart pounding against my back. He climbed out and smiled apologetically: "I'm sorry I had to jump in on you."

One of the German prisoners stood up whimpering. His left arm dangles by a shred. On the ground were five still figures. Near us Chaplain George Quinlivan of Cohoes, N.Y., knelt in prayer by the dead and then helped attend to the wounded. Even with two direct hits our causalities were light, considering the fact that Mt. Brolo was now our battalion fortress.

When the tanks broke through the beach defenses, Bernard had ordered the troops by runner to evacuate the flats and make their way as best they could to the mountaintop through the enemy guns. Major Lynn Fargo of Ripon, Wis., sank wearily beside a slit trench where a young soldier slept. "I'm so tired my legs feel like they're off at the hip," the Major said. "E company is cut up. I was there. I was in the flats when the tanks ran down the beach, shooting up everything. I was right behind them, but they didn't see me." "They say a regiment is in the next valley," someone said. "God, that's the best news I ever heard," Fargo sighed.

We walked up to Bernard's command post. "All the enemy is trying to do now," he said, "is get away. If my men have the strength, I've got the will to go after them. We'll keep pecking away and give them more hell than they are looking for." There wasn't much left to give them hell with. The artillery was gone and machine gunners and riflemen were running out of ammunition. "Let's go up and take a peek at the situation," the colonel said to Fargo.

"If you don't mind, sir, I think I'll sit right here and think of cold malted milk."

"Son, you've got more guts than a sausage mill," the colonel said softly, looking down at Fargo.

Upon the slope came squads carrying two mortars, with all the mortar ammunition that was left—twenty-two rounds. "Good boys!" exclaimed Bernard. "Just put them inside our little old last stand circle and then knock hell out of that bridge to the west. We won't be able to knock it out, but we can keep them from bringing stuff down the road." The mortars were set up and began firing at the bridge. Fargo checked off each round as it was shot.

"Lordy, that's a pleasant whistle," Fargo grinned. Up the hill came Lieut. Jesse Uglade of Greeley, Colo., platoon leader in company E with fourteen men following him. They had escaped from the flats. And there came Lieut. Thomas R. Rodgers of Danville, Va., whose gunners had fought with the enemy tanks; and Second Lieut. Eric Tatlock of Cardiner, Me., who had helped in the fight to protect the ammunition dump. "We beat off two attacks on the ammo dump," Tatlock said. "Engineers, artillerymen and every man who could handle a gun was fighting. We were cut off twice, but they didn't get through until we were ordered to evacuate."

Even as they withdrew, five groups tried to carry ammunition up the hill by hand. Only two succeeded, through the machine gun and shell fire burning mountainside. Pfc. James Heppler, 534 Narnett St., and Pvt. Harry W. Honn, 5524 Michigan Ave., both of Kansas City, gathered in the tight little circle and began digging foxholes. Heppler had bagged some snipers with his machine gun and was helping protect the artillery until the tanks broke through. Honn had knocked out one machine gun nest with his mortar.

Most of Company E, led by Lieut. Alexander Russel of Jacksonville, Ill., and a company under Capt. Burleigh Packwood of Billings, Mont., made their way to the high ground., scaling the northern slope of the mountain after dark. All over the hilltop was the sound of digging by the men from the broken beachhead below. Rifles and machine guns kept chattering through the whole night. We lay in our slit trenches, dozing and wondering if the morning would bring another attack. Soon after dawn an observer came running to Bernard's command post.

"There are troops moving on the road with vehicles, sir," he said. "I can't tell yet whether they are doughboys or not, but those damned vehicles look like jeeps to me."

"Pass the word along. There may be American troops on the road," the Colonel ordered. "Tell the men not to fire and to keep under cover. I'm going down to see."

With Second Lieut. Herbert B. Stranahan of Brookline, Mass., and Pvt. Aldo R. Benedetto of Staten Island, N.Y., we worked our way down the mountainside to a ledge overlooking the road—and there were the American troops who had fought all day and all night along the coast road to reach the embattled battalion. Bernard's regimental commander wrung his hand.

"You did a great job," he said. "You had us plenty worried, but the boys fought like hell to get to you. They were so tired they could hardly walk."

"I knew you'd get to us," Bernard said.

"Well, we've got plenty of rations and plenty of water. Get your men off the hill and we'll feed them. We'll take care of the wounded. If you'll go back to the bridge you'll find food and water. I know you are hungry."

"If you don't mind, Colonel, I'd like to look after my men first."   ☐

Spadafora, Sicily, August 16 — At 11:33 a.m. today a 155-millimeter Long Tom belched flame and smoke in a vineyard near here and the first shell from American artillery screamed into the mainland of Italy. The honor of pulling the lanyard for the U.S. Seventh Army's first shot went to the Colonel and commander of a field artillery regiment. And the honor was shared by fifteen men of Battery D, manning the big gun which is nick-named Draftee.

"I'd like to fire that first shot on Italy," the Colonel said when the Long Tom was wheeled into position. "Do you mind, son?"

"That's all right, sir," replied Pfc. Elbert Keel of Atoka, Tenn., who pulls the string on Draftee.

"Just give it a yank?" the colonel asked.

"Yes, sir," replied Keel. "Just jerk the string and get your arm out of the way of the recoil."

When the colonel yanked the lanyard the long barrel recoiled with a roar and dust billowed up from the plowed earth in the vineyard. A few seconds later the shell smashed into the Villa San Giovanni railway and ferry termi-nus on the eastern coast of Messina Straits, which were being used by the enemy to remove men and materials from Sicily. The order to fire was given by Battery Commander Lieut. William B. Dougherty, Dallas, Tex. After the colonel fired the first shot, Keel took over the post and the gun pumped many rounds into the Italian mainland in the opening of the artillery assault to silence enemy guns on the mainland and smash the harbor.   □

Allied Headquarters in Sicily, [late August] – Out of the conquest of Sicily came a by-product of great value to the Allies in the Atlantic and Pacific theaters of war—greater co-operation and understand-ing between the U.S. Army and Navy. Perhaps more than any other single campaign Sicily showed the absolute necessity for, and the dividends to be reaped from, the close coordination of sea and land power. There were mis-understandings and differences during the Sicilian operations, but in the end they were solved satisfactorily.

An Army officer, after finishing a conference with a naval lieutenant commander on plans for a landing operation behind the lines on the north coast of Sicily, exclaimed:

"I had some terrific arguments with that guy. He wanted to do things his way—and I wanted to do them my way. We damn near came to blows sometimes. But you know, he's one of my best friends now. We're begin-ning to understand each other's problems a lot more and we worked out our differences to the satisfaction of everyone." And then he added: "I don't need to tell you the Navy has been doing one hell of a job in the cam-paign."

With each amphibious operation, the technique of both Army and Navy is improved. The Sicilian invasion was much smoother and landings were made with greater precision than when American troops invaded North Africa last November. There, many units were landed far wide of their objectives. On Sicily each division was set in at the exact spot as planned; moreover cruisers and destroyers supported the landing parties with terrific fire power concentrated on enemy strongholds.

There always was liaison between land and sea forces unless communications were knocked out. When troops went ashore in assault boats, there were Navy men in the first wave to set up beach-to-ship communications; Navy men accompanied artillery observers to help direct fire from cruisers and destroyers. The most vivid personal recollection of the Navy's role in giving the Army fire support was when a task force made an amphibious landing behind the enemy's lines at Brolo on the road to Messina.

We reached our objective at dawn with a surprise landing. Then in the early afternoon the enemy counter-attacked our beachhead in force with support from tanks. A young lieutenant called the command post. "Unless I can have help," he said, "I can't hold out another five minutes. Can't the Navy give us help?" From an observation post on Mt. Brolo a Navy observer radioed the ships hidden in the mist offshore and before the five minutes were up the guns were hurling salvo after salvo into the attacking enemy. Under this terrific barrage they withdrew. The troops were jubilant over the Navy's quick response. "Jeeze!" a doughboy murmured in awe. "I thought I'd heard the sweetest sounds on earth when I listened once to Benny Goodman but those Navy guns have got Benny's boys beaten."   □

Allied Headquarters in North Africa, [late August] –
[Editor's Note: Don Whitehead returned to Algiers after the Sicily campaign ended and as preparations were being made for the first attack on the Italian peninsula at Salerno.]

Medical science moved up within range of the guns of the enemy during the Sicilian campaign to perform miracles of surgery which undoubtedly saved many lives. Among the dusty mountain roads field medicos set up tented hospitals—often with their own artillery roaring about their ears and frequently with enemy shells bursting nearby.

It took steady nerves to stand in those shelters and operate on wounded men. Teams of skilled surgeons, however, showed it could be done, and thus a new technique of "front-line surgery" was perfected by the U.S. Seventh

Army. Army authorities say it worked "at peak efficiency." This new phase of medical care for battle casualties resulted from a modification of the original casualty evacuation setup. Under the original setup the wounded were transported by ambulance to operating stations five or six miles behind the front, and no matter how carefully or rapidly they were evacuated were subject to a certain degree of shock. The "front-line surgery setup" made it possible for them to receive expert attention within one or two miles of the enemy guns, and the minutes saved resulted in saving a proportionate number of lives.

"The establishment of these complete operative units," said Col. Edward D. Churchill of Boston, Mass., surgical consultant with the surgeon's office for the North Africa theater, "did away with the shock and lapse of time we formerly had to deal with."

Each operating unit was equipped with modern sterilizers, tables, instruments and batteries of lights, and functioned independently. Under the arrangement followed in the Sicilian campaign, the surgical platoons broke away from their hospital units upon arriving in a combat area and set up their stations as near the front as possible. When a seriously wounded man was taken from the field of battle he was given immediate treatment, while the less seriously injured continued on to stations further in the rear. The front-line stations gave treatment for severe shock, compound fractures, abdominal and chest wounds, head wounds, performed amputations and handled cases of gangrene and uncontrollable hemorrhage.

A large share of the credit for their success, of course, goes to the first aid men working with the troops in the lines and the litter bearers who brought the wounded out under enemy fire. Much of this evacuation work had to be done at night. Too much praise, however, cannot be given the surgeons who worked under the most trying conditions in their front-line stations.

One day four German planes dived to bomb and strafe a vehicle stalled near one of these units. Clouds of dust and smoke rolled over the operating tent. When the attack was over, I was among those who rushed over to see what damage had been done to the hospital. We found that shrapnel had sliced holes in the tent, but inside the surgeons were going calmly about their work as though nothing had happened.   □

Allied Headquarters in North Africa, [late August]–
The United States Seventh Army—created for the conquest of Sicily—reached maturity in the thirty-eight days of battle between the invasion land-

ing July 10 on the beaches of southern Sicily and the occupation of Messina. From a virtually unknown quantity as a team, the Seventh Army developed on the field of battle into a hard-hitting, well-integrated force which drove straight through bitter enemy resistance with only two serious checks to the steamroller advance. And if the Sicilian campaign proved anything, it was this: The American doughboy, given experience, is the equal of, if not superior to, any soldier the Axis can produce.

He earned this recognition the hard way on those rocky, steep, heartbreaking ridges which corrugate the island of Sicily like the wrinkles on an old man's gnarled hand. The conquest of Sicily was primarily a doughboy victory. The infantry did the job with able and brilliant support from the artillery, engineers, Navy, and Air Force, but still the foot soldier fighting wearily across ridge after ridge was the decisive factor in ripping nine Italian divisions and three and a half German divisions, which Hitler gambled on holding this important Mediterranean bastion.

The doughboy, doughfoot, foot-slogger, dogface, or whatever nickname you choose to call him by, fought brilliantly and he fought heroically. That is no hackneyed, over-dramatic description of what the infantry did on Sicily. In calm, deliberate retrospect, the achievements on Sicily remain as thrilling, as vivid and impressive as they were when I watched them on the spot. There were mistakes, there were breakdowns in coordination, but on the whole these faults were minor and were being corrected as the campaign neared an end.

One of the most encouraging aspects of the campaign—outside the accomplishments of the doughboy—was the close liaison between the Army, the Navy and the Air Force, an indication itself of the maturity of this man's Army. And it isn't paradoxical at all for an Army to be both young and mature; for an Army comes of age when it knows the tools with which it must work—and uses them to the best advantage. If the conquest of Sicily may be taken as a gauge of what we may expect from American troops in future operations, prospects are favorable, for on the proving grounds of Sicily an American Army was tested and it came through the test with spectacular success.

I was lucky enough to be on the scene for the two most crucial battles of the Sicilian campaign, and so I was not only able to get observations of men on the scene, but I watched the battle from close range and was in position to draw my own conclusions. In both cases they were the same: Our infantry fought magnificently and the artillery was tops. The first battle began developing twenty-four hours after we landed, with the enemy forming up to attack our central bridgehead on three sides. That was the most critical period perhaps in the entire invasion and at that time the veteran First Infantry Division in the central sector did not have but very few of its tanks and guns ashore, and the beachhead was less than five miles in depth.

The Forty-fifth Division on the right flank and the Third Division on the left had landed successfully with considerably lighter opposition than the First Division, but there were still gaps between the divisions which had not been closed, in which the enemy could throw flanking forces. With more than one hundred tanks, including Mark VI Tigers, the Germans launched their attacks the second day against the central sector. The infantry fought tanks with rifle grenades, hand grenades, machine guns, rifles and pitifully few antitank guns.

Shoving down the Gela Valley, the German tanks drove to within 1,000 yards of the beachhead, shooting up stores and vehicles. They ran over troops in their foxholes, but the doughboys held on. Artillery emplaced in the sand dunes smashed at the tanks over open sights and drove the attack back while the Navy lent a hand with salvos from destroyers and cruisers. For ten hours the central beachhead was in danger of being collapsed under the furious enemy assault, but the attacks were beaten off and the First Division began its fight inland across the ridges. The beachhead was saved.

Reviewing the situation later, Maj. Gen. Terry Allen, commander of the First Division, remarked matter-of-factly, "the situation might have been damned serious. As it was, it was only embarrassing." The First Division figured again in the second official stage of the campaign—the Battle of Troina. Troina is an ancient, rocky fortress-like city which sits atop a cliff twenty miles west of Mt. Etna. It dominates all the approaches including the single east-west road paralleling the main north coast road, and overlooks what some military men called "one of the greatest natural defensive positions in the world."

The Germans chose to make a fortress of the city and to make their bid to halt the American advance on the Troina line. The German High Command issued orders that Troina should be held "at all costs." There was to be no retreat. And so on August 1, the battle for Troina began when one battalion from the Ninth Division moved toward Troina and met bitter resistance from the Germans dug in trenches, caves, gullies, culverts and dry ravines. With this battalion stopped, the First Division moved into action with the fierce mountain-fighting Goums [Goumiers] from French North Africa on their left flank.

The battle raged for five days until it seemed that both sides would collapse from exhaustion. It seemed incredible that troops who had marched and fought over the rough country all the way from the beaches could continue to attack the enemy night after night and then meet the enemy's counter-attacks. In those five days the Germans made more than twenty counter-attacks. But they did endure it and on the morning of the sixth marched into battered Troina, where the miserable inhabitants lived in gloomy cellars, in the cathedral's tomb-like basement and in the shattered stone houses. The Germans' Troina line was broken. And to the north, too, there was bitter fighting with the Forty-fifth Division adding new laurels to its record.

The performance of this division won the admiration of every soldier in the Seventh Army. It came direct from the United States for the Sicilian invasion without previous combat experience, but the troops fought like veterans. Their greatest work was "Bloody Ridge" before San Stefano, where they scaled the steep slopes of a high ridge to root the Germans off in one of the bloodiest engagements of the campaign.

Then the Third Division, which was first into Palermo, moved through to continue the drive toward Messina with two amphibious landings behind the enemy lines, and crossing roads through the mountains to knock the enemy off the ridges dominating the coast road. This was tortuous, hard mountain fighting, enough to test the mettle of any soldier, with the enemy always having to be driven off high ground on which he could look down on any attacking force.

Handsome, hard driving Maj. Gen. Lucien Truscott, a native of Chatfield, Texas, engineered the Third Division's brilliant drive on Messina and he was enthusiastic over the showing made by the doughboys. "Our troops were magnificent," Truscott said the day after his men captured Messina to conclude the conquest of Sicily. "Our men are as good as any army in the world today, and they are better equipped.

"The showing of the Forty-fifth has proved that our troops are ready for combat when they arrive from the United States. Our training program is basically sound at last, with the realism that was needed."

Truscott said he had been a severe critic of the Army's training prior to the draft because he did not feel it was realistic, that it did not produce initiative in officers, and that it did not prepare the troops for the sights and sounds of actual combat. "Again now our young officers are learning to take responsibility and to use initiative," he said. "It is difficult to get officers to use initiative on the battlefield, but our young men are coming through in great style. They are developing fast."

There is no doubt that the Army gained a lot of confidence in the march across Sicily—and a great deal of savvy, too. While there was nothing new tactically developed, the Army learned better how to use the tried and proven tactics against an enemy putting up bitter resistance in the final days of the campaign.

The day before Troina fell, I asked Maj. Charles "Chuck" Horner of Doylestown, Pa., what was the main difference between the fighting on Sicily and in Tunisia where his battalion also was engaged. "The main difference," he said, "is that we are a lot smarter now than we were in Tunisia. We know better how to fight the Germans and how to take care of ourselves. We don't butt our heads against a stone wall trying to reach an objective. We know how to go around it and attain the same results." This is another way of saying the American troops have reached maturity.   □

Allied Headquarters in North Africa, [late August] – After the Americans had smashed the enemy's Troina line in the bitter five-day battle which decided the fate of Sicily, a haggard German prisoner with red-rimmed eyes was trying to explain why the defense had broken. "We never had any rest," he said. "Your infantry attacked by day and night. They kept coming. We would stop them and then they would come back again." He closed his eyes and shuddered and went on: "But the most terrible of all were the guns. The artillery never stopped, and you can only stand so much of that hell."

Two nights before, I had sat on a ridgetop before Troina with Maj. Charles "Chuck" Horner of Doylestown, Pa., and we listened to the thunder of our guns behind us, to the never-ending parade of shells passing overhead and dropping into the enemy's positions. "We think we're having a tough time," Horner said. "But imagine what the Germans are going through under that barrage."

From the first shell fired in the Battle of Tunisia until the fall of Messina in the conquest of Sicily, American artillery has played a brilliant, consistently spectacular role in the successes of the American troops. In both the Tunisian and Sicilian campaigns the verdict of military men has been that our artillery is as good if not better than the artillery of any other army. Certainly the enemy has been unable to match it. Perhaps the most stirring artillery action in all the Sicilian invasion occurred on July 11, the day after our troops landed and established their beachhead at Gela in the central sector of the American front. The enemy tried to wipe out the Gela beachhead attacks from three sides. We had only a few tanks ashore at 8 a.m. when the enemy attacked with one hundred tanks, including several of the big Mark VI "Tigers."

But we did have a large part of our artillery ashore and in the final analysis the artillery turned the tide of battle after forty German tanks had been driven to within 1,000 yards of the beachhead. The spirit of the artillerymen is fine, and they make a competitive game out of their gunnery, with each gun crew trying to outdo the others in the battery.

It's an old story that one German prisoner captured said, "I have only one request before I'm sent away. I'd like to see the Americans' automatic artillery." Of course, the Americans have no automatic artillery, but the boys at the guns work them so rapidly they might as well be automatic. During the Battle of Troina I ran across a gun crew that might be considered typical of all gun crews in the artillery. They called their howitzer "Bleepo III" after a comic page dog.

"But this dog don't wag its tail," said Sgt. William L. Thomas of East Liverpool, Ohio.

Thomas said his crew had set up the gun with camouflaged nets in a little valley west of Troina. They lounged about with their shirts off, their bare backs bronzed by the hot sun of Africa and Sicily. All clustered within ten yards of the gun, ready at any time to jump to their position at a moment's notice. "The boys wore out two guns in Tunisia," said Thomas. They first saw action on George Washington's birthday at 3:30 p.m. in the Thala Park where they fired their opening shot at the enemy. "We made an 800-mile march in four days with no rest," Thomas recalled. "The rain was pouring. We had one helluva time. Finally, we pulled into position and started firing.

"The Germans were trying to get into Tébessa and they put us into the line to help stop them. We fired five rounds and then they began to retreat." Pfc. Alton J. Russ of Ash, N.C., grinned and said: "I think we blasted them that time." The other members of the gun crew lounged about in the shade of olive trees. They were Pvt. Charles Higgs, Amsterdam, N.Y.; Pvt. Donato J. Toto, Boston, Mass.; Pvt. Armand Pielads, Roslindale, Mass.; Pvt. Leo Schwartz, Brooklyn, N.Y.; Cpl. Robert M. O'Hairen, Providence, R.I.; Pfc. Cornelius Obermeier, Pittsburgh, Pa.; Pfc. James Ward, Reidsville, N.C.; and Cpl. Carmine V. Lerelia, Boston.

The telephone rang. Thomas picked it up. "Fire Mission!" he barked. The men jumped to their feet and took their posts. Commands were snapped.

Russ, Higgs and Godin put a shell into a tray and Toto rammed it into the gun. Obermeier stuck in a powder charge. Zerella set the range. Then Pielads jerked the lanyard and the big gun roared. Thomas listened to the observers report.

"Left, 14-3-6-7!"

The men grabbed the tailplate of the gun and turned it a few inches. The range checked. Then the crew methodically began firing. As the last shot was fired Donato grabbed the phone and spoke to Lt. Leon R. Birum, Union City, Ind., the battery firing executive.

"What's the matter with No. 1," he jibed. "Their girdles too tight?"

Donato laughed, "He says we got a little head start."

"Now ain't that just too bad," grinned O'Haire, and Thomas took the phone to speak to the lieutenant.

"Cease firing," he told his men. "Mission accomplished. We were shooting at an enemy strongpoint."

"Did we do any good?"

"Well, the mission was accomplished," Thomas said. "That means we knocked hell out of 'em."   □

Allied Headquarters in North Africa, September 3 – The Allied landing in Italy today was the fruition of plans laid well over a year ago in many parts of the world. In the words of an official spokesman, "Don't get the idea that this is a new campaign or a new 'second front.' That started a long time ago when we first came to North Africa." The special communiqué announcing British and Canadian troops had pushed across the narrow Straits of Messina from Sicily, whose conquest was finished only seventeen days ago, emphasized the same point with the words, "Allied forces under the command of General Eisenhower have continued their advance."

Most significant perhaps was the fact that Gen. Dwight D. Eisenhower began the actual smash at Hitler's so-called "European fortress" with by far the biggest, most powerful, most versatile, single air force ever massed to support an army in the field—an air force whose leaders could claim to have reduced the once-dreaded German air force as a vital factor in further operations anywhere in the Mediterranean area. This air force has given southern Italy a long "softening up" process with special emphasis on the destruction of airdromes, from which the Luftwaffe could menace an invasion fleet and landing armies, and rail and other communications by which the enemy could dispatch reinforcements, weapons, and supplies to any threatened point.   □

Allied Headquarters in North Africa, September 3 – It was only a hop, skip and a jump for the Allied force across the narrow Straits of Messina into Italy on the seventeenth day after the first doughboy patrols marched into bomb-gutted Messina. The Allies didn't even wait to clear away the terrible wreckage and the litter of enemy equipment on the shores from which they embarked for this great new move against the Axis.

When the armada moved across the strait under a starlit sky with flashes of guns sparkling like fireflies against the dark hills on either side of the water, they left behind Messina's harbor cluttered with sunken ships. Preparations were under way to continue the drive across the strait before the retreating enemy had a chance to recover from the shock of the beating. The water across which the invasion was made is less than two miles wide at its narrowest point and in some places is only ten-feet deep.

From the docks at Messina the strait looks like a broad, placid river. Italy's mountains rise abruptly on the other side. With field glasses you could see small boats, barges and ferries on the opposite shore and columns of smoke rising from bursts of American artillery which kept harassing fire on the enemy withdrawing into the mainland. With the air force and artillery pounding the mainland and neutralizing the enemy's counter fire from batteries hidden in the hills it was no risk of men or equipment to concentrate small boats along the west shores of the strait for this invasion.

The boats were able to cross the strait within twenty minutes in a quick shore to shore dash. The hills above and to the north and south of Messina provided good hiding places for artillery to lob shells onto enemy positions and with aerial and ground observation it was no great task to pick targets. □

With the U.S. Navy Invasion Task Force, September 9 — American and British troops fought their way onto the mainland of Italy south of Salerno before dawn today behind a barrage so heavy that ships five miles back at sea trembled and shook with the concussions. As I write this in the first light of day the guns are still thundering and troops hold the bridgehead onto which are pouring more troops, guns and armor from a mighty Allied armada.

Although the message from Admiral Sir Andrew Browne Cunningham, commander in chief of the Allied Mediterranean Fleet, saying the armistice with Italy had been declared was received shortly before midnight, fighting is bitter and destroyers are engaging the coastal batteries. So either the Italians in this sector have not been advised of the armistice or else the guns are manned by the Germans.

The storm broke shortly before midnight, after the invasion convoys had steamed across the placid sea with little to remind the troops and sailors that they were participating in a great Allied amphibious invasion to crack Hitler's European fortress. Enemy planes dived in to drop bombs near our ship and ack-ack brought three of them plunging into the sea. The bombs fell harmlessly into the water and our great fleet steamed slowly into the Gulf of Salerno with the dark shadow of the Isle of Capri on our left. From the deck we could see gun flashes on the mainland, and we knew that the enemy had not been caught by surprise and that he was waiting.

Then came the electrifying news of the armistice with Italy. The word spread around the ship swiftly and injected an almost gay note into this solemn business of invasion. The message said: "An armistice with Italy has been declared. Operations now in progress are to proceed as ordered, but Italian armed forces, including aircraft, should be treated as friendly unless they take hostile action or threaten hostile action. Plans for the covering fire on the beaches are to proceed as ordered, but coastal batteries should not be engaged unless they open fire."

There was speculation that perhaps the troops might get ashore without having to fight their way to their objectives. Many officers aboard our ship foresaw the possibility of the Germans having to retreat quickly to northern Italy, with the Italians out of the war. We stood in the dark deck discussing the armistice as the hour drew near. But then there were three flashes from the shore and shells whined across the ship. Two more passed over and fell astern. "Order the destroyers to return the fire," snapped the rear admiral in command of our force.

Our ship came to a halt and then began to lay a smoke screen. A great fire blazed up ahead and there were explosions in the city of Salerno. Our guns had not fired; so obviously the enemy was carrying out demolitions. Flashes of gunfire ripped along the coast and sounds of explosions and gunfire rolled across the water. Our destroyers moved into position and began hammering the coastal batteries. A British Monitor moved in and hurled steel at the enemy as red, green and white flares looped across the sky.

At 2:17 the rear admiral ordered his assault boats to "go ahead with the landings as planned." And signal lamps flashed word to the troop-carrying vessels. The fires in Salerno and south of the city blazed up fiercely at times, outlining the dark shadows of boats in the water.

And then the barrage on the beaches opened up. Never have I witnessed anything like it either in Tunisia or on Sicily. And none of the British officers or American naval men on board had ever seen anything equal to the eruption of explosives on the beaches ahead. Lt. Robert M. Wiley of Ballston Spa, N.Y., gazed at the display in awe. "They unloaded hell, death and destruction," he said, and that is what it was—hell, death and destruction.

At first it fell on the beach near Salerno, and then it fell on the beach to the south. Rocket shells fell by the hundreds. Nothing could have lived through that barrage and at 3:40 a.m. the first wave of troops landed on the northern-most beach and waves piled into other barges to the south. The enemy had left anti-personnel mines on some of the beaches, and machine guns and batteries not caught in the barrage also opened fire. The battle of the mainland was under way. British commandos and American Rangers under Lt. Col. Bill Darby of Fort Smith, Ark., swarmed ashore and fought their way into their objectives. We moved out of the North African port two days ago and assembled in convoy, and early the next morning we were under way.

Since this American Fifth Army under Lt. Gen. Mark W. Clark is a mixture of British and American ships—there were about as many British aboard our ship as Americans. Although our vessel was crowded we had luxuries we hadn't anticipated. There was even hot and cold fresh water for shower baths. For between-meals entertainment there was an excellent library of several hundred volumes and a movie every night. We saw Harriet Hilliard in "Juke Box Jennie" the other night. Harriet would not get a good start on one of her swing numbers than an alarm would come over the loudspeaker. But soon the men would come straggling back, the projector would take off his steel helmet and the show would go on.

It was mid-afternoon when we sighted the dim outline of a mountainous island and our skipper, Commander Edward H. Eckelmeyer of Philadelphia, identified it as the Isle of Capri. As dusk fell and a half moon illuminated the sea it was almost impossible to realize that this warm, serene night was the night for invasion. ☐

With the U.S. Navy off Salerno, Italy, September 9 – The invasion of Italy is one of the most brilliant triumphs in the history of the United States Navy. Putting troops, guns, tanks, and supplies ashore on the beaches at the Gulf of Salerno climaxed perhaps the most intricate, complex, and delicate naval operation ever carried out by any naval power.

The massive scale of this amphibious landing—dwarfing anything yet attempted by the Allies—was enough alone to place a terrific responsibility on the Navy. It involved detailed planning, timing and teamwork of almost unbelievable proportions. But besides transporting an army from North Africa and setting it ashore ready to do battle, the Navy also protected the cargo en route to Italy and then helped it launch the invasion with support from guns of cruisers and destroyers.

The story of the Navy's part in the invasion of Italy is one principally of behind-the-scenes toil of officers and men working day and night, planning and executing thousands upon thousands of minute details leading to the spectacular job of getting an army across the Mediterranean onto enemy soil. An army doesn't just march aboard transports and set sail for an objective. Actually, amphibious invasion begins on the enemy beach and works back to the point where the army loaded into ships for the move. This is not the anachronism it sounds. The reason is simple:

First the army must decide where it wants to go, on what beach the troops are to be landed, and what objectives must be taken. It must decide which troops are needed ashore first and what equipment is necessary for them to do the job. It must decide when guns, tanks, trucks and supplies are needed and where. If the army wants infantry assault waves to be followed by artillery, tanks, and trucks in that order, then the navy organizes loading schedules to confirm beach needs. Thus landing plans work back from the beach to the loading points. There is a reason for every soldier, every gun, every box of ammunition, every tank being aboard a certain ship in a certain place. For beach landings are made on railroad time schedules even in face of heavy enemy fire. Once the operation begins, it must go on.

The beachmaster is the Navy's equivalent of the train master in a busy railroad terminal, except the train master doesn't have people shooting at him as he handles traffic. There is a beachmaster for each of the beaches on which troops are landing. Going ashore with the assault troops, naval beach parties set up shore-to-ship communications, make a quick hydrographic survey to determine the best landing points, set up navigation lights to mark the landing points, control beach traffic, assist in evacuating the wounded, and work with enemy engineers.

Handling beach traffic is one of the most vital phases of the landing operations, for the beaches must not become clogged with ships and supplies, and at the same time the navy must see that the army gets what is needed at the proper time. Any serious breakdown on the beach would imperil the entire operation.

Lt. Col. James H. Brower of Rochester, N.Y., marine officer and liaison between the Army and Navy, was one of those who helped draft the Navy's loading plans. "We learned one hell of a lot in the Sicilian operation," Brower said. "This time I think we've made a great many improvements."

One improvement Brower devised was a logistic chart for each vessel with a deck diagram on the reverse side showing the exact location and name of equipment and material with which the vessel was loaded. With a copy of this chart, the beachmaster is able to tell at a glance what a ship is carrying, where it should be unloaded, and how. In the war room aboard the flagship, Brower has a large wall chart listing each vessel and its contents. He can tell at once which ships are unloading and what army has gone ashore.   □

With the United States Navy in the Gulf of Salerno, Italy, September 9 — The determined courage of American naval men in taking ships onto the invasion beach in the Gulf of Salerno under direct enemy fire won the praise today of British troops. With the cool determination of veterans the youthful crews of the amphibious vessels unloaded an English division to hold part of the Allied invasion front in the face of bitter German resistance.

A young British lieutenant returned to our ship after he was wounded in the early morning landing. He was painfully hurt, but he wanted to tell how the Americans helped him and his men on the beach. "The Americans aboard our ship were wonderful," he said. "As we started in for the beach, 88-millimeter guns opened up on us at 300 yards and followed us all the way in. The skipper did not even hesitate in the face of the heavy fire.

"We beached and got all our vehicles off the craft, but some of them stuck in the soft sand and we were having a hard time getting them dug out. The crew left the craft and came ashore to help us. They did not have to do it, but they did, while the skipper waited for them. Then an 88 shell burst in the ship and I was wounded along with a few other men. Only then did the skipper pull away from the beach."

It took courage for the Navy men to get this British division ashore, for the Gulf of Salerno has been a devil's cauldron of smoke and flame and cannonading and bombing since the invasion armada steamed into position early this morning. On this part of the front the British ran head-on into a Panzer Grenadier division which had rushed up batteries of 88-millimeter guns to cover one sector. Fighting has been savage throughout the day, British cruisers, destroyers and gunboats dueling with German shore guns. The cannonading began shortly after midnight and has continued without pause.

The Italian naval commander at Salerno has been taken prisoner, but as yet we have had no clarification aboard our ship of Admiral Cunningham's message last night saying an armistice had been reached with the Italians. "Maybe," said one wag, "it would be better for us to fight without an armistice."

There are still some Italians fighting alongside the Germans, and it is not clear whether they know of an armistice. When the sun came over the hills this morning it disclosed the invasion armada to the enemy. Hundreds of ships anchored in the glassy waters of the gulf. They stretched as far as the eye could see, and as each hour passed more arrived. They came in great convoys and then anchored to wait their turn to go to the beach.

As troop, tank and vehicle carrying vessels moved toward the beach, destroyers shuttled back and forth near the beach, blasting the enemy and trailing black smoke to screen the ships from enemy observers, lashed to barrage balloons inland, and escorting ships to their positions. When American fighter planes came over to give aerial cover they shot down the balloons.

The enemy guns in the hills back of the plain and beyond Salerno had the range of the beach and kept pouring shells into the landing areas and at the vessels heading for the beach. The enemy prepared for invasion on these beaches, for they were mined and the waters were sown with mines, which had to be cleared. The landing proceeded smoothly on "Red Beach" and troops pushed inland to take objectives astride the main road and on the high ground south of Salerno known as Monte Giogi. But on the right flank of this force at "Green Beach" the enemy had a concentration of 88s firing directly into the beach, with infantry deployed in the groves, and the troops fought their way inland slowly.

At noon the enemy counter-attacked behind strong artillery support and the troops fell back to the beach, destroyers, cruisers and gunboats again moved in to give support to this weakened sector. Under these conditions it was necessary to abandon the original "Green Beach" and to move unloading operations further south. During the intense excitement of this grand-scale invasion operation the flagship of the American rear admiral directing one of the task forces gradually moved near the beach until we were only a few hundred yards off shore.   □

Salerno, Italy, September 9 — Benito Mussolini ended his spectacular career as Italy's "Il Duce" a tired, beaten, rather comical figure riding to prison in the backseat of an ambulance. The bald-headed, big-jawed, one-time strong man of Europe who built an empire and then saw it crumble around him, didn't even get to make one of his theatrical exits. He did not even get to make a speech or play the role of martyred hero. He just faded into oblivion as the prisoner of four big carabinieri, to play no role in the swift succession of events which tumbled Fascism's rotten facade, placed King Victor Emmanuel in power and led to Italy's withdrawal from the war.

His son-in-law, Count Galeazzo Ciano, former foreign minister, was made a virtual prisoner in a Rome apartment, while his pro-Nazi daughter, Edda, wept hysterically over the collapse of her playhouse. For Mussolini the end came swiftly on the night of July 25. He was taken into custody by a mere captain of carabinieri as he walked from Villa Savoia after a conference with the King. The captain was polite but firm in insisting that Il Duce step into the ambulance—so coolly insistent that Mussolini acquiesced without a struggle.

And he drove off into the night with no crowds to cheer him and no one even to notice his departure from the scene. He was just a bald-headed, big-jawed little man riding in the backseat of an ambulance with four big carabinieri.

This was the story told me today by a young Italian naval officer just returned from Rome and vouched for by his superior officer. They were both surprised that the outside world had not heard it before. (The Berlin radio on September 9 broadcast its version of Mussolini's downfall declaring that he was "dragged by brute force" from the royal palace, strapped to a stretcher and spirited away in an ambulance. His removal, the broadcast asserted, was the result of a secretly planned coup d'état by the King and Marshal Gen. Pietro Badoglio.)

He told me the story while standing on the main street of Salerno a few hours after German troops had been driven from the outskirts of the city which they ransacked before leaving. "I swear every word is true," he said. "Everyone will know the story sooner or later so I might as well tell you. All Rome knows it by now."

On the night of July 24 the Italian Senate met to consider the country's military and political future. Fascism was tottering. Mussolini no longer held the whip in hand and in fact had no control either over the country or the party he created. His enemies had at last become vocal and there were men to speak out against him. There were long speeches, arguments, and discussions lasting through the night into the next day. The fate of Italy was being decided and Mussolini had little voice in that fate and little persuasive powers.

Roberto Farinacci, perhaps the most rabid of all Fascists, led the Fascist minority. Dino Grandi, former ambassador to Britain, championed the anti-Mussolini majority. "Farinacci made an impassioned plea to place Italy's entire military and political future into the hands of the Germans," said my informant. "He said the Germans were strong and would restore Fascism to its former glory and that this was the only hope to save the deteriorating political and military situation." To this Mussolini and the Senate said no.

And then Grandi made an equally impassioned plea. He spoke for several hours, setting forth the view of those clamoring against Fascism, against Mussolini and against German domination of Italy. He read a proclamation which would place the country's military and political future in the hands of the King. To Grandi's proposal, Mussolini said no. Five senators said no. Nineteen said yes. And Count Giacomo Suardo, president of the Senate, voted neither no nor yes. And as these men left the Palazzo Venezia nineteen turned and walked one way. Six, including Mussolini, walked in the opposite direction. And the man who voted neither no nor yes strolled away alone.

Ordinarily, the naval officer continued, Mussolini visited the King on Mondays and Thursdays for conferences. But on this day, Sunday, he received an urgent call that the King wished to see him immediately. The little monarch did not wish to wait twenty-four hours to discuss with him important matters. And so Mussolini hurried to the Villa Savoia. This time, for some reason, he had a stronger guard accompanying him, and the people, who were accustomed to seeing him pass on the streets of Rome, noted this and wondered. When Mussolini reached the Villa Savoia, he hurried from the automobile into the place while the bodyguard waited outside. He was closeted with the King for several hours.

Meantime, after the decisive defeat in the Senate, Farinacci went to the German commander in Rome and a few hours later was on his way to Germany dressed in the uniform of a captain in the German Army. A few days later over the Munich radio Farinacci pleaded with the Italian people to trust the Germans because they would restore Fascism and Italian glory.

When Mussolini concluded his conference with the King, he came out the door and walked to where he had left his automobile and special guards. But his car was not there. An ambulance stood in its place with a carabinieri captain beside it. Mussolini, my informant said, appeared startled. The carabinieri captain stepped forward and saluted. "I think, your excellency," he said, "this automobile is more suitable for your safety than the other one."

"Nonsense," Il Duce snapped. He looked about and saw only royal police. "What is the meaning of this?"

"Well, sir," said the young captain, "I must tell you this car is much better than the other one." Mussolini looked into the eyes of the determined, insistent young captain and what he saw there made him give a shrug of resignation. "Mussolini stepped to the door of the ambulance," the officer concluded, "and the captain opened it. Inside were four big, handsome carabinieri. Mussolini stepped in. The door was shut. The ambulance drove off the grounds—through the rear gate—to prison."   □

Salerno, Italy, September 10 — German soldiers rode through the streets of Salerno machine gunning civilians and Italian soldiers as well before they were finally driven out of the city this afternoon in the second day of bitter fighting on this northernmost sector of the Allied invasion front. Against desperate opposition, the Allied troops slowly deepened their invasion bridgehead. Weeping women, who said the Germans robbed them of all of their food two days ago, gave our troops the same sort of riotous welcome they received when they entered the towns of Sicily. Even while machine guns rattled at the edge of the city and shells burst nearby, people came from their houses to greet the troops.

The mayor, Fascist leaders and wealthier people fled when the Allies began the invasion. Those who greeted us were the poor people who had no means of transport or money with which to get out of the danger zone. So they stayed in shelters while the Germans stripped their homes of silver, linen, food, wine, and anything else of value they could find. The people cheered the troops as their liberators and they were bitter toward their former Allies. Unarmed Italian soldiers wandered about the streets or gathered to talk with British Tommies and exchange souvenirs.

I entered the city this afternoon from the flagship of the American rear admiral commanding the naval task force and was accompanied by Lt. Col. of Marines Jim Brower, Rochester, N.Y. We climbed into a small landing craft in the gulf and were piloted to the beach. An Italian civilian on the beach frantically signaled that there were land mines where we were headed and then pointed out a safe lane. A British naval officer later said the civilian had saved several craft from hitting the mines.

"Maybe," said Brower as he stepped ashore, "I'm the first Marine to land on Italy."

"Well I know I'm the first citizen from Greensboro into Salerno," Morton laughed.

We walked into the center of the city. There were a few Allied soldiers and Navy men on the streets and a few hundred civilians. Machine guns were still popping outside the city. Three American representatives of the Allied Military Government (AMG) had already arrived with troops and posted proclamations. Italian carabinieri police who had been disarmed by the Germans wore civil police armbands and were keeping order.

Lt. Col. Thomas A. Lane, Washington, D.C., AMG chief for the Salerno district, was busy organizing the civil government which bogged down completely after most of the officials had fled. He was sided by Capt. Augustine Riolo, Endicott, N.Y., and Second Lt. Donald Murray, Los Angeles, Cal. They entered Salerno when the Germans and British were still fighting in the outskirts and began to set up the civil affairs organization.

The people lived in terror the last two days as the Germans looted homes and stores, dynamited water mains, stole all the food, and confiscated all vehicles and gasoline. "The Germans machine gunned civilians walking down the streets." Capt. Riolo said, "and they cleaned out the town. These people haven't eaten for two days, and they are looking to us to take care of them." An Italian colonel said the situation in Naples was desperate with the Germans pillaging the city and threatening destruction of Italian troops whose ammunition is running low. The civil authority has broken down completely, and Naples has become a virtual battlefield.

With the armistice, Italian naval and army officers with a few minor exceptions appeared to be giving full co-operation to the Allies and willingly turning against their one-time ally. In some cases it was reported the Germans were forcing Italian units to continue the fight, machine gunning them if they refused. Capt. Riolo said, "They expected us to land in this area because of the heavy bombings and said they were ready to fight with us, but if they were ready to fight they could do nothing after the Germans took their guns and ammunition." The senior Italian naval officer in charge of Salerno port conferred with the American vice admiral and gave him valuable information on the naval situation including charts of minefields along the coast.   □

With Allied Armies in Italy, September 12 — The first American evacuation hospital to follow the troops in the invasion of Italy began receiving patients today in canvas-walled wards. Tents and equipment came ashore on the invasion beach last night and less than twelve hours later, casualties returning from the front lines were receiving expert care from the staff directed by Lt. Col. Paul K. Sauer, New York City.

Overnight a modern hospital had sprung up in the plain over which the American troops had pushed back the Germans only two days before. It would have been operating sooner except that battlefield priorities delayed the arrival of equipment. Sauer and his staff landed in Italy at 2 p.m. on invasion day and spent the next forty-eight hours peeking out of slit trenches while enemy guns shelled the beach area, and planes bombed and strafed around them. "We got a warm reception," the gray-haired hospital commander said with a smile. "When we got ashore we found the enemy was only 800 yards ahead of us. It was an exciting introduction to war."

Sauer brought his hospital from the United States to North Africa last May, and then he was selected to bring the first evacuation hospital into Italy with the Fifth Army. Coming ashore, the doctors were machine gunned and strafed as they crouched in landing boats. The vessels were used for landing all types of Army personnel and were not marked with Red Crosses, so the enemy had no way of knowing it was a hospital unit.

In the plain where the hospital now sits they watched America troops battle German tanks which counter-attacked in a desperate effort to break the Allied bridgehead. When they got ashore there was nothing for them to do but dig in and wait for equipment to follow them ashore. "So we spent our first forty-eight hours on Italian soil in foxholes," Sauer said. "Then our tents and equipment arrived late yesterday. We worked all night setting them up."

Occasionally they have to break off work and jump for foxholes when enemy planes dive in to strafe nearby targets, and bits of shell shower down from an anti-aircraft barrage. Even as Sauer told of the trip to the beach, there was the stuttering of machine guns from the skies. Two Spitfires were on the tail of a Messerschmitt 109 which had tried to sneak in to attack the beaches. The Spitfires poured a hail of bullets into the enemy plane and then the German pilot bailed out and the ship crashed.

"When our nurses come ashore tomorrow from the hospital ship we will have all personnel on hand and give the wounded or ill men the best care," Sauer said. Near Sauer's evacuation hospital, Maj. J. W. Pickens of Cleburne, Tex., had a divisional hospital clearing station operating with a capacity of one hundred beds, and from these hospitals, the casualties are being cleared to the hospital ships to be taken to station hospitals in Sicily or North Africa.

With Pickens was 2nd Lt. Oran C. Ogdin Jr., Parkersburg, W. Va. "I have been with this outfit over a year," Pickens said. "I thought they were good, but not so good as they are. They have done a great job under fire.

"When we were coming in one of our small boats was sunk by direct 88-millimeter gunfire. Two of my men swam back into the sea to save the lives of two men who couldn't swim, and were drowning. One company of officers was caught in machine gun fire during a tank battle, and we've been bombed and strafed, but the men have gone right ahead with the work."

Ogdin came through two harrowing experiences with only a couple of slight wounds which did not keep him off his feet. He was on the beach when a shell burst within a few feet of him, but was only grazed by the shrapnel, then later a German plane dropped a bomb which hit beside his slit trench. It blew him into the air just as a tree trunk fell into the trench where he had lain. "It felt like the whole plane was falling on top of me," he said. "It was a miracle that I got out of that one." □

Aboard the U.S.S. BISCAYNE in the Gulf of Salerno, September 16 — This bombers' alley is a red hot spot on the world's battlefronts—a ship-filled, smoke-hazed stretch of water through which the Fifth Army is being funneled onto the mainland of Italy. On the maps it's the Gulf of Salerno, but to American sailors it is Bombers' Alley, the lane down which the enemy roars through blistering anti-aircraft fire to hit at the ships pouring men, guns and tanks onto the invasion beaches.

Seven days after the first assault troops swarmed over the beaches to establish a bridgehead on Italian soil, the enemy still is blasting at our ships from the skies with hit and run attacks by small forces slipping through the Allied fighter protection. Five and six times each day the ship's loudspeaker crackles with the general quarters alarm. Sailors boil up from the lower decks to their battle stations. Portholes are closed, hatches are closed and the gunners point their weapons at the sky waiting for the attack.

And then the ship is tense with expectancy, shipboard life freezes into hard resistance. Small boats scurry away from the large ships. One moment there is the calm inaction of peace. The next moment the lid is blown off with a gush of anti-aircraft from hundreds of guns as enemy planes come within range, usually diving out of a bright sun. That's when your stomach turns into a hard knot and you crouch involuntarily, watching to see if a bomb is dropping your way, while the smaller ack-ack guns hammer away and the larger guns cause the ship to shudder.

The crew of this ship are supremely confident that they are riding a "lucky ship." "They can not do anything to our ship," declared Harry Murphy of Brooklyn. "She's got a charmed life." At least a dozen bombs have dropped within one hundred yards of the ship, and one came so close it lifted the stern out of the water, but no harm was done. The Germans don't always miss. However, our ships' losses have been far below expectations for operations of this magnitude, I was told by a ship's officer.

If fire breaks out aboard a ship among the first to reach her usually are the damage control officer and his fire and rescue party. The efficient officer has a reputation among his shipmates as a man without nerves. He takes his men in to fight the fires regardless of danger, and sometimes when others think the situation is hopeless. When fire broke out aboard a British ship the other day, the fire and rescue party went to the scene. Clifford B. Barnhill, of Bremerton, Wash., was hoisted on the deck of the abandoned vessel with a water hose and he began pouring water into a compartment stored with ammunition and powder bags.

The fire party tossed some powder overboard and within a short time had the fire under control, saving the valuable cargo. The men of the Navy have to move fast when things get to popping along Bombers' Alley. There's no time to think. One of the most important fleet defenses lies in airplane recognition. When a plane comes hurtling across the gulf, the gunners must be able to tell at a glance whether it's a Messerschmitt, a Focke-Wulf, a Spitfire or a Warhawk. Considering the speed with which the plane moves, there are few mistakes in identifying hostile and friendly planes.   □

Aboard the U.S.S. BISCAYNE in the Gulf of Salerno, September 16 — The Germans are believed to be using a new type of radio-controlled aerial torpedo against the Allied invasion fleet in the Gulf of Salerno. There have been previous reports the Germans were experimenting with an aerial torpedo, but this is the first time, it is believed, that it has been used in actual combat.

Several naval officers said they saw a winged object, like a small plane, flying toward a boat. It passed overhead, wheeled, and then dived. It is believed the torpedo is controlled by radio from a plane flying at a high altitude, with the pilot controlling the projectile.   □

Capri, September 22 — Young Henry Ringling North is having more adventures in the Mediterranean as a lieutenant in Uncle Sam's Navy than he ever had operating the big top with his brother, John Ringling North. Ringling Bros. and Barnum & Bailey's circus is just a sideshow compared with his extravaganza on the invasion front and North is top man in one of the daredevil acts.

Two days ago, he rescued Tito Zaniboni from the island of Ponza, sixty miles north of Capri, where he was held as a prisoner because of his attempt on the life of Mussolini in 1926. North brought Zaniboni, his beautiful daughter and the Duke of Camerini from Ponza to Capri, thus saving three of Italy's most bitter anti-Fascists. North was the first American on the island of Ponza. He went there with a naval task force to see if it was still German-held. German planes flew over the motor launches as they sped toward Ponza, but did not attack them. "We found that the Germans had gone," North said, "but for some reason they had not taken Zaniboni or the Duke of Camerini with them."

Except for betrayal by his secretary, Zaniboni might have ended Il Duce's career that day in Rome when he calmly prepared to assassinate the Fascist chief. Zaniboni installed a precision rifle in his office across from the balcony on the palazzo Venezia. He knew the exact time Mussolini was to appear. An expert rifleman, he expected one shot to be sufficient. But he had in his employ a young secretary addicted to gambling, who was in debt and desperate for money. He learned of Zaniboni's plan and sold out his employer for enough money to cover his gambling debts. Police arrested Zaniboni before he could fire a shot.

Zaniboni spent sixteen years in solitary confinement. About two years ago he was moved to Ponza. Prior to the mission of Ponza, North and another officer went ashore at Amalfi and started to the town of Cava, thinking it was safely in the hands of the Allies. They walked into a barrage of mortar fire that had them sweating and then the Germans dropped shells around them as they scrambled back to their boat. North has had too much to do on his Navy job to give much thought to the big top. "Things move too fast over here to worry about the circus," North said.   □

Capri, Italy, September 23 — With a good supply of soap and cigarettes an American soldier or sailor can barter his way through Capri's best society and spend his leave in luxury on this Mediterranean beauty spot. For two years soap and tobacco have been rarer than tourists on this playground island.

When ships or boats put in at Capri's small harbor, the men wander through the novelty-filled shops, which are doing a rushing business. Caprians, joyfully anticipating a speedy return of the good old tourist days when the war ends, point out the villas owned by Gracie Fields and Mrs. Harrison Williams and think it quite a joke that a British officer has taken over the villa which once belonged to Count Ciano. Many villas are thrown open to the American visitors in a gay welcome to the "liberators," but there probably is none happier to see the Americans than Mrs. Theodore Catuogno and her daughter, Constance of Philadelphia, who are the only American citizens living on the island. The Catuogno villa is a gathering place for young officers with leave from sea duties.

Mrs. Catuogno and Constance came to Capri for a two weeks' visit, fell in love with the island, and have been here six years. "Our friends urged us to leave when the war began," the mother said. "But we thought the war would be over in a short time. I did not think Italy could possibly stay in the war more than two months. Then when we wanted to leave we couldn't." The two women received an allowance from Theodore Catuogno, who formerly operated Philadelphia's Rittenhouse [hotel] along with Mrs. Catuogno's brother, Vincent Bruni. But since the Germans occupied Rome they have been unable to get funds from the Swiss legation. "Because we had an Italian name," says Constance, "not many people on the island knew we were Americans. We want to get back to America as soon as possible."

Lieut. (Jg) George Steele of Fairhaven, Mass., and Lieut. (Jg) George Patterson of Macon, Ga., dropped by to eat grapes from the Catuogno vineyards. "When we heard there were Americans on the island," Steele said, "we dropped by just to be able to talk to someone from the United States." They had been on a sightseeing trip in town with Lieut. (Jg) Bob McLeod of Minneapolis, Minn., and Lieut. (Jg) Giles Peresich of Biloxi, Miss. "I did not think there was any place left in the world like this," McLeod said. "You can see Naples from here and still you feel the war is far away. Yet the Germans left the island only ten days ago, after dominating life on Capri." Mrs. Catuogno said that "if the Germans got drunk and created a disturbance no one did anything to them. I guess the Fascists were afraid of them, although most Italians hated the Germans and wouldn't speak to them on the street." □

With the United States Navy in the Gulf of Salerno, September 26 — The once beautiful port of Naples is now a ravaged city of horrors. Desperate German troops—ruling the tortured city by terrorism—are spreading destruction, machine gunning women and children and forcing soldiers and civilians alike into slave labor battalions with death for those who refuse. This is the story brought from Naples by terrified refugees who escaped in fishing boats, risking drowning at sea rather than face the fury of their one-time Allies. Many of the refugees were not so lucky. The Germans tossed hand grenades into their boats as they attempted to slip away from the harbor or machine gunned the frail craft.

The apparent aim of the Germans, infuriated by the Italian armistice with the United Nations on the eve of invasion, is to wreak vengeance on the Italian people and to destroy Naples as much as possible so that nothing of value remains when Allied troops take the city. The port is rapidly becoming a shambles, refugees say, and harbor facilities are being blasted and burned day and night. Ships are being sunk in an effort to block the harbor entrances and the waters are mined to delay the Navy's making use of the harbor as a supply base. Great clouds of smoke drift over the city and make the smoke pouring from Vesuvius seem a puny effort. The rumble of demolitions is plainly audible on the island of Capri, which is becoming a haven for hundreds of refugees. One refugee, who asked that his name be withheld for fear of reprisals against his relatives held by the Germans, told this story:

"There are many bodies of dead Italians lying in the streets of Naples. Some of them were shot down for no reason except that they were walking in the streets. I saw a German shoot an Italian soldier who still had a rifle. A young man ran to pick up the rifle and he was killed too. I saw a German soldier flip a cigarette butt into the street. A youth stopped to pick it up and he was shot. There is an absolute reign of terror existing. Food stores are being looted and the people are starving in their homes, afraid to come out on the street.

"The Germans are forcing every able bodied man to 'volunteer' for labor battalions. They are taking them north as pioneer troops and perhaps to force them to work in German factories. These people are becoming nothing more than slave laborers.

"A few days after the armistice some of our troops fought the Germans in Naples. But they had little ammunition, since the Germans controlled the supplies. The Germans soon overpowered them."

Allied bombings smashed most of the harbor facilities, sank many ships in the gulf and alongside docks and battered the railway terminals. What the planes did not destroy the Germans are trying to finish and from all reports they are setting the torch to many non-military buildings such as the Naples Opera House. Great fires are burning in the southern part of the city where the Germans blasted a torpedo factory, the military arsenal, gas works, engineering works and many oil storage centers around the railway yards. Obviously Naples' primary value to the Allies is in its large harbor. Since the invasion, all troops, armor guns and supplies have been moved across the beaches in the Gulf of Salerno by shallow draft amphibious operations vessels that can unload cargoes at the docks, speeding up the flow of supplies and material to the Army.

The food situation in Naples is acute. No supplies are moving into the Metropolis from the farms, where there are abundant harvests of grapes, apples, peaches, nuts and vegetables. Disease is rife among the malnourished people to increase the fear and misery. Many refugees arriving at Capri are being segregated for fear disease will spread to the little playground island. The influx of 100 to 200 persons each day is putting a strain on Capri's slender food resources. The refugees arrive with only small bundles of valuables, fifteen or twenty persons crowded into a small boat.   □

Allied Headquarters in North Africa, October 1 – Clearing of the harbor of Naples will eliminate a grave problem of troop supply for the Allies. Since the invasion began in the Gulf of Salerno on September 9, every ton of shipping to feed and equip the Fifth Army has gone across the beaches in the slow and laboriously-painful process of supply by small boats and vessels. Once engineers and salvage crews remove wreckage from a portion of the harbor and dock area, deep-draft vessels will be able to tie up and unload swiftly.

The Germans have sunk many ships in the harbor and have demolished as much of the port as they could, but Navy men agree it is almost impossible to make a port completely useless. Harbors at Tripoli, Tunis and Bizerte were left in shambles by the retreating enemy but still the Navy managed to clear channels quickly and open them to Allied shipping. Naples' capture came none too soon for supply problems were multiplying with the approach of bad weather and rough seas. When I left the Gulf of Salerno four days ago the wind was whipping up heavy waves which were tossing the small ships about. Sweating crews were almost frantic, trying to keep shallow-draft supply vessels from being smashed or capsized on the beach. Flat-bottomed amphibious craft not intended for heavy seas became almost unmanageable.

A great part of the supplies for the Fifth Army has been carried from North African and Sicilian ports. The small vessels were driven onto the beach and after they were unloaded and the supplies were reloaded into trucks, they were driven along dusty roads to supply dumps. Supplying that great army across the beach was one of the great accomplishments of the Navy and Merchant Marine of the campaign. Crews labored day and night on the beaches to keep the supplies. It was one of the invasion's weakest links. But now, relief is in sight. In the calm, protected waters of the Gulf of Naples big vessels soon will be able to land their cargoes directly onto land. The fall of Naples was a Fifth Army victory second only to establishing the mainland beachhead. □

Allied Headquarters, Algiers, October 16 – One American P-38 lightning pilot, Maj. William L., Leverette, thirty-three, of Tallahassee, Fla., knocked down seven enemy planes in one action last Saturday when Lightnings bagged seventeen Junker 88 dive-bombers about to attack an Allied convoy in the Aegean Sea, Allied headquarters disclosed today. Five were downed by Second Lieut. Stroy Hanna, twenty-three, of

Westfield, Ind.—the full complement to become an ace—and three by Second Lieut. Homer L. Sprinkle, twenty-two, of Potosi, Mo. Only eight of the Stukas escaped in the mad aerial battle.

Squadron Commander Leverette said his squadron had just arrived over the convoy fifteen ahead of schedule when Sprinkle called to him and reported "Bogies at 1 o'clock." "We call unidentified aircraft Bogies," Leverette continued, "and there was a cloud of them headed our way. I saw they were Stukas. I called to Second Lieut. Wayne L. Blue of Tecumseh, Neb., to take three ships and give us top cover.

"We got in behind them without being seen, but we missed seeing a Junker 88 behind them. We peeled off in the middle, and I got two of them before they even knew we were there. The gunner in the first plane started to fire, but stopped as soon as I let go.

"I turned to the left and poured it into a third plane. He went into a deep spiral. I looked over my shoulder just in time to see the first one crash into the sea. We came back at them again and I got on the tail of another. I got a couple of others, and then got number six, but the last was the best. I got in some good shots, and set his engine on fire."

Hanna made one pass without getting in a shot, but on the second dive he shot down a Stuka. Another came into his sights, and "I let him have it, and both the pilot and gunner were shot out of their seats." Sprinkle shot down two Stukas and then tore the wings off a third.   □

Allied Headquarters, Algiers, [October] — More than 500 Allied vessels including warships and merchantmen were used to get troops and supplies ashore during the first phases of last month's Salerno landing, the American and British Navies revealed today in describing the spectacular support given the operation by the two Navies. Two of Britain's mightiest battleships, the *Valiant* and *Warspite*, mingled their terrific broadsides with those from the American cruisers *Boise*, *Philadelphia* and *Savannah* and almost a score of destroyers to help turn the tide of battle when the enemy was threatening to smash Lt. Gen. Mark W. Clark's bridgehead.

The two battleships joined the Allied force pumping shells into German positions on the sixth day of the invasion, and they arrived just as the Nazis were making their bid to crack the bridgehead. Actually, the joint naval announcement was a modest reference to the part played by the warships in smashing German resistance and opening the way to Naples.

Not as spectacular but even more important than the two-day appearance of the *Valiant* and the *Warspite* was the job done by the cruisers and destroyers in laying down fire support. Their guns roared day and night while the operation was in progress. Admiral of the Fleet Sir Andrew Browne Cunningham was in supreme naval command with Vice Admiral H. K. Hewitt, USN, in immediate command of the Western Task Force divided into two sections: The Southern Attack Force under Rear Admiral John L. Hall Jr. aboard the *U.S.S. Samuel Chase,* and the Northern Attack Force under Commodore G. N. Oliver, R. N., aboard *H.M.S. Hilary.* There was an unusual situation in Oliver's command, for Rear Adm. Richard L. Conolly, although senior to Oliver in rank, volunteered to serve under the commodore. Destroyers taking part in the action were the *Plunkett, Niblack, Benson, Gleaves, Mayo, Wainwright, Triple, Rhind, Knight, Woolsey, Ludlow, Edison, Nicholson, Bristol, Cole, Bernadou* and the *Dallas.* The cruiser *Boise* was under the command of Capt. N. L. Thebaud, the *Philadelphia* was under Capt. P. Hendren, and the *Savannah* was under Capt. Robert Cary. "Covering and supporting gunfire from the warships played an immense part in the eventual success of the operation for at times the troops ashore were held up and were unable to advance in the face of strong German resistance from carefully prepared and sited positions," the announcement said.

Even enemy tank attacks were broken up by the pounding from the warships. The ships engaged shore batteries at point blank range and poured tons of shells into enemy positions. The cruiser *Boise*'s participation in the Salerno action marked her entry into a new war theater after her unparalleled record of having been chiefly instrumental in sinking six Japanese warships in twenty-seven minutes during the October 1942, battle off Cape Esperance, Guadalcanal. Battered and torn, the *Boise* came home after she had been given up for lost when she became separated from her cruiser-destroyer task force which intercepted the Japanese force. In helping destroy two Japanese cruisers, a light cruiser and three destroyers, she lost three officers and 104 men in the violent night battle. □

Allied Headquarters, Algiers, [October] — Corsica's dead-end kids, lean from hunger, their tough and bony bodies covered with tattered and patched rags, helped liberate their homeland from the Nazis. Now they want to follow the French Army into France. A delayed story sent here from Corsica by Capt. Karl Quigley, American liaison officer with the French, said of these Corsican teen-agers and their guerrilla bands: "One sees them everywhere. They are standing by the roadsides looking for lifts toward the front (the story was written while fighting was still going on in Corsica). They are in the hills marching doggedly through the rain squalls that appear and disappear continually. They are traveling only in one direction . . . toward the Boche [French pejorative term for the Germans] who for more than three years has made their lives hell.

"These kids with their hunting knives hanging from worn leather belts and Sten guns or German rifles slung over their hunched up shoulders, are fighting a war. Until now they have fought it better than the Italian Army with all its modern arms and classy equipment. They are up forward where the going is tough and they are behind the Nazi line that stretches across the northern end of this mountainous terrain.

"When they get caught their lives are not worth a damn. Jules Andreani is seventeen. He turned seventeen last month and his family in Bastia gave him the kind of a birthday party one can scrape together in an occupied land. He turned up at this tiny partisan outpost looking hungry and tattered. He had spent thirteen furtive days in the hills to the north sniping at what Germans he could find. He had on a pair of Nazi boots and carried a German Mauser rifle made in Erfurt in 1913. He is cocky as hell.

"He strutted about the farmyard that is the home of a company of tough Moroccan irregulars. A French colonel came up and asked him what was going on up forward. The kid spat on the ground before he answered, but when he began to talk he knew what he was talking about. He drew a rough map on the muddy ground with one of his newly-acquired boots and when he was through he paused to wipe the boot off with his hand.

"He explained where the machine gun positions were and swaggered a bit as he explained where German snipers had been hidden—but were hidden no more. Then the colonel took him into a wooden barracks which once had been Italian. When he came out he wore a Moroccan djellaba, homespun burnoose of the French Colonial Army's famed Goumiers [Second and Fourth Moroccan Infantry Divisions of some 10,000 men]. He had enlisted in the Army and was going back as a guide.

"I asked him if he were satisfied. He began his answer with a word untranslatable and unprintable.

" 'Next year I'll be a sergeant,' he said. 'Next year when we are in France I'll be a sergeant.'

"I looked at the colonel dripping beneath his pale blue kepi. He smiled at me through the downpour. He didn't have to come out and say the kid was right. The kid knew it and the colonel knew it and the rest of the world that lay behind them as they climbed into trucks to move off did not matter at all." ☐

Algiers, October 21 — Lt. Gen. Mark W. Clark's Fifth Army has won a behind-the-lines victory of transportation and supply. In a race with winter and harassed by many handicaps, including enemy fire, the Fifth Army's supply men have kept supplies flowing steadily into Italy. Their greatest achievement came when they shifted the supply route from across the Gulf of Salerno beaches into the devastated port of Naples. A few days after the Army reached that port, a liberty ship had snaked its way in and unloaded its cargo.

A company of amphibious ducks under Capt. Mahlon Fisk of Little Rock, Ark., handled a big part of the tonnage going onto the beaches in the early days, bringing food, water, gasoline and other supplies—even 105-millimeter guns to help the infantry blast the enemy off the beaches. A duck [amphibious truck] driven by Pvt. Floyd L. Browning, Houston, Tex.—"The Sea Horse"— came ashore with one such gun, and eleven minutes later it was blazing away. Within seventeen minutes it had knocked out two machine gun nests and one enemy "88." The ducks were loaded and placed in the water twelve miles from shore at 2 a.m. In the darkness they slipped in unobserved by the enemy— who was positively flabbergasted when the gunfire suddenly broke loose.

After the enemy was driven from Naples, engineers, salvage crews and Italian workers plunged into the job of clearing wharves of wreckage and debris and cutting a lane for shipping through the sunken hulks of ships. Before Naples fell, transportation experts had solved one problem—they recalled a branch railway line from Paestum, where supplies were being unloaded on the beaches, to Salerno. They took the flanged wheels from damaged railway cars and welded them to the brake drums of G.I. trucks for locomotive power. The trucks were able to haul five cars laden with ten tons each. Five trucks became locomotives.

Then the men under Lt. Gen. R. H. Clarkson of Santa Fe, N.M., Fifth Army transportation chief, repaired a steam locomotive which could haul 250 tons of freight. There was no electricity in Naples—so three Italian submarines were brought in and their 750-kilowatt generators provided the power. The commanding general of the port of Naples said when he reached it that "the Army has taken over the greatest concentration of port ruins in the history of war."   □

Naples, October 24 — Practically every doughboy here says Naples is about the best town he's seen since he left home. In a popularity vote among American troops, such romantic points as Algiers, Tunis, Oran or

Casablanca would run a poor second. Why? Well, mainly the friendliness of the Neapolitans and the abundance of comely girls. After almost a month of Allied occupation, Naples slowly is recovering from the horrors wrought by the Nazis. Many of the city's scars are disappearing. Debris and wreckage are being cleared away.

Commenting on the efforts of residents to make the Americans feel at home, Pvt. Donald Connor of 12371 Birwood Avenue, Detroit, said: "If we want directions to reach any place, they not only give the directions but go out of their way to take us there themselves. The day we got here, we couldn't find but one guy could speak English, but he took the day off to show us around."

The pretty girls appear in large numbers, and they are no less friendly than the other Neapolitans. Joe Yank likes that. The ladies at home will be interested to know that Naples has a seemingly inexhaustible supply of good silk stockings. They sell for around $2.50 a pair—and they are not rationed. Nor are there runs on the stores, for most Naples women go barelegged. Usually, their shoes are wood-soled "wedgies" with cloth or leather straps.

Small shops are reopening and displaying stocks of souvenirs, the prices of which have soared. In many cases the Allied Military Government (AMG) has stepped in to cut profiteering and set ceiling prices. But price control is difficult. "When we first arrived," said Pvt. Delmar Richardson, Fort Wayne, Ind., "we were buying silk stockings for 50 cents a pair. But everything has doubled or tripled in price since then." At the city's new restaurants, food is scarce. Business is far from normal, too, although the markets have ample stocks of apples, nuts, persimmons, mangos and other fruits. □

With the Allied Fifth Army in Italy, October 26 –
Opening the assault on the enemy's strong upper Volturno line, Lanky Lt. Col. Llye W. Bernard of Highland Falls, N.Y. sent his rugged infantry battalion up steep 1,600-feet slopes today and his boys batted the Germans off. They tramped through the hills in darkness last night to get into position, stumbling over rutted, dusty roads and bending under their heavy burden of battle equipment.

On their right and on their left, other troops moved into line to await the signal for attack which would break the lull on the Fifth Army front. An artillery barrage opened at dawn, crashing and echoing through the valley in a rolling thunder unbroken for an hour. When the morning mists lifted, the attack began. The Fifth Army once again is on the move along the historic road to Rome in a slow hill to hill advance which is only beginning to develop.

Under the gray curtain of clouds, our dive bombers came over in wave after wave. Near their targets they swung into echelon and then one by one plummeted toward the earth in screaming dives to unload their bombs on the enemy around Mt. Nicola, Mt. Gaievola and Mt. San Angelo in the vicinity of Pietravairano. It was an impressive display of air power and air superiority. As the bombers came in, Spitfires wove a pattern of protection above them. Not a single enemy plane opposed the Allies and not a single plane was lost.

From an observation post high up on the mountainside, Lt. Col. John W. Hansborough of Tyler, Texas, and Lt. Col. Kenneth Wade of San Diego, Calif., watched the bombers at work. "They put on a beautiful show," said Hansborough. "I never have seen closer liaison and co-operation between ground and air forces." Pvt. Lester Couch of Kentucky paused in his march into line to watch the bombers and a grin spread over his beet-red face as he observed, "we've been marching a mighty long time, but it's worth it just to see those boys at work." The narrow country road winding to the front line was jammed with an incongruous assortment of traffic. Civilians hurrying out of the battle area rode past on bicycles laden with bundles, or carried their belongings in bags and boxes. Pack trains of mules carrying ammunition, guns and supplies filed along the side of the road. Jeeps and trucks snaked through the lines of civilians and animals and occasionally detoured into plowed fields to get around bulldozers widening the little road.

Although this veteran division which was moving into action had been fighting for about a month, the troops still had a spring in their step and paid little attention to the shells falling nearby. At the foot of the hill a burning ammunition truck, hit by a shell, sent a column of black smoke into the sky. "The boys in the truck got out all right," said Sgt. Frederick Bell of Pecos, Tex. When the attack opened, the troops had to cross a small open valley to storm one of the commanding heights overlooking an important crossroads and railway line. The Germans tried to halt the advance with machine gun and mortar fire, but Col. Bernard's men overcame opposition at the foot of the mountain and began working their way toward the top. Capt. Burleigh Packwood of Bozeman, Mont., and his company reached the top first and drove the Germans from the peak. Then they dug in to protect troops on their left.

Around the mountain trail to the south more troops moved toward the line in single file while Lt. Col. Lionel McGarr of Phoenix, Ariz., watched.

From the east side of the Volturno, where another division was attacking, came the sound of small arms and mortar fire and staccato bursts of machine guns. "They are having a scrap over there," McGarr said, "but everything is going all right. We got all our first objectives less than three hours after the attack started.

"The boys went up the hill like mountain goats. They are getting to be better mountain fighters than we even figured."

While the fighting since Salerno has been tough, many soldiers believe the hills of Sicily were worse than those here. "At least these hills are not so close together and we have not had to march such long distances," said Capt. Edwin Nichols of San Francisco. Medical men have found the terrain better suited to the evacuation of wounded than Sicily's saw-toothed ridges because jeep ambulances can be driven near the fighting troops. "That's a great help to litter bearers," said Capt. William H. Miller of Woodstown, N.J., whose job is to see that cases are moved quickly from battalion aid stations to clearing stations. "Those boys are doing a fine job under fire." The troops gained their objectives in the opening attack with light casualties.   □

With the Fifth Army In Italy, October 28 — On rain-swept and sodden recently-taken heights, American troops beat off German counter-attacks last night and opened the way for other units of the Fifth Army to press steadily forward against the Germans' upper Volturno line. Under dripping skies, the Yanks fought their way up 1,800 feet of slopes to capture the second of three mountain ridges controlling an important section of the vital road to Rome.

(Allied headquarters at Algiers announced yesterday that the Fifth Army had occupied two stretches of high ground facing Massico Ridge—one in the Francolise area and the other, known as "Mad Dog Hill," near Raviscania. Massico Ridge is one of the anchors of the new Nazi mountain line.)

Infantry went into the attack with Sherman tanks following close behind the first line troops to give them fire support. Not since the Fifth Army landed in Italy have tanks given such close support to attacking ground troops. "The tanks did a great job," one officer said. "They came right in behind our troops to shoot up enemy positions and help clean out opposition pockets."

A battalion led by Lieut. Col. Lyle Bernard, of Highland Falls, N.Y., stormed the hill yesterday and drove the Germans off. Last night the enemy counter-attacked, but their forces were driven back. Then they tried to infiltrate the American positions but were unable to break the tight defensive positions. The attacks gave the Fifth Army positions dominating other high ground and a firm hold from which to smash at the main upper Volturno line. The Germans were reported to be suffering heavy casualties and indications were their supply situation is extremely bad, largely because of the steady hammering of Allied air forces.   □

With the American Fifth Army in Italy, October 29 –
The Germans have flooded ten square miles of the famous Pontine marshes near Rome which Mussolini reclaimed in his plan to give land to the people. This was but one of the many obstacles the tightening German defense was preparing for Rome, which many expect to fall this year, but only after many bloody battles are fought across central Italy.

Rugged mountains stand before the American Fifth and British Eighth Armies. South of the Apennines, there are only two routes of approach to Rome, and both are dominated by towering mountains which must be swept clean of the enemy before troops can advance in the valleys. Cold and heavy rains already are complicating the army's problems of combat and supply. Chilled autumn winds are adding to soldier discomfort.

Nevertheless, the Fifth Army is keeping steady pressure against the Germans in the upper Volturno River region with a series of attacks to capture mountain ridges dominating the Garigliano River Valley. Once through the upper Volturno line, the Allies will force the Germans to fall back behind the flooded Garigliano River line, which may be hinged on the ancient city of Cassino. The present series of attacks are swinging like a hinge to the west against Mt. San Croce, a 3,000-foot extinct volcano overlooking the Garigliano Valley.   □

With the Fifth Army on the Volturno River, November 4 –
In a sweeping midnight attack preceded by a terrific artillery bombardment from hundreds of guns, American units of the Fifth Army completely smashed the Nazis' upper Volturno River line last night and thrust the Germans back toward their new Cassino defense line. As the creeping barrage moved forward across the river and the flat valley separating the Volturno from the rugged hills, American doughboys waded the river and slipped into the shadows of the vineyards.

There boobytraps and mines left by the Nazis took a heavy toll among the Americans, but at dawn the doughboys had worked their way across the 1,500 yards of flat lands and were inching up the mountains where the Germans sprayed them from machine gun nests. Venafro fell to the American attack in a house-to-house battle with close artillery support breaking up one Nazi counter-attack.

One Austrian who surrendered there said he had heard over the radio that the Tri-Power conference at Moscow had refused to recognize Germany's annexation of Austria and that his country's independence would be restored. Under those circumstances he and his countrymen no longer had reason to fight, he said. At 10:30 p.m. we climbed into a jeep convoy and drove down the dim road toward the Volturno. Nobody said much. A cold, raw wind blew up the valley. Dark shadows loomed ahead and became jeeps or trucks moving back from the front line. The river was a bright ribbon to our left. Our observation post in a thicket of thornbush and scrub oak was not more than one hundred yards from the river where the troops were going to cross.

The barrage began at midnight. Hundreds of guns poured tons of shells into the enemy. The noise was terrific, and the mountains formed a perfect sounding board. Flames and showers of sparks across the valley made a fantastic display. The barrage was to advance some 300 feet every six seconds in order to stay out in front of the infantry. But some of the shells began falling short. "For God's sake," yelled the colonel. "Get that fire lifted in front of that outfit."

But there was no communication. The telephones were dead, and the radios wouldn't work. A tank had run off the road in the darkness and had chewed up the telephone wires. Our shells began falling farther inside the enemy area. "That's better," a captain said. Finally, a line was opened to one unit. "Tell them to be alert on the phone," the colonel said. "They have no one there right now," someone said. "They all are on the move to a new location."

"Oh! Hell!" the colonel snorted. "Clarke, go down to the river and find out what's going on. Dammit, we've got to have information. Need any help?"

"Naw. I'll be all right." He walked into the darkness. It was 3:20 a.m. Capt. Clarke reported back that Lieut. Col. Ed Bird of Des Moines, Iowa, had all his outfit across the river and that Major Floyd Sparks of Iowa and his unit were well advanced. Then came word that Col. Bird's outfit had walked into a booby-trapped vineyard. Cunningly wired traps and mines were taking a toll as our troops tried to work their way out toward the enemy.

Shortly after dawn a report came that Major Sparks had reached his objective, but was having to clean out the enemy holding the high ground above the ridge, while Col. Bird's unit worked along the ridge toward the town of Roccaravindola. The Germans had dug in the town and were sweeping the approaches with machine gun fire. In the valley a column of black smoke rolled up. "What's that?" the colonel asked.

"Jerry has blown the bridge."

"That's a good sign. That means he does not intend to stay."

"Look!" someone shouted. A column of Germans was climbing the hill toward the town. Obviously they were going to reinforce the town's defenders. "Get some fire on them fast," the colonel ordered.

Within three minutes mortars and high explosive 37-millimeter shells began bursting along the slope. Then the Germans came running down the hillside in wild disorder. Shell bursts followed them. "Those gunners," said the colonel, "get the gilded bird cage with the stuffed canary as first prize." □

With the Fifth Army in Italy, November 12 — A lot of legends are growing up around American soldiers of World War II and one of those men likely to become a legendary character is Chaplain Delois Marken of the Cottage Grove Avenue Church of Christ, Des Moines. He believes his place is in the front line with the combat troops, and that is where he stays most of the time. "There is no greater place for worship than a foxhole," the chaplain said. During one intense enemy barrage, Marken scrambled into a slit trench with an infantryman who trembled as he prayed aloud. "I guess you think I'm a sissy," the soldier said, "but I lost my best pal yesterday and I guess it sort of got me down."

"That's okay, son," Marken told him, "I pray, too. Let's pray together." And that's what they did.

When the German collapse came at Cap Bon in Tunisia, Marken was watching Allied troops trying to handle thousands of prisoners marching in to give themselves up. Everything and everyone was [*sic*] confused. An officious little German major, noticing Marken's Lieut. Col. insignia, approached. Apparently he did not notice the cross on the other side of Marken's collar.

"This situation is terrible," the German major declared. "There is no organization. It is inexcusable. Such confusion would not be permitted by the German Army."

"Yes," Marken retorted, "yes, we are inexperienced at this sort of thing and there is great confusion. But we had heard over your radio that Germans would fight to the last shell and the last man. We had poor information and were not prepared for such a situation as this."

Then Marken pointed to the cross on his collar. "I came here to bury you fellows, not to watch you surrender."

Pfc. Ken Pfeiffer has cut hair all the way from Aurora, Ill., to Italy and for the first time since he's been in the Army he got a barber shop of which he was proud. He set up shop in one of King Victor Emmanuel's palaces. Instead of the usual ration box seat for customers he has a real Italian barber chair with a big mirror against the wall. In one corner is the usual collection of six months old magazines which is found in any barber shop at home.

In the past year, Ken figures he's cut 14,610 heads of hair. Usually he gives the men the kind of haircut they prefer. But he had a colonel once who was almost bald and sensitive about seeing anyone around with more hair than he had. "So I damned near had to shave the head of everybody in our outfit," Ken laughed. Originally Ken was in the armored force as a tank driver and he came on the African invasion with a tank destroyer unit. When not busy at his regular duties he would set up shop under a tree and put up a sign, "Free Haircuts, No Tips." Now he has a full time job as Fifth Army barber and charges twenty-five cents for each haircut. The money goes into the company fund.

Major Edward L. Austin, son of Vermont's Senator Austin, is developing into one of the Fifth Army's experts on the use of big thirty-two-ton tank destroyers. After the Salerno invasion beachhead was established, Austin was promoted to command a tank destroyer battalion and his outfit has seen plenty of action. He was perhaps the first tank destroyer officer to use his guns as artillery as well as antitank weapons. That was early in the Tunisian campaign. Austin saw his first action with the French at Pichon. He landed on Salerno Beach with the first tank destroyer units. Germans shelled the ship he was on and the vessel lost its anchor, hit a false sandbar. When the gate opened to let the vehicles ashore, a jeep ran into the water and disappeared, so the ship had to back off under fire and try another landing spot. □

With the U.S. Fifth Army in Italy, November 13 — Bitter fighting developed today along the central sector of the Fifth Army front as the Germans threw in strong counter-attacks, pounding the American and British defenses with heavy artillery and tanks. Late in the day the situation still was confused as the Allies wheeled up artillery to counter a move by the enemy striking north of Mignano on the road to Rome. First reports said both sides were suffering fairly heavy casualties. This latest enemy counter-attack came as the Allies edged through rugged mountains toward the main enemy defenses of the Garigliano river "winter line." On the western flank, American troops trapped a company of Germans in the mountains, killed thirty of them and wounded thirty. The others fled and were caught in their own minefields, inflicting other casualties.   □

With the U.S. Fifth Army near Mignano, Italy, November 14 — Rain fell from the gray, sullen sky in a steady, depressing drizzle and low-hanging clouds closed in around the mountain peaks on which American doughboys were fighting today to dislodge the Germans hidden in strongpoints blasted from solid rock. The roads to the front were sloppy strips of mud. But traffic moved slowly forward with supplies. The days old artillery dueling persisted.

We splashed up the muddy roadway to a little farmhouse in the shelter of a protecting rock ledge. Ahead loomed Mt. Lunga, where the Yanks were fighting to oust the Germans. To the right was Mt. Rotondo, which our troops had captured in a costly battle. A group of young officers stood solemnly in the farmyard, rain dripping from their helmets, waiting for a conference inside to break up. Soon, they will be leading their troops forward again.

Lt. Lewis Horton, Pageland, S.C., stared at the gray, wet mountains. "A hell of a time to be fighting a war," he said. "Yeah, but we have been lucky," someone said. "Our boys have got new equipment. What about the equipment?"

"Well," said Horton, "every man got an overcoat, three blankets, a shelter half, a field packet, two suits of long underwear, combat boots, a pair of wool gloves and a raincoat."

In a room of the farmhouse, Lt. Col. Lionel McGarr of Phoenix, Ariz., and other officers bent over a table, examining a map by the light of a lamp, although it was midday. "The Germans are dug in here, intending to stay," McGarr said. "We have found some of their observation posts dug into six feet of rock with roofs of crossties, sandbags and rocks. They had rugs on the floor and the walls were painted. Each had large stocks of food and water. The boys drove them out of one artillery observation post that had all the comforts of home almost, and two telephones. The phones were still ringing as our men walked in. They had left in such a hurry they didn't have time to destroy the place. But most times we have to drive them out with grenades."

"What's this about Footsy Britt?"

"Footsy had himself a time," McGarr chuckled, referring to Lt. Maurice Britt of Lonoke, Ark., star end for the University of Arkansas in 1939 and 1940 and later a member of the Detroit Lions professional football team. "Footsy's company was attacked twice on Mt. Rotondo by about one hundred Germans who broke through the line and were over-running the right flank of the company. They'd slipped in at night under cover of darkness and fog.

"With eight men, Footsy plowed into them machine guns and hand grenades. He got eleven himself and his men knocked off sixteen others. They broke up the attack and saved the position."

Grenade fighting is becoming more and more common to the doughboys. One company used 500 grenades in one day's fighting recently. The officers agreed that the Germans have changed their tactics against the Americans since the campaign in Sicily. There, night actions were an American specialty. But here, the Germans send in groups of ten to fifty men to attack four and five times each night. "Keeping the front-line troops supplied is a problem," said Capt. Mackenzie Porter of Berkeley, Calif. "We've even used the cooks of the supply personnel as carriers to get the stuff to the front. With the troops being counter-attacked four and five times a night, no one could leave the position."

Later, we stood chatting with Cpl. Harry McQueen, Champagne, Ill. Suddenly, a shell whistled toward us. We ducked for the stone archway. One reporter slipped and skidded headlong into a mudhole. Then we felt pretty foolish because the shell had passed over and McQueen hadn't even deigned to duck. He grinned, "we sort of get used to that around here."

McGarr came out and looked down the valley toward the enemy positions. "The Germans are well-disciplined, well-trained fighters, but if you keep plugging they'll break," he said. "They are not supermen by one hell of a long way. Our boys can take them any day in the week but you've got to keep slugging to do it." ☐

With the U.S. Fifth Army near Mignano, Italy, November 15 — Among the men who live with death at the front lines, there are few who have a tougher, lonelier, more unglamorous existence than the boys who trouble-shoot the battle zone communications lines.

None has a more vital job than those who string and maintain the telephone lines through trees, across rocks, along ditches and over mountains right into forward positions. There is never any trouble finding the front; just follow the telephone lines and where they end is the front. The first thing any commanding officer wants from army to corps to division to battalion to company is communications. If they are good, the wireman has done only what is expected; if they are bad, then he is blamed all down the line until they are good again.

A few miles from Mignano, Sgt. Harold Allen, Decatur, Ill., and seven other men lay in slit trenches alongside the shell-battered road for five days, trouble-shooting the telephone lines leading from their regiment into the front line. Whenever a shell or mortar bursts or a vehicle rips out a section of wire, they crawl from their slit trenches to find the break and repair it. Allen and his men have developed a burning hatred for tanks.

"About all they are good for in this country is to rip up our telephone lines," Allen growled. And whenever a tank crawls up to fire at the enemy, it draws artillery fire around Allen and his men.

Lieut. John C. Perkins, Bowling Green, Ky., regimental communications officer, figures his men string an average of twenty miles of telephone lines a day. During the Sicilian campaign, they strung from 800 to 1,000 miles of wire, about equal to the distance from Memphis, Tenn., to New York. Some of the wire is strung from spools, hauled by jeep and carried by mules, but much of it is strung on foot and by hand.

During the first ten days of the Italian campaign, Perkins' section laid down 300 miles of wire from the regimental command post to the assault companies. Lines also are laid to any attack unit such as artillery pack trains and reconnaissance troops. These are the temporary lines in the battle zone. Once the fighting has moved forward other wire men follow and replace the light with heavy field wire on telephone poles.   □

With the Fifth Army in Italy, November 16 — Determined to hold their Garigliano River line all winter if possible the Germans have concentrated the bulk of their defensive strength along the Fifth Army front in a desperate bid to halt the Allied advance on Rome. This strategy became increasingly clear today as American and British patrols probed the enemy's so-called winter line—a deep series of pillboxes, gun emplacements, trenches and barbed wire entanglements blasted out of the rocky mountains. For the first time since Allied troops fought their way ashore on the beaches of

Salerno the Germans have fallen back, while they fortified six positions—and no one has any illusions about the bitter, bloody battles that must be fought before the enemy is dug out of the hills.

The valley running from Cassino to Rome between towering fog-covered mountain masses is the natural road for the army to follow. And because it is the natural avenue to Rome the Germans have thrown up their heaviest defenses and massed the greater part of their troops in the vicinity with the Apennines on their left flank standing as a guard against the British Eighth Army. In addition to holding the strong positions on heights commanding the valley the enemy has had a friendly ally in the weather. Steady cold rains have swollen streams and inundated bypasses along the Fifth Army's supply lines as well as subjecting troops to exposure in muddy trenches.

But for the first time in a week the skies were clear today and a bright sun shone on the muddy front giving the doughboys and Tommies a chance to dry their clothing. Also for the first time in several days the air force had a chance to strike at the enemy. The strain on the troops had been great and the rugged mountain fighting is underscoring once again the fact that war is a grim game for tough resilient youth.   □

With the Fifth Army in Italy, November 16 — With their advances now measured in yards instead of in miles the road to Rome has become by far the toughest route of battle any American troops have fought on in the Mediterranean theater. Neither Tunisia nor Sicily presented the difficulties which the Allied troops must overcome before they drive the enemy into northern Italy and it is becoming obvious that neither of those campaigns cost the blood this drive will cost.

The difficulties are the weather, terrain and well-trained, well-disciplined enemy dug into strongpoints of solid rock in numbers greater than the Germans have previously congregated along a single front in this theater. The roads to the front are slimy brown strips of mud. Each small stream is a traffic bottleneck. The Germans blew the bridges which engineers have had to replace with temporary structures.

Rains have turned the countryside into muddy bogs. Day by day it is growing colder in the towering, cloud-swathed mountains where the doughboys and Tommies are fighting tenaciously to rout the enemy out of his strongpoint. The weather has weakened Allied air power which was one potent weapon the Germans were unable to match. Allied war planes have been grounded much of the time by rain, fog and low-hanging clouds which reduce visibility.

It is true the weather is the same on the enemy side of the line and their troops are uncomfortable too, but their communications are not hampered by demolitions. Their troops are in well-prepared positions which give them shelter from the elements. Some of their outposts have been found even to have rugs on the floors and large stocks of water, food and small luxuries.

Since they are attacking, the Allied troops cannot prepare shelters to protect them from the rain, cold and exposure they are enduring in open slit trenches and in rock crannies in the mountains. Because of the apparent quality and numbers of enemy troops, the Allies are unable to crack the Garigliano River line by sheer weight of numbers. The terrain favors the defenders, for they hold the heights and Allied troops must always fight their way up slopes in the face of direct enemy fire. In many places the Germans have dugouts similar to the old First World War type opening onto systems of trenches.

The weather, by grounding fighters and bombers, is of distinct advantage to the Germans, freeing them from the steady hammering of the lines and communications that cost them so heavily during the summer and early autumn. The slow Allied advance meanwhile is giving the enemy time to prepare additional defenses beyond Cassino, a hinge of the Garigliano line. Present indications are, therefore, that the Fifth Army will have bitter, costly fighting all the way to Rome.   □

With the Fifth Army near Venafro, Italy, November 16 — Christmas has arrived for the American doughboys in the front lines. Great loads of yuletide packages bearing postmarks of hometowns from Maine to California are being rushed to the front by truck, mule train and hand to cheer the boys now living in cold, foggy weather in ankle-deep mud.

It was pouring rain today as we skidded in a jeep along a rough muddy trail to the foot of a mountain near the front line. For some reason this sector of the front was fairly quiet and the guns were not booming strongly as usual. In the doorway of a barn on an improvised table Pfc. Herman Sumner, Cranberry, W.Va., carefully wrapped a package.

"Sending that one home?"

"Naw," he said, "I'm wrapping this for the sergeant."

Sgt. Thomas Wallace, Walnut, Iowa, held string in his hand. "I'm sending home bed spreads for the folks," he said, "I have one for mother and another for my wife. I hope they get there in time."

Most of the boys are sending packages home to parents, friends, wives. Tons are arriving here with each mail delivery. They are taken into the front line with rations and distributed. They ignore the warning "do not open until Christmas" and strip off the paper to get at candy, cigarettes, cakes and other gifts.

Pvt. Louis Laudone, New London, Conn., was feeling gay. "We are getting our presents a month sooner than we expected," he said, "but that's all right by us." Laudone wrapped a package carefully, tucking the paper in to make neat corners. "I'm sweating one out myself," he said. "I know I've got one on the way, but it hasn't arrived yet. The boxes are getting here pretty regularly and of course none of the boys wait for Christmas to open them."

Sgt. John Boyd, Sparta, Tenn., said he mailed a package home two weeks ago with souvenirs from Italy for his wife and a "toy horse with a monkey on his back" for his son. "The boxes were coming in fast for three or four days," Boyd said. "Most of the boys are getting cigarets, candy and wrist watches. I'm hoping maybe the folks will include a watch in my package."

It is the second Christmas away from home for many. "I guess we can stand another over here if we have to," said St. Sgt. William Schaffer, Des Moines, Iowa. Pfc. Tony Zalewski, Detroit, began kidding the boys. "Seems to me there are few packages from Iowa, but I guess there's not much in that state anyway," he said. "That's what you think," retorted Pvt. James Linsville, Marshalltown, Iowa. "As a matter of fact, Michigan is only attached to Iowa for ration purposes."

But underneath the banter and wise cracks was a warm feeling of cheerfulness as the men stood around watching Christmas packages being wrapped while a cold dismal rain fell outside the doorway and guns boomed in the distance.   □

With the Fifth Army in Italy, November 18 — The first WAC [Women's Army Corps] to put foot on the continent of Europe was Pvt. Lora O. Howieson, 2501 Cobden Street, Pittsburgh, Pa., who thinks it is "pretty wonderful" to be among the first contingent of WACS to arrive in Italy. Private Howieson with fifty-four other WACS, two officers and one Arab dog nicknamed Doublement arrived late yesterday and spent today getting quarters in order while a buzz of excitement ran through the ranks of lonely males around Fifth Army headquarters.

"We thought we were going to be left in North Africa and forgotten," Private Howieson said. "And we are pleased to be back with our friends who left us when the Fifth Army invaded Italy." Officers who led the WAC contingent are First Lieut. Cor Foster, College City, Pa., and Second Lieut. Miriam Butler, Reno, Nev. "It has been wonderful getting to Italy and one of the most exciting experiences of our lives," Foster said. "There was a race to see who got ashore first and Private Howieson won by a couple of steps." □

With the Fifth Army in Italy, November 19 — American engineers are still chuckling over the ruse they pulled on the Germans in the first crossing of the Volturno River by Allied troops. "That was the only real fun we've had on this whole invasion," said Lt. Col. Robert E. Coffee of Brookings, S.D., whose battalion has done just about everything but whip up a chocolate fudge cake on the march from Salerno. Coffee's men helped put the Fifth Army across the Volturno three times but the first crossing was the toughest. That's when the boys had to outwit the enemy. They had practiced bridging streams back in the United States and in Tunisia, but practice and performance under enemy fire are not exactly the same.

On the morning the troops crossed the Volturno to attack, the engineers went in with them to build a bridge across the stream but enemy observers spotted them and began pouring shells into the position. The engineers suffered some casualties from shell fire and several vehicles were hit. The Germans drove them back. Coffee talked the situation over with Major Vernon L. Watkins of Sturgis, S.D. The enemy fire was too heavy to send men into it, but the Army had to have a bridge across the Volturno for supply vehicles and armor.

After nightfall the engineers moved back to the river and fogged up the area with smoke pots. They laid out a regular smoke screen—and before long the enemy opened up again with artillery to plaster the area. They kept it up all night. But Coffee and his men weren't there. They had moved up the river a short distance to an alternate site and were calmly putting in their bridge without the slightest disturbance. "We didn't even hear a machine gun bullet except for a few strays," Coffee says. "By 7 a.m. we had a bridge ready for light traffic and before many hours passed they had a 300-ton bridge in place and vehicles were pouring across."

But bridge building is only one of many things engineers are doing in this war. They have won a great deal of respect for themselves by their work in the Tunisian, Sicilian and Italian campaigns. Many infantrymen will tell you that "this is an engineers' war." By that they mean the Army could not move without the engineers to build the bridges, repair demolition, build roads, clear mines, provide water and do all the other chores which engineers are doing even to painting signs.

It is axiomatic that no army moves faster than its supplies, and supplies cannot move unless there are roads open. So it is the engineers' big job to keep the supply routes open by repairing the damage done by the enemy. Heavy rains have increased the engineers' problems on roads where the Germans blew every bridge and even dynamited the smallest culvert and in addition the Germans have a habit of shelling the areas where the combat engineers are at work on a bypass or a bridge installation near the front line.

Before an attack the engineers must send out their own reconnaissance parties to check on the best river approaches to locate mines and minefields and to check on enemy demolition. Capt. Claude De Cory of Lead, S.D., is an expert now at reconnoitering but he and his men are lucky if they come back without being shot at. Among those who work with him are Sgt. Jim Merril of Hot Springs, Ark., and First Lt. William Mangler of Daytona Beach, Fla., Pvt. William Schmit and Pvt. 1st Class Clarence Roen, both of Hot Springs, Ark. "Our toughest assignment was that first river crossing," De Cory said. "The Germans made us go for cover that time." After the Volturno crossing, demolition became more and more the problem in one stretch of fifteen miles. Engineers had to build eleven bypasses around blown bridges and culverts. Later they put bridges across them.   □

Fornelli, Italy, November 23 — The doughboys are fighting an inspiring battle against two enemies on the Italian front—one against the determined Nazis and another against the weather. For ten days the weather has been more savage than the enemy, despite the increased use of German artillery. And the weather more than the enemy has slowed the Fifth Army advance down to patrol action except on the extreme right flank where the troops still are fighting their way up slimy slopes beyond the little town of Cerro. Sleet, snow and rain—torrents of rain—have made battle conditions almost impossible and have imposed terrific hardships. The battlefields are quagmires. The roads have been churned into mud bogs. The small mountain streams have become sullen, brown rivers of destruction.

I slopped through water and mud to a regimental command post today to see for myself what conditions are like on the extreme right flank of the American line. In a drafty, damp building a red-haired kid from Vermont sat reading a letter from home. His boots were two balls of mud and his clothes were soaked. His hands were blue from the cold, for he just had come in from the field.

For thirty days his unit had been fighting through mountains, virtually isolated from the rest of the army. They had the hard, dangerous, back-breaking mission of capturing a mountain through which there were no roads. They made their own trails and were supplied by pack train through some of the roughest country American troops ever have fought across. But they whipped the enemy and came through with amazingly high morale. The kid sighed and thoughtfully folded the letter and slipped it carefully into a wallet. "The folks back home do not quite know what we are up against, do they," he said. "It looks like they think we are having a picnic and that it's all over but the shouting. I wish they could see for themselves what it is like out here."

Then he smiled and said, "But do not use my name. I do not want to hurt my family's feelings." I knew what he was thinking—he was thinking of the cold rain, sleet and snow high up on those mountains beyond us where his outfit was fighting and where he would have to return in a few hours. He was thinking of the rains that lashed them day and night, rain that sometimes turned to hail or snow, and of the water-filled slit trenches where the men had to lie during enemy shelling.

He was thinking of men with only one or maybe two soggy blankets to wrap around them at night and no change of clothing. And of the troops who had no dry shoes or socks and whose feet after several days began to swell until they could no longer wear shoes. Trench foot the medics call it—the same ailment that troops suffered from in the last war. At least one man wrapped his sore feet in rags and kept going anyway.

The rains have increased the army's problems many times, not only in maintaining the individual soldier's fighting efficiency, but in supplies as well. The engineers maintain a constant watch over the bridges and the crews splash through mud to help push stalled vehicles or to fill in deep ruts cut by tanks and trucks. Along the road can be seen the results of the troops' efforts to fight the weather. But their slit trenches alongside soaked shelters are filled with water. They must dive in them in case of enemy shelling or an air raid.

Clothes droop forlornly from lines where they were hung days ago to dry—and still hang. Through ankle deep mud the men walk along the vital lifeline, keeping traffic moving. At one point the engineers had thrown a cable across a swirling river and hooked on a jeep trailer as a ferry—the only slender link of supply for troops in the mountains until a bridge could be built. Before that they threw rations across the stream by hand.

At another point the engineers built a bridge over a rain swollen stream under direct fire from enemy guns. Now traffic was going across, although the drivers were warned that they were under enemy observation. Capt. A. T. Chavez of Albuquerque, N.M., kept a watchful eye on the span. "They dropped a shell twenty feet from the bridge yesterday," he said. "Now I'm holding my breath." Slowly and laboriously the army is pushing forward—but as the kid from Vermont said, it is no picnic. ☐

With Fifth Army at Fornelli, Italy, November 24 – The "battle of the house" was one of those savage, isolated fights which characterize present operations along the Germans' touted winter line—one of many patrol skirmishes in which Americans excelled.

The battle site was a three-story stone farmhouse in a muddy field between the little towns of Rochetta and New Rochetta. The action occurred a week ago, but troops in the rain-swept hills were still talking about it today. Twenty-four Germans caught twelve Americans in the house. For three and a half hours the Americans fought like their pioneer forebears fought when their cabins were besieged by Indians. When the fighting ended only four Nazis were alive. "Because of fights like that one," said Lieut. Fordyce Gorham of Williamsport, Pa., "German officers issued orders that there were to be no more patrols into our territory. We gobbled them all up on three straight nights. We captured or killed every man in four enemy patrols. Not a man got away. That sort of discouraged them."

In this fight, a young lieutenant led his reconnaissance patrol of eleven men toward the German line. They had tommy guns, pistols, knives and grenades. The lieutenant's name cannot be told. He is dead now. But he had accounted for a German officer, several of that officer's men and an Italian traitor. As his men slipped into enemy territory, they saw Germans approaching from Rochetta. Then they saw others coming toward them from New Rochetta, and a third bunch from another direction. Outnumbered two to one, they slipped into the farmhouse, hoping to remain undetected so that they could continue scouting.

But an Italian civilian had seen them. He led the Germans to the house. "The enemy surrounded the place and the German officer and the Italian came up and knocked on the door," said Sgt. Henry S. Furst of Ephrata, Pa. "When no one answered, they kicked the door in and then the lieutenant opened fire. He killed the German officer and the Italian. That's when the battle began." The lieutenant and his men retreated up the steps to the second and third floors to wage one of the strangest scraps yet fought in this campaign. Some Germans set up a machine gun and sprayed the house while others tried to get in. Every time they tried they met a burst from a tommy gun. They lobbed concussion grenades through the windows. When a grenade would fall into one room the Americans would rush into another, wait out the explosion, then rush back to toss grenades at the enemy.

One German detail was throwing grenades from a blind spot beneath a window. "I'll take care of the devils," the lieutenant said. He leaned out the window and threw a grenade into their midst, but before he could duck back inside a bullet killed him. Sgt. Donald B. Greaber, of Salt Lake City, took command, and the fight went on. As it intensified, Sgt. Theodore Bachenheimer of Hollywood, Calif., volunteered to try to escape and go for reinforcements. He dashed out and ran through a hail of enemy fire. But when Bachenheimer and reinforcements arrived, Sgt. Greaber and his men had everything under control. The battle of the house was over. The Germans had been caught in their own trap. □

Fornelli, Italy, November 24 — The little Italian house near the front was a temporary refuge from the cold and the rain. Through the storm came the muffled booming of artillery. The pot-bellied charcoal stove took the chill from the air and steam rose from the wet, woolen uniforms of the soldiers standing nearby. We were talking of the bravery of men who had fought their way through the mountains for thirty days under great hardships to drive the Germans back toward Cassino.

"I keep talking of a sergeant I knew," said Chaplain Delbert Muehl of Hopkins, Minn. "I saw a story from home the other day about some man who had refused to be inducted into the army because he felt that his wife came before his country, and that he did not owe his country anything. That hit me pretty hard because, you see, I remember this sergeant. I knew him in Africa—a big, good-looking, cheerful kid, who thought there was no place like the United States. He joined one of the toughest outfits in the army. His father was a colonel in the artillery and I guess he kinda wanted his father to be proud of him.

"He got into the fight on Sicily and was wounded in the knee. The doctors wanted to send him back, but the sergeant did not want to go back and have to be reclassified. He begged so hard that the doctors finally relented and let him stay. When he went back to North Africa, after the fall of Messina, that knee was in bad shape, and every once in a while it would buckle under him. But he would not leave the outfit, and he came along when we came on the invasion of Italy. He was with us when we went into the mountains, the roughest country any of us had ever been in before. We had to pull ourselves up many of those rocky mountains with the enemy looking down on us.

"The mountains were so steep in one place that five of our twelve pack animals actually fell off. I watched the sergeant climbing the steep slopes. He would fall down time after time as the knee gave way under him. But each time he would get up and go on. And he made it through those mountains, although I know his knee was in terrible shape, and was causing him great pain.

"I saw him again the other day as the boys were going in to attack the mountains, where the enemy had dug in behind a minefield. He came limping toward me and I saw he had no shoes on. His feet had sweated so much he had taken off his shoes and wrapped his feet in rags. But he would not quit. When he came up to me, he grinned and said, 'well, I've made it so far. I guess I'll keep going.' And he limped on up the mountain. But this time he didn't get to the top with his pals. Shell fragments cut him down. That's why it hits me pretty hard when I hear of someone who says he does not owe his country anything. I keep thinking of the sergeant."   □

With the Allied Expeditionary Force in Italy, [November 26] — Casey has gone to bat against the enemy in the invasion of Italy, but unlike Mudville's famous hero, this Casey has not struck out. He is Lt. Col. John W. Casey, Chicago, former St. Louis advertising man now antitank officer for the Fifth Army. Casey's thirty-two-ton M-10 tank destroyers have done and are doing a great job in driving the enemy toward Rome and his battalion commanders are furnishing textbook material on the versatile use of antitank weapons when there are no tanks to fight. Under Casey's direction, the tank destroyers are radically altering old concepts of their proper use. Originally they were regarded as a special purpose, semi-independent force whose sole duties were to engage enemy tanks in combat.

But that idea is being changed. Casey's tank destroyers are used not only in defensive roles but also for general division reconnaissance, for direct support of infantry in attack and as artillery. The tank destroyers had their great day in the invasion of Italy when they helped halt the German tank attack which threatened to smash the American beachhead in the Gulf of Salerno October 14 and 15. The M-10 Tigers—so-called because the tank destroyer insignia is a tiger crushing an enemy tank in its jaws—look much like Sherman tanks except that long three-inch high velocity guns poke out of their turrets. The tank destroyers weigh the same as the Shermans and are powered by two Diesel engines. The gun has an indirect range of 14,500 yards, a direct range of about 2,000 yards. When the fifteen-pound projectile hurled by the tank destroyer gun smacks an enemy tank with a direct hit that tank is literally destroyed. Already tank destroyers have been given official credit for destroying thirty-one tanks, two guns, four vehicles, three machine gun nests and several mortars on the Italian mainland.

As yet, the tank destroyers have never been given full credit for the job they did in helping break up the big threat to the invasion forces when German armor drove toward the beach down the V-shaped junction of the Sele and Calore Rivers south of Salerno. When the attack began to develop and it was apparent where the enemy was to hit, forty-eight tank destroyers were sent into position on the right side of the V back of the Calore, and thirty were put on the left side behind the Sele. Later twenty-four more were thrown in to bolster defenses on the left flank.

"The tank destroyers dug in right behind the infantry," Casey said. "It was a classic example of using the tank destroyer in close support of infantry and it bucks up the morale of the troops to see those big TD's [tank destroyer] with them." While artillery blasted at the enemy from the beaches, the tank destroyers were firing at them from both flanks. The enemy was caught in a box of terrific fire. On the first day of the attack the TD's destroyed fourteen enemy tanks in the Sele-Calore pocket while the M-10 Tigers accounted for eight more on the left flank. During the first week of fighting they bagged twenty-five enemy tanks. Since then, enemy armor has been no great factor in the fighting, and although they have bagged thirty-one tanks to date, the TD's have not lost a single M-10 as the result of enemy tank fire. Before the Sele-Calore fight was over, Casey was in it himself as a battalion commander. His own tank destroyer smashed eight enemy tanks.

He came along on the invasion and landed as a Fifth Army observer pending the consolidation of the bridgehead when he was to resume his normal functions as tank destroyer officer for Lt. Gen. Mark W. Clark. "I think I was the only man who came ashore and didn't see a shot fired," Casey chuckles. "I just happened to be in one of those little spots on the beach where there was no fighting." But it was not long until he was in the thick of it. He accompanied an American force into the town of Persano which was cut off by an enemy attack into the Sele-Calore salient. For a time it seemed the entire force would be wiped out or captured, but after nightfall they fought their way out.

At headquarters Casey gave a clear picture of the grave situation. Many had thought Persano was in the hands of American troops and that there was no threat in that sector. He was then put in command of a TD battalion which went into the line on the left flank of the American defenses. Six tank destroyer men won Silver Stars for their heroism in the Sele-Calore action when their destroyer moved into the open and knocked out five enemy tanks while under artillery and small arms fire.

The six citations read pretty much like that of Staff Sgt. Raymond G. Murphy of Jacksonville, Fla., which said, "Staff Sergeant Murphy, while commanding his tank destroyer, caused his destroyer to be moved into the open in the face of five enemy tanks and under artillery and small arms fire and by so doing was able to destroy all five enemy tanks and one ammunition vehicle. During all this time Murphy was subjected to artillery fire, small arms fire and fire from opposing enemy tanks. Murphy's gallant and aggressive action removed the menace to our infantry and was an inspiration to his comrades and reflects the finest traditions of the Army of the United States."

The other five were Sgts. Edwin A. Yost of Gorham, Kan.; Technician 5th Grade Alvin Johnson of Granbury, Texas; Pvt. Joseph R. O'Bryan of New Haven, Ky.; Pvt. Claude H. Stokes of McAlester, Okla., and Pvt. Clyde T. Stokes, brother of Claude. Claude was assistant gunner in the destroyer. Clyde passed the ammunition.

When he returned to his regular post as antitank officer Casey turned his battalion over to Maj. Edward L. Austin, son of Vermont's Senator Austin. Most of the men with Casey are young like Austin—Maj. John C. Niehaus, Chickasha, Okla.; Maj. John W. Dobson, Greensboro, N. C., former University of Richmond football star; Maj. Charles F. Wilder, Hollywood, Calif.; Capt. Fletcher B. Emerson, Houston, Texas, and Capt. Charles H. Lydard, Westfield, Mass. These men support Casey's idea of using destroyers in whatever way they can be effective when not engaged in antitank defense.

While running the Fifth Army tank destroyer Training Center, Casey developed the use of the destroyers as artillery when others thought the TD's should be confined to antitank work. With support from General Clark and other staff officers, the tank destroyers were integrated with divisional artillery to double the fire power of the artillery battalion. "It didn't make good sense to have these huge expensive units' fire power waiting around for something to do when there were no enemy tanks around."

Casey is a cool, unruffled man but it burns him to hear the M-7, a 105-millimeter howitzer mounted on a tank chassis, called a "tank burster," or a tank-destroyer. "The M-7 is solely an artillery weapon," he said. "There is now only one tank destroyer and that is the M-10." Casey should know. He was in the original cadre that founded the Army's first tank destroyer school at Camp Hood, Texas. ☐

With the Fifth Army near Mignano, December 3 — This is a valley of hell—a man-made hell of thunder and lightning belched from hundreds of Allied guns hurling steel at the enemy. The roar of their volleys rips and tears and beats at your eyes until your head rings. It seems the guns are everywhere, in every clump of trees, in every gully along each trail. For many hours they have been pounding, pumping tons of explosives into the German positions on Monte Camino, on Monte Maggiore and in the Liri Valley beyond, in a sudden, savage outbreak of the Fifth Army along the road to Rome.

For almost three weeks the rains came. Steady, cold downpours bogged the front in a morass of mud, turned mountains into slippery barriers and halted Lt. Gen. Mark W. Clark's troops as they came up against the enemy's strong River Garigliano defenses which they had intended to make their winter line. The enemy had orders to hold at all costs. But as the rains fell and the majority of the troops rested from mountain climbing, the Fifth Army slowly drew up guns, ammunition and supplies over roads which were almost impassable at times. It was a painful, arduous process.

When trucks and jeeps could go no farther, mule trains carried supplies into the mountains. When animals could no longer scale the steep slopes, supplies were hauled up by doughboys clawing their way up the mountains on foot. The task that lay ahead was to break open the road to Rome—Highway No. 6, which curves beneath towering mountains through Mignano and on to Cassino, lying beneath a mountain on which St. Benedict built a monastery and founded his ancient order.

From observation posts on Camino and Maggiore the Germans looked down on Mignano and Cassino Road. From these vantage points, too, they could see every move made by the Allied troops in the valley south of Mignano. Before the British and American troops and armor could move on Cassino it was necessary to control the heights west and east of the valley. So the Fifth Army trained its "Long Toms," 155-millimeter howitzers, and 105's on Monte Camino and Monte Maggiore. More than 800 guns were wheeled up for the artillery assault while the doughboys and Tommies got set. Then the British advanced on Camino Wednesday night. But the enemy strongly held on to the heights. It was a coordinated American and British attack. Today the troops fought their way up Camino while the doughboys on their right stormed Maggiore's heights. Before the infantry left their foxholes for the dawn attack, artillery crashed out in a tremendous symphony of death and destruction. It was a barrage so intense that German prisoners taken from their foxholes were stunned and in some cases unable to resist.

The barrage was the greatest ever laid down before American troops, military men said, and it is being compared to the barrage Gen. Bernard L. Montgomery's Eighth Army laid down at El Alamein, Egypt, where Marshal Edwin Rommel's desert army was smashed. The artillery of one American division alone hurled 250 shells for each of its 200 guns and that was only a twenty-four-hour supply—a total of 4,000,000 pounds of explosives to be hurled into the enemy lines while the small hand of the clock made one revolution on its dial. That is why this is a valley of hell.

The guns never cease their striking. Whole batteries of them roar in unison with a concussion that shakes the earth. Driving through the valley today was like running a gantlet of guns, and while weapons dealt smoke and flame in the valley, heavier guns farther back sent clouds rolling across. For each enemy shell that landed, Allied artillery pumped across at least thirty. Along the road, doughboys had taken refuge from the rain in caves chiseled out of the soft limestone by the Italians and Germans. The Italians had used the caves as storage places for vegetables, fruit and grain. When the Americans came along, they moved into them and used them as command posts, medical stations and billets.

In one large, roomy cave Capt. Cecil Shustick, Columbus, Ohio, and Lt. Samuel C. Clarkson, Lebanon, Ky., set up a medical detachment station. On a little ledge a charcoal fire was burning to take the damp chill from the air. They had a piece of canvas hung over the opening. As I entered, an Italian woman was excitedly bestowing thanks and gifts of nuts and fruit on them. They had treated her daughter for a toothache. □

With the Fifth Army in Italy, December 6 — With excellent observation from towering Mt. Maggiore, American artillery rained shells today on one—if not the only—escape route for the Germans on the south side of the Garigliano River. From their hard-won heights the Yanks looked down on a bridge across which the enemy troops must withdraw with their equipment to escape the closing grip of Allied troops wiping out resistance in the dent driven into the German winter line. On Mt. Camino the British virtually have surrounded one group of Germans holding out on a pinnacle above "Monastery Ridge," so-called because of an old monastery on its barren slope.

The British took the ridge in the first assault, but were driven back by heavy mortar fire. They won back the ridge, on which virtually the only cover was provided by the walls of the monastery but enemy mortar and shell fire set the monastery afire and the British had to withdraw from it again. They worked their way around the ridge, however, to bypass the strongpoint. The maneuver left the Germans strangled, but still holding the positions even though their supply lines were cut. The first surge of the new Fifth Army attack put the Allied troops in a strong position along the west side of the Mignano-Cassino road. □

With the U.S. Fifth Army, December 8 — A gray-haired brigadier general, an old infantry man himself, declared today the doughboy's capture of La Difensa and Maggiore mountains on the road to Rome was one of the greatest achievements of the infantry in this war. The Battle of Lookout Mountain, he said, could not be compared to the fight which began five days ago and ended with the American troops holding the great mass which overlooks the Mignano-Cassino Road and the valley beyond. "Pile three Lookout Mountains on top of each other," he said, "and you get an idea of what those boys did." He talked to us on a muddy hillside near the front as other infantry moved from their positions to attack the heights north of Maggiore. "I would be ashamed for you to give my name and say I was there because they are the ones who did the job and they deserve the credit. They had some tough times in Tunisia, but I haven't seen anything to compare to this operation. It was guts all the way."

The attack began on Maggiore and La Difensa on the morning of December 3 with the heaviest artillery barrage of the Italian campaign. On top of these two great masses, towering above the others north of the main highway, the Germans were able to observe the movements of the Allied troops. After the attack began, rain fell to make the operations even more difficult for the Americans. "The roads were terrible," the general said, "and it was a disheartening thing to see some of the supply dumps we built up with so much effort wiped out by enemy artillery fire.

"The general attack caught the Germans by surprise. They were expecting us to attack but didn't think we would move when we did. The initial phase went well right up the slopes of Difensa, and two units were on the peak and spread over Maggiore before the Germans realized they were there. Our boys dug in during the night and the next morning went after them in hand-to-hand fighting to clear them out of caves, dugouts and pill-boxes. There were a lot of snipers, well concealed, and they had to be found one by one. It took the doughboys four days to get them out. No one can imagine the terrain without climbing it himself. It took sixteen hours for troops to carry a box of 'C' rations two miles to the peak and return to the supply dump at the foot of the mountain.

"In some places, the troops had to pull themselves up the slope by means of a rope tied to trees or rocks. That's bad enough without any load on your back, but they were carrying equipment and supplies. The litter bearers did a magnificent job. It took six men to carry a stretcher off Maggiore with four men in reserve to rest the others. Often they were under mortar and artillery fire."

The general told of one captain who started up the slopes with forty men carrying supplies to the advance troops. Slipping, scrambling up the trails, they were caught in a concentration of enemy fire. Each time they picked up their burdens and tried again. Finally, the captain was killed, but at the end of fourteen hours, his men completed the mission.   □

With the Fifth Army near Mignano, Italy, December 9 – German front-line soldiers are pinning their hopes of a victory for the Fa-therland on a great offensive next spring, which they call "vergel-tungschlacht"—a war of revenge. They are told—and they believe—that Germany is husbanding its forces for one great and final desperate attack. Prisoners volunteered this story today while being questioned by American officers.

If the German troops question the current lack of Nazi planes over the front it is because of "vergeltungschlacht." If there are no tanks it is because of "vergeltungschlacht." If there should be no food, ammunition, artillery support, or supplies, the reason is that these things are being saved for the great day when Germany will lash out with another mighty blow to crush her enemies. Every shortage is explained to the German troops in terms of saving material for the war of revenge.

It seemed incredible to me that the Germans could believe those things. But they do. Out of 169 prisoners questioned, however, only fifteen said that they still thought Germany could win the war. The others said they believed their fatherland would lose, but their guess as to how long the war will last ranged from two weeks to two years. Most of the Germans felt as did one prisoner captured at Maggiore. He came from Hamburg and was brought to this front on November 17. He said that unless the "vergeltungschlacht" wins for Germany "the fatherland is lost." On a visit home a few days ago, he said, he saw the results of the steady pounding of the British and American air forces and found that Hamburg was virtually a shambles. A row of hotels near the railway was intact, he added, but the railway station was destroyed and almost all of the city leveled except for some homes in the suburbs.

Another German was captured on Mt. Camino. He surrendered to the Yanks when he saw that his position was hopeless. "Germany can last another two years," he said. "Germany is one great armament factory and even after those severe air blows the country is only groggy, and will not be beaten in a few months. We have become fatalists. We have lost our homes and our property and have nothing more to lose, so why should we worry about this little bit of life?" □

With the Fifth Army in Italy, December 16 — Italian forced labor battalions are being driven under German guns to complete new defenses around and beyond Cassino before the Fifth Army completely smashes the Garigliano line, it was learned here. Escaping from the labor gang and slipping through the German lines, an Italian high school boy and a thirty-one-year-old University of Naples student reported to American officers that the Germans were building up a complex system of trenches, machine gun nests and gun positions to guard the approaches to Rome. Haggard, frightened and thin, the two said they braved death to escape from the gang, with which they had been working since Naples' fall.

This is the report they gave of the enemy's frantic effort to hold up the advance of the Americans and British: From October 4 to 13 they were with a gang of 300 Italians working along the Rapido River near the town of Cassino. There they cleared trees, vines and shrubbery from the left bank of the stream to give the Germans a clear view of the approaches and to remove cover helpful to attacking troops. Then they dug a system of "T" trenches near the river edge thirty to forty feet apart so that every foot of the opposite bank could be covered by fire. The Nazis had the Italians cover these trenches with branches to hide them from observation planes. From October 13 to November 21 the two worked in the hills west of Cassino building small forts of lumber covered with concrete.

In one area alone they helped build thirty-five such miniature forts, fifteen in a second area and thirty in a third. These small strongpoints are about six feet long, three feet wide and six feet high—big enough for at least one machine gun. Slots in the concrete give the gunner a view of his area of fire and the forts are so placed that the bands of fire are interlocking. After that period the Italians were put to work on antitank ditches, underground ammunition dumps, minefields and laying of barbed wire. Because of the intensity of the American artillery fire the Germans are being forced to put much of their stores, ammunition and food underground, either in caves or in dugouts built by Italian laborers.   ☐

With the Fifth Army near San Pietro, Italy, December 16 — A little band of doughboys filed around the mountainside, dirty, unshaven and stumbling with fatigue—the survivors of the only platoon to fight its way into the shattered town of San Pietro. Somehow they managed to get through the murderous enemy fire which poured down on them when they attacked the gray town sitting on the side of Mt. Sammucro. They dropped their rifles and gear and sat down to wait for someone to tell them what to do next. But first you had better hear about San Pietro and then you can understand what these men have been through—Pfc. Casimer O. Trevino of Benavides, Tex., Private Cecil P. Gilbert of Philadelphia, Miss., Private Glen Boke of Covington, Va., Private Joseph Meunier of Westerly, R.I., Private Jessel Baker of Wichita Falls, Tex., Private Ross Adkinson of Hix, W.Va., and Private Joseph Chicacchio of Watervliet, N.Y.

San Pietro is the key to control of the Liri Valley south of the main German stronghold of Cassino. The Germans have made it a stronghold in their winter line. In the town itself the enemy has machine gun nests and underground kitchens and stores of ammunition and food. Around the town on the rocky-terraced lower slopes of Sammucro they are entrenched in caves and dugouts, with machine gunners barricaded behind rocks and logs.

Yesterday at noon American infantrymen attacked San Pietro. The battle has raged for two days and still San Pietro has held out in one of the bloodiest fights of the entire Italian campaign. The attack began with a heavy barrage pounding the slopes around the town and beating the town itself into a shell. And then the infantry went into action with tanks giving them support—except that the tanks never were able to give much help. Mines, the enemy's antitank fire and mud had the armor pretty well bottled up. Capt. Charles Beacham of San Antonio, Tex., led the first company into the attack on San Pietro from the south while other troops worked their way along the slopes above the town in the face of murderous fire. "We started out all right," said Trevino. "I was with the captain and two bodyguards. We advanced right up to the edge of the town and there was a little draw which we had to cross."

"There was no cover anywhere," Gilbert said.

"No, there was no cover," said Trevino shaking his head. "Capt. Beacham led the way and we ran across the draw into the edge of the town one by one until one platoon of the company was in town."

"That's when everything opened up on us," Chicacchio said. "They laid mortar fire on us and were shooting from caves and from houses," Trevino continued. "There was nothing we could do but get out. There were not enough of us to hold the town and the rest of the company was pinned down by machine gun and mortar fire."

So the men dashed back across the draw with machine gun bullets whipping around them and scattered to find cover. Some threw themselves on the ground to escape the hail of lead. "There were booby traps all around," said Chicacchio. "A lot of the boys got caught in minefields. Some of us crawled more than 400 yards on our bellies to get out of the area. I saw one man in front of me blown straight up in the air by a mortar burst." Slowly the men made their way back across no man's land to their own lines to report and wait for further orders while other troops moved in to continue the attack on San Pietro. No one knew what had happened to the platoon sergeant who leaned against a wall in the town, firing his carbine from the hip and shooting three Germans. "He stayed behind to take care of the wounded," Trevino said. ☐

San Pietro, Italy, December 18 — American doughboys have won one of their bloodiest, bitterest and toughest battles of World War II on this one hundredth day of the Fifth Army's invasion of Italy. In all the fighting from the beaches of Salerno to the Garigliano River, none has been so packed with drama and heroism as that of this forty-eight-hour span, nor has any been so costly in American lives as the battle for San Pietro, which ended today shortly before we walked through "Death Valley" to reach this pile of misery and rubble that once was a town.

The Americans walked into this battered, filthy, stinking little town at the bottom of Mt. Sammucro to find that the enemy had pulled back toward Cassino, giving up a key position in the winter line which the Nazis had hoped to hold weeks longer. Although the town fell yesterday, when advance guards entered on the heels of the retreating enemy, its capture was recorded as of today. The name of San Pietro will be remembered in American military history along with such names as Fondouk, Bizerte, Tunis, Gela, Troina, Salerno and Naples. The name of this little village will never be forgotten by the American soldiers who took part in the battle for it.

We picked our way with a patrol and first aid men through fields ripped by mortars and shells and strewn with the still bodies of doughboys who fell in the bloody, savage fighting. The fierceness of the fighting was written in those fields and in jagged piles of masonry in the town. Neither Tobruk nor Bizerte nor Battipaglia nor Troina were as ripped and torn and pulverized by explosives as this gray, little town overlooking the valley approaches of Cassino. The Americans call it "Death Valley" because death was on the rampage for forty-eight hours as they stormed this enemy fortress ringed by fortifications dug into the terraced slopes commanding the Liri Valley. Before the U.S. Fifth Army could advance along the road to Rome, this fortress had to be reduced.

The battle began three days ago when the Americans attacked at midday behind a heavy artillery barrage. Casualties were heavy and some companies lost all their officers, either killed or wounded. While one group worked its way slowly along the slopes of the mountain from the east in the face of heavy fire, another attacked from the south out of the valley. Both ran into murderous fire from enemy machine guns and mortars hidden in the caves. One company, led by Capt. Charles Beacham, San Antonio, Texas, reached the edge of the town in the first drive, but had to withdraw in the face of direct fire.

After two company commanders were either killed or wounded, Second Lt. Eden C. Bergman, Clifton, Texas, took over their commands, reorganized the troops and led them back into the fight. He took his men deep into the German lines, but had to draw back again when he had only seven riflemen left. Held off in the first assault, the troops prepared for another attack.

"We ran into a veritable nest of machine gun positions," said a colonel from Texas. "They had built emplacements into the hills with interlocking bands of fire and the positions were protected by barbed wire and fields of anti-personnel mines." This colonel added: "We could have penetrated the Germans' outside line of defense in the first assault if we had wanted to pile up bodies until the troops would have to walk over them. But we try to save as many men as possible." When the attack began, the colonel happened to have a telephone to his ear and he could hear the men in line calling for artillery fire, yelling, "My God, when are we going to get artillery support?"

Within five minutes the artillery was laying down a barrage and mortars were firing into registered targets to help beat off the enemy.

Three times the Germans attacked on the lower slopes of Sammucro and three times they were beaten back. While the fight was raging on the lower slopes, an equally fierce engagement was taking place on the peaks hundreds of feet above, where a unit led by Lt. Rufus Cleghorn, Waco, Texas, occupied positions a week ago. "Rufus the Loudmouth" the doughboys call this 220-pound, barrel-chested, former athlete from Baylor University who has been recommended for promotion. Cleghorn has a foghorn voice and during the heat of battle he climbs on the highest rock, shouting curses at the enemy, screaming insults and throwing rocks and hand grenades. The first day he and his men beat off seven counter-attacks. The slopes of the mountain were strewn with German dead, mowed down as they attempted to retake the heights.

"Those boys used sixty boxes of grenades in about a week," said Capt. William R. Lynch, Huntsville, Texas, who had charge of seeing that they received ammunition and food supplies. "That's about 2,000 grenades, or the number a division would normally use in the combat period. Besides the grenades, they used three times the number of mortar shells they would normally expend."

Yesterday afternoon at exactly 6:53 the Germans below on the slopes came out of their cages and dugouts to make a counter-attack. The battered, weakened doughboys, trying to join their comrades on the peaks, made a stand and fought off three attempts to break their lines. Nobody knew it at the time, but that was the last desperate stab of the enemy.

For his cool, daring leadership in organizing the defense and encouraging the men under intense enemy fire, thirty-one-year-old Lt. Henry C. Bragaw, Wilmington, N.C., like Cleghorn, is being recommended for promotion. Bragaw is a slender, soft-voiced Southerner who was a horticulturist on a North Carolina plantation before the war. He sports a fierce red handlebar mustache which is his identification with the troops.

Other officers praised Maj. David Frazior, Houston, Texas, who, they said, "had done everything from chuck grenades to direct artillery fire." Supplying these troops was a tremendous problem and it required two men carrying supplies to keep one man in the line fighting. Cooks, clerks, drivers and other rear area troops were drafted to carry supplies up the mountain. Each man would carry a box of rations or a can of water plus a bandolier of ammunition, mail and grenades stuffed in his pockets. It took them seven hours to make the round trip and in some places they had to pull themselves up steep slopes, hand over hand, by ropes tied to trees or rocks. Battered by artillery and mortar fire, hammered by infantry attacks—and unable to pierce the American lines—the Germans pulled back from the San Pietro defenses toward the Rapido River line before Cassino.

Today under gray skies we walked around a muddy trail to the edge of the valley where Lt. P. C. Hough of Fredericktown, Mo., had a company preparing to move in the direction of San Pietro. Foxholes dotted the olive grove and soldiers lounged near them. Two litter bearers came up the trail carrying a soldier who had fallen in "Death Valley." Hough watched them pass and slowly turned to follow their progress up the slippery path. "There goes my best friend," he said simply.

We climbed over a low stone wall and skirted the edge of the bank into the next broad field. Shells and mortars had gouged holes into the earth so that there were not ten square yards in all that area unmarked by explosives. The Germans methodically had dropped their shells to cover almost every inch with shrapnel. Against the bank lay an American soldier with his knees drawn up to his chest. A few yards from him the earth was stained with blood. Beyond were other doughboys, some of them looking as if they were sleeping peacefully. We scrambled across a thirty-foot-deep ravine and found an old cobblestone pathway leading around a ridge to San Pietro. We walked slowly, watching for trip wire and mines.

At one place the Germans had strung barbed wire across the trail, so Farnsworth Fowel of C.B.S. climbed over and I started to follow when Homer Bigart of the *New York Herald Tribune* cried, "Watch out!" There in the trail on the other side of the wire was a teller mine with a threadlike trip wire attached to a detonator. We stepped carefully over the wire and walked up a winding path to the edge of San Pietro. Along the side of the road were huge caves which the Germans had used as ammunition storage dumps, living quarters and gun positions.

Around a curve of the road were two General Sherman tanks. In the attack on this fortress they had almost reached the town when they were hit by antitank fire. We climbed across the rubble toward the center of the town. There were no streets. Stone masonry and debris were piled ten feet high. We walked across these piles of wreckage, sometimes in what was once a street and sometimes across what once was a house. How anyone managed to live through the bombardment of San Pietro defies the imagination. But as we climbed over the wreckage, men, women and children came crawling from cellars, caves and dark holes that had been their homes for days. They had terror stamped deep into their thin, miserable faces. They brought out strong red wine and forced glasses into our hands. They did not have to force wine on me after that long climb. And then everybody gabbled at once until there was bedlam in that street of horrors.

Not a house in San Pietro stood whole and undamaged and none I saw ever will be fit to live in, but the Germans had built their defenses around and in the town and the Americans had no choice but to beat the fortress to pieces. A young, barefoot mother, with her child nursing at her breast, came to beg for food. But we had none. At the edge of that hell of wreckage we found the great Church of the Archangel Michael, with its dome and ceiling smashed and debris piled high. In one niche in the wall was a figure of St. Peter and below it a plaque saying this was a gift from San Pietro immigrants who had made their homes in the United States. A Madonna, said to have worked miracles, was the only thing left intact in all that wreckage. □

With the U.S. Fifth Army in Italy, December 22 – The Fifth Army's advance on the road to Rome is going to be the same bloody, slow, costly battle it has been all the way from the beaches of Salerno. This is becoming more and more evident as the days pass and the Army is able only to inch forward against the Germans entrenched in strong mountain positions which flank Highway No. 6 running up the valley through which the Army must pass.

The Fifth Army has stormed one mountain stronghold and wiped out an enemy dug into caves with hidden machine gun nests, only to find another on the next ridge. There can be no blitz warfare here to sweep the Army forward in a great smashing drive. There is no terrain suited to tank warfare. Tanks must travel roads covered by antitank guns and our artillery is being hit without being able to hit back. Thus the fight for Rome is strictly infantry warfare. The Germans must be dug from their caves one by one with hand grenades in close-range fighting. Head-on assaults against such positions are costly and slow. The Germans organized their defenses in the mountains paralleling the Garigliano River and in the heights above Cassino and called them their "Winter Line." There the enemy intended to hold the Fifth Army for the Winter. Orders went out to hold at all costs, and the German still is a disciplined enough soldier to obey his orders. □

The Fifth Army Front in Italy, [December 23] – Lt. Gen. Mark W. Clark made a dawn-to-dusk tour of the Fifth Army front today acting as a military Santa Claus in presenting over one hundred decorations, promotions and battlefield appointments. Wading through thick mud and driving a jeep over a fifty-square-mile area to reach the men in the most forward areas, the Fifth Army commander personally carried Christmas greetings to his American, British and French troops. An unusual incident occurred when he interrogated prisoners of war within an hour after their capture when four Germans were brought to a French regimental headquarters while he was visiting there. Through an interpreter he found that the Germans were in Russia thirteen days ago. Going from regiment to regiment, Gen. Clark walked up to surprised French officers and men on the crests of mountain ridges and to gun positions from which artillery was firing upon the Germans. Along the twisting, muddy front-line roads, he greeted the men, and told them he hoped they would be home by next Christmas after winning the victory.

Two Americans of Japanese descent were among the men promoted by Gen. Clark for outstanding battlefield leadership. The men, both of whom were made captains, were A. Fukuda, 1960 South King Street, Honolulu, and H. Kawano of Pearl City, Oahu. Clark told them the 300th Infantry Battalion had done a fine job and that the U.S. Army was proud of the unit. Clark also visited hospitals, going through the wards to wish the patients a Merry Christmas and a quick recovery. □

With U.S. Fifth Army in Italy, December 23 — When the slim, bespectacled doughboy walked through the gate of the Institute of the Good Shepherd in Naples, cries of "Luigi, Luigi, Americano, Americano," rose in shrill treble voices and orphans came running to greet their friend. It's always that way when Pvt. James Louis Wingate, twenty-five, Baltimore, visits his little friends in the big house overlooking the beautiful Gulf of Naples. They know the smiling soldier will have caramels or hard candy or chewing gum or money with which to buy good things to eat.

Yesterday was different. This time they were going to give Luigi a Christmas party. At other orphanages, Americans were giving parties for children but at the Institute of the Good Shepherd, the children were giving a party for their Luigi. And so they lined up to bring gifts which they had made or bought with pennies hoarded for months—giggling little girls who are among Italy's thousands of war orphans. One gave Private Wingate an embroidered silk purse. There were beautifully embroidered handkerchiefs, delicate little handmade good-luck pieces which Neapolitan mothers usually hang around the necks of their children.

And then one tiny three-year-old tyke came slowly forward, holding out a doll with a pink dress and a blue ribbon in its blond hair, a doll for Wingate's daughter, Frances. But the three-year-old wasn't looking at Luigi. Her eyes were devouring the beautiful doll and you knew she wanted it herself, terribly. Her eyes were brimming as she held it out to Luigi. Wingate saw the tears, too, and the look on the child's face. "No thank you," he said, "you keep the doll for your Christmas." But the little girl shook her head and pressed the doll into his hands and the Mother Superior said, "You must take it. They bought the gifts for you and they really would be unhappy if you refused." And then the little girl echoed all the others with "Buon Natale" and everybody laughed while Luigi exclaimed over his gifts.

"I guess this is one of the happiest Christmases I ever had," Wingate said. "I happened in here one day and I was the first American these children ever had seen. They crowded around to take a look at me and I gave them some caramels. Then I got to coming back regularly until they got to expect me. I'm pretty lucky with dice, too, and I'd bring my winnings up and give the money to the Mothers Superior to buy food with. They don't get much to eat." Wingate looked at his gifts and swallowed hard, "and I never expected to have a Christmas like this in Italy."   □

With Fifth Army in Italy, December 27 — The little men from the Hawaiian Islands who have fought in the Italian invasion to prove they are as good Americans as any other doughboys have won their place so far as their fellow-fighters are concerned. From the beaches of Salerno right into the Nazi winter line these troops of Japanese descent have fought and are now fighting some of the hardest battles of the entire campaign. They have asked no quarter, nor have they received any. They rank on a par with other troops for endurance, skill and ability—and they have the added incentive of their effort to prove themselves good soldiers.

Their first commanding officer was Lieut. Col. Farrant Turner, forty-eight, of Honolulu. He led them on the invasion and stayed with them through some of the hardest fighting in Italy. But in the rugged country now embraced by the front a man near his fifties can hardly expect to stand the physical strain of mountain warfare as a field commander. Reluctantly Turner gave up his command to Maj. James Gillespie of Des Moines, Ia., one of the most popular officers in his division. But Gillespie suffered an attack of stomach ulcers and in turn gave over the command to Maj. John A. Johnson, Jr., whose home is at Kanai in the Hawaiian Islands.

During the fighting at the second crossing of the Volturno River Major Gillespie was seriously ill, but stuck to his command throughout the operation. Johnson took command of the unit while a captain, but was promoted to a major as the result of his leadership during this campaign. He had been with the outfit for several years—having been one of the officers who trained some of the men in the National Guard. He was well known in the islands as a member of the University of Hawaii football team in 1936. "The boys feel they are on the spot and that they have a personal duty to make the people at home feel they really are as much Americans as anyone," Johnson said. "They are no different from any other soldier, but they have that added incentive to fight—because some of their fathers are in internment camps at home."

These island troops do not like to be called "Japanese-Americans" nor do they like to be regarded as different from any other troops. About ten per cent came into the army from the Hawaiian National Guard while the others entered through Selective Service. About seventeen per cent of them are college men. Some operated or worked on plantations, some were school teachers and others were in business. Since landing in Italy the unit has won a reputation for its close fighting and on more than one occasion the men have frightened German troops with their wild cries. In one attack German troops fled in disorder, leaving machine guns and equipment behind them. ☐

With the Fifth Army near San Vittore, December 29 — Another Italian town died today beneath terrible, crashing explosions of American artillery. The mass of rubble and debris has a name—San Vittore—but that is about all that is left to identify the once peaceful place except a church steeple. Artillery men call today's kind of barrage a "serenade." Hundreds of guns were thundering and the explosions were echoing as the shells crashed into enemy positions. It was truly a serenade— of death and destruction. San Vittore was caught in the same unhappy state as San Pietro, which American guns reduced to appalling wreckage. The Germans had made the town the center of another fortress along the road to Rome and to demolish the fortress the town itself had to be destroyed.

For two thunderous minutes San Vittore was battered by tons of explosives and lost in billowing smoke, dust and flame. When the guns had stilled and the smoke drifted away there were only gaunt jagged walls, houses with roofs smashed and streets piled high with debris. The serenade preceded a move by troops under Maj. David Frazior of Houston, Tex., to enter the town with a strong patrol led by Lieut. Richard Dashner of Waco, Tex. San

Vittore has been the hot spot on the Fifth Army front since the capture of San Pietro. It lies on the southern base of a hill in which the Germans are entrenched in caves and dugouts. The enemy also is strongly situated on a ridge to the east of the town. Frazior sent a patrol into San Vittore yesterday, but the doughboys ran into fierce enemy fire, lost two men killed, and had to withdraw under a smoke screen.

Before dawn today Pvt. Fred Costello of Beaumont, Tex., led a second patrol into the town and while the men were searching the buildings, Costello climbed into the church steeple to inspect the countryside. He saw Germans moving into the town. The Germans discovered Costello's patrol and pinned the Americans down for several minutes with intense fire, but they also managed to withdraw from the town. I found Frazior's headquarters just as he was going to enter the town behind the heavy barrage. With him were Dashner and two platoon leaders, Second Lieut. Cecil Mitchell of Napoleon, Ohio, and Sgt. William Ingram of Mexia, Tex. He led us through shell-ripped olive groves to an observation post overlooking the town. Behind, the troops moved into position for the thrust on the town. At the observation post Sgt. Edmond J. Boles of Waco, Tex., and Sgt. O. L. Brotherton of Mexia, Tex., waited for the operation to start. "We'll go into the town right behind Major Frazior if the patrols are able to stay this time," Boles said. Pfc. Clifton E. Sheeler of Cockeysville, Md., stayed by the field telephone and Sgt. Pat Barry of Beaumont, Tex., brewed coffee while he waited for the guns to open up.

At 2:30 p.m. the artillery let loose and the gunners pulled out all the stops. Lieut. Col. Aaron W. Wyatt of Tarrytown, N.Y., jumped into a foxhole beside me. "Give 'em hell," shouted Sheeler as the explosions crashed through the valley and smoke obscured the little town. Occasionally the smoke drifted away and the buildings became visible. A big structure in the front of the town, which looked like the municipal building, had half its roof gone and gaping holes in the walls. The entire character of the town quickly changed. Now it became an ugly, broken, dead city. Soon the explosions lifted from the town onto the hill where the Germans were dug in. Then Major Frazior's troops in front of us came out of their foxholes and moved toward San Vittore. ☐

With the Fifth Army in Italy, December 29 — Fast thinking and Texas double-talk are a good substitute for secret code when telephone communications go out at the front. Capt. Jalvin Newall of Huntsville, Tex., proved this at Mt. Sammucro when telephone lines to the battalion command were knocked out by mortar fire. Newall's men had gone down from the Sammucro peak to a hill on the lower left. Just when things began to look pretty bad, in the early morning his telephone to the battalion command went out. The only communication left was radio, but he didn't want to risk giving the enemy information and thus expose his men to danger. So Newall called Lt. Richard Burrage of Waco, Tex., and said:

"Listen, Dick. Now get this straight. I started to the postoffice to deliver mail and ran into the roughest road you ever saw."

"What's that again?" Burrage asked. "I thought you said something about going to the postoffice."

"That's exactly what I said," replied Newall and by this time Burrage began to understand what was happening.

He carefully noted the message and then went into a huddle with Maj. David Frazier of Houston. Together they realized that Newall meant he had started for his objective and run into trouble.

"Okay, go ahead," Burrage called back on the radio.

"I don't know whether to leave the mail on the road or bring it back. Maybe you'd better notify the Postmaster," said Newall.

From this Burrage and Frazier figured Newall was trying to tell them he wanted to know whether he should leave the men in position or withdraw them and wanted a decision from the commanding officer. "I've been down to see Jerry Sadler," continued Newall. "I found thirty-seven letters from Able, fifty-two from Baker and forty-three from Charles. I got the solitaire grease and I'm afraid when the sun comes up it will melt and I'd like to get it back to the kitchen before it spoils."

That one was not so easy to unravel, especially the part about Jerry Sadler, who is a well-known figure in Texas politics. But finally Burrage and Frazier had it. They decided Newall had seen Jerries in the saddle of the mountain where the doughboys were, but the strength of the A-B-C companies was so low he was afraid that when the sun melted the mists off the mountain the Germans might open up and inflict heavy casualties. Newall thought perhaps he had better bring his men back to the crest of the mountain before the Germans got the range. His messages were relayed to the commanding officer and the order went back. "Leave the mail on the road. Do not bring it back." So Newall left the mail on the road for two days in order to beat off a counter-attack and hold the post that had been won.   ☐

Three

CASSINO AND ANZIO,
JANUARY–FEBRUARY 1944

With the Fifth Army in Italy, January 5 — Savage fighting flared suddenly on the Fifth Army front today in a renewal of the Allied drive toward Cassino on the road to Rome. The infantry attacked under the heaviest enemy artillery and mortar fire seen on this front in many weeks. For the first time doughboys were beginning to encounter the enemy's concrete machine gun emplacements—pillboxes built by forced Italian labor. An officer said the only way to reduce the nests was to storm them head-on and toss grenades into the gun aperture to destroy the crew.

The thrust came after a night of torrential cold rain which bogged the front in mud and increased the difficulties of the foot soldiers. Streams which had subsided during the past few weeks suddenly rose to flood levels and impeded progress. Low-hanging clouds in the morning kept Allied airpower shackled but at noon the clouds lifted, permitting fighter-bombers to roar in on three missions and pound the German guns emplaced on the hills.

As soon as the American and British troops moved out of their positions the Germans turned loose a heavy concentration of mortar and artillery fire. The thrust moved forward into the face of this intense thunder of explosions and once again the Fifth Army was battering at the line of strong defenses guarding the approaches to Rome. The Germans concentrated their fire on the roads leading to the front line and kept up a steady pounding. The sudden Allied thrust quickly brought a bag of prisoners, many of whom appeared to be youths under twenty. The Germans seem to have many machine guns in this area. In some cases one crew was found operating two or three guns covering strategic approaches to heights which the doughboys and Tommies must capture to control Cassino and break the enemy defenses.   ☐

San Vittore, Italy, January 7 — American troops fighting from house to house in a bitter battle which raged for nearly three days captured the village of San Vittore yesterday, killing or capturing virtually all the German defenders. Control of San Vittore put the Fifth Army a step nearer Cassino and wiped out German resistance in one of the toughest fortresses in the enemy's winter line. More than one hundred prisoners were taken during the battle thru the gray stone houses and at least an equal number were killed in the savage fighting that swirled thru the streets, into houses and up on rooftops.

But, though the Germans fought well, they did not fight wisely because the doughboys trapped them and only a scattered few Germans slipped thru the ring of steel which closed around the shell smashed town. While the battle roared around the town, terrified, miserable, and hungry civilians crouched in dark cellars and caves where they lived for days. The Germans had forced them from their homes to convert each house into a small fortress. Some 200 women and children crept into the dark, smelly sanctuaries to wait for the tide of battle to roll over. They were too frightened to come into the open today for the Germans were dropping shells among the already wrecked buildings to harass the victorious Americans.   □

San Vittore, January 7 — Lieut. Gen. Mark W. Clark's Fifth Army was a step nearer Cassino—and Rome—today following the capture of San Vittore, one of the toughest German defense points in their entire winter line in Italy. San Vittore, scene of savage fighting in one of the bitterest small-scale struggles of the Italian campaign, officially fell to Gen. Clark's men at 3:37 p.m., Thursday, but it really surrendered at 1 p.m. The Germans had been ordered to fight to the last for the honor of the regiment, but under the relentless pressure of the Americans their commanding officer, a tall, blond young Austrian Nazi from Vienna, sent word to his men that they might surrender if they were trapped. And the greater part of them were trapped, only a scattered few Germans slipping through the ring of steel which the doughboys closed around the ruined village.

More than one hundred prisoners were taken in the town alone during the battle, which raged from house to house and along rooftops. Some of them surrendered without putting up a fight, but other Americans had to make three attacks on one pillbox to silence it. Hugging close to walls and dashing into doorways when shells whistled by, Homer Bigart of the *New York Herald Tribune* and I walked through the streets and in one dark, cavernous dwelling found more than one hundred men, women and children—Italian civilians— a wrecked people so poor they had been unable to flee from the town as hundreds had done. They simply had no place to go except these cave-like cellars when the Germans ordered them from their homes months ago.

The only food I saw was a little corn, onions and peppers and fruit. The children looked thin and emaciated and most of the men and women were gaunt and hollow-eyed from the nights of disturbed sleep and hunger. They were too frightened to come into the open today, for the Germans were dropping shells among the already wrecked buildings to harass the victorious Americans.

As the battle rages on outside San Vittore, the pungent odor of death lies heavy over the entire town. In this town, too, the trail of death, destruction and famine shows the trail the Germans have taken. Each time a shell crashed into the town or moaned over, the crowds shrank back into the darkness of their dirty, ill-smelling cellars. The children whimpered and their mothers pulled them close to them, looking at us with pleading eyes as though we could bring them comfort.

I entered the village this morning to find the doughboys exhausted from the hard fighting. I found one dark-haired, handsome sergeant leaning against a doorway as though he would sink to the floor in fatigue if he took another step. His young face was covered with a four-day growth of beard. He was Sgt. Francis Poll of Byron Center, Mich., one of the first American soldiers to enter San Vittore after the attack began last Tuesday night. Sgt. Poll's commanding officer, Lieut. Irwin Hall of Central Square, N.Y., had entrusted the sergeant and Staff Sgt. Albert Stagle of New England, N.D., with leading a spearhead into the attack. They were lucky to come back.

Coming into town, I passed more than a score of German prisoners who were captured in their machine gun nests. Guarding was a group including Private Levat of Rochester, N.Y., and Pfc. Salvatore Fiore of Westport, Conn. "We made three straight rushes and the third one did the job," grinned Sgt. Levat in commenting on his unit's attack on a German pillbox. "We killed one German and captured six in that one nest.   □

At the Fifth Army Front, January 8 — American troops held their grip on the slopes of 900-foot Mt. Porchia today with the same determined spirit of the young captain who led them up the rocky hillside under heavy enemy fire. Mt. Porchia, two miles southwest of San Vittore, is one of the toughest nuts on the Fifth Army front. It sits in a plain before Cassino like the back of a sinister pre-historic animal rising out of a swamp and is one of the heights guarding the approaches to the city. The attack on Porchia opened at 8 o'clock Tuesday night when troops under Col. Lyle J. Deffenbaugh of Council Bluffs, Ia., and Lieut. Col. Elton Ringsak of Grafton,

N.D., moved onto the Cassino plain under bright moonlight with tanks giving them fire support.

Thursday morning they had reached the foot of Mt. Porchia. One unit under Capt. James W. Wilson of Lexington, Ky., moved partway up the mountain but had to withdraw under intense enemy mortar and machine gun fire and regroup for another move against the heights where the Germans had dug machine gun nests and sniper holes. While Wilson regrouped his men, Capt. Ralph C. Fisher of Hyattsville, Md., stood up before his detachment and shouted, "I'm going up that mountain." Fisher started straight up the slope of the northeast corner with his men right behind him. They battled their way through enemy machine gun nests straight to the objective and the Germans have never been able to dislodge them. Only half the men who went up the mountain with Fisher reached their goal because of the heavy enemy fire. But those who did dug into positions and quickly prepared to stave off counter-attacks.

Thursday night at about 8 o'clock the counter thrust came—with the Germans attacking Fisher's group both from along the ridge and from the lower slopes. Maj. Thomas W. Hoban, Cleveland, Ohio, estimated that the enemy had five to one superiority even though heavy artillery fire had decimated the ranks of the Nazis' defending battalion. To make up for these losses the Germans called up every possible replacement—mule skinners, truck drivers, messengers and mess boys—put guns in their hands and sent them into the counter-attack. Fisher's men were forced down from the ridge in the first rush of the enemy and had to crawl into rocky niches on the ledges below, but after seven hours of fighting they climbed back.   □

At the Fifth Army Beachhead South of Rome, January 23 — Twenty-four hours in the life of a war correspondent is not particularly important to anyone but the correspondent himself—but this chronicle will give newspaper readers a glimpse of how their news is gathered in this theater of war. As an explanation to all editors of correspondents on this show: there have been thousands of words written, but finding a means of getting them back to Naples is another matter. Perhaps today there will be a speed boat or plane or ship which will carry back the copy we have been unable to file by radio.

For several hours we have been going around with our mouths open in amazement over the ease with which the Army and Navy managed to land troops behind the enemy lines. I landed with the second assault wave at 2:10

a.m. but did not see a shot fired. We just walked. That's how easy it was. After more than twenty-four hours ashore I have been able to get only 250 words of copy out by radio. Radios seem to have a peculiar way of losing all contact with the world during a time like this when you have a big story to tell.

Correspondents attached to the Fifth Army drew lots to see who would win a place with the amphibious force. There were several places open. I was one of the lucky ones and was assigned to an advance unit. Others were placed so as to spread the coverage over all units of the invading force. We did not know when or where we were going but we were told confidentially about the amphibious operation by which the Fifth Army hopes to smash into the enemy's flank and thus open the road to Rome.

As I write this it appears that the planners of this operation conceived a brilliant one, for it has gone better than anyone could have dreamed. I drew a unit commanded by Lt. Col. Lyle W. Bernard of Highland Falls, N.Y., an old friend from the Sicily campaign and one of the ablest and toughest soldiers I've ever seen. "This may be the toughest thing we've hit yet," Bernard said. "But I've got men who can do the job if anybody can." I figured it would be wise to stick close to this tall, lean soldier who had come up the hard way because he seemed to have a charmed life. He and his second in command, Maj. Lynn Fargo of Ripon, Wis., have come through some hair raising experiences together unscathed. They have that certain something called battlefield luck.

It doesn't take long for the reputation of good fighters to spread through the army and these two have that reputation, along with their entire unit. They make a remarkable team and work together as though reading each other's thoughts at times. We went aboard ship and that night we lounged in our little stateroom and drank very bad gin and very bad cognac and talked far into the morning, and Fargo said: "War has taught me never to judge a man until I know what he is made of and it has taught me a strange lesson, that men are bound closer together in time of war. It should not take a war to bring them together, but that is what is happening."

Next morning our ship steamed out to sea to convoy with the invasion fleet and steamed toward Rome. Everyone spent most of the day sleeping or lounging in bunks, resting for the test ahead because we thought this would be the toughest landing any of us ever made. We did not see how the enemy could be unaware of such an armada. And then Bernard called his officers into the wardroom to give them a briefing on the operation and to explain his plans in detail. "There can be no withdrawal and there will be no surrender," he said. "We've got to root the bastards out with mortars and even bayonets and it will be a hard job. I'm not trying to paint a tragic picture but that's the way it looks and you might as well have it straight."

After the briefing, a poker game started. Some men read, others wrote letters to their wives or sweethearts—thinking perhaps they might be the last letters they would receive from them. Col. Charles Martineau of Elizabethton, Tenn., went about the ship quietly talking to the men. A few hours before he had held mass on an altar improvised on the hood of a jeep. Then it was time to disembark. Our ship stood at anchor about four miles off the coast. We were to land in the vicinity of *Nettuno. We strapped on musette bags, slung a blanket roll over our shoulders, checked our canteens. Each man had two days' emergency rations composed of three bars of concentrated chocolate and three boxes of K rations.

A bell sounded and we filed onto the dark deck and stood at the rail as seamen lowered the assault boats. There was not a sound from the mainland and the only lights were stars studding the black sky. We clambered down a swaying net into the boat and were jammed in tightly. The men did not talk much, but stood swaying with the boat. Then I heard the seamen say, "This boat is leaking badly. We'll never make shore. I knew I'd get a tub like this one." But finally the leak was plugged and the boat moved on inshore with others in V formation. At 1:45 a.m. the Navy loosed a barrage on the beach and then we thought the Germans would answer with coastal defense guns, but nothing happened. Not a shot was fired from the shore.

Then the boat hit the beach and Bernard shouted "everybody out fast!" We surged toward the front of the boat but the ramp stuck. "Follow me over the side," Bernard shouted, and jumped into the shallow surf. The soldiers swarmed over the side and splashed ashore. I dropped into hipboot water and then fell headlong as the weight of my pack and bedroll threw me off balance. A soldier raised me to my feet and shivering with cold, I hurried after the troops already filing across the sand.

Later we learned that the troops to our right and left walked into mines but apparently our strip of beach was unmined for I did not hear any explosion or see a shot fired by our troops although there were occasional small arms fire off at our flank. We just marched in single file across the low marshy land, stumbling through bogs and water filled shell pits in what must

---

*Editor's Note: On January 22, 1944, American forces of General Mark Clark's Fifth U.S. Army and Don Whitehead landed at Nettuno, a small seaport immediately south of Anzio, while the British landed just to the north of Anzio, which explains his frequent references to Nettuno rather than what was later called the Anzio Beachhead. As would happen later in December 1944 with the Battle of the Bulge, Whitehead was not there (he had been recalled to Allied headquarters in Naples, and then to Algiers) in early February 1944 and thereby missed a major scoop—the massive German counter-offensive at Anzio, which was not safely repelled until February 17.

have been a German artillery range. Finally we stopped and there I decided to wait for dawn and write my first dispatch to be filed by radio. All of us were soaked and for two hours we hopped and jumped about trying to warm our frozen feet and legs, excited by the lack of enemy opposition and the swift advance of the troops.

The sun felt good when it rose across the misty horizon. Still there were no reports of enemy opposition except in a few isolated cases where troops ran into a few Germans who were not even aware we were landing behind their lines. Our men just kept marching straight to their objectives while armor, guns and ammunition poured ashore on a precision schedule, and then we waited to see what the Germans would do about this threat to Rome and to their Cassino lines. □

At the Fifth Army Beachhead, South of Rome, January 23 — Our landing was accomplished with clock-like precision from the very first, with a calm sea aiding Allied troops. Not until 8:50 a.m. on Saturday was there any real sign of enemy resistance. From out of the sun came five Focke-Wulfs in a screaming dive on the beach. Anti-aircraft guns from sea and land loosed a terrific barrage at the hurtling planes, which dumped their bombs and roared away. Within the next two hours the Germans attacked twice more.

I landed in the second wave with troops led by Lieut. Col. Lyle W. Bernard of Highland Falls, N.Y., who told his men before they left their ship: "There is to be no withdrawal and there is to be no surrender." We clambered down nets on the sides of the ship shortly after midnight and crouched in assault boats, awaiting the time for the rendezvous. The Navy had brought an armada into position under a starlit sky and anchored a few miles offshore. It was a precision maneuver, seldom seen in difficult amphibious operations.

Then, at a signal, the assault boats moved inshore, looming dark in the water and leaving white wakes. Tense and silent soldiers, watching for the enemy to open fire, waited for those first flashes of guns shooting from the shore. Shortly before 2 a.m. the boats close to the shore loosed a terrific barrage on the beach and explosions pounded against our eardrums.

"Now they'll open up on us," Colonel Bernard muttered, staring into the darkness ahead. But there was only the sound of the assault-boat motors and the thumping of the water against the blunt noses of the craft. It was uncanny. We had expected the Germans to be waiting on the beaches, as they were at Salerno, but this time they were not ready. (Italian civilians in a little town occupied by American troops said that the Germans had never appeared much interested in this stretch of coastline and that those garrisoned in the town had left last Tuesday, a later dispatch reported.)

The entire operation was a marvel of coordination between the Army and the Navy. Many army men said that it was more nearly perfect than any that they had ever witnessed. As far as I was able to observe on a small sector of the front, there was no single hitch, on either sea or land, and troops rushed to their objectives as fast as they could walk through unfamiliar, marshy country.

But this initial advantage, while cheering to officers and men, did not dispel cautious awareness of the danger that is sure to develop when the enemy counter-attacks—in all probability with armor, for this country is flat country, excellent for maneuvering armor. A few hours after the initial assault, the roads in the area were heavy with guns and trucks moving toward the vague line known as the front and antitank guns speeding into defensive positions.   □

With the Fifth Army's Amphibious Forces South of Rome, January 23 — We walked in behind the German lines early today with hardly a shot being fired in a most sensational amphibious operation. It was so easy and simply done and caught the Germans so completely by surprise that as I write this dispatch six hours after the landing American troops are literally standing with their mouths open and shaking their heads in utter amazement. "Maybe," said Lt. Col. Edgar C. Doleman, "the war is over and we don't know it." A Fifth Army infantryman who made other amphibious landings said, "I still don't believe it."

The doughboys swarmed ashore at 2 a.m. expecting to have to fight their way in over the beach through barbed wire and minefields. I landed with the second wave at 2:10 a.m. Then we began walking, expecting each moment that the enemy would open fire with a blinding flash of fire. But we just walked. Nothing happened in my sector. There were only a few scattered shots fired and most of them came from our own tense troops.

To our north there was the sound of gunfire, but it was very light and at this early stage there was every indication that Lt. Gen. Mark Clark's Fifth Army had pulled a brilliant maneuver to hit the enemy from the side and open the road to Rome. The next few hours will decide that when the expected German counter-attack develops. Moving swiftly in from the beach, troops in this sector reached their objectives without even making contact with the enemy except for opposition from two or three Germans. At dawn a swarm of fighter planes swept over to give protection to the invasion fleet. Even before dawn the artillery, armor and advanced guns, were ashore and rolling into position. The whole thing was like a perfectly coordinated practice maneuver without even simulated opposition. And Army men praised the manner in which the Navy got them ashore right on schedule. □

With the Fifth Army on the Beachhead South of Rome, January 24 — Italian civilians in a little town occupied by American troops said today that the Germans never appeared much interested in this stretch of coastline and that those garrisoned in the town [Nettuno] left last Tuesday. The civilians had another report that a battalion of the enemy was preparing to move in today, but the Allied landing Saturday beat them to the punch.

This was my fourth amphibious operation. It followed two in Sicily and one at Salerno, and I never saw anything to equal the precision and ease with which the Army and Navy coordinated their efforts to put a strong force ashore and catch the enemy with no defenses prepared whatever. German Field Marshal Albert Kesselring must be blushing tonight for his failure to plug the chinks in his coastal fortress. The landing was so smooth that an observer might have thought it was a peacetime maneuver without even simulated opposition.

I landed with Bertham Brandt, young photographer making his first amphibious landing. As we walked across the dunes with enemy guns silent he said: "This is not right; I don't like it." A doughboy turned and said: "It ain't right, all right, but I like it." □

On the Fifth Army's Beachhead South of Rome, January 24 — American doughboys battled all night to hold on to vital bridges along the Mussolini Canal which the Germans attempted to seize with counter-attacks but at dawn today the Americans still held the bridges and had thrown the enemy back. Furthermore they tightened their hold on this beachhead as more guns and supplies arrived in a growing threat to the Germans' grip on Rome. In one sector four bridges changed hands three times in a succession of attacks and counter-attacks which began after dark last night and continued almost until dawn. Each time the Americans were thrown back by tank and infantry assaults, they returned to battle the Germans back from the hotly-contested objectives.

Doughboys under Major Oliver G. Kenney of Berkeley, Calif., had reached their objective the morning of the landing by a swift march across the flat marshland near Anzio. They were well ahead of schedule when they dug in near the Mussolini Canal to meet an expected counter-move by the Germans. One of Kenney's units was attacked by infantry and tanks but held on until the enemy worked around on the flank and forced them back. Then the doughboys pushed the Nazis back with a vigorous counter-thrust with close support from tanks. Capt. C. Elmore, Lexington, Ky., took two canal bridges and after a see-saw battle ended up at dawn in control of both points. These clashes, however, did not involve any large concentrations on our side and as yet the Germans have not thrown in any great number of troops against the bridgehead, although we can expect them.

In just forty-eight hours this chunk of Italian coastline, which a few days ago was a barren, shell-pitted artillery range, has become an amazing landscape bristling with guns and swarming with troops, jeeps and trucks. It is not even recognizable as the same land I saw when the sun came over the horizon two days ago and revealed a great invasion fleet lying offshore and landing craft disgorging their barges onto the beaches. Now each road and lane is busy with traffic. Familiar signs point the way to this or that regiment battalion or attached unit. Military police direct the flow of traffic as casually as I saw them on the streets of Naples. The seeming confusion of the initial landing has settled into the orderly, smooth movement of an army well established. Except for occasional hit and run raids there is little in the rear areas to disturb the remarkable calm.

Up forward, however, it is another story. On a trip to the front I watched the doughboys moving into new positions. White and gray plumes of smoke rose from German shelling. Most of the German shooting was 88-millimeter bursts at our fighter-bombers and fighters which have been coming over steadily. In two hours at the front lines no shells came close enough to give anybody the jitters. A shell screamed into a field one hundred yards away while troops ducked for cover but the shelling was not intense and I found officers and men in high spirits.

You could walk from one farmhouse to another in perfectly clear view of Velletri, Genzano and Albano, towns high on the Alban Hills between us and Rome, without a shot fired at you. The front was a pleasant change from the place where we spent last night. The stillness of 3 a.m. was shattered by a rending roar of a German 150-millimeter shell and the room was filled with a sailing window, blinds, dirt and other items that barely missed your correspondent and Lieut. Col. George Gardes of Needham, Mass.

At one command post concealed in a grove of trees, tall, bearded Lieut. Lewis F. Bixby, one-time reporter on the Kalamazoo, Mich., *Gazette*, sauntered in with a report on a reconnaissance mission he made during the night behind enemy lines. With Sgt. Verel E. Billerbeck, Martinton, Ill., Bixby slipped 3,000 yards behind the lines to obtain information. "Once a group of Germans walked to within twenty feet of us. We could have knocked them off but it was not our mission to fight. Finally the Germans went away." Bixby and his men lay beside a group of Germans and watched them shooting toward American lines. "I've seen the Germans do a lot of shooting," he said, "but that is the first time I ever sat behind them and watched them at work."

Italian civilians evacuated from the Anzio area four months ago have begun to filter back into their homes and are giving the Americans a warm welcome. "When we came in," said Pvt. Rocco Zito, Utica, N.Y., "one old woman stood by the roadside and kissed the hand of every soldier who passed. I guess there were about 200 of us and she did not miss a man. They say the Germans took their chickens, cheese and wine. Rofuoni Loreto, a gray-haired farmer, said he had been in Rome two days ago. "People are praying for the arrival of the Americans," he said. □

With the Fifth Army South of Rome, January 25 – In four days Lt. Gen. Mark W. Clark's Fifth Army troops have established such a strong beachhead south of Rome that the German grip on the capital is menaced and enemy troops along the main Cassino front are threatened with being trapped if they cling to their positions in the hills. This is an optimistic view, but the manner in which the Americans and British gouged a hole in a short time and consolidated their position leaves no alternative but to be optimistic. The Allies smashed in from the sea at probably the most vulnerable spot in all the German defenses in Italy and moved swiftly to take advantage of the element of surprise.

Men, guns, armor and supplies have poured across the beach in an unbroken flow and in such proportions that no one I have met has any fears that the Germans ever will be able to threaten a breakthrough such as endangered the Salerno beachhead. Actually, we expected an attack at dawn on the day of the landing. But none came. And as this is written four days later the Germans still have been unable to launch an attack in force to halt the advance of Allied troops who have pushed out to widen and strengthen the vital beachhead.

Within these four days the Germans lost their best chances for pushing back the Fifth Army—for the critical period in any amphibious operation is that time between the landing of assault troops and the arrival of guns, tanks and supplies in strength. That period is past in this operation. Whether the Germans can concentrate enough force against the beachhead remains to be seen, but at this phase it appears unlikely and this feeling of confidence runs through the entire section of the Fifth Army whose job it is to hold and widen the bridgehead.

Results of the amphibious landing have given the Allies many advantages. Some of them were these: The army advanced more than thirty miles toward Rome with exceptionally light casualties. A strong force was able to bypass the enemy's mountain defenses and avoid a slow, slogging fight up the valley on a single front. The move has threatened to bottle up the Cassino sector and isolate parts of at least five enemy divisions which have held up the Allied advance for weeks on the winter line. And the Allies hold the small but valuable port of Anzio.

There unquestionably will be much hard, bloody fighting ahead before the Fifth Army can enter Rome, but the amphibious move has gone far toward breaking up a stalemate. There are two possibilities for German moves to counter the beachhead threat. One is to pull back from the Cassino front and put up new defenses before Rome. The other is to throw enough men, guns and armor around the beachhead to seal it off while still battling to hold the Cassino front.

Already the enemy is pulling back reserves from the Cassino front to this area and troops are reported marching up the road from Frosinone while others are converging on this front from other directions. The principal reasons the Fifth Army has been able to accomplish so much infiltration in such a short time are that the landing caught the enemy by surprise, that troops experienced in amphibious operations moved swiftly, that the Army's supply system is excellent and that the Navy did a magnificent job in getting the army and supplies ashore.

The surprise element was not so much in the fact that a landing was to be made behind the lines as in the place and time. It is becoming apparent that the Germans expected a landing somewhere north of Rome and pulled out all defenses along this strip of coast to leave a vulnerable opening. Optimism on this front is due largely to the fact that the Army is well ahead of its timetable both in progress on land and in pouring supplies over the beach. The real test, of course, will come when the Germans attack in force against the beachhead. Then will come the decisive phase of the campaign.   □

On the Fifth Army Beachhead South of Rome, January 25 –
Out in the flat fertile plains south of Rome American troops supported by tanks are having to blast German machine gunners from every farmhouse in their drive across the Mussolini Canal. Hastily throwing up a defense against the swift Fifth Army drive inland from their Nettuno beachhead, the Germans have evacuated Italians from their homes and turned each building into a fortress which the Yanks are attacking with tanks and machine guns. For the first time in the Italian campaign the Americans are fighting over country suitable for tanks, and armor is being used effectively to support infantry advances. Armor aided the doughboys in their push last night into enemy territory.

Late yesterday afternoon two units commanded by Capt. Burleigh Packwood of Billings, Mont., and Capt. "Footsie" Britt of Lonoke, Ark., moved across the Mussolini canal to seize two road junctions. Fifteen minutes after their attack began the fighting started and it continued all night long but the Yanks drove the enemy back from house to house to reach their objective, even though the Germans threw in reinforced units in an effort to halt them. "Packwood chased the Germans all the way back to the objective," grinned Lt. Col. Lyle W. Bernard. "The boys went ahead against heavy machine gun and armored car fire."

"Our men ran the Germans from house to house," said Capt. Charles Noble of Santa Ana, Calif. "When things got too hot in one house the Krauts would drop back to another."

In one house the Germans had five machine guns set up. Packwood sent one unit under Lt. Philip Horan of Akron, Ohio, out to clean them out with tank support and the troops assaulted the stronghold, driving the Germans out.

During the night the enemy brought troops in by truck and dropped them behind the doughboys on lateral roads but in each case Packwood or Britt would send men back to wipe them out. □

On the Fifth Army Invasion Beachhead, January 27 –
For anyone who wants to see a lot of action in a little time from all sides there is no better spot than a beachhead—this beachhead in particular. Like a newsreel that runs twenty-four hours a day, Mars is grinding out a super-colossal special feature of life and death, thrills and chills—and a dash of comedy.

All you have to do is put on a helmet and step out under the clear blue sky and things begin to happen. It's best to wear a helmet, for around this neighborhood the flak rains down like hail when the Army and Navy really get warmed up with ack-ack guns on the enemy planes. For those who do not care for too much fresh air there is a grandstand view from any waterfront window of the colorful stucco villa which is occupied by the war correspondents assigned to cover this operation.

We moved into our new quarters with the beautiful sea view from another villa which trembled like a palsied old gentleman in a windstorm every time the guns began to roar. And then, too, the Krauts were throwing shells around promiscuously and some of the boys felt that our northeastern exposure was a little too exposed for comfort. Perhaps it was a good idea, because the day after we left the delightful villa with its atrocious paintings a shell passed through the walls and smashed up the gents' room. But there were some differences of opinion last night when the Krauts paid an early evening call with their bombers. That's when it began to appear as though this noncombatant unit was a prime military objective.

First, the Germans hung out their flares to light up the shoreline and the ships at sea. That was when I was trying to heat a mess tin full of meatballs and spaghetti over a fierce little flame of primus, while Slim Aarons of *Yank*, the weekly army newspaper, opened a tin of peas. We heard the plane diving and the whistle of a bomb, and a half dozen of us piled into a narrow hallway, flat on our faces. Somebody stepped on my back and then Slim's wrist watch, and about that time the bomb hit in the street outside and a chunk of plaster slapped me on the head.

The concussion blew the windows and shutters open and knocked a candle over on the bunk of Burgess Scott, a *Yank* reporter, and set it afire to violate all blackout rules. By the time we got the lights out another plane was diving, and the Navy, which had been tending to its own business, decided that enough was enough, so every gun they had opened up.

A few seconds after the second batch of bombs hit nearby we were scrambling for the air raid shelter on the floor below and I discovered that I was still balancing a plate of spaghetti and meatballs through the melee without dropping a single meatball. When the raid was over everyone began trying to figure out why the Jerries selected our villa for a target, when somebody noticed that outside at the waterside there is an old pier which in starlight or under a flare probably looks like a ship tied up to the shore. We are thinking of going down and persuading the engineers to maybe blow the thing up, but they would probably say it would be a good idea to leave it there and let the Germans waste their bombs on it.   □

Allied Headquarters in Italy, [January 27] — American troops had battled to within 500 yards of Cassino from the north today and Allied Headquarters announced that the core of the Germans' Gustav line was "seriously threatened." The Americans and French tore wide gaps in the Gustav line in bloody fighting in the mountains to the rear of the stronghold despite a hail of fire from German six-barreled Nebelwerfer mortars and self-propelled guns manned by a "last ditch" garrison fighting from the ruins.

At the same time other Americans were making a direct frontal attack on the ancient city guarding the open Liri Valley. To the north, meanwhile, Allied troops enlarged their Anzio bridgehead in the face of desperate German counter-attacks and engaged in hard fighting in several sectors. One of the German counter-attacks thrown back was just west of Littoria. With their Cassino front near collapse the Germans were throwing attacks against the beachhead with increasing strength as new elements arrived in the enemy line in an effort to seal off the most serious threat to Rome.

On the comparatively quiet Eighth Army front along the Adriatic the Allies had the enemy jumpy and nervous. The Nazis were shooting off flares frequently at night, and there was much movement of enemy transport behind the lines. (German nervousness frequently is a sign of an impending Allied offensive.) Fighting grimly to halt Lt. Gen. Mark W. Clark's Fifth Army at Cassino, the Germans threw in counter-attack after counter-attack on the American flanks. But the Americans and French to the north widened the breach in the Gustav line to three miles, capturing several heights near Terelle. The Americans crossed the Cassino-Terelle Road and Terelle itself was almost surrounded after the capture of a series of heights on Mt. Castellone, a 2,300-foot peak where one hundred prisoners were taken.

Cassino faced encirclement if the Germans continued to fight to the last man as they gave every indication of doing. The Americans coming down from the mountains were in a position to cut Highway No. 6 to Rome behind the defenders. The highway already was of little use to the Germans since it was under the command of Allied artillery on the slopes above. But despite the threat from every side the Germans contested every inch of ground and burrowed in the ruins like the Russian defenders of Stalingrad. They had to be cleaned out of caves and dugouts one by one in the vicinity of Mt. Manna, and out of the Monte Villa barracks to the north of the town. From 50 to one hundred bombs smashed into wireless installations at Durazzo on the Albanian coast when Liberators of Maj. Gen. Nathan F. Twining's Fifteenth Air Force set out to wreck that Nazi communication center in the Balkans.

Mitchells [B-25 medium bomber] blocked the Appian Way eleven miles south of Rome at Albano and Warhawks bombed Cisterna where American troops fought on the outskirts of that Appian Way town. ☐

With Allied Invasion Forces South of Rome, January 27 — Hospitals and hospital ships in the Allied invasion area south of Rome have been the targets of German bombers. The enemy already has attacked three hospital ships with bombers, and I just have returned from an evacuation hospital where shells whine viciously overhead. One exploded nearby as two teams of surgeons carried on their work in the operating tent.

The job of caring for battle casualties went on without slackening, despite shells and ack-ack shrapnel which peppered the tents and wounded one sergeant. American evacuation hospitals already have set up and are caring for casualties, but the pressure upon the hospital staffs in this operation has not been nearly as heavy as it was at Salerno. ☐

Naples, February 8 — When the great invasion of the European continent begins, one of the big responsibilities of the Allied air forces will be to prevent any concentrated use by the Germans of rocket-propelled glider bombs. There is no breach of security involved in saying that this new aerial weapon of the Nazis is a potent threat against shipping. The Germans know it and the Allies know it.

An invasion fleet at anchor is like a flock of sitting ducks unless air cover can intercept the control plane from which the gliders are directed by radio. Anti-aircraft fire is only partly effective against the small winged projectiles, because they sweep down on their targets swiftly and are difficult to hit. As a matter of fact, it is usually only a lucky hit when one is stopped by ack-ack fire.

The Germans used glider bombs against the invasion fleet at Salerno and again at Anzio during the Fifth Army's behind-the-lines thrust. Censorship prevented disclosure of the full effectiveness of this weapon until Winston Churchill announced its use at Salerno. Again at Anzio, correspondents with the landing forces were forbidden to say the Germans were using rocket bombs against shipping. A directive said no mention was to be made of the glider projectiles. Since then, however, these restrictions have been lifted. Now the correspondents may tell something in detail of what the rocket bombs are like and how the Germans use them.

From descriptions pieced together by several eyewitnesses who have watched these winged weapons attack, it is learned the bomb is about twenty- to thirty-feet long, with tail fins acting as a stabilizer and rudder. It has a wing-spread of some fifteen feet and in flight it looks like a small plane. Apparently it is armor-piercing. At Salerno, one of them that hit a ship penetrated thick steel deck-plates and exploded in the craft's interior.

The bomb is attached to the belly of a twin-engine Heinkel bomber, which is equipped as a control plane. When still some distance from the target, the bomber plane's pilot releases the glider and drops the flaps of his plane's wings to slow his own speed, until the bomb shoots ahead into the pilot's vision. From the time of its release, the glider apparently is controlled visually and directed by radio. The glider can make a sharp turn to swoop in on its target from the side, if necessary.

Except when the control plane is in trouble from fighter attack or ack-ack, or the glider is hit by shrapnel, the bomb appeared to observers to be under excellent control at all times. This does not mean the rocket bombs always score a hit. They don't. Many of them fall harmlessly into the sea, either because the pilot loses control at the last minute, or because they overshoot the target.

Whether the enemy can muster a large fleet of rocket-bomb gliders for use against an invasion is not known, but it is logical to assume—and the Allied air forces must go on the assumption—that the Germans can concentrate large numbers against an invasion armada. And the air forces must be prepared to protect shipping from this type of attack.

Witnesses tell of a red-and-green glow at the tail of the glider when the rocket is in flight. This apparently is caused by the propelling charge. At the Anzio beach, Captain Clark Neal of Clarendon, Ark., was standing at the rail of a ship late one afternoon when the Germans came over with glider bombs. "I saw one of the bombs heading for a ship near us," he explained. "It made a screaming sound in flight and looked like a small plane. At first, I thought it was a plane that had been shot down and was falling into the water. There was a light in the tail end which changed from green to red. It looked like a faint tracer."   □

Algiers, February 8 — There is no longer any need for American soldiers returning to the United States to feel uneasy about what they will find in that strange land. All the answers are condensed in a booklet known as Soldier's Guide to the United States, compiled by an anonymous member of the Forty-fifth Division somewhere in Italy. The booklet is a double re-verse on all those booklets the boys received when they left home, guiding them through England, Egypt, India, North Africa, Persia and other far-away places. Following is an expurgated condensation of this new guide:

INTRODUCTION

"You have been assigned to duty in the United States and the helpful rules of conduct contained in this pamphlet will be of great assistance in cement-ing a greater friendship with the civilian population. The impression you create will cause the native to judge all soldiers, therefore it is important to be polite, courteous, generous, but at all times firm. Naturally, having been overseas, you have automatically become a leading authority on practically everything, and your opinions will carry great weight. A practical plan of entering into any conversation is to preface all remarks as follows:

" 'Now when we landed in North Africa' or 'When we landed in Sicily.' This will silence all other conversation and secure instant attention, espe-cially when a slightly loud tone of voice is used. In anything in the ensuing monologue about invasions you must always remember that you landed in the first wave. These things are hard to check.

RELATIONS WITH CIVILIANS

"Be generous with your cigarettes and especially kind to children. Small boys sometimes attempt to loot the glove compartment of a jeep, but may be easily discouraged by a kick in the groin.

HISTORICAL BACKGROUND

"The United States was discovered and immediately had trouble with the In-dians. It seems that eventually they were all placed on certain tracts of land where oil was subsequently discovered. Of course, the Indians were immedi-ately chased out and later rounded up and placed in the Forty-fifth Division.

FOOD

"The staple articles of diet are meat and potatoes, and pie. This is very mo-notonous. Everything is rationed, but you will soon make your black mar-ket connections and do all right.

LANGUAGE

"The American language is difficult, but you will soon pick up enough to make your wants understood. As to pronunciation, some vowels are pro-nounced separately and then again others are not. Other points to note are:

"Oy is pronounced erster.

"Oi is pronounced erl.

"C before aou is pronounced as c before a o u.

"Z is pronounced, but you won't run into this one often.

CHARACTER

"The American is highly individualistic, but is friendly and courteous. For example, if you call up an American and say, 'Can you line up a couple of dames for tonight?' you will generally find out that yours will turn out to be an awful looking dog.

WEIGHTS AND MEASURES

"One kilo equals two pounds, two pounds equal one kilo. One quart—you won't see this much; practically everything comes in fifths now.

WATER SUPPLY

"Drink only water which is obtained from an engineers' water unit. As these are practically impossible to locate, you better lay off the stuff.

HYGIENE AND HEALTH

"Malaria, take aspirin tablet.

"Sandfly fever, take aspirin tablet.

"Dysentery, take aspirin tablet.

WATERBORNE DISEASES

"These diseases are borne by water, take aspirin tablet.

CITIES

"The principal cities are New York.

"With the above hints you should get along quite well with the Americans. One splendid way to ingratiate yourself with soldiers you will meet there is to ask if they've been overseas. When they reply in the negative, just sneer."

□

Four

OPERATION OVERLORD:
THE D-DAY LANDINGS IN NORMANDY,
APRIL–AUGUST 1944

London, April 30 — *[Editor's Note: The Associated Press called White-head to London to cover the ongoing preparations for D-Day.]* London has a case of nerves—invasion jitters—caused by the terrific strain of waiting—waiting for the great Allied blow against Hitler's fortress. London has waited almost four years for the day that is approaching when British, American and Canadian troops will swarm across the beaches to batter at German defenses. Now the remaining period of waiting is imposing a heavy burden on nerves already worn by years of conflict, by savage air blitzes, by retreats and defeats and slow turning of the tide to the point where the man in the street could see a hope of final victory.

The newcomer to London senses the strain of the invasion wait in watching the hurrying crowds on the streets, seeing faces in the subway with that little drawn look about the eyes and mouths, and hearing explosive arguments which break out with the slightest provocation. And the contrast between the faces of people on the streets in the United States and London is startling. On the sidewalks of New York, Washington, Los Angeles or in small towns, people's faces have not become marked by the long strain of the war. Even in their hurry they seem relaxed, without the restlessness which is found here.

The awareness of the impending invasion has been forced on the people in many ways during these past few weeks, particularly in the non-stop pounding of Europe's invasion defenses by American and British air forces and in tightening security measures. Londoners know the pressures of the last few months have put an added strain on nerves, and they will be glad when "it" happens. "It" always means the invasion. "It's this way, guv'nor," a cab driver explained. "This is like waiting for your wife to have her first baby. And there's nothing to do but wait."

That probably is the simplest explanation of how the average man feels about invasion jitters. But there likewise is a sense of satisfaction that the hour of decision is approaching; that the end of long and bitter fighting is in sight, and that the enemy's nerves must be frayed far more than their own by constant aerial pounding and the threat of invasion which hangs over them day and night. ☐

London, May 6 — Tunis fell one year ago—on May 7, 1943—and the first anniversary of that Allied victory finds Gen. Dwight D. Eisenhower preparing his armies for the greatest gamble in military history—a smash against the continent of Europe. The leader of the long-awaited invasion will be playing with gigantic stakes when his legions sail against the enemy. No other American general ever was called upon to risk so much in manpower, in ships and guns and materials produced by the hand of American labor.

The fall of Tunis was just the opening scene in the tremendous drama now developing on this troop-packed island, from which the blow will be struck. What the result will be none can say. But New Zealand Prime Minister Peter Fraser voiced a sober viewpoint when he told a London press conference, "I cannot say whether the impending attack on Germany is to be a success. We all hope and believe it will be. If it is not, we will have to set our teeth and go into it again."

But the gamble will be made. All odds have been assessed in months of careful study, planning and preparation. All the risks have been calculated, even to the varying heights of the tides. Tens of thousands of troops and millions of tons of supplies and tools of war have been piled up in England in preparations for D-Day. And after studying the odds, Eisenhower and his generals are confident that the great gamble will succeed. That confidence had its birth in Tunisia when the American, British and French troops smashed the armies of Field Marshal Erwin Rommel and Col. Gen. Jürgen Von Arnim and captured 248,000 enemy troops.

The final crushing attack in Tunisia began at 3 a.m. on May 6, last year, after an armored division shifted from the Eighth Army front to the First Army, and the American Second Corps switched in secrecy to the north to drive against Bizerte. Within thirty-six hours the Allied drive had crushed the German resistance. Bizerte and Tunis were swarming with Allied troops. On that solid foundation of triumphs by Allied arms, Eisenhower began planning for the invasion from England, assembling armies and weapons. One year ago Allied armies freed one continent of the enemy, and today they are preparing to free another.   □

London, May 12 — The troops which America will send into the invasion of Europe form "the best equipped army that ever existed," according to Brig. Gen. Henry Benton Sayler, General Eisenhower's chief ordnance officer. "We're all set," said Sayler, whose responsibility it has been to build up the vast stocks of guns, tanks, ammunition, trucks and spare parts for the smash across the channel. "We've got more tools of war, gear and spare parts than any armed forces ever had before." The vast supplies are stored in warehouses, in bomb-scarred buildings, in great piles along England's winding roads.

"We hope and believe that we have overestimated our needs," said Sayler, whose home is in Washington, D.C. "But the people at home should know that, if we have underestimated those needs, then our reserves will be wiped out and the real reserve will be on the production line at home." The fifty-year-old one-star general has been working in the background for months preparing for the European invasion. His name isn't widely known at home, but his responsibility in the great invasion will be tremendous.

Sayler, a native of Huntington, Ind., was a graduate in West Point's class of 1915 which produced General Eisenhower, Lieut. Gen. Omar Bradley and Lieut. Gen. Joseph T. McNarney. He was an artilleryman in the first war but has been in ordnance since 1921. He helped mount the North African invasion. "We are much better prepared than we were then," the general said. "We went in 'cold' then but now we have teamwork and are able to do our work with a surprisingly small number of problems because each man knows his job. One of the most important of Sayler's responsibilities is an organization which can maintain and repair ordnance in the field—particularly in combat areas. □

London, May 15 — The day is drawing close when thousands of American youths—some hardened by months of training, some in actual combat—will storm the beaches of Europe in the supreme test of the infantryman in World War II. The hopes of millions rest with G.I. Joe, the guy who will carry the great burden of battle, take the hardest blows of the enemy, endure the greatest hardships.

The infantryman will have every reason to assist him that American ingenuity and mass production have been able to devise, thousands of planes supporting his attack, great navies to give him fire support, masses of artillery and hordes of tanks. But those weapons will be in a supporting role. The big job still will have to be done by G.I. Joe with his rifle, tommy gun, bazooka, machine gun, and mortars.

When D-Day comes and the mighty blow is struck, G.I. Joe will begin the great adventure. And it will begin something like this: Just as he has done many times, Joe will get aboard an invasion craft—but this time it will be the real thing instead of an exercise. And when night falls the boat will pull into a convoy of hundreds of other small boats heading for the enemy-held shores. Joe and his buddies are in the assault waves, ready to hit the shore shooting. They don't carry much except their weapons and ammunition and emergency rations.

Overhead is the drone of many planes, and then flares light the heavens as the enemy comes spying out the movements. As the assault boats near the shore the Navy's big guns open up with a thunderous barrage against gun positions and machine gun nests.

Shells scream into the water. Terrific explosions rend the air as one ship hits an enemy mine. Rockets shoot into the air along the coastline as the Germans signal the assault is hitting. A shell catches a small boat. The wounded scream. Men flounder in the water. But Joe and his buddies can't help them. The rescue job is for the Navy. Nothing must stop these men from getting ashore.

Then the darkness of land looms. The boats run onto the shore, the ramps fall and Joe and his friends crouch low and wade through the shallow surf. Behind them roar the Navy's guns. Shells whine overhead. Nostrils smart with the sting of cordite fumes and every man's heart is pounding with excitement and fear. Not cowardice, but the strong impelling feeling of fear that wipes out fatigue. A bangalore torpedo explodes and men are pouring through a gap in the barbed wire. Machine guns spit at them and orange tracers stab the darkness. A bazooka gunner sends a rocket crashing into a machine gun nest and the gun is stilled.

While the infantrymen stumble through the darkness, engineers are clearing a lane through the mines and taping off the safe paths for those who follow—getting the shores ready for the tanks and trucks and jeeps and tank destroyers and ducks and self-propelled artillery. Joe and his friends will keep pushing forward in the darkness, fighting to get as far as possible before dawn when the enemy can see their movements. And their legs will be weary. The packs will be heavy. Ammunition and tommy guns and bazookas will weigh a ton—but they must keep going forward.

There will be quiet, shy youths who suddenly step from the crowd to become leaders. Men who never impressed anyone in training will be heroes and fight with a bravery none had suspected. And Joe and his buddies will find they have a strong bond between them. They have fought together and seen their friends die and they have killed Germans together.

But the infantry's job will have only begun when they get ashore. Then they must reach their bridgehead objectives in long hours of fighting and dig in to meet the inevitable enemy counter-attack. That's a big job for G.I. Joe, a tough, bloody job. But he's the man who can do it. He did it in North Africa, in Sicily, and on the beaches at Salerno where the 88s were waiting.

It's the long road home—and that's really where he wants to be.   □

Aboard an Invasion Ship, June 3 — Newspaper correspondents accompanying the American assault forces on the invasion of France were whisked out of London May 29 with only an hour's notice—and so tight was the secrecy that none knew whether he was heading for the real show or just another exercise. Although all had been waiting for weeks to be called to join the units to which they had been assigned for the great expedition, almost everyone was taken by surprise when the call finally came.

I received a telephone call at my London flat at 9:30 a.m. and Lieutenant Colonel Jack Redding, a former reporter for the *Chicago Herald American*, chatted casually for awhile and then said, "I'd like you to come over in an hour, and it would be a good idea to bring along a musette bag. You might go out of town for a day or two."

The other correspondents were at Redding's office when I arrived. John O'Reilly, of the *New York Herald Tribune*, remarked that he had "sent a thousand dollars in money orders out to be pressed" in a pocket of a suit. He was permitted, under escort, to return to his hotel to salvage the money orders, and others were escorted to pick up forgotten papers or uniforms they had neglected to bring along. None was permitted to make telephone calls or write notes, and no one was allowed to leave the hotel room except under escort.

We each received a Supreme Headquarters, Allied Expeditionary Force overseas visa which said: "No correspondent may quit the overseas theater during the validity of this overseas visa without the express permission of the supreme commander." Then we were loaded into jeeps and under the watchful eye of a security officer began the long drive from London. Only Lieutenant Sam Brightman, former Washington correspondent for the *Louisville Courier Journal*, knew where we were going.

In camp for an overnight stay, Captain Robert Hughes, of Greer, S.C., chief field censor of our sector, read us the stringent rules of censorship by which we must abide. The next day the group of about twenty correspondents split up to join various units. We were driven by back roads and winding lanes to avoid towns and were finally delivered to the unit which was making preparations to board ship.

"I've been throwing another extra sock in my bag each time I heard the rumor we were leaving," said Major Owen B. Murphy, of Lexington, Ky. "Now that you boys have shown up I guess it's official this time."

John Thompson, of the *Chicago Tribune*, and I met the commanding general of the unit. He gave us the warmest welcome ever received in any outfit.

"Regard yourselves as members of this unit," he said. "You have complete freedom of movement and I want you to get all the information you can. We are ready to help you all in any way possible. The people at home won't know what is happening unless you are given information and I want them to know."

Then the general smiled.

"You both know how to take care of yourselves and won't forget to duck. But if an unlucky shell should get you, we'll do all we can. If you're wounded we'll take care of you. If you're killed we'll bury you. Meantime, we'll feed you and see you get what you want." □

Aboard an Invasion Ship, [June 5] — The morale of American troops is running high as the vast invasion fleet prepares to move through the channel to storm Hitler's fortress Europe. There's no doubt about it. Doughboys are ready and their spirits are up. They can see the beginning of the end of war. It's not a false optimism. They know what lies ahead of them, that many will die on the beaches of Normandy. They know the Germans are going to throw everything in the book at them to smash the invasion, but still they are grimly confident.

They feel this is the road back home, home which most of them have not seen for many months. Most of them never have been in battle before, but their ranks are toughened by a hard core of veterans who learned to fight across the battlegrounds of the Mediterranean.

The quality, the variety and the amount of equipment are almost beyond belief. Never has the United States sent an army into battle so well equipped. Capt. Victor Briggs of 433 Central Park West, New York City, summed it up when he said, "we're ten times better right now than when we were in Sicily. We've really got the stuff. It takes more to knock out one of our companies now than it would have to knock out a battalion in Sicily."

For weeks the Allies have been assembling the invasion fleet in every port in England. "I wouldn't want to be on the receiving end of the stuff we're going to throw on the beaches," said Major Paul Gale of Lynn, Mass. "It will be terrific."

We boarded our ship at midday today after all the troops were loaded. They lounged on bunks in holds, reading, sleeping or arguing. Some played cards; others rolled dice. In the bottom hold the Army had set up a miniature sponge-rubber model of the beach and countryside which our troops are to attack. Made from hundreds of aerial photographs, the model shows in detail each hedgerow, tree, house, barn, church and lane.

Sprawled around it were soldiers studying its features. They were leaders of assault groups which will land in the initial waves. There were Capt. Briggs, Lieut. Clarence M. Bloch of Beckley, W.Va., leader of a mortar platoon; Lieut. Ralph W. Vernon of Hyattsville, Md., leader of a mortar section; Lieut. Donald E. Jennings of North Olmsted, Ohio, an assistant section leader.

With them were Lieut. Bennett Atkinson of Chester, S.C.; Lieut. Marion Skinner of Paducah, Ky., and Lieut. Anthony Lechtenberg of Ponca City, Okla.   □

General Montgomery's Headquarters, June 6 – Gen. Sir Bernard L. Montgomery, leading Allied armies in the grand assault on France, believes Field Marshal Erwin Rommel—the Desert Fox he trapped on Africa's sands—will try at once "to knock us back into the sea." The little gray general who chased Rommel across North Africa predicted to correspondents May 15—twenty-two days before the invasion—that the German general entrusted with ground defenses in the west "will commit himself on the beaches."

"He is a disrupter," General Montgomery said, "and to disrupt the invasion he will try to hit us early." The general based his prediction, made public today, on a long study of Rommel's methods in battle, and of the man himself. "I have supreme confidence," declared the hero of El Alamein, who broke the back of the German desert army there and then pursued him to the ultimate Afrika Korps disaster at Cap Bon.

Monty studied the characteristics, habits and fighting methods of Rommel—he even kept a picture of the Nazi general above his table in his desert caravan—and came to know him as an impulsive commander who preferred the quick decision to slow slugging. Montgomery told the correspondents that his battle plans were based on a study of human nature. "It is important," he said, "to know human nature and what men can do—to get him into the right places doing the right job."

As no two men are alike, so General Montgomery believes no two divisions are alike. "You may think so," he said, "but I assure you they are different. The commander who thinks divisions are all alike will lose battles. No division is equally good at everything. One division does one thing well, another does another thing best. And it is the commander's responsibility to see that the right divisions are in the right places at the proper time."

General Montgomery praised the leadership of Gen. Dwight D. Eisenhower in drawing the British and Americans close together, asserting: "We are the only two peoples in the world who could have done it—teamed up for this great show." Wearing his familiar battle dress, he spoke in sharp, clipped sentences and declared, "I have supreme confidence" in the outcome. Montgomery expects a hard fight, sees the German soldier as good as any in the world, but he believes the German high command is not up to its old standard. "Put the German on some ground," he said, "and let him stay there long enough and it takes a bit of doing to get him off—it takes a bit of doing." □

With the American Army in France, June 7 – The rugged, independent peasants of Normandy, who refused to knuckle under to German authority, are overjoyed at the arrival of the Americans. There are 1,900 civilians still living in one village, from which the doughboys today cleared the last snipers, digging them out of basements, churches, bedrooms and shops from which they were firing through windows at our advancing troops. Most civilians had gathered in a large farmhouse at the edge of town to escape the fighting in the streets.

Despite the fact that the Germans were sniping from civilian homes, only one civilian was killed—because the artillery refrained from opening fire on the houses. Men, women and children gathered in the farmyard to chat with the troops, stopping to get water from a pump that was kept busy all day. And they watched the endless procession of infantry, guns, armor and trucks passing along a narrow dusty lane to the not far distant front.

Capt. Leonard Peters of Boston arranged to feed seventy of the town's populace at an army mess because they were unable to return to their homes to get food. The mayor, M. Hubert, said that the Germans with few exceptions had treated the people reasonably well if they did what the Germans ordered. The men were all forced to work for the German Army three days a week, and most of them were employed in the past months helping build beach obstacles, pillboxes, blockhouses and dugouts.

Unlike the Germans in North Africa, Sicily and Italy, the Germans here paid for what they got from the farmers and townspeople and, under strict orders, acted very correctly. The mayor said that there was one case of rape and one of robbery, but that the perpetrators were not Germans. He pointed out that the people of this sector, which is a rich farmland specializing in dairy products, have plenty to eat. They were eager for such luxuries as candy and cigarettes, however.

The Germans did not disturb the herds of cattle and few of the animals were killed during the fighting. Though the Germans acted correctly, the people said they put pressure on them when they wanted something. The former mayor, for example, refused to give a radio to a German officer and he was removed from office. Mayor Hubert is not a collaborationist, however, but accepted the office because his son was being held in Germany as a prisoner, the people said.

Whether the Germans knew the Allies were to attack yesterday was not clear, although three regiments had moved into this area for maneuvers. The day before D-Day, the commanding officer came to the mayor and told him there would be practice shooting in the area the next day, but that the people should not be alarmed. The officer requisitioned six animals to carry supplies to the men and arranged for two others to carry them food at noon.

Supporting the theory that the Germans did not suspect the invasion is the fact that the officers and men made no effort to pack personal belongings or get personal papers in the homes in which they were billeted. Also no effort had been made to evacuate civilians in this particular area.   □

With the American Troops in France, June 9 – Four days after landing amid bitter fighting on the beach the American troops in this sector have launched an attack to push their beachhead deeper into Normandy. This was accomplished as a result of the unprecedented speed with which troops, guns and supplies were landed once the crust of the enemy's opposition was broken. Never before have troops, guns, armor and supplies been put ashore with such speed, despite a slow beginning and when the enemy was fighting to crack the American landings.

I believe the Germans now have lost their chance to break the beachhead. They lost that chance the first two days of the invasion when they committed their reserves to desperate battles. The doughboys charged across the beaches and the enemy was unable to launch a counter-attack. Allied air support is magnificent, and not a single enemy plane has been seen over this beachhead during the daylight hours since the landing in this sector. Indications show that the Germans are unable to rush in heavy reinforcements with any speed because our air forces have bombed the railway lines.

The Germans are fighting guerrilla warfare in a desperate attempt to stop the steady progress of the stout-hearted Americans and they are making great use of snipers. The enemy is fighting from trees, hedgerows, buildings and farmhouses and sending snipers to infiltrate our lines to harass the rear, but they have been unable to halt the advance. There was one verified case of a sniper being found garbed in the clothing of an American soldier.

Outside the town in this area the Germans are spotting our advance from dugouts. During an exchange of fire, six enemy soldiers came out with their hands up in surrender. A platoon led by Lieutenant Robert Brown, of Jackson, Miss., was fighting for an assembly area when a sniper opened up from behind a bush. Lieutenant Brown silenced this fire.

The German sniping technique is to leave one or two men with machine pistols, rifles and ammunition hidden in the trees or along the thick hedgerows which border Normandy's narrow, winding lanes. If a large body of doughboys passes, the snipers hold their fire. They wait for small groups of men, walking singly and in pairs and then they open fire. But the doughboys stalk them down, and few snipers come back alive. Most of them are very young or men in their forties and fifties. During the night the Germans send sniping patrols to rough our lines, but these tactics, while irritating, have not stopped the infantry.

The other night a German patrol slipped behind our lines along the hedgerows and surrounded one unit's command post where Major Frank Callicco, of Utica, N.Y., was in command. It was about 1 a.m. They sneaked in and covered Callicco and his men with machine pistols. "You are prisoners," a young German said in English, and ordered Callicco and his men to accompany them. Callicco had other ideas. The major suddenly grabbed the machine pistol from his captor and tried to shoot him, but the gun jammed. He beat the German over the head. Another German grabbed him from behind, and Callicco tossed this one over his head.

In the meantime the other boys were in action, too, and when the fracas was over the major and his men had taken the Germans prisoners. Now the boys are calling him Major Muscles Callicco. Never before have the Germans used such tactics against American troops, but this country lends itself to this type of fighting. The hedgerows are very thick and each neat field is bordered heavily by trees or shrubbery instead of fencing. Green oak, beech and elm trees provide cover for snipers.

One eighteen-year-old sniper was hiding in a field toward which our unit was moving to set up a command post. He opened fire and a doughboy shot him through the heart. Even as his heart was bursting through the bullet hole in his chest the German was frantically trying to get his first-aid kit. Then he collapsed. Another sniper in the same ditch started running, and a tommy gunner shot him down.　　□

With American Troops in France, June 10 — I had seen enough of our beachhead from a foxhole so I went up in a Piper Cub today to take a look at the wedge driven into continental Europe and what I saw was both beautiful and awesome. From a low altitude I got a better perspective of the magnificent job the doughboys have done. As I flew over the area with Lieut. Oscar B. Rich of Foley, Ala., we saw Yanks attacking below us toward a forest where the enemy was believed to have hidden tanks and infantry.

We saw armored vehicles rolling slowly along hedgerows raking the undergrowth with machine gun fire to drive out snipers while behind them came doughboys taking cover in trees and hedges as the attack moved forward. Rich swung out over the beach and there stood our tremendous invasion fleet stretching as far as I could see. Ships were moving in to discharge their cargoes and small boats scurried around, weaving white wakes about the bigger ships which were pouring more men, guns and supplies ashore. □

With American Troops in France, June 12 — Tech. Sgt. Alex Stout of Opelousas, La., is still seeing stars. The sergeant thought he was looking at the Milky Way when at close range he saw Gen. George C. Marshall, Gen. Dwight D. Eisenhower, Gen. Henry H. Arnold, Lt. Gen. Omar N. Bradley, Adm. Ernest King, Rear Adm. Alan G. Kirk and lesser lights when they paid an unexpected visit to the beachhead to see the progress of the American advance. They stayed more than three hours visiting the second front, and the sergeant helped them prepare a lunch of hot C rations, the regular G.I. Joe diet. Sgt. Stout also supervised the task of providing hot water and towels for the four-star and lesser generals, but after it was over he did not have much to say. It was pretty much of a shock.

The high-ranking Army and Navy officers came ashore shortly before noon in a duck. They came up on the bluff to the Air Force landing strip, where an air evacuation plane loaded with eighteen American and German wounded was getting ready to take off. Pvt. Louis Weintraub, 395 St. John's

Pl., Brooklyn, a former *Washington Post* photographer, now with the Army Signal Corps, was taking pictures of the evacuation plane. "I looked up," said Pvt. Weintraub, "and saw all that brass coming toward me. I almost dropped my camera, but I managed to start shooting them. But, Brother, I was shaking like a leaf."

Sgt. Reg Kenny, 49 W. High St., Somerville, N.J., photographer for the army newspaper, *Yank*, felt pretty much the same as Pvt. Weintraub, but they had presence of mind enough to ask the generals for a ride and climbed into the convoy with them. "That guy Arnold is all right," Pvt. Weintraub said. "He let me sit by him in his command car and I took the whole trip with him."

Gen. Eisenhower climbed into the evacuation plane and looked it over. He expressed pleasure with the setup. He viewed the German coastal defenses—machine gun nests, blockhouses and gun emplacements. Inspecting the location of an 88-millimeter gun, he remarked, "That's terrible. Our boys would not do it that way." From the landing strip the generals drove to American headquarters, where the sergeant had hot water and towels waiting for them. "I didn't expect to find hot water at the front," Gen. Eisenhower told the sergeant.

After washing up and having lunch, the officers drove to Isigny, which was captured by the Twenty-ninth Division. The town was still burning as they entered it. A French policeman saw the four stars on the leading car and saluted. The civilians sensed this was an unusual visit and waved and clapped while police kept them on the sidewalk. Gen. Bradley jumped out of the car and looked about, but the others kept their seats in the cars, viewing the ruins, talking to civilians and waving to passing soldiers. The troops along the road looked up with shock in their faces as they recognized the high-ranking generals. Then they grinned and saluted. From Isigny the generals drove back to the beach and took an amphibious duck out to the ship which had carried them to France.   □

With American Forces Near Cerisy Forest, June 12 – The Germans pulled back so rapidly through the Cerisy Forest area before the advancing United States Second Division that they had no time for demolitions and, in contrast to Nazi withdrawals in Africa and Italy, the enemy left few mines behind. (This was the first disclosure that the American Second Division was fighting in France.) Keeping steady pressure on the enemy, the doughboys have made fast gains through the green hedge—

grown Norman countryside and, still pushing forward past the Cerisy Forest, have driven the Germans back to a point where only their long-range guns will be able to shell the landing beach.

We had suspected Cerisy Forest to be a hiding place for German armor, infantry and antitank defenses, but the American troops swept through with only light opposition. East of the Cerisy Forest the doughboys captured one of the largest ammunition dumps to fall into Allied hands. There was growing belief the Allies gained a strategical surprise in landing and caught the Germans without any reserve strength in this area.

The Second Division showed up exceptionally well. They were trigger-happy and nervous at the first shooting and at the slightest movement ahead of them, but after the first half day of hearing guns, seeing shells explode and hearing bullets whiz by, they settled down.

The division had its shakedown battle in capturing Trévières, four and one-half miles from the coast. The Germans had turned the town into a strongpoint. In bitter fighting the Americans left it a shambles of bullet- and shell-pocked buildings. After capturing the town, the boys of the Second Division drove on and through the Cerisy Forest, wiping out pockets of German snipers and resistance as they moved forward in a swift advance.

I have just made a tour of the central beachhead and what I saw left me with the belief the Germans have lost their chance to push us back into the sea. They lost that chance during the first three days. Now our armies have landed in such strength that the most perilous period has passed. The swiftness with which American troops, guns and supplies were put ashore this past week despite many handicaps is reassuring for the future.   □

With American Forces in France, June 13 — With magnificent air support and by gaining strategical surprise in opening the Western front, Allied forces on the beachhead have outstripped the Germans in the initial buildup of troops and supplies and were set for the enemy's first major counter-attack today aimed at slicing the beachhead in two parts.

The enemy put in an attack toward Carentan with elements of an SS division driving toward the Vire River flowing between the beachhead on the Cherbourg Peninsula and the beachhead east of the peninsula. The attack was preceded by an artillery barrage on the town of Carentan, but the enemy was unable to match the strength of American gunfire and there was confidence that the attack will be beaten back. The beachheads were linked two days ago, but now the Germans are trying to split them again. But this counter-attack has come six days after it was anticipated by the commanders.

Plans were made to meet a heavy counter-attack by D-Day-Plus-One, but it did not develop because the enemy was unable to move troops into the area fast enough. The air forces had battered supply lines so hard their movements were slow. And only now are American troops beginning to feel strong enemy pressure. Except for bitter fighting on the beach, American troops since the landing have kept the initiative and this counter-attack does not mean they have lost it. But for those who might be overly optimistic, it is a warning that the German buildup is beginning and there is bloody fighting ahead.

The attack began against the American 101st Airborne Division east of the Vire River—and it came six days after anticipated. During these precious days our Army has been able to build up reserves of men, guns, armor and supplies. Those were days of decision when the entire operation hung in the balance. But the enemy was unable to move swiftly enough and with sufficient punch to disrupt the landings.

"God and the Air Corps are on our side," one officer said. "God gave us the weather and the Air Forces took care of the enemy's movements by strafing roads and blocking lines of transport. Only military idiots would have made a landing where we did on the peninsula. But we knew the Germans thought that, too, so we did it. The paratroops did a magnificent job of tying up enemy reserves while the assault troops got across the causeways and lagoons and moved inland for a junction."

The troops assaulting the peninsula moved so swiftly the enemy was unable to destroy causeways and left many guns which had never even been manned. Once the landings were made, the enemy began throwing in defenders, building up from the left flank of the beachhead to the right as they are able to move them into the area, and resistance is stiffening as the days pass.

On the other hand, the Allies were able to build up beachhead strength during the period the Germans were unable to offer any real resistance beyond hard fighting on the beach where the First Division and elements of the Twenty-ninth Division landed. The Americans have met few of the Nazi fanatical diehards. The troops have been a strange mixture of Poles, Czechs, Austrians, Tartars and Mongolians. The average German prisoner taken on this beachhead has no real faith in a Nazi victory. One old German soldier captured had been in the service for fourteen years. With tears streaming down his leathery face, he surrendered because he said he believed that Germany was whipped. □

With American Troops in France, June 14 — The night-mare days of the beachhead landing are past, but everywhere I find the troops afraid that the people at home are too optimistic. We hear that the re-action to the beachhead fighting in both England and the United States is that the war is all over except for a few messy details and that the public's feelings have bounced like a rubber ball. They should be feeling good that the Allies grabbed a hold on the continent without the blood bath that many predicted. Actually, there was only one sector of the American front where there was any bitter fighting getting across the beaches—and that was where the fighting First Division and elements of the Twenty-ninth smashed head-on into a reinforced German division waiting on the beach.

The assault troops who battled their way from the beach that first day should have a ribbon to wear as a special mark of distinction. It was a battle in which the doughboys overcame every obstacle the enemy could put in his way. But this is only the initial phase of a giant operation. The greatest bat-tles lie ahead with the enemy slowly being hemmed in on all sides. The real tests will come when divisions are hurled against divisions in titanic strug-gles. While a most critical period is behind us, the situation cannot be re-garded as past the dangerous stage until the Allies are able to build up huge reserves and burst out from their bridgehead.   ☐

With American Troops Somewhere in France, June 14 — More than anything else, the men who came safely through the bloody beach battle in our sector on D-Day want their sweethearts, wives and parents to know that they are all right. As usual, a soldier generally is more worried about not worrying the people at home than about himself and his first thoughts, once the greatest danger is past, are of those he loves.

Capt. William Collins, Chicago, was pinned on the beach by heavy enemy fire for more than four hours and somehow he came through it un-scathed. I saw him with his unit and he said, "Look, will you just say for me, 'Dear Marge, I am all right.' Will you?" I told him sure I would. Then wise-cracking, cheerful Capt. Max Zera, who talks Brooklynese but comes from New York City, called me over and suddenly became serious. "Mama's going to be awfully worried about me," he said. "She knows now that my outfit came in with the first waves. Just let her know that I am well and was not hurt." Mrs. Zera, your son is getting along fine. Cpl. J. B. Johnson, Port Arthur, Tex., looked up from a foxhole and grinned, "Tell 'em at home I'm having a happy birthday."   ☐

Isigny, France, June 14 — General Charles De Gaulle visited his homeland today for the first time in four years and countrymen lined the streets of beachhead villages shouting his name. The ovation was dramatic. The tall, lean leader of the French Committee of National Liberation appeared unexpectedly, but news of his trip across the channel swept through Allied-held territory in a few hours. Wherever he went, crowds gathered to catch a glimpse of him and call greetings.

Cries of "De Gaulle, De Gaulle" swept the streets. Old men and women came stumbling out of the wreckage of their homes and business houses. Children ran yelling out of the rubble and clambered across the debris to see this man whose name obviously was magic to them. The people were begrimed and ill-dressed and the wreckage accentuated the dramatic background of the French fight for liberation. There was no mistaking the spontaneity of the welcome.

The voices of the people rose in a shout as De Gaulle appeared.

"Vive De Gaulle."

"Vive la France."

"Vive l'Amérique."

"Vive la Grande-Bretagne."

"A bas les boches, à bas les collaborateurs."

It was a chant that ran through the crowd and then as though it was a theme song for the occasion came the sound of voices singing "La Marseillaise."

De Gaulle stepped from a jeep and the gendarmes were unable to hold the crowd back. They surged forward to speak to the general and shake hands with him as he stood under a shell-dented street lamp in the town's battered square. De Gaulle urged the people of Bayeux, the first city in France liberated by the Allies, to help in the battle to free the country, William Stewart, Canadian press correspondent, said in a dispatch from the beachhead. The general said he had come to Normandy to salute the city of Bayeux and he announced the appointment of a local representative. "You have seen the enemy flee from here and he will flee farther," De Gaulle said. "We will fight to the end. We will fight by the side of our Allies for the sovereignty of France so that our victory will be the victory of a free people."

Trees were strung with tricolor banners. Some of the people wept openly. De Gaulle stood bareheaded beneath a French flag mounted with the Blue Cross of Lorraine. He had the Stars and Stripes and the Union Jack at his sides. At the end of his brief speech he joined the people in singing "La Marseillaise." De Gaulle drove into Isigny (eighteen miles west of Bayeux) with a group of French Army officers in three jeeps and an amphibious naval vehicle guarded by an escort of dusty American military policemen armed with carbines.   □

With American Troops Near Isigny, June 15 — American doughboys surrounded for forty-eight hours have fought their way through the enemy to rejoin their unit. Even the Brigadier General tossed hand grenades at the Germans. It is unusual for one-star generals to be with small assault elements probing deep into enemy lines, but in this beachhead battle many strange things happen. One reason for the doughboys' successes is that their officers lead them into action.

One outfit was being troubled on its right flank by the harassing fire of snipers, machine guns and mortars, so it was decided to send a group under the command of Maj. Anthony Miller and Capt. Alexander Pouska Jr., both of Baltimore, to probe a sector across the Vire River. Under cover of darkness, the infantrymen crossed the river in assault boats without opposition, but after advancing about 1,000 yards they ran into a hail of fire from automatic weapons. During the fighting, the group split, one making its way back across the river while the other continued.

The general (whose name cannot be told), Miller and Pouska had 150 men with them when the first fight was over. The next morning they were contacted by Capt. John C. Brashears of Baltimore, a liaison officer. Brashears had crossed the river and reached the unit. When he started back along a wooded lane he turned a curve and ran head-on into a German sergeant with five men. "The sergeant and I were both as scared as hell," Brashears laughed, "but his surprise lasted longer than mine. I shot him with a rifle and then ducked into a hedgerow to make my way back to where the general and our men were."

The unit sent out patrols but they ran into fire from all directions and the fire was particularly heavy from the lane where Brashears shot the German sergeant. So Brashears and Sgt. William McAtee, also of Baltimore, organized a combat team and went out to clean up the area. They ran into fire from a farmhouse nearby. "A rifle grenadier slipped up to within fifty yards of the Germans and laid a grenade among them," Brashears said. "Then one of our men threw a hand grenade at close range. When we moved up there were three or four dead Germans in the farmyard. The others had cleared up."

The groups started to make their way back to their own line, but the general decided to make one more try at reaching the objective, although they had used up their emergency rations and were running short of ammunition. The Germans had cut a gap in the hedgerow outside the village and had set up fields of fire commanding the approaches. The group worked around them as night was fading only to find themselves in the midst of both German and American artillery. So they dug in for the night. The next day the general, the major and the captain brought their men back safely.   □

With the American Troops at St-Sauveur-le-Vicomte, June 16 — Bitter fighting for the Cherbourg Peninsula reached a sudden crisis today when American troops burst through fanatical German resistance to within about six miles of the Germans' last escape corridor. The break in the virtually stalemated fighting in this sector came with dramatic suddenness this morning when stubborn enemy resistance crumpled before the steady pressure of doughboys. The forward surge carried our troops across the Douve River and into this shell-smashed town which sits astride the main highway running south from Cherbourg. There is no indication yet how many enemy troops or how much equipment will be trapped if the breakthrough should carry on across the peninsula.

The Germans clearly faced a crisis in trying to keep their badly-mauled troops from being split on the peninsula. This new push by the Americans has created a grave problem for the German command. It must throw in new reserves to check the rush by a quick shifting of forces or leave its troops in the northern part of the peninsula to shift for themselves as best they can.

The Germans have made a general move to bring up reinforcements. Whether they will be able to counter this new development and contain our advance remains to be seen. Indications are that the next forty-eight hours may be decisive, as to whether the Americans will be able to continue to roll forward across the peninsula and close the last gap. Normally violent reaction from the enemy could be expected in the next few hours.

The advance into St-Sauveur was swift and dramatic across the green countryside ripped by shrapnel and machine gun bullets and strewn with the bodies of Germans mowed down as they lay in the woods and hedgerows trying to halt the doughboys and units of the crack shock troops. But the Yanks were not to be denied in their westward thrust across the peninsula because they kept pressure on the Nazis until they cracked. Then the advance burst forward like waters from a broken dam.

This town now—except for doughboy patrols moving through it—is a shattered, beaten city of death. It died under the terrible weight of artillery and lies gray, ugly and torn—a horrible scar in this beautiful little Douve River valley. Its destruction was inevitable because the Germans turned it into a strongpoint and were fighting bitterly from house to house to try and save it.

The town was entered at 12 o'clock noon when first units of shock troops crossed the river led by Lieut. Eugene Doerfler, Hays, Kans. The unit which entered the town was under the command of Capt. Clyde Russel of Iowa who followed Doerfler across the bomb-shattered bridge at the edge of this mass of ruins.

The Germans were throwing cooks, truck drivers and supply troops into the line in a desperate effort to stem the advance. In many of their front-line units they had a large percentage of Russians, Poles, Czechs and other nationalities. But behind this strange assortment of troops were tough, fanatical Nazis, manning heavy machine guns and mortars. They were the backbone of the defenders but even they cracked finally under relentless pressure.

I walked into town shortly after noon and what I saw made me think of what General De Gaulle had told people of ruined Isigny when he looked at the wreckage of their homes and business houses—"These are sufferings which every part of France will have to bear before final liberation." I drove to the front behind swiftly moving assault troops along roads strewn with wreckage of German light tanks, guns and trucks. There even was one mess truck smashed before it could escape. Hedgerows and trees along the road were clipped by a scythe of machine gun fire and twigs and branches were scattered on the paved surface. Bedding, clothing, stationery, shoes, helmets and gear were scattered as though flung away by men in their frantic fight.

In deep grassy ditches along hedgerows lay stiffening bodies of the defenders of the fatherland, frozen in grotesque postures. And near one dead German a doughboy had hung a mirror on a hedgerow twig and was calmly taking a shave. On a hill above St-Sauveur I climbed into the gray tower of an ancient chateau and looked out a little window at the valley below. Across the winding Douve River lay the beaten town, hazy in the smoke and dust of battle.

German shells were falling on the hillside below—shells from 88s and mortars. Six frightened horses in a nearby pasture ran frequently about seeking escape from the thunderous noise. In a clump of bushes behind the chateau our mortars were sending shells whining overhead. Sgt. Sam Berkowitz, Cleveland, Ohio, had used an old house as an observation post for artillery fire on the town. "I saw one house which looked like it was full of Germans," he said. "I called for fire and the first shell was a direct hit. I didn't see any of them come out."

Pvt. Eddie Bisso, Jr., Queens, N.Y., listened to the mortars and then looked at St-Sauveur. "Those guys behind us are in the rear echelon now," he grinned.

I climbed down from the tower and joined the troops moving into town. We hugged embankments for cover from snipers but about 200 yards from the river bridge we came out on an exposed road. Machine guns rattled off to our right and bullets snapped past. I fell beside the road with Lieut. George Scalf, Nashville, Tenn. He poked his carbine over the bank and searched the bushes for snipers. There were no other shots our way so our group continued across the half demolished bridge into the mass of wreckage that once had been a town.

Walls of many buildings were shot away completely, leaving gaunt skeletons exposed. Furniture, bedding, household goods and debris were piled up in a hopeless scramble. There was not a building standing whole and the streets were clogged with debris. Hobbling about in the wreckage was a lieutenant colonel. He had jumped into France D-Day and had broken a bone in his foot. It was encased in a plaster cast and he was on a crutch but still with his troops. Praising his men for the job they had done, he sent units forward to keep the Germans on the run.

Then the Nazis began to rain mortars and 88s on the town and we hugged the walls and buildings while bursts threw a gray film of dust over us. ☐

With American Troops Southwest of Carentan, June 17 – Fighting, the toughest and bitterest of any on the entire American front, continues in this sector. The roads are littered with German dead, mowed down by the withering fire from tanks. At least 500 dead Nazis are piled up in the ditches and hedgerows where SS troops and parachute troops fought fanatically in a mad effort to break through between two beachheads two days ago.

But as the Germans advanced along the hedgerows and under cover of bushes American tanks ran up and "gave 'em the garden hose"—sprayed the area with more than 60,000 rounds of .30 caliber machine-gun bullets. "The Krauts fell from trees and out of the hedges like flies," said Capt. Harry Vold, of Cleveland Heights, Ohio. Time after time the tanks charged, crushing Nazis under their steel treads.

The battle was raging for a crossroads about two miles southwest of Carentan and that was where Tank Commander Sgt. Wilbur K. Rockwell, Antrim, N.H., and his gunner, Corp. George W. Smith, Silver Creek, Miss., set an American beachhead record by knocking out three tank-mounted

105-millimeter German guns at 1,000 yards with three shots. "Smith the gunner knocked them off like pigeons on a fence," grinned Cpl. Patrick J. Brogan, Buffalo, N.Y.

The Yanks were hard pressed and when the tanks rolled up they stood up in their foxholes and cheered wildly. You'd have thought you were at the Giants-Dodgers game," said Pvt. John Boretsky, Brooklyn. ☐

With American Forces in France, June 17 – The American Army has 3,283 killed and 12,600 wounded in opening the Western front in Normandy, Lieut. Gen. Omar N. Bradley said today. The total of 15,883 casualties was for the first eleven days of the campaign, and included reports up to midnight last night, Gen. Bradley said. He paid high tribute to the courage of doughboys in establishing the beachhead on the European continent.

Gen. Bradley appeared before beachhead correspondents in a group for the first time to discuss the campaign. He said that casualties on the central beachhead where the American First Division and elements of the Twenty-ninth Division landed had run higher than anticipated. This casualty report confirmed Gen. Bradley's confidence before the invasion when he predicted that the Continent could be invaded without creating the bloodbath which the enemy insisted would result and which many persons expected.

Gen. Bradley's first words to the correspondents who gathered in the tent under the shade of a huge beech tree were in praise of his doughboys and parachute troops and their leaders. "Only by guts, valor and extreme bravery on the part of the men and their leaders involved were we able to make the landing a success," he said, "and I cannot say too much for the parachute troops who dropped in the rear and made the job easier for the beach troops. They did a marvelous job."

The General disclosed that since D-Day there had been two critical periods when the Germans might have created a serious situation by an attack in force. The first period, he said, was when the doughboys fighting their way ashore in the central beachhead were encountering a reinforced Nazi division. This was where the First Division and supporting elements of the Twenty-ninth fought their historic beach battle. The second critical time was when American forces were trying to make their junction of beachheads secure north of Carentan. This was a soft spot at the time because it was a junction point between the American Seventh Corps on the Cherbourg Peninsula and the Fifth Corps on the central beachhead. The General declared emphatically that he thought the enemy now had lost his chance to drive the Allies back into the sea and that the beachhead now was absolutely secure.

Since their landings American troops have captured and evacuated 8,500 prisoners, Gen. Bradley said. Using a twig from a beech tree as a pointer in the manner of a schoolmaster, he outlined the situation to correspondents. He estimated the number of German divisions in France to be at more than sixty, with sixteen divisions or elements fighting against the entire Normandy bridgehead. The general declared the enemy would be unable to move all his divisions in France into the Normandy front because defenses must be manned in other parts of the country, and garrisons have to maintain control of the civilian population. Gen. Bradley gave high praise to the Navy's support of the assault troops, recalling that some warships ran to within 500 yards of the beaches pouring shell fire into enemy strongpoints. He lauded the air forces which kept the enemy's reserves from forming in front of the assault waves.

Discussing the situation on Cherbourg Peninsula, where the United States Eighty-second Airborne Division captured St-Sauveur-le-Vicomte yesterday in a surge threatening the enemy's last escape corridor, Gen. Bradley said the Germans might fight for the port of Cherbourg as long as possible even though the peninsula were isolated. He said Cherbourg has strong all around defenses prepared with big guns pointing out to sea, and many anti-aircraft batteries. The indications are, he added, that the enemy's strength on the Cherbourg sector runs well into five figures. Should their escape corridor be closed on the west side of the peninsula, there is a chance that the Germans might try to evacuate by small boats at night. He said operations were proceeding pretty much as planned except that last minute changes had to be made when the Germans moved two new divisions onto the peninsula to support the single division that had been stationed there. □

With the American Troops on the Cherbourg Peninsula, June 17 — With breathtaking swiftness and courage the magnificent fighting Ninth Infantry Division broke through with the aid of the Eighty-second Airborne Division to close a fist of iron on the neck of the Cherbourg Peninsula where thousands of Germans are threatened with entrapment. With machine guns and cannon raking this corridor, which has only one main exposed road running down the western coastline, the enemy's last exit route virtually was closed.

Thus twelve days after the invasion the doughboys of the veteran Ninth Division which fought in North Africa and Sicily have smashed through stubborn German defenses in a brilliant move with the Eighty-second Airborne, which fought in Sicily and Italy. The whole advance during the last thirty-six hours has been so sudden and swift that it is confusing even to those of us watching the drive. But briefly here is what happened during those vital hours.

Thursday the doughboys were locked in a bitter hedge-to-hedge battle across the green bullet-stripped fields littered with the carcasses of dead cattle. Progress was slow, with every hedge a strongpoint where the enemy made a fanatic fight. This was particularly true of enemy machine gun and mortar squads who are one hundred per cent Nazi. Our advance was so slow it was almost a stalemate. Then late on Thursday the German resistance began softening up. Friday morning the dam broke. The Germans suddenly caved in. They began a wild effort to pull away from the terrible pressure the Americans were keeping on them. The Americans swept forward, and 82nd Division units drove through St-Sauveur. Once it was a lovely little village on the west bank of the meandering Douve River, but when I entered it with parachute troopers it was a shattered, lifeless thing of ugliness. North of St-Sauveur the doughboys broke across the Douve River by riding on tanks and firing their machine guns as the machines lumbered through the shallow waters and rolled on westward in the drive to shear off the peninsula.

This was the break they had been fighting for, and it was being exploited as swiftly as possible to keep the enemy disorganized and rocking back on his heels. Now the Americans are looking down on the sea with direct fire on the crossroads about a mile northeast of St-Lô-d'Ourville, which is southwest of St-Sauveur. When it became apparent that the Germans were trying to pull out of the area, with heavy movement on the road, including some vehicles less than eight yards apart, Allied air forces went to work on them. The Germans countered with the heaviest show of daylight fighter strength I have seen since D-Day—four Focke-Wulf 190s.

Civilians filtering through the lines reported tonight that civilians had begun evacuating Cherbourg on orders from the Germans. They said roads out of Cherbourg were lined with civilian carts and trucks loaded with people and belongings. Most are heading for rural places or to Les Pieux and Bricquebec in hopes of finding sanctuary.

There were no authentic reports yet on what the Germans are doing in Cherbourg or whether any demolitions are in progress in the harbor area, which obviously the enemy wants to deny us as long as possible. The next logical line for a last-stand defense of Cherbourg would be in the vicinity of Valognes, northwest of Montebourg. The latter now is securely in American control. North of Valognes is high plateau ground which dominates the terrain rolling down to Cherbourg.

The swift advance of the Americans threw the Germans into such confusion that some captured troops didn't even know who their commanders were or where they were supposed to go. One officer was told to pull back his troops to Ste-Colombe, which is a mile and a half north of St-Sauveur. But at that time the town already was in American hands. When told we held the town, the bewildered German exclaimed: "I don't believe it." When the Americans stormed across the Douve River to drive the Germans off the high grounds on the other side, one German raged: "You crazy Americans! This is not war, it is madness!"

The advance was so fast the doughboys did not encounter any demolitions or mines. Near Orglandes, northeast of St-Sauveur, they captured a complete German field hospital in which there were about a hundred wounded, some of them American paratroopers and medics who jumped behind the enemy lines D-Day. The Ninth Division encountered hard fighting today in making the last advance to high ground overlooking the sea but they would not be stopped. However the Germans managed to extricate three batteries of 88s before they were overrun although not all the crews were able to get away. There are no indications yet that the Germans are trying to make a general evacuation of the peninsula or intend to give up Cherbourg without a bitter fight. Troops now in the line against the Americans may make a sacrifice stand.

In other sectors of the American beachhead doughboys made local gains to straighten out their lines. In the Carentan sector they moved well beyond the Vire-Taute Rivers canal. The Ninth Division which was identified today as being on the beachhead originally was composed of men largely from New York and Pennsylvania with artillery from the New England states but the flow of replacements during the North African and Sicilian campaigns has made it an all-American division, with men from every state in the union and the District of Columbia. One of the division's combat teams landed just east of Algiers in the invasion of North Africa while another landed at Port Lyautey, French Morocco. Both had hard fights to take their objectives. Later the entire division went into action in Tunisia. In Sicily the division helped in the capture of Troina, the battle which broke the back of enemy resistance on that island.   □

With U.S. Troops on Cherbourg Peninsula, June 18 – American troops, which cut through the Cherbourg neck in a "last-mile" drive, have beaten off the first fanatical German attempts to break out of the peninsular trap. The American Ninth Division solidly sealed the last enemy escape corridor today, capping a dramatic and historic three-day drive westward to the sea. The Yanks cut the peninsula's west coastline highway last night and officially reached the sea at 11 p.m., to climax the swift thrust. Now the stopper is in the bottle and the big question is how long it will take to clean out stubborn resistance and smash through to Cherbourg.

I visited the closed corridor today with other correspondents and got an idea of the confusion which enveloped the Germans when the American advance swept forward so that the last of the enemy units were literally running in circles trying to find a way out of the trap. The Americans cut the western coastline road in two places—at Barneville and at St-Lô-d'Ourville-and immediately got set to repulse the Germans' counter-attack, which came today. It literally was a massacre—the massacre of St-Jacques-de-Néhou. That is where the Americans battered the Germans in one of the bloodiest encounters of the invasion. St-Jacques-de-Néhou lies directly north of the St-Lô-d'Ourville crossroads where the doughboys first sliced across the peninsula road to cut off the enemy escape route. There, near St-Jacques, the Germans made their bid to escape. Before telling of this bitter engagement, there is some background which should be given.   □

With American Troops on Cherbourg Peninsula, June 18 – American troops have cut through the Cherbourg neck in a "last-mile" drive and have beaten off the first fanatical German attempt to break out of the peninsular trap. The American Ninth Division solidly sealed the last enemy escape corridor today, capping a dramatic three-and-a-half day drive westward to the sea. The doughboys cut the peninsula's west coastline highway last night and officially reached the sea at 11 o'clock in the evening on June 17 to climax the swift thrust. Now the stopper is in the bottle and the big question is how long it will take to clean out stubborn resistance and smash through to the port of Cherbourg.

I visited the closed corridor today with other correspondents and got an idea of the confusion which enveloped the Germans when the American advance swept forward so that the last of the enemy units literally were running in circles, trying to find a way out of the trap. There was no way out except to overrun the Yankees' strangling line to the sea—and the Germans already had tried that and failed.

The Americans cut the western coastline road in two places—at Barneville and at St-Lô d'Ourville crossroads, where the doughboys first sliced across the peninsula road to cut off the enemy escape route. There, near St-Jacques, the Germans made their bid to escape, under orders rumored to have been from their high commander. But before giving an account of this bitter engagement, there is some background which should be given.

When the Ninth Division burst through stubborn German defenses on Friday and swept forward toward the sea, units of the division drove to the high ground east of Barneville, while another unit pushed on to a ridge northeast of St-Lô d'Ourville. Then units of the northern force pushed on into Barneville, while southern troops moved into St-Lô d'Ourville, thus cutting the coast road in two places.

In the meantime the enemy's 77th Division attempted to withdraw south to La Haye du Puits, but the routes of withdrawal already had been cut by doughboys moving much faster than the enemy had anticipated. The German Seventy-seventh Division made a desperate effort at 6 a.m. today to break through the doughboys' wedge of steel. Their infantry, supported by armor, moved southward.

In the early morning haze, a battle of small-arms fire broke out. Then the bigger guns engaged in the fighting, and for a confused, exciting time, the battle raged seemingly in all directions. The battle raged for about two hours, with the Americans putting their heaviest mortar-fire concentration on the enemy since the original landings. On top of this, the artillery called for "a serenade," while the infantry had orders to hold on at all costs. When the artillery calls for a serenade it means that every gun in the group drops its other missions and begins firing on the area where the danger is greatest. This particular serenade poured more than 1,000 shells on the Germans.

The enemy attack wavered. It slowed. Then it broke under this awful pounding. The German columns began pulling back. The fields around St-Jacques are littered with German dead. Their bodies lie along the hedgerows and in meadows splashed with the rainbow colors of flowers. Their attack was mass suicide. After this abortive attempt to break out of the trap, the enemy began moving north on the roads to Bricquebec, while other columns poured into the same town from the other side. The Allied air forces immediately pounced on this tempting target. Fighters and five bombers smashed at transports converging on the town, and, as one officer said, "The fliers had a field day."

Meanwhile, in the corridor occupied by the Americans between Barneville and St-Lô d'Ourville, the infantry was flushing out small groups of Germans and destroying isolated points of resistance. The enemy was so confused that many prisoners said they did not know who their commanders were or where they were supposed to go. Americans were behind Germans and Germans were behind Americans. But the major difference was the Yanks knew their mission while the Germans did not know which way to turn.

The main road from Barneville to St-Lô d'Ourville was cut at 10 o'clock last night, and an example of German confusion was that when our troops reached the St-Lô d'Ourville crossroads they captured five Nazi military police who had been put there to direct traffic down an escape route to the south. By coincidence, it was almost four years to the day when British troops used the same crossroads as a defense point to hold the Germans while other troops were being evacuated from the Cherbourg Peninsula to England.

The Americans cut the peninsula at the exact point where they had planned before the invasion—although the commanding officers of the various units did not know where this point was when studying the tactical problem. Before they left England they worked out attack problems on sand tables showing simulated terrain in this area. "When we reached it," an officer said, "it was like coming home. Every officer knew where he was and what he had to do."

With John Thompson of the *Chicago Tribune* and William Stoneman of the *Chicago Daily News* I climbed to a hilltop overlooking the sea and gazed down on the escape corridor which had been closed by the doughboys. Officers leading the assault units which first cut the western escape road were Capt. Robert Hilpert of Washington State, Lieut. Lawrence McLaughlin of Boston, Mass., Lieut. William Klauz of New York City and Capt. Jesse Niven of North Carolina. I visited the command post of this unit concealed in a thicket not far from the battlefront. "The boys did a grand job," said Maj. H. A. Schmidt, Altoona, Pa. On a nearby telephone Maj. Arthur D. Jackson, Jr., Richmond, Va., warned the unit that enemy tanks were reported nearby while Capt. John Boland, Burlington, N.C., kept close tabs on the progress of the men cleaning out the blockade area. One officer, whose name I cannot reveal because of his rank, laughed and said, "We heard over the B.B.C. this morning that the Ninth Division had cut the peninsula."

"The news came in," he added, "just as we were having a counter-attack by the Germans who were trying to cut through south. For a time we wondered who was trying to cut whom."

In a tall elm tree, Lt. George Connolly, Arlington, Mass., had an observation post, observing the effect of artillery fire on enemy positions. We had taken over the area where the enemy manned positions, expecting a possible landing from the west side of the peninsula rather than the east. With Connolly were Pvt. William Wilson of China Grove, N.C., and Pvt. Lawrence Hickey of Yonkers, N.Y. Below us lay the narrow corridor which the doughboys had closed to the enemy and beyond was the blue sea. Behind us, American guns rumbled and shells rustled over to burst in enemy positions.

Fires burning in the area of St-Lô d'Ourville threw a pall of smoke into the sky and there were other fires burning in the green countryside, testifying to the accuracy of the U.S. batteries. From the north came the steady thumping of our bombs falling on enemy columns and the rattle of strafing, with the whining dive of planes. And while the harsh sounds of war beat in waves over our little hill there came from the trees the cheerful melody of songbirds singing in the green branches.

On the thirteenth day of the invasion, tough, hard-fighting American doughboys crossed the peninsula which the enemy fought bitterly to defend. Late yesterday afternoon, units of the Ninth Division had reached Besneville, which is four miles from a strategic crossroads near St-Lô d'Ourville and six miles from the sea. While the Germans were completely disorganized, and with hardly a pause, the American troops kept moving down the sloping fields and along the hedgerows, shooting up small knots of Germans making a frantic last stand. They crossed the last main highway on the west coast and kept pushing on to the sea.

The dramatic, swift advance was like a fist of iron smashing through the neck of the peninsula and the Germans were unable to stop it with their last, gasping defense. The Americans immediately began consolidating their positions to keep the enemy from making any stampede rush to escape southward.   □

With American Troops, Advancing toward Cherbourg, June 19 — With the shelling of the city itself, the battle for Cherbourg began tonight. Two weeks after landing on the Normandy coast, doughboys were almost within sight of the port city as a result of one of the most sensational advances the American Army has made in this war. American troops drove northward today to within eight miles of Cherbourg and began shelling the port with big guns.

It is a thrilling sight to see the Army moving up fast to take advantage of the breakthrough to the coast-troops marching along roads which a few hours ago were in enemy hands while guns, armor and trucks roll forward with them. There is no estimate as yet of the enemy dead. The fields, hedgerows and ditches hold the secret—bodies are lying where they fell because no one has had time yet to collect them. There was hardly a pause from the time the Americans smashed their way across the neck of the peninsula and beat back a frantic German effort to escape from the trap of steel, until they wheeled and swept toward Cherbourg.

They captured today at least 700 German prisoners, whose units had been disorganized by the American breakthrough. In three campaigns I never have seen an army take so swift and decisive advantage of a breakthrough as the Americans have done in the last two days. They are not giving the enemy a chance to recover from the blows he suffered when the doughboys knifed their way across the peninsula. A stream of prisoners slogged along the roads, doughboys covering them with tommy guns. The prisoners' faces showed their bewilderment.

The roads were littered with the wreckage of German vehicles and equipment. Some sectors resembled the scene in Tunisia when German resistance broke suddenly and confusion swept the ranks of Col. Gen. Jürgen Von Arnim's and Field Marshal Gen. Erwin Rommel's armies. Dejection and confusion were apparent among some of the enemy troops. They simply were not prepared for the drive that trapped them, and they were unable to react to the situation. One division made a desperate escape attempt, but it was so badly mauled that it fell back to the Cherbourg line.

Hitting northward from Barneville, one of the main points on the main west coast road cut by American troops Saturday night, the doughboys swept through Bricquebec. The fleeing Germans did not put up a fight for the town. Cutting of the Bricquebec-Valognes Highway denied the Nazis another major communications route and made the supply problem much simpler for our advance units.

Prisoners coming back from the front rode on fenders and hoods of trucks and were coming in so fast the units did not know how many they had. The advance was so swift one unit's command post was moved three times during the day. Once they found thirteen Germans hiding where the command post was to be set up.

One group of doughboys captured a field hospital and found thirty-five wounded American airborne troops who had been captured on D-Day. The men said they had received good medical treatment and their wounds were well dressed.

This last-ditch defense line before Cherbourg will be the battleground deciding the fate of the city. Its old positions possibly have been improved by the Germans, but already Americans are bombing and shelling enemy objectives in the city itself. Cherbourg, however, was not being shelled indiscriminately. Definite targets, such as fuel dumps, ammunition stores and strongpoints had been selected. □

With the American Forces in France, June 19 – Representatives of Gen. Charles De Gaulle's provisional government have already moved into liberated sections of Normandy to set up political control of civil affairs, although the provisional government as yet has not been recognized by the United States. François Coulet, who was secretary-general of Corsica and sub-prefect for that area, has arrived in Bayeux to take over duties as commissioner of the republic for the Region of Rouen. Obviously this is a coup d'état for De Gaulle, who simply brought his men into the beachhead when he came ashore last week and set them to work as rightful directors of French political affairs. Under present plans De Gaullists will occupy key political posts in each region as it is liberated.

These representatives will be appointed by the provisional government which does not plan to hold local elections until all France has been liberated. "Until the whole of France has been liberated and Frenchmen who are prisoners in Germany have been returned to their homes there can be no universal election," Coulet said in an interview today. "They should have voice in the selection of officials. We'll probably keep the districts as they have been set up by Vichy," Coulet said. "They are economic for administrative purposes."

In addition to directing civil affairs, Coulet's organization intends to enlist a territorial army as a small token force to help the Allied military keep order. "There will be no mobilization," Coulet said. "We'll call only for volunteers because we have a harvest at hand and men are needed on farms." Coulet said he saw no reason why there should be any friction between his organization and Allied military civil affairs. As he put it, "Allied civil affairs represents the army while I represent the French people."

In Bayeux Coulet removed the sub-prefect from office and appointed in his place a young native of the region, a well-to-do farmer named Triboulet. The sub-prefect was removed because he was too close to the Vichy regime. Just what would happen if Allied civil affairs appointees are not suitable to the De Gaullists is not exactly clear. The point has not yet arisen. But if they are able to show that the officeholder had "acted against the interests of the Allies" then the civil affairs officers have no alternative but to get rid of him. According to the civil affairs officer, Coulet said, there has not been a single case of opposition to his office from the old Vichy elements, and he knew of only one case where a collaborationist was manhandled by patriots after the Allies liberated this area.

While the Normans are undoubtedly pleased with the arrival of the Allies they are not demonstrative and have been rather reserved. They are definitely anti-German and anti-Vichy, from my impression, but there has been no wild acclaim of the Allies as liberators. Whether the people are De Gaullists or not is difficult to say. They gave the general a spontaneous enthusiastic reception when he visited the beachhead last week, but there are many who say they are interested only in the liberation of France and not in politics. □

With American Forces before Cherbourg, June 20 – American troops driving within only four miles of Cherbourg today heard the thunder of explosions from the port, and civilians straggling through the lines said the enemy had begun demolitions in the harbor. The deepest point of the spectacular breakthrough had not yet reached the highest ground from which forward elements might see the city itself.

Moving across hedgerows and green fields, and past peasant cottages with roses in bloom, the doughboys slowly closed the trap on Cherbourg. Already the Americans are within the outer rim of Cherbourg fortress—prepared positions where the enemy is expected to make a final bitter stand on order of the high command to fight to the last. But strangely enough, some positions were unmanned when our troops approached them.

Artillery began pounding the last east-west lateral road over which the Germans might move their troops and equipment to Cap Lévy, east of Cherbourg, or to Cap de la Hague, jutting out on the west tip of the peninsula. Our guns rolled to engage the Germans in and around Cherbourg itself. The enemy's last chance for escape is by sea at night from Cherbourg fortress— the escape route four years ago for British troops trapped on the peninsula by the German breakthrough in France. But they must escape at night if at all, and in small craft. The Allied air forces rule the air by day and the navies would be able to deal with any large-scale escape by sea. With the enemy trying to ruin the port facilities by demolitions, the smoke of explosions hung over the city.

Despite efforts of the Germans to evacuate civilians, approximately 6,000 French citizens were reported clinging to their homes and ready to take their chances. The Americans were receiving aid from French patriots. Many Frenchmen, some of them veterans of the last war, volunteered their services as scouts and guides—even as front-line troops to fight alongside the Yanks. "They drifted in by ones, twos, and threes, begging us to let them help in the capture of Cherbourg," one officer said as we stood near where the guns were booming at the front. "They know the country well and we see no reason why they couldn't help fight for their homes and country. They are in a weird assortment of uniforms, but they know how to fight."

As we stood at a command post in a quiet, peaceful orchard near the front, a high-ranking officer suddenly said: "Listen!" Then the artillery broke out in a roar. They were playing a "serenade" for the enemy—every gun in the area being turned on an area in the Cherbourg line. "And in a few minutes the Air Force will bomb hell out of several of their positions," the officer said.

Thrown into confusion by the swift drive of the doughboys, the Germans have been making a desperate effort to prepare Cherbourg's defenses for a last stand fight, with army, navy, air corps and labor troops. They ordered all civilian men out of the town Saturday night and instructed women to leave by Sunday. Apparently the Germans had pulled together remnants of everything left on the peninsula and were drawing them back for the defense of the port city. But hundreds of troops were unable to get out of the Allied trap. They were wandering around waiting for someone to pick them up. They were usually unarmed and confused about what to do.

Late this afternoon doughboys had not run into any well-coordinated defense and there were strong indications that the Germans had not yet recovered from the confusion of the beating they took when the Yanks smashed across the neck of the peninsula and then started north. And yet in driving toward this front one could see sharp contrasts of peace and war. War, it seemed, had leapfrogged across this lovely countryside.

In some places there were ugly shattered houses, burned fields and charred vehicles—the evidence of the savagery of battle. Around the curve of the road you felt you were in another world. Children waved gaily from trim yards of peasant cottages where roses bloomed in profusion. Cattle grazed in the fields and there was not a sign of destruction. Flowers bloomed in profusion along the roads and each cottage seemed to have a flower garden riotous with color. Civilians waved at each passing jeep or truck and sometimes children tossed roses at us.

But there is something sad and depressing about driving through such a lovely country and seeing what war can do to the people. And perhaps the

saddest sights of all are to be seen in the wrecked towns. Civilians are returning to their ruined homes now. They fled when the war neared but they
are straggling back with pitiful bundles and carts full of household goods. In
one town a child sat on a pile of debris laughing and waving gaily at the passing convoys. Behind her a woman, obviously her mother, picked aimlessly
in the debris looking for something to salvage from the wreckage. At another place a man and woman tugged at the heavy stones and broken timbers
trying to get order out of what once had been their home. They heaved together at a huge timber but could not budge it. They looked at each other.
Then the man shrugged and they walked slowly out into the street hand in
hand.   □

With American Forces before Cherbourg, June 21 –
Powerful American forces were drawn up before Cherbourg tonight,
preparing for the kill—getting ready to hurl an overpowering weight of men
and metal on the trapped German garrison that is entrenched in its last-stand
defenses. Civilians straggling through the lines said that within the city the
Germans were preparing for a street-by-street defense, knocking holes in
the corners of buildings and setting up machine guns and antitank guns to
cover the approaches. Supreme headquarters in its midnight communiqué
said, "Allied forces made further progress in the battle for Cherbourg, and
the area held by the enemy is steadily diminishing. Our advance up the entire peninsula has been rapid."

With methodical precision the American doughboys closed in on the
heights overlooking Cherbourg and encountered the cove of the enemy's
last line of defenses—blockhouses and concrete pillboxes. For the past
twelve hours they have been probing positions, locating strongpoints and
getting ready for the final thrust. The fall of Cherbourg now is a matter of
time. That much is apparent. There is little chance for the enemy to make a
"Stalingrad" of the city because the Americans have superior hitting power
on land, sea and in the air.

Thus, fifteen days after the first landings in Normandy, the doughboys
are ready to batter down the gates of the city whose control would give the
Allies a valuable point of entry for supplies. But, as the Americans tightened
their arc of steel about the German perimeter of defenses, they met stiffening opposition from strongpoints fixed so that the lines of fire crisscrossed,
with each point supporting its neighbor. As yet the Americans have made
no effort to smash the Cherbourg line. Forward patrols have found enemy

pillboxes clustered in each defensive area, most of them apparently having been previously prepared, but some very recently constructed.

In drawing back on their inner defenses, the Germans gave up much ground and several strongpoints which, it seemed to the Americans, they should have tried to hold if they intended a do-or-die stand. Obviously the enemy had not recovered from the confusion and disorganization which followed the American breakthrough to the west coast and subsequent drive northward. Many guns and much material which might have been saved by an orderly retreat have been left behind.

The fight has gone out of many of the Germans, who have seen the hopelessness of their position. In one case doughboys surrounded four tanks. The crews surrendered without trying to fight. Another time a German captain and eighteen men with only one gun among them surrendered, because they were cut off from their unit. Maj. Harry Blevers, former Waterloo, Ia., high school athletic coach, said many Germans were taking advantage of the confusion in their ranks to escape and surrender. "They slip away from their columns when marching at night," he said. "Their officers had kept them in line by threatening retaliation against their families if they did not fight."

There have been some cases, however, of Germans putting civilian clothes over their uniforms and going into the woods as snipers. "We caught five in one group who had civilian clothes over their uniforms," said Maj. Ernest King of Mullins, S.C. "They were hiding in the woods and shooting at our boys, who at first thought they were Frenchmen."

Harry Harris, Associated Press photographer of 32 Sixty-ninth Road, Flushing, N.Y., found them very annoying at Barneville. "While we were eating, the Germans kept coming in and wanting to know where they could surrender. We couldn't eat for those lugs," exclaimed Harris.

On the British-Canadian sector to the east of the Cherbourg Peninsula, heavy fighting continued in the Tilly-Caen sectors, but the series of attacks and counter-attacks left the front virtually unchanged. Cherbourg was becoming a sort of European "Singapore." The Germans apparently had not anticipated having to defend the city from the landward "back door." At least seven great coastal batteries pointing out to sea make it nearly invulnerable to direct naval attack and the Americans pressing in from the south found the flanks on both sides of the peninsula guarded by extensive minefields and tank obstacles and ditches. In capturing Valognes the Americans discovered an elaborate underground fortress with heavy gun positions just outside the town where the road slopes down toward the sea. As at Singapore, however, all guns pointed toward the sea, useless for defense against attack from the rear.

Cherbourg, which once was the third greatest port in France and which will be of prime value to the Allies in landing heavy equipment and reinforcements, shook to the blasts of German demolitions. Naval sources declared, however, that such eventualities had been considered in advance and said they were confident that no matter what the Nazis were able to do, Cherbourg could be put back into working order quickly. They have encountered and mastered similar situations elsewhere, such as at Tripoli, in Libya, and Naples. It is known that the Germans do not have sufficient ships in Cherbourg to block the harbor by sinking them, and a twenty-five-foot tide is counted upon to make it relatively easy to open at least a high-tide channel.   □

With the American Forces before Cherbourg, [June 22] (2 p.m.) — By land, and air Americans unleashed a mighty attack on the fortress of Cherbourg today. At 12:40 p.m. (6:40 a.m., Eastern War Time) waves of American and British medium bombers and dive-bombers roared in and began the pounding of fortifications in the Cherbourg line, a pounding which continued for eighty minutes. And when the bombers had stopped, the artillery opened up and battered at the line in thunderous, drumming explosions. Behind the artillery the doughboys moved up and began storming the German defenses.

This was the great assault intended to crush the last German resistance before Cherbourg—a mighty land and air assault greater than any since the Allies fought their way onto Normandy's beaches. The doughboys were drawn up this morning waiting for the air bombardment and then the artillery barrage which covered their advance. The barrage pounded the line until the infantry advanced to within close range of its objectives and then was lifted.

Late yesterday the doughboys, driving northward east of Cherbourg, broke through the Cherbourg line to cut the Cherbourg-St-Pierre-Eglise Road and block any German escape or any move to bring in reinforcements from that direction. They were not giving the enemy time to get set, for they were attacking while the Germans were still confused and disorganized from the swift breakthrough across the peninsula.

One high officer said the Germans' backbone of resistance on the Cherbourg Peninsula was smashed June 16 when the Americans crashed through in the Orglandes-St-Sauveur region and battered their way to the sea, sealing off the peninsula. "Once my men cut across the peninsula," the officer said, "Hell—I could have held the peninsula against all the Germans in the world. The crux was on June 16—that was when we broke their back. We had to take a lot of chances, but we did it."

The enemy was so completely disorganized by the breakthrough they never have been able to collect themselves to hold back the American rush north to throw an arc of steel around Cherbourg. The German defenses ran roughly from Fermanville, east of Cherbourg, down to Gonneville, and then curve to Hardinvast, Ste-Croix-Hague and up to Gréville on the coast west of the port. Behind this defense line the Germans sat in concrete pillboxes and blockhouses when the great assault opened.

"We could not have done the job we have done without air support," the officer said. "But it's going to take a damn good bunch of doughboys, engineers and artillery to finish this job."

A thrust last night on the east side of Cherbourg drove to a road two miles from the sea at Haulucas. And then the attacks today smashed in from the south. One thrust moved in on the north banks of the Divette River, with the high ground immediately outside Cherbourg as the first objective, while a twin drive hit directly north and east of the Divette River. The Army had planned to call in the Navy to pour in fire from the sea, but the operation developed so swiftly the ground forces could not wait. Precautions were taken not to bomb Cherbourg itself, but to concentrate on strongpoints in the arc facing the American lines.

The Germans were believed caught as the British were at Singapore—with heavy naval guns in the casements unable to traverse to fire inland. They had batteries of these guns in thick concrete forts, but they were useless in the attempt to stop the Americans driving in from the south. □

With American Forces Storming Cherbourg, June 22 (6:08 p.m.) — The battle for Cherbourg raged to a thunderous climax tonight, with battle-stained doughboys closing in on the port city in a savage attack which began at 2 p.m. (8 a.m., New York time). As I write this dispatch, Long Toms and 105-millimeter guns are blazing and the doughboys are blasting at the enemy's Cherbourg defenses with bullets and explosives. Death and destruction are rampant in the arc of defenses the Germans are manning. The attack climaxes the spectacular doughboy drive which opened eight days ago and has swept to the gates of the city. This was the historic march by infantry and supporting branches—a victory dash unmatched on the French beachhead except by the courageous assault of the troops who fought their way ashore June 6.

It began at noon of June 14 when our troops opened their attack that drove westward across the Cherbourg Peninsula to shear off the northern part. This is a day-by-day account of that swift drive:

JUNE 14–15: While one unit was putting pressure on the enemy around Montebourg on the eastern side of the peninsula, others opened an attack westward in the general area of Orglandes. These latter were the Ninth and Eighty-second Divisions. All the afternoon of the 14th and the next day fighting raged across the hedges and green fields. The Americans fought forward slowly against bitter opposition. Late on the 15th the German opposition began to soften under the massed American fire

JUNE 16: Suddenly the enemy defenses cracked south of Orglandes. The doughboys swept forward to cross the Douve River at St-Sauveur-le-Vicomte.

The enemy was in confusion. The bodies of enemy dead were strewn in fields and ditches. This was the big breakthrough. It developed all along the front into a rout. The swift American advance overran and surprised German units. The roads were littered with enemy trucks, tanks, guns, equipment and clothing in vast disarray. Prisoners came in by the hundreds.

JUNE 17: At 11 p.m. on Saturday night American troops reached the sea, capturing St-Lô d'Ourville and Barneville on the western coastal road and driving a wedge clear across the neck of the peninsula.

JUNE 18: One German division, ordered to try to escape to the south, attempted to break out of the trap. It made a heavy attack, which the Americans beat off with massed artillery and mortar fire. German dead covered the fields. Those who remained alive began retreating. They fell back to the Cherbourg line, with the Yanks pursuing them and giving them no chance to recover.

JUNE 19: Steadily pressing north on the western side of the peninsula, the Americans overran Bricquebec and cut another main lateral road.

JUNE 20: The Germans began pulling back on the east side of the peninsula and the Americans captured Montebourg and Valognes, two main towns south of Cherbourg. Montebourg, where the Germans fought bitterly house-to-house, was left behind as a broken, torn town in which hardly a building remained intact.

JUNE 21: The Americans edged up on the Cherbourg line and began probing its defenses slowly. They closed an arc of steel around the city, broke through the defenses on the east and west and cut the lateral coast roads, completely bottling up the Germans within Cherbourg.

JUNE 22: The Americans launched an attack by air and land to smash through the defenses of Cherbourg. Although the land assault was preceded by heavy bombing and massed artillery fire on enemy strongpoints, the infantry met resistance from pillboxes and began methodically cleaning them out, one by one.

This was the great assault to crush the last German resistance in Cherbourg.   □

With American Forces Advancing on Cherbourg, [June 23] (1:20 p.m.) — American troops widened the breach in the Germans' Cherbourg line today in an advance that carried spearhead forces to within 2,000 yards of the great port city. The entire enemy front has broken down into hard knots of resistance, some of which have been bypassed by American troops and are behind our lines. Enemy defenses showed signs of crumbling soon after the Allied drive broke through the perimeter of Cherbourg's defenses last night.

With medium bombers, dive-bombers, artillery and mortars hurling tons of explosives into their positions, the Germans were literally fighting with guns in their backs—if they leave their posts their officers have been ordered to shoot them down as cowards. The American spearhead from the south carried to the railroad southeast of Octeville on the outskirts of Cherbourg, and was strengthened this morning when one of the enemy's strongest points was knocked out after being bypassed.

This strongpoint consisted of steel-reinforced concrete emplacements which covered the doughboys' approach to Cherbourg from the south. The advance units fought their way by it and left it for others behind to clean up. For a time yesterday the advance units were almost cut off from supplies by the fire from this fort. But early today waves of medium bombers roared across the bright blue sky and once again the thunder of bomb explosions made the earth shudder. And when the attack from the air ended the American infantrymen moved in to clean up the position. They found four German non-commissioned officers left in the strongpoint, all dazed by the shock of the bombing and the fight gone out of them. All others in the position were dead.

East of Cherbourg the Americans shoved forward a little more than a mile, with the front there broken into confused pockets. From the west our troops moved on the heights of Mont du Roc. They were now fighting on the west and on the south in sight of Cherbourg. The confusion of the front lines was evident when I tried to get forward to advanced elements with two other correspondents. We turned off the main road to a winding dusty lane, but we got no farther than the ridge from which we could see shell bursts ripping into the enemy positions.

As we drove along the road about two miles from the spearhead, the enemy began shelling the area. Shells began whistling across from both directions. To the east there was a lively machine gun and small-arms battle in progress at one of the pockets bypassed by our troops. We took cover behind an embankment while dusty doughboys crouched and ran to shelter in an antitank ditch dug by the Germans. The soldiers shouted to us not to move over in that direction as engineers were blowing up enemy pillboxes. It is necessary to destroy the pillboxes as they are cleaned out. At first the troops left them intact, but found that the Germans slipped back into them under cover of darkness.

Within the last twenty-four hours the Americans have taken more than 1,200 prisoners. The number of enemy dead within that defense of death is not known. The Cherbourg line was a death trap for hundreds of Germans who did not accept the ultimatum to surrender which was offered to them before the doughboys threw in their heavy attack.

Last night American artillery erupted with a heavy barrage against the strongpoints to help the doughboys in their push forward. The guns rumbled all night long and the air trembled with concussions. Then, this morning, under clear blue skies, medium bombers roared over in waves again blasting enemy positions. Our most advanced elements pulled back to a safety zone to permit the bombers to go to work, then they went forward again when the bombers had finished their job.

There is no grand surge forward against Cherbourg. That is not the way this fight is progressing even though our troops have blasted a wedge deep into the enemy's lines which is in depth all the way back to the city itself. When the doughboys reach the city they expect to have to fight their way from house to house unless there is a sudden collapse of the enemy such as there was at Cap Bon. Cherbourg is doomed as an enemy stronghold. That much is certain, although the Germans still have a hard knot of resistance holding out in the most intricate maze of defense systems most of our troops have encountered since they landed. Six-feet-thick concrete pillboxes and gun positions are staggered in depth on commanding ground with fields of fire interlocking, so that if one position is knocked out the troops come under fire from another.

Each of these strongholds is a self-contained unit. The doughboys found them well-stocked with ammunition and supplies after they had blasted out the defenders of many of them who were thrown into the line in a last-minute desperate effort to stave off the American advance.   □

With the American Forces before Cherbourg, June 24 – French civilians in Cherbourg have hidden stores of wine and champagne which they are eagerly waiting to uncork when the Americans arrive. This was the news brought from Cherbourg today by a young Cherbourg merchant who slipped through enemy lines to offer his services to the Americans and to give them all the information he could to aid in the capture of the city.

"There are 5,000 civilians left in the city," he said. "Most of the townspeople fled to the country to escape possible bombings and shellings but those who are left are waiting to give the Americans a big welcome."

The Germans have mined the approaches to the city, he said, and prepared the buildings for house to house defense by knocking holes in the walls from which to shoot machine guns and rifles. The merchant asserted, however, that he doubted the enemy had the manpower to man all of the defenses. About the only business operating in the city now under siege are a few cafés patronized by the Germans, he said.   □

With American Forces Entering Cherbourg, June 25 – American forces entered Cherbourg, late this afternoon. With artillery battering the enemy's collapsing defenses, American troops clawed into the city from south, east and west and clamped a firm grasp on the vital port. The Germans' stand or die defenses slowly withered under the terrible pounding from our big guns and mortars until at 6 p.m. (noon, New York time) there were only two strongpoints at Fort du Roule and a few other scattered defense points holding out against the relentless doughboys. There remains tonight the slow job of cleaning out the main part of the city and the shelling of the enemy guns which are still firing.

Cherbourg lies under a pall of dust and smoke from fires kindled by artillery explosions and from demolitions of the Germans. Hundreds of prisoners are streaming back to prisoner cages. There is no estimate of the number, but they are being rounded up in groups of twenty, fifty and one hundred at a time, wherever the doughboys go. There are many others dead among the positions hammered by our big guns. But Cherbourg proper is untouched by our artillery fire which is concentrated on points of resistance.

Late this afternoon the Germans blew up Fort des Flamands. A mighty explosion ripped out the sides of the fort and clouded the eastern half of the city in dense smoke. Cherbourg's basin was an inferno of artillery explosions, flames, smoke and dust today—a spectacular and awesome sight.

And then, when the troops began the final attack at 2 p.m., a sudden quiet descended over the battlefield—a ghostly sort of silence which was unbroken for minutes by the noises of battle. The only sound I remember was the crunch of shoes on the gravel as the doughboys marched on Cherbourg. Even though they were told to stand by their guns or be shot as cowards, the Germans broke under the steady hammering of artillery and pressure from the doughboys, and did not put up the house-to-house defense many expected them to do.   □

Cherbourg, June 26 (11:31 a.m.) — Cherbourg is a rubble-filled, smoking battleground over which rolls the thunder of crashing enemy artillery shells and the sharp rattle of machine guns as the Americans move from house to house cleaning up the last fanatical Nazi resistance in this port city.

At 11:30 a.m. today we cannot say that Cherbourg is entirely ours. The American forces who stormed up the peninsula and fought their way into the city late yesterday afternoon have virtual control, but there still remain stubborn groups of Germans who have not yet surrendered. They are holed up in houses and in concrete pillboxes on the beach, fighting to the last, while from Cap de la Hague the enemy's artillery is now throwing heavy shells into the city. Their concussion is shaking the wooden box on which I am writing this dispatch a few yards from the English Channel.

Across the street is the Amiot aircraft plant, or what once was a plant; now it is a charred and burning ruins, sabotaged by the Germans in the last hours in Cherbourg. Down the road less than one hundred yards our tanks are sitting on the beach near knocked-out enemy strongpoints, blasting at machine gun nests that still are holding out. The rattle of machine gun fire breaks out intermittently.

The tanks helped the doughboys fight their way through tough, scattered knots of resistance to enter the city late yesterday. When the Germans began firing from houses along the route of advance, the tanks rolled up and blasted the positions. In one house a German officer and three enlisted men lay dead with bullet holes through their foreheads, neat round holes put there by an American expert rifleman. The officer lay with a champagne bottle in one hand, a rifle in the other. He had decided to fight to the last. The resistance is disorganized. The defenders, still manning their guns, are German fanatics, trapped like rats. There is no escape for them. They are the last doomed defenders of Cherbourg.

No one should ever forget the battle for Cherbourg. It is a classic example of American courage and initiative. I have seen a lot of towns fall in Africa and Sicily and Italy, but none thrilled me so much as the entry of the American troops into this city. Of all the places stormed by skill and courage, this ranks at the top of the list. Now the defenders are in their last dying spasm of resistance. Their only hope is to deny the Allies the use of the port for a little while longer.

The Americans won control of Fort du Roule late last night, thus wiping out one of the enemy's strongest positions in the perimeter of defenses. Within this great concrete and steel pile the Germans had been able to hold out even while those behind them were being overrun. But even yet all the Germans have not been dug out of the maze of tunnels and interconnected chambers of the deep fortress. There were reports that the Germans had recaptured Fort du Roule last night, but this proved to be untrue.

"Any talk of the Germans recapturing Fort du Roule is nonsense," declared the officer commanding the troops who had fought their way into the upper part of the fortress whose naval guns pointed out of thick concrete walls just south of the city toward the sea. Even while the Americans were in control of the upper part the Germans were still firing from the lower levels. "We put a charge of TNT on the end of a pole and dropped it down to the gun opening," the officer said. "Then we pulled a string. It damn near deafened me, but that gun never fired again."

A German prisoner declared the lower chambers of the fortress could not be reached from the top and that supplies were brought down into it from a tunnel leading from the railroad station thousands of yards away. Apparently the fortress was neutralized now, but there were still enemy troops within it who will have to be dug out when the secret entrance to the interlocking rooms and levels is found.

With two other correspondents I tried to reach Cherbourg on the main highway from the south. But from the west an enemy anti-aircraft gun was raking the approach with bursts of fire. Artillery observers were searching for this bypassed position which was endangering columns coming up behind the advanced units. By a circuitous route we drove to the very beach which yesterday was being pounded by Allied warships knocking out a battery of guns. Around the gun positions were concrete pillbox domes which had been manned until this morning, when tanks came up and blasted out the defenders. Dynamite charges then had destroyed the pillboxes. Private Noah Stonum, a tank gunner from Elgin, Ill., helped put one of them out of commission.

Across the water we could see the old French forts on the breakwater. White flags of surrender fluttered from them. Fort des Flamands looked like a pile of debris. The Germans blew it up yesterday as the doughboys closed in.

The first unit into this section of the city was led by Lieut. George Myers of Cincinnati. This was the spearhead that sliced off the eastern part of the city. "Damn it, I wanted to wade in the English Channel today, but machine guns from the pillboxes were still firing this morning," one officer growled.

There were surprisingly few mines and booby traps left by the Germans to hamper the American entry into the city. Most of the opposition was from machine gun nests and guns in the forts. The unit here has found only two booby traps so far and the only mines were those in front of the smashed beach defenses.

Coming into the city the doughboys hit one tough knot of resistance with a German colonel and 300 troops holed up in a building and armed with machine guns and rifles. "We just brought up tanks and boys with automatic Browning rifles," said Lieut. Benjamin Westervelt of 418 Stockholm Street, Brooklyn, "and poured fire through the windows and doors. That got 'em. The colonel came out to surrender his men. They poured out of there through the windows and doors in streams."

The unit kept one of the prisoners and when a pillbox strongpoint was encountered he was sent forward to tell the defenders that unless they surrendered tanks would be brought up and all of them wiped out. "We got fifty-six of that bag," Lieut. Westervelt said. "We did the same thing at other places, too, and this man convinced more than one hundred Germans to surrender." There were few civilians in the section of the city we visited, but those on the streets were giving a warm welcome to the Yanks.	□

Cherbourg, June 27 — A warm sun bathed the Place de la République and doughboys strolled through Cherbourg's main square today, relaxing from the battle while a tall American sergeant played nostalgic melodies on a piano accordion to the accompaniment of guitars strummed by a doughboy and a young Frenchman.

That was the story of Cherbourg this pleasant afternoon. There were few sounds of battle. The guns had stopped their roaring and the city was as quiet as any peaceful community in the United States. Little groups of soldiers and civilians were laughing and chatting about the troubadours in the glass-littered street. Sgt. Ivan Broten of Isanti, Minn., played softly on the accordion. Sgt. Charles Horvatich of 184 Forty-ninth St., Pittsburgh, and his French companion couldn't understand each other's language but their guitars blended sweetly.

Our troops wiped out the last German resistance in the arsenal area this morning, ending the fight for Cherbourg, and as we entered the city today labor battalions were already at work cleaning up the debris on the streets.

American, British and French flags are flying in all the streets. Some of the tricolors were crudely stitched pieces of bunting which obviously the townspeople had made just for this day—when they could say their homes had been liberated. Flags came out of hiding and began waving from windows as troops moved through the city. "When we'd come to a street intersection flags would be stuck out of the windows behind us," said Pvt. Thomas Harney, 12 Lawrence St., Yonkers, N.Y.

One of the last places in the city where the doughboys had to fight was the Gestapo headquarters and a pillbox just down the street from it. A unit under Capt. Milton Holladay, Lexington, Ky., cleaned out this strongpoint. The Germans in the Gestapo headquarters finally fled through an underground passage to the City Hall in an attempt to escape, but they were captured there.

"We had to fight all the way in," said the tall Kentuckian, "and when we reached this street they opened fire on my men from the pillbox at the entrance of the headquarters and at the end of the street."

Holladay called on tank destroyers to come up and give his doughboys a hand, so Lieut. R. B. Fullerton, 3833 Yakima St., Tacoma, Wash., brought up one of the destroyers and blasted at the pillboxes to quiet their fire.

In the Gestapo headquarters Holladay's men found an American medic who had been held prisoner for four days. He said he knew the German captain commanding the pillbox at the end of the street and believed if someone talked to him he would surrender with his men. The German had lived in New York and knew English well. Lieut. Harry Aschkinasi, 1561 Sheriday Ave., New York City, went into the pillbox.

"The German captain had a bottle of brandy," Aschkinasi said, "and he was slightly tipsy. We talked for a half hour. I told him he didn't have a chance, and might as well give up. The captain said that if he had good German machine guns instead of old French weapons he never would surrender. Finally he agreed and came out with his troops."

The Germans had lived in comfort with plenty of food and liquors. In every place we have been there were stores of sausages, butter, loaves of bread, and canned goods. Many beds had bright-colored down comforters covering them. □

Cherbourg, June 27 — An inspection today of Fort du Roule disclosed stocks of ammunition and a huge inventory of stores worth millions of dollars. And all the mysteries of this fort, the Germans' strongest bastion guarding the southern approaches to Cherbourg, have not yet been solved by American forces, now swarming the underground chambers driven into a cliffside and reinforced by steel and concrete. The deep tunnels held enough food, ammunition, guns and other supplies inside the deep tunnels to have kept a large force supplied for months. There are thousands of cases of cognac, fine French wines, champagnes and liqueurs and vast stores of everything from shaving cream to torpedoes. Officers have not yet located the passages leading to all the series of levels, and there is the possibility Germans may still be inside the fortress. But they made no move to destroy it before our troops broke in.

Cpl. James Bresnahan of Waterbury, Conn., led a group of us through one of the great series of chambers, 300 feet below the cliff top where the Yanks first broke into the fortress. Thick steel doors were blasted open, and inside was an intricate, amazing installation. The main tunnel was 200 yards deep, thirty-eight feet high and equally as wide. Off the main tunnel were other rooms of the same height and width and about fifty yards in depth. An overhead crane was electrically powered for moving heavy weapons or ammunition from one part of the tunnels to others.

An electric light system was found, along with telephones, automatically controlled ventilators and water mains. By lantern light we walked through the tunnels. They were littered with clothing and equipment of the fortress's defenders. Double-decked bunks ran along the sides of most of the tunnels where the men lived. Their personal belongings were strewn about in disarray. Some of the Germans had wrapped packages and addressed them to friends and relatives in Germany, but were caught before they could send them out. They contained pieces of silks and satins, cigars, tins of food and trinkets.

Maj. Glenn Plumlee, Birmingham, Ala., walked into a great chamber stacked high with ammunition of all kinds, from shells for huge guns to small arms cartridges. One chamber that had been occupied by marines contained twelve large torpedoes hanging on the walls in racks. Down the main corridors the walls were stacked high with boxes of radios, combs, lotions, soap, matches, cigarettes, chewing tobacco, playing cards, toothpaste, shaving cream, razor blades and hundreds of other items. Much of these huge stores will be a blessing to American troops, who are short on items available in quantity inside Fort du Roule. Almost all the bunks had food about them, and the lockers had half-eaten cans of preserves and foodstuffs.   □

Cherbourg, June 29 — Enemy troops making their last stand on the Cotentin Peninsula in the Cap de la Hague area northwest of Cherbourg were reported receiving supplies today from planes flying by night.

East of Cherbourg, Americans finished mopping up and took 1,102 prisoners yesterday while caging 450 more in other sectors. Strong artillery concentrations silenced German guns holding out at Fort Central.

Indications were that the die-hard elements at Cap de la Hague were preparing to make a stand on the Vauville-Beaumont Hague-Gréville line. They are the escaped remnants of four German divisions shattered in the Cherbourg trap.

The enemy's artillery was silent last night, but it is known that he has two 280-millimeter railway guns somewhere near Auderville. He also has twenty to thirty light and medium tanks on Cap de la Hague. The entire northern tip of the peninsula now has been cleared except for those at Cap de la Hague.   □

With the American Army in France, June 29 — Five years of war have wiped out the cream of German youth and now there is "a missing generation," in Germany—those youths of twenty to twenty-eight years who form the backbone of any great fighting force.

This statement came today from an American staff officer who has watched more than 37,000 enemy troops pass through the prisoner cages since the doughboys stormed the beachhead of Normandy twenty-three days ago. And he asserted there is only one conclusion to be reached from the prisoners taken—the cream of Germany's armies is gone, slaughtered or captured in the abortive campaigns in Russia, killed in the hot sands of the western desert, or lost in North Africa, Sicily and Italy.

Most of the prisoners either are very young, many of them eighteen to twenty, or they are well past thirty years. The oldest prisoner was sixty-nine. The officer's observation was made as the doughboys were driving the last of the peninsula defenders onto the very northwestern tip of Cap de la Hague. There were an estimated 3,000 Germans left in the pocket with only one avenue of escape—and that by sea at night when the Allied air force is unable to observe the movements of small boats.

While the enemy has buried the finest of his soldiers, the American armies still have their youth, and in the opinion of this staff officer that makes the great difference in the armies of Germany and those of the United States. Man for man, he said, the Germans are licked in the quality of troops.

Although the entire American front was relatively quiet, doughboys were put in the attack in the St-Lô sector to straighten out the lines by capturing enemy-held positions. In the early morning, dive-bombers roared in to pound strongpoints and then artillery laid down a heavy barrage in advance of troops, signaling the flare-up of activity on the southern front.

Defenders of Fort Central on the mole at Cherbourg were blasted into submission today by the heavy guns and the way was opened for minesweepers to clear the harbor waters of any mines which the enemy might have left behind. Dock repair crews already have moved into the city to get busy on the sabotaged harbor, where the enemy set off demolitions, wrecked cranes and workshops, and sank ships in an effort to block the harbor.

One of the surprises of the Cherbourg campaign has been the enemy's failure to strew the path of the confused retreat with minefields such as the Germans used in North Africa, Sicily and Italy. One officer said the Germans had strung up wire and hung out minefield signs in many places which were not mined. "This was just a lot of eyewash for Rommel when he made his inspection of the west wall defenses," the officer said dryly.

Evidence of German confusion after the American breakthrough June 16 at St-Sauveur-le-Vicomte has been cropping up in many places. One of the most striking cases was in an American's capture of an enemy hospital containing 2,300 wounded. The officer who inspected it reported that the hospital was "in bad shape," without even any record of officer casualties. Many patients had not had their bandages changed in five days and there were cases of gangrene as a result of lack of proper care and organization. □

With the American Forces in France, June 30 — Allied forces have killed, captured and wounded an equivalent of seven full German divisions since the invasion of France twenty-four days ago. Giving Field Marshal General Erwin Rommel's Normandy defenders a severe mauling, Lieut. Gen. Omar N. Bradley's troops alone captured more than 38,000, killed an estimated 10,000 and wounded at least 12,000. The greater number of these were bagged in the swift drive on Cherbourg.

Figures on the casualties inflicted on the enemy by the British have not been released yet, but the American totals run much higher than on the British front, as the result of the Cherbourg trap being sprung. The total American catch likely will run more than 40,000 when the Cap de la Hague area finally is cleared out. An American staff officer said that German divisions which were destroyed were the 352nd, the 709th, 243rd, Seventy-seventh and Ninety-first. Killed, captured or wounded Germans in other enemy units were estimated as equaling two additional divisions.

The enemy's wounded were estimated conservatively at three for every man killed. In contrast, Allied losses have been relatively slight, the officer said. Since D-Day, the British have destroyed 106 German tanks and damaged another 192. A tank is not counted as destroyed unless it is burned out or engineers have blown it up. This loss represents a serious blow to the Germans.   □

Somewhere in Normandy, June 30 — Monsieur le Comte, who is a millionaire with one pair of shoes to his name, spoke for all the French in Normandy when he said: "We are very rich and yet very poor." Rich in tradition and national pride, rich in fertile land and sturdy Norman buildings, but so poor that Monsieur le Comte walks about in skiing shoes he once reserved for holidays in Saint-Moritz. "They are all I have left," he said.

The count, who is in his seventies, rode to Cherbourg in a jeep yesterday and was as excited as a child. He said it was his first automobile ride in four years. The count owns a château in Normandy but is no better off than his tenant farmers. Here was no collaborator. He was a firm friend of the captain who drove him to Cherbourg on official business. On the way he described what it was [like] to live four years under German domination.

"Living in the richest part of France, we never lacked for meat or bread," he said in English, which ran into French when he became excited. "It is the little things like shirts. I was unable to buy a shirt for four years, and now I have only five. If the war lasts another year I'll have no shirts."

Some things are obtainable in the black market but at outrageous prices—3,000 francs for a pair of shoes, 140 francs for a package of cigarettes. "That's why patriotic French people resorted to barter," he explained. "You have some cheese; I have some nails; we exchange."

His château first was occupied by the Germans and now is used by the Americans, but the count waits patiently for the war to pass him by. He said he had no complaint to make about the Germans. "They were very correct," he said, "but of course they were Germans, and we do not want them."   □

With the First Division in France, July 2 — When the history books are written about the great invasion of France, you may never read of Joe Dawson. But no history will be complete without him. Thirty years old, Joe is a black-haired, lean-faced captain from Waco, Texas, a former oil region geologist.

Commanding Company G of the Fighting First Division, Joe led the first unit to come off the beach that bloody morning of June 6. He was that one lone man out in front of the tens of thousands of doughboys [who] poured into Normandy. Joe and his men faced murderous fire to open an assault on Germans hidden in trenches, pillboxes and concrete and steel blockhouses. Here's what that means:

When the doughboys hit the beach on D-Day, the Germans in strong positions poured direct fire onto the beach with machine guns, rifles, mortars and artillery. The Yanks had landed from a heavy sea, crossing mined log and steel barriers. Shore gravel rose sharply from the water's edge offering slight cover, and behind that embankment thousands of troops lay pinned to the beach.

Joe's commanding officer quickly assessed the situation. "Gentlemen," he said, "we are being killed on the beach—let's go inland and be killed."

So at the head of his company, Joe walked straight into an enemy minefield and across barbed wire to draw the lead fire. His men followed him. Joe doesn't know I am writing about him. As we talked today he said, "Give my men all the credit because they deserve it. They did a great job." But in Joe's story, I also hope to picture his men.

Of the push, Joe said: "Things got to moving so fast I don't remember just what did happen. It was cops and robbers stuff all around."

Anyway the men entered Colleville, which was lousy with Germans. They fought a pitched battle all day and all night and clung to their positions—even when our own Navy began pounding the town with big guns, hurling shells all around them.

In a church, Joe met a burst of fire. A bullet grazed his left kneecap and lodged in his right leg. And Joe kept right after the Germans, firing blindly. When the enemy ran out and crossed a hedgerow, Joe ended this little fracas with a grenade, while his men fought furiously around him.

"We got an anchor in the town and I built up firepower around it," Joe said.   □

St-Sauveur-le-Vicomte, July 3 — In a Fourth of July eve burst of fireworks, doughboys drove south tonight along the western coast of the Cherbourg Peninsula toward the pivotal crossroads of La-Haye-du-Puits while mauling the enemy with heavy superiority of artillery.

The troops surged forward on a ten-mile front and captured the village of St-Jores, ten miles west of Carentan, in the early morning hours and then closed in and seized hills overlooking La-Haye-du-Puits, hub of a network of roads important to movement of German men and material.

Two months ago French patriots said Marshal Erwin Rommel had inspected these positions and expressed pleasure at their strength and strategic location. The doughboys captured some Poles in the early hours of the push but after that hit a tough line of German resistance. The enemy pulled back Russians, Poles and other "ersatz" troops to eliminate any soft spots in the line.

It was officially disclosed that the Germans had brought one full division from Russia to throw against the Allies. Some prisoners captured today had only arrived in the line last night and barely had had time to get into their fortifications before they were hit by this new attack. Other prisoners were taken from the remnants of units which managed to escape the Cherbourg trap sprung June 16, when the Americans smashed across the peninsula neck to the sea. The advance moved to within three miles of the town's limits after the right flank succeeded in breaking through a narrow corridor between the marshlands at St-Sauveur-de-Pierrepont, southwest of here.

In the early morning mists, sodden troops moved into battle in a driving rainstorm. Water dripped from trees and hedges and the lowlands were turned into bogs which impeded progress of the troops. Heavy armor was mired and the air forces were prevented from giving support. The attack began at 5:30 a.m. (11:30 p.m. Sunday, Eastern War Time) after a thunderous artillery barrage which raked enemy positions. Rain and fog hampered observation on the targets but hundreds of guns pounded those already spotted.

I watched troops move down a road into a battle laden with machine guns, mortars and ammunition. Water ran from their helmets and their uniforms were dark and heavy with rain. Their shoes sank into mud on the roadside and made little squishing sounds as they slogged along. Their packs looked heavy and water-soaked and occasionally a soldier slipped and slid in the oozing brown mud. Fog and rain muffled the sound of guns and shells. They made a dull heavy thump instead of the sharp clear crack heard on a clear day.

In a tent hidden under a dripping elm an officer sat on his ammunition case studying red, blue and black pencil marks on the map, with lines marking rivers, bridges, forests and towns. He was seeing those men moving from hedge to hedge, the river they had to cross, the enemy sitting behind machine guns in fortifications dug into the hillsides. He was seeing marshlands and bridges and winding roads and gun firing. To him, the map was a battlefield.

He pointed to a narrow bottleneck between the marshes.

"That's the tough spot," he said. "They knew we had to come through that narrow neck of land, and they were waiting with machine guns. The boys fought like hell and then broke through. Now they are moving along fine."

Some of the doughboys had waded through the marshes in water hip-deep and chest-deep, with guns held above their heads, while bullets spattered around them. And then they had driven the enemy back. Once again the doughboys were in a hedge-to-hedge fight against snipers, machine gunners and mortars. In the first surge they captured more than one hundred Germans. "We've hit an all-German outfit," an officer said. "They've taken everybody out of the front lines except the Germans to make things as hard for us as possible."

"That's okay by us," someone said. "We'd rather kill Germans than those ersatz troops."

The new attack by the doughboys began one week after the capture of Cherbourg while the enemy still was reeling from that swift blow. The move gives a clear indication of the Americans' intention to keep hitting the Germans and if possible give them no chance to get set. □

With American Forces at Balleroy, France, July 3 – One of the strangest battlefield scenes in all the invasion of France occurred in no-man's land near here when eight German nurses captured in Cherbourg were returned to the enemy lines.

For thirty minutes the guns stopped roaring, snipers held their fire and the mortars were silent while two ambulances and a jeep rolled down the lonely road between the lines. A few hundred yards beyond Caumont the procession stopped and Capt. Quentin Roosevelt, son of Brig. Gen. Theodore Roosevelt, and Capt. Fred Chercke stepped out.

They were met by two German officers who had a party of enlisted men well to their rear. The enemy officers saluted stiffly. One said in English, "It's a very hot day, isn't it?"

"Yes, it is," Capt. Roosevelt answered.

And then the German nurses climbed from the ambulance and walked down the road to the German lines. The German officers saluted formally, wheeled and walked away. A few minutes later the guns began booming again.

So far as is known here, this is the first time in World War II where German women have been returned to the enemy. There was no effort at an exchange because the Germans never have captured any American nurses.

This was not an act of chivalry on the part of the Americans. As a matter of fact the Army was glad to be rid of the eight women, who would be only a minor nuisance if held and no one saw any reason why they should be detained since they were non-combatants.

They were captured in an enemy hospital at Cherbourg, but as soon as the Americans were able to handle the enemy wounded they were brought to a rear area and negotiations were started to get them back to their own people. They ranged in age from thirty to fifty-eight. The eldest nurse was a veteran of the First World War, when she served in Russia, Bulgaria, France and other fronts. Most of them were tearfully happy when informed they would not be held prisoners but would be returned to their own lines.

They stayed in an American hospital commanded by Col. Richard Johnson of Chicago, and were under the supervision of Maj. Esther McCafferty of Wilmington, Del. They were given American cigarettes and food and were shown about the hospital which caused one of them to exclaim: "Mein Gott, did you bring all this with you?"

I saw them near the front when they were given a rest while waiting for negotiations to be completed for their transfer. One thirty-year-old woman with streaked blonde hair, a broad forehead and a square jaw, could speak English.

She had been in England to learn the language. Her name was Herta Wist and she was from Karlsruhe. Her husband, a marine captain, had been captured in the arsenal at Cherbourg. Before becoming a nurse a few weeks ago she entertained German soldiers as a pianist. She wore silk stockings with a run in them. On her white jacket was a ribbon given for meritorious service.

"Do you want to go back to Germany?" I asked her.

"Oh, yes, yes, I want to go back. After all, I am a German," she said.

"When do you think the war will be over?" I asked.

"I hope the war will be over very soon," she answered.

"You hope it?"

"I hope it."

"Wouldn't you feel safer in England than in Germany?"

She shrugged. "Everybody would rather be home."

She said everyone in Germany talked of the war and the bombings and were tired of fighting.

"They hope the war will be finished soon in Germany and also in France," the nurse said.

"Do you think Germany will win?"

She shrugged again. "I don't know."   □

With American Troops outside La-Haye-du-Puits, July 4 — Doughboys, battling forward hedge by hedge through heavy German mortar and machine gun fire, moved within two miles of La-Haye-du-Puits today as hard fighting raged along a twenty-five-mile front on the southern part of the Cherbourg Peninsula from Carentan to the sea.

Having gained two to four miles, the Americans sealed the fate of La-Haye when they fought to the top of Hills 121 and 131 and overran positions which Field Marshal Erwin Rommel had inspected and found satisfactory two months ago. Quick-fuse shells from American artillery smashed and sprayed the enemy in ditches and hedgerows.

With a group of artillerymen atop Hill 131 I watched the battle below, moving toward La-Haye. Smoke poured from the town. Through field glasses I could see the spire of a church and the wrecked railway station.

On the road leading west on the next ridge, enemy trucks, self-propelled guns, half-tractors, horse-drawn artillery and motorcycles and carts were moving out of the town. Some Germans were riding bicycles, and there even were herds of cattle in the procession that was hurrying out before the Americans enveloped that avenue of escape.

Farther east smoke was rising from shell bursts where the Americans had pushed south through marshlands and driven the Germans back about a mile farther from Carentan. German artillery has been shelling that area daily in an effort to destroy bridges over the Vire River.

The assault in this sector was led by a gallant lieutenant colonel who limped across the fields on a crutch. One foot is in a cast that reaches almost to his knee. He broke a bone in his foot on D-Day, but returned to his unit and continued to lead his men. To see this man limping into battle was one of the most stirring sights of the entire campaign.

Reaching the hilltop observation post before La-Haye was something of an adventure. With an Australian correspondent I drove along back roads from which German mines had just been removed and reached a unit command post in an old farmhouse. A log was burning in the fireplace and a grandfather clock solemnly ticked off the seconds while a group of officers leaned over a table, studying their maps.

In the courtyard soldiers lounged about, cleaning mud from their caked uniforms and shoes. Chickens clucked unconcernedly in the barnyard, and a white-nosed black kitten looked sleepily from the hayloft.

Pvt. Eddie Bisso, New York, showed me with a map how to reach the observation post. "Go down this road," he said, pointing, "then go down that one. You'll see some white papers on the side of the road. They're booby traps. A little farther is a piece of lumber in the road. There's a mine under it, so don't run over it. When you get to the crossroads where there is a dead German, turn right and keep going."

We followed Eddie's directions and reached the base of Hill 131. There a soldier told us to follow a wire up the hill. We climbed a path through cool shadows of pine and elm trees. One could almost imagine that the war was far away, except for the crash of artillery shells over the hills and the rustle of shells passing overhead. Along the path were slit trenches and discarded German equipment strewn around shelters vacated by the enemy. At one place we found a German radio, its antenna still up and earphones lying beside it as though the enemy operator had been surprised by the Yanks, or else had fled without trying to destroy the equipment.

We pushed through the underbrush to the top of the hill and there in a scrub pine thicket was a group of observers looking down on the rolling country beyond which were Germans. The country looked too lovely to be a battlefield, but from the trees and hedges rose smoke from shell bursts and mortar fire. Guns thundered and there was the rattle of machine guns and small arms.

We lay on a soft matting of fern fronds in the warm sun and watched the enemy moving along the road with shells bursting nearby and tried to follow the progress of the troops through hedgerows. Powerful glasses pulled the scenes up.

Beyond La-Haye lay the town of Lessay, near the coast, and as I looked at the white buildings across the ridgetops there were tremendous flashes and smoke boiled up. Then I saw our bombers overhead.

Little Cub planes floated lazily over the enemy lines with nothing in the air to disturb their leisurely observation of enemy gun positions and movements. □

With the American Troops near La-Haye-du-Puits, July 4 — The beachhead battleground has a new arrival, a seven-pound patriot born almost in the front lines. His name is Daniel Jean and he kept an American doctor from his duties for two hours while making his arrival just as American troops were liberating his home from German control.

Maj. Daniel McIlvoy, Springfield, Ky., was going to visit a front-line unit two nights ago when an excited Frenchman rushed out of a little farmhouse and told the doctor his wife was having her child and would he deliver the baby?

The major got the chaplain's assistant, a private who speaks French, and followed the Frenchman into the house. In the rays of a flashlight McIlvoy delivered the child.

"It was a boy," grinned McIlvoy, "and they named him Daniel in my honor." □

First Division Command Post in France (Balleroy), [July 4] — Heroes of the Fighting First Division who led the American assault on France and lived to cross that hellish strip of beach where so many fell, stood in the shade of the tall Normandy elms Monday and received an accolade from Gen. Dwight D. Eisenhower.

They had tried to clean the stains of battle from their clothing for the occasion, but still their uniforms showed that they had just returned from the front, not far away.

No one cared about spit and polish with these men—least of all General "Ike," who pinned Distinguished Service Crosses on the chests of twenty-two and gave the Legion of Merit Award to two others. These were the elite of the infantry regiment. They had come through a test as great as any soldier ever faced and by their courage and leadership had opened the way for thousands of troops to follow. They stood at attention on the lawn of an old gray chateau when jeeps carrying Gen. Eisenhower, Lt. Gen. Omar N. Bradley and Maj. Gen. Leonard T. Gerow halted before their ranks.

General "Ike" jumped out, smiling. He wore a garrison cap, an air force jacket belted at the waist, and his trousers stuffed into parachute trooper boots. The three generals shook hands with Maj. Gen. C. R. Huebner, commanding the First Division, and an officer began reading the names of men receiving the awards.

"Brigadier General Clift Andrus . . ."

I remembered that thunderous morning of D-Day when this tall, square-jawed man moved up and down the beach with absolute disregard for his own safety, organizing the troops and moving them inland against strongpoints which were pouring murderous fire into our ranks.

"Colonel George A. Taylor . . . "

The colonel had stood on the beach where thousands of men were pinned down by enemy fire and said in a quiet drawl: "Gentlemen, we are being killed on the beaches—let's move inland and be killed." His men surged forward and broke the German defenses.

"Lt. Col. Herbert C. Hicks, Spartanburg, S.C. . . . "

Troops of his command spearheaded the assault on the Atlantic wall, and his gallantry and that of his men contributed greatly to D-Day's success.

"Maj. Charles E. Tetgmeyer, Hamilton, N.Y. . . . "

Under heavy fire Tetgmeyer covered the length of the beach administering to wounded, then went repeatedly into the mine-strewn water to pull out wounded.

"Capt. Victor R. Briggs, New York City. . . . "

His unit was the first to come off the beach and he deliberately walked away across a minefield alone to draw enemy fire and give his men a chance to move up behind him.

"Capt. Kimbell R. Richmond, Windsor, Vt. . . . "

His assault boat grounded 400 yards from the beach. He and his men swam on in through artillery and machine gun fire and then attacked.

"Capt. Thomas M. Marendino, Ventnor, N.J. . . . "

He led his men in a charge up a slope and overran a German strongpoint under heavy fire.

"Lt. Carl W. Giles, Jr., Gest, Ky. . . . "

His landing craft was sunk by enemy fire. He swam ashore, pulled to safety three men hit in the water, and with most of the officers of his unit casualties he assumed command and carried out the mission.

And so on down the list to Pfc. Peter Cavaliere, Bristol, R.I., who went forward to set up an observation post, was surrounded by Germans, shot eight, and clung to the position.

As Gen. Eisenhower moved down the double rank he spoke a few words to each man, asking him his job and where he was from in the United States. After pinning on the medals, he called the group around him.

"I'm not going to make a speech," he said, "but this simple little ceremony gives me opportunity to come over here and through you say thanks. You are one of the finest regiments in our Army. I know your record from the day you landed in North Africa and through Sicily. I am beginning to think that your regiment is sort of a praetorian guard which goes along with me and gives me luck.

"I know you want to go home, but I demanded if I came up here that you would have to come up with me. You've got what it takes to finish the job.

"If you will do me a favor when you go back you will spread the word through the regiment that I am terrifically proud and grateful to them. To all you fellows, good luck, keep on top of them, and so long."   □

On the Normandy Front, July 4 — For almost two years the townspeople in the village of Les Pieux have filed past a little cemetery and placed flowers at the base of crosses in the churchyard. The inscription on the crosses read: "Those who died for the country deserve our prayers." They are the graves of American fliers whose planes crashed near the village November 12, 1942. This is the story told by the people of Les Pieux.

On that November afternoon a flight of American bombers droned over. German anti-aircraft batteries opened up on them and for a time it looked as though the enemy's defenses had no effect. But suddenly two of the bombers burst into flames and crashed nearby. Frenchmen took the bodies from the wreckage. They arranged a mass funeral in the gray stone Catholic Church but when they arrived at the church in their Sunday best, German guards refused them entry.

The bodies were then buried in the churchyard. Each Sunday when the flowers are in bloom French civilians come and drop them on the graves. Each week the local butcher spends two hours tending this little American cemetery.   □

With American Troops outside La Haye-du-Puits [July 5] — American troops, fighting across Normandy's sun-washed fields in an effort to trap enemy troops still fighting in La-Haye-du-Puits, have left but one narrow escape corridor for the enemy. Even this one road to the south is under the direct fire of guns of American troops who have driven to the east and southwest of the crossroads town. Yesterday doughboys captured the railway station and railyards in the northern part of La-Haye but after holding it for several hours they pulled back to await further progress.

For a time one of the hottest battlegrounds on the entire front was along the sunken road in the marshland southeast of La-Haye where our tanks caught a large German patrol this morning. The tanks sprayed the Germans with machine guns and wiped out almost the entire group, although the Germans fought savagely. Capt. Chester Pasternik of Chicopee Falls, Mass., discovered one of the prisoners taken was a cousin.

The greatest advance of the day was southwest of Carentan where doughboys, sweating under a blazing sky, battered their way forward hedge by hedge for 2,000 yards. The Germans threw in a sharp counter-attack and pushed the Americans back 500 yards, but the doughboys held on to a 1,500-yard gain which was aimed at bursting through marshland bottlenecks.

On other sectors of the American front the doughboys drove forward in the third day of the attack and captured the town of Culot, four miles south of Carentan, after beating back a strong enemy counter-attack.   □

Bolleville, France, July 6 — Nobody ever heard of Bolleville except a few Frenchmen until the doughboys moved in today on their way to La-Haye-du-Puits, which the Germans don't want us to have. It's just a gray cluster of houses on the roadside with the spire of a square church jutting into the sky above gray slate roofs—a lonely, sad hamlet of vacant houses looking tired and somber.

Occasionally a jeep dashes up the road before the enemy can get the range for a shell. At a road intersection a soldier lounges against an embankment, taking shelter from occasional shells which crash nearby. He looks curiously at our jeep as it stops.

"Where's regimental headquarters?" we ask.

He shrugged. "Don't know," he says. "Back there somewhere." He waved vaguely down the road over which we'd driven without seeing markers.

"What's up ahead?"

"Germans," he said.

More shells fell near and we jumped from the jeep into a ditch beside him. "Sort of hot, isn't it?" we said.

"It's hotter up the road a little way." Then he grinned and said, "our command post is in a house just around the corner."

We walked down a lane and through a barnyard into the courtyard of a small house. Doughboys were resting from battle. They'd just come out of the line after leading an attack toward La-Haye a mile away, and they were tired. One youth lay sleeping just inside the door of the house on a bare floor. Another had a broken mirror propped up on a stone and was shaving in a bucket of cold water.

Lieut. N. E. Otto, Chevy Chase, Md., talked to two French civilians.

"These guys say there are about two dozen Germans still hiding in a barn over there," Otto said.

"Well, check on it," somebody said.

A lieutenant colonel rose wearily from in front of a map on which he had marked the positions of our troops. "These babies are tough," he said. "They are all Germans and are fighting in every hedge. Know what they do? They get an embankment under the hedges and set up machine guns covering every field. Soon as our boys move into the field they open up on all sides."

He rubbed his hand through his hair. "They are pretty good, but we are learning how to take care of them. We learned a lot in these last two days. Our casualties today are less than a fourth of what they were yesterday. That means we are learning."

We walked back into the sunshine of the courtyard and he turned to Pvt. George Decrocker, Kalamazoo, Mich., and said: "Decrocker, tell him about those Germans you captured." The tall, strong-jawed youth with a three days' growth of beard on his chin hitched the carbine on his shoulder and smiled.

"We were working through the hedges yesterday and I saw two Germans walking along a hedgerow. I went over and jumped across the hedge and landed right in the middle of a bunch of Germans. They threw up their hands and I counted seventeen. There were a few too many for me, so I called for the boys to come over and help march 'em back."

By this time a small crowd had gathered around.

"I'll tell you who did a great job," said Maj. R. E. Jess, Raleigh, N.C. "It was the medics."

He pointed to Capt. J. G. Moore, Berkeley, Calif., and Chaplain Jerome Healy of Canon City, Colo.

"My boys did fine work," Moore said. "They go right into the front to bring back wounded. Some of them have been wounded, too. They have to carry litters from 200 to 300 yards to jeeps and then bring the wounded to the casualty clearing station."

The major interrupted. "Yeah, and this guy goes out himself and gets the wounded just like his men. He wouldn't tell you that. And so does the chaplain."

Healy, who taught at Holy Cross Abbey in Canon City, smiled. "Well, when they are short of litter bearers and need help I go out and give 'em a hand," he said. "You know, I even learned how to give plasma."

The little farmhouse trembled with the crash of shells. Bolleville looked ever sadder and more dismal in the late afternoon sun. Tomorrow these men will have moved on in an attack against the enemy, leaving Bolleville forgotten on the roadside—a name only a few people ever will remember. □

With American Troops outside La-Haye-du-Puits, July 7 — The Germans are making a miniature Stalingrad of the crossroads town of La-Haye-du-Puits and when the thunder of battle has rolled beyond, it will be a torn and beaten pile of wreckage. The Germans decided to make a stand in La-Haye and in the heights and hedgerows around this highway junction, and that means death for any city in this war, where artillery seeks out enemy strongpoints and pounds them mercilessly.

Our advance elements drove into the outskirts of La-Haye today after other troops had pushed forward in a slow, bitter battle to win objectives to the southwest and southeast of the town. They fought from house to house with machine guns, bayonets and hand grenades, rooting out the enemy who was making a desperate bid to hold his strategic position. In each house, or pile of rubble that once was a house, the Germans had set up a strongpoint.

"This is tougher than the Cherbourg defenses," said Capt. Donald Bovee of St. Johnsbury, Vt. "This fighting is the hardest we have hit yet."

The enemy is making a desperate stand to hold on at La-Haye as long as possible and delay the Americans from breaking out of the Cherbourg Peninsula bottlenecks which are hemmed in by marshy lowlands. But despite the stubborn defenses, the doughboys are making progress in the envelopment of the town.

Our infantry has had one of the hardest fights of the campaign in seizing the heights about a mile southwest of La-Haye. In this rolling country of thick woods and hedgerows, the Germans had built underground strongpoints—dugouts reinforced with thick logs over which the earth is piled. They are built so that grass and flowers are grown over them. They blend with the terrain and are barely visible at one hundred yards.

The Germans counter-attacked late today in an effort to retake the heights but ran into heavy artillery fire and determined American resistance.

Near La-Haye the Germans battered holes through the walls of houses and ran tanks into them to make small fortresses in the path of the American advance. But despite this defense, the Yanks captured the heights and then dug in to hold on to their gains.

Already La-Haye is virtually destroyed from the pounding of artillery at the end of the fifth day of attack. But as in Cassino the enemy has taken shelter in the ruins and is fighting from house to house in obvious desperation to deny the doughboys control of this communications center.

But the American troops are closing slowly around La-Haye, and the hour of decision is drawing near. ☐

With the American Troops in France, July 7 – The invasion of France has proved that the basic training of the American Army is sound.

In the thirty-one days of battle in Normandy, Yank doughboys have whipped veterans with five years of war behind them. The American invasion forces did have a hard core of troops who had fought in North Africa, Sicily and Italy, but the greater part were "green divisions"—men who never fired a shot in anger until they hit the beaches.

These doughboys have learned fast. They have made mistakes and know that war is different than field maneuvers at home. When a man plays for keeps, he soon learns that crashing explosions and whining bullets are things that kill and maim. Changed now are thoughts that months of training were just monotonous grind and trouble, and that officers just were being too tough with drills, rehearsals, rifle practice, marches and maneuvers in England.

Before the invasion Lieut. Gen. Omar N. Bradley expressed confidence in the infantry; he said American troops were ready for the job ahead of them. General Bradley, who is largely responsible for invasion training, was the commanding officer of the infantry school at Fort Benning, Ga., before he went to North Africa to take over command of the American Second Corps.

Doughboys aren't supermen, none thinks he can whip ten Germans single-handed—any front-line soldier would laugh down anyone who suggested it. The German is termed a good soldier, a tough enemy. But, odds equal, the Yank thinks he is a better fighting man than the German.

Britain's Gen. Sir Bernard L. Montgomery before the invasion said that if the Germans were put on a piece of land and left there long enough, "it takes a bit of doing to get them off." Although the Germans were in France for four years, Americans are doing that bit.

Observe the work of the Fourth and Seventy-ninth Infantry Divisions and the 101st Airborne Division on the Cherbourg Peninsula: the 101st spearheaded the invasion. Its men dropped behind the lines to disrupt communications, knock out concentrations, and prevent massing of reserves— protecting the landing of the Fourth Division.

Both divisions did a job. They won the beachhead and opened a path for other troops. Then, in the big drive on Cherbourg, the Fourth and Seventy-ninth teamed with veterans from the Ninth. Those "green divisions" burst through some of the strongest fortifications on the entire beachhead. It was the first time they had hit anything like those fortresses, but the doughboys went through. The gains were made against troops seasoned in the battle of France, in Poland, Russia and Italy, and the campaign was impressive.

American troops admit they still have much to learn but they feel assured their basic knowledge will carry them through. □

With American Troops in France, [July 7] – Throwing armor into the attack across the Vire River, Lt. Gen. Omar N. Bradley's American troops battered the enemy back today southeast of Carentan and captured the town of St-Jean-de-Daye. The swift attack of the doughboys across the Vire River east of the town and over the thirty-five-foot Vire et Taute Canal north of St-Jean swept the enemy back and placed our troops beyond marchlands through which they had to fight their way.

At noon our troops were astride the main road from St-Jean-de-Daye to St-Lô about eight miles to the south, and across the lateral east-west road just south of St-Jean. With a firm bridgehead across the river and canal, the Americans committed armor to the battle and sent tanks rumbling across bridges erected by engineers yesterday in spectacular defiance of German artillery and mortar fire.

The tanks smashed their way along a dry ridge running from Cavigny to Saint-Gilles, blasting at the enemy, who was dug into hedgerows along the high ground. The advance continuing south and west of St-Jean, is straightening out a bulge in the American lines northeast of St-Lô while other American forces are battering at the enemy all the way from the Vire River westward to the sea.

On the west our troops continued their enveloping operation against La-Haye-du-Puits with no immediate reports of advance elements having penetrated beyond the outskirts of the town, where they fought house to house battles yesterday, digging the Germans out of the rubble and wreckage.

There was no official confirmation from front-line troops whether the main north-south road out of St-Jean-de-Daye had been cut by our troops, but positions of the advance elements place them near the highway.

Regrouping during the night, the doughboys continued a hedge to hedge assault at dawn all along the line to slowly push farther south. The slashing attack and spectacular bridging of the river and canal apparently caught the Germans by surprise and now they are trying desperately to stem the advance by leaving suicide squads behind to disrupt elements following up the assault troops.

"We are running into a well-trained enemy," an officer said. "They lie hidden in a hedgerow or tall grass until our assault troops pass them by, then open up shooting from the rear. Our men don't have much sympathy for an enemy who shoots them in the back."

The Germans had no concrete positions in this area, but had dugouts walled with thick logs, trenches and foxholes from which they fight with machine guns, machine pistols and mortars. The advance carried well past small hamlets and La Goucherie, west of St-Jean-de-Daye.

Success of the attack lay in the magnificent job the engineers did in bridging the river and canal when the doughboys had a bridgehead only 400 or 500 yards in depth. When the request was made for a bridge behind the Infantry, the engineers' commanding officer declared that if the Infantry would put down a smoke screen, his men would bridge the canal, even though the area was under small arms fire and enemy shelling.

At 5 a.m. yesterday the request was made for the smoke screen at 5:30 a.m., and it was right on schedule. Twenty minutes later the engineers had a bridge across the canal.   □

St-Jean-de-Daye [July 7] — In the lonely Place Du Marché in the center of this broken little village there was only one living thing when the doughboys moved through the streets today—a brown kitten, looking forlorn and bedraggled in the wreckage. It curled in a shattered window and looked inquiringly at passing troops as though searching to find a friend among all the destruction. If anyone stopped nearby the kitten would jump from the window and rub against his legs.

All the people fled from this village when the thunder of guns drew near. They left their shops and houses and went into the country to find safety from the battle that raged about their homes.

Our troops captured St-Jean-de-Daye this morning in a drive across the

Vire River and the Vire et Taute Canal which began yesterday morning. The doughboys battled their way west and south, driving the enemy back with another desolate village behind them. Soon the villagers will come straggling back to their homes and some order will be brought out of the wreckage. But now St-Jean-de-Daye is deserted except for troops moving along the road. Under the direction of a lone M.P.   □

With the American Troops in France, July 8 — Field Marshal Rommel had planned before the invasion to smash the Allies' armada and equipment while it was still afloat and attempting to reach the beaches. By building up the Atlantic Wall fortifications he had hoped to make the coastal defenses of France impregnable to attack—so strong that the Allies would not even be able to break through from the beaches.

This was disclosed in a captured report by Rommel to his field commanders on April 22 after he had inspected the Atlantic Wall and expressed satisfaction with it. In discussing the beach defenses, Rommel declared in his report: "Again I have to emphasize the purposes of these defenses. The enemy will most probably attempt to land by night and by fog after a tremendous shelling by artillery and bombers. They will employ hundreds of ships, unloading amphibious vehicles and waterproofed and submersible tanks.

"We must stop him in the water, not only delaying him, but destroying all his equipment while it is still afloat. Some units do not seem to have realized the value of this type of defense."

This was an unusual passage in the report, since Rommel, so-called master of mobile warfare, was emphasizing the importance of a static defense and apparently relying on this to whip the Allies on the beaches. The report confirms the belief expressed by Gen. Sir Bernard L. Montgomery before the invasion that Rommel would try to destroy the invasion forces on the beaches. But Rommel put too much faith in the Atlantic Wall, without mobile reserves within striking distance to back up the front-line defenses.

"Almost without exception unusual progress has been made in all sectors of defense groups in accordance with the seriousness of the situation," the report read. "I have expressed my satisfaction to the commanders and troops for the fine coordination of all the available forces and the clever employment of the civilian population."

Regarding this, he said: "In the short time left before the enemy operations start, it is necessary that all commands employ every single man at the utmost for the reinforcement of all defense areas and to use any one of the civilian population who can be used. Most units have acted accordingly, but I still noticed some who did not comply. One company, for instance, is still training its troops two hours in the morning and two hours in the afternoon in contrast to the divisional order which allows only one day a week for this purpose. In this company's beach sector, obstacles are very thinly spaced and there are no obstacles at all against airborne troops in the rear areas. This is against all orders and must be changed."

"The time seems to be near," Rommel said, "when the coast will no longer be capable of being penetrated, because of the strength of its obstacles and the fortress-like defenses, and the enemy will have to employ numerous airborne troops to solve the problem from the land. It may be that the enemy shortly will launch a mass attack by simultaneous employment of all their strength and put into action a mass of their airborne troops on the first day. It may be to crush units manning the coastal defenses in the sector between the sea and land by mass employment of divisions attacking in the direction of the coast so as to succeed in breaking open the coastal defenses.

"The enemy is capable of landing three divisions from the air in any chosen area within three minutes and of forming units of battle shortly after landing. As airborne troops are committed mainly on moonlight nights or at twilight, or at dawn, it will be necessary to be especially watchful at these times." □

La-Haye-du-Puits, France, July 9 — Skylarking infantrymen on captured bicycles and German shells are giving combat military police a traffic problem in this blitzed village.

The village itself has been devastated by the rocking artillery and aerial bombardment and nothing is moving in the deserted ruins except crouching doughboys and five young screwballs whizzing around town on German bicycles, heedless of occasional sniper bullets. This is their day to celebrate—they found a bottle of cognac in one enemy dugout—and they are making the most of it.

"Look out or you'll get yourself killed," shouts Pfc. Joe Harshkowitz, thirty-two-years old, of 772 Henry Street, Brooklyn, a military policeman directing traffic at the center of town in front of a shell-racked cathedral.

French inhabitants of the town fled so quickly they had no time to gather many personal effects and the gaping doors and blasted windows disclose interiors disordered by German looters. Some of those Germans now are lying dead by their gun positions, with the rain dripping off their upturned, ghastly faces.

Tech. Sgt. John H. Strouss of Muncie, Pa., just returning from a sniper hunt, told of the tactics used in the desperate attempt by the Germans to hold this supply channel.

"Most of their snipers held their fire until we got in the center of town," he said, "then they cut loose on us all at once. You never can tell where you will find those babies. Some even have been hiding in the big chimneys of those old houses. They take a pot shot and drop back into the chimney."

Maj. Francis Jenkins of Charleston, S.C., declared: "In this town the enemy had organized especially strong in an old château and it was here we had the roughest time.

"They were able to stand up under our shelling and bombing because of the depth and strength of their shelters. They would just go inside until the bombardment was over and then come out ready to catch our infantry moving in as soon as the shelling lifted. They had all roads mined and plenty of automatic weapons and 88s that covered the north part of town.

"The troops ahead of us—they really did the main job of cleaning out this place—finally located this 88 by the château and their riflemen shot up its crew. After that they pushed right through and after taking a batch of fifty-seven prisoners kept right on going.

"Mopping up, however, has been something of a job. Those Germans are extremely tricky. We clean out one house and the Nazi slips into it from another side. They know the town backward and forward. It is slow going to root them out—pick and shovel work. We had some casualties but fewer than expected."   ☐

With the American Army in France, July 10 — Breaking through the Germans' strong defenses around La-Haye-du-Puits, American troops drove south today along the road to Lessay, opening a broad exit through the base of the Cotentin Peninsula.

Stubborn enemy defenses cracked open when the doughboys stormed through La-Haye and then began moving ahead swiftly against scattered knots of resistance. The Germans began falling back to their next line of defense. All along the American line from the Vire River in the center of the Normandy front, to the sea on the west, the Yanks were smashing at the Germans in a cold drizzle. Fog hung low over the marshy lowlands, reducing visibility and muffling the thunder of hundreds of guns.

All last night and today the Americans kept heavy artillery pouring fire on the enemy's positions. There was an almost steady crash of guns and there rarely was a time when one hundred rounds a minute could not be counted. Guns, trucks and armored rolled along the muddy roads, churning up a brown ooze. The long columns caused one to marvel at the mass of equipment concentrated in Normandy, which only a short time ago was only a beachhead.

South of St-Jean-de-Daye American troops were supported by tanks and armored vehicles, which patrolled roads and lanes with their guns spraying the enemy's hiding places in trees and hedgerows. The fighting moved south of Cavigny in this sector after the Americans yesterday beat back a German counter-attack in which twenty Nazi tanks were used.

"Our artillery kept the Germans in muddy foxholes for three weeks and they were rarely able to get out," said Lieut. E. J. Karrigan of Aberdeen, S.D., former managing editor of the *Aberdeen American News*. "They say they never experienced anything like our artillery fire which keep pouring in day and night."

Prisoners said they had been able to get only one hot meal a day and that was delivered to them at night from kitchens in the rear. One fanatic prisoner from an elite SS unit was arrogant when captured in the St-Jean sector and boasted that the Germans would win the war.

"But he changed his tune when he got to the rear areas and saw our equipment and supplies along the road," said Capt. John Carbin, 389 Communipaw Avenue, Jersey City, N.J. "He began writing and became more dejected every mile. I never saw a man change so fast."

Karrigan said the Germans not only were booby-trapping bodies of the dead but "even booby-trapped the body of one German that wasn't dead. When the Americans approached he raised up and showed them the booby-trap wire which would have blown him up if anyone had moved him."

The drive toward the south from La-Haye put the Americans in control of one of the enemy's strongest defensive positions along the entire line and uncorked one of the three exit corridors from the peninsula. From a map study it appeared the enemy's next strong defensive line south of La-Haye is likely to be at Lessay where there is another bottleneck between marshes and the sea. Lessay is about four miles south of La-Haye and an important road junction.   □

With American Troops North of St-Lô, July 11 — The American First Army attacked at dawn today toward St-Lô behind the drumroll thunder of hundreds of big guns, and fighting raged across a forty-mile front in the Cherbourg Peninsula to the sea.

I have just returned from a visit to forward units and early reports were that our troops were making slow but steady progress toward objectives north and east of St-Lô, center of an important network of roads, and one of the strongest German points on the entire front. Gray, threatening skies prevented close support by dive-bombers.

The G.I.s came out of the soggy foxholes at 6 a.m. after their artillery had sprayed the Germans with a terrific barrage which still was crashing at noon. In almost two years of war I never have heard such a steady blasting of big guns. "There's just no use trying to sleep," said Maj. Paul Krznarich of Mesa, Ariz. "They have been shaking the ground all night."

It seemed that there were guns in every field. I tried to count reports of 105-millimeter Long Toms during a sixty-second period but gave up at the count of seventy because the crashes were blending together in an unearthly cacophony. It was impossible to tell whether two or ten guns were firing at the same time.

A heavy concentration of artillery was thrown at the Germans on St-André-de-L'Epine about two miles northeast of St-Lô, where the enemy had a strong position in the path of the foot-sloggers' advance.

Armor went in to support the infantry and "hose" hedgerows with machine gun bullets, looking for German snipers. When necessary, the troops dynamited paths through hedgerows for tanks to plow through into the next field. The Americans smashed into elements of SS troops, sent in to stiffen lines.

On the western end of the front, where the doughboys broke through the enemy's anchor positions at La-Haye-du-Puits, the advance south continued with the enemy falling back on the next line of defense. This is likely to be the high ground behind coastal Lessay, which sits in a bottleneck of an estuary and marshlands. South of Carentan, American troops fought their way down the Périers Road to the vicinity of the village of La Maugerie, eight miles from Carentan.

Spread of the attack along the central beachhead front broke a comparative lull there of about three weeks, and increased the tempo of the drive south from the neck of the Cotentin Peninsula. Now the American advances are becoming a grave threat to the lateral road network between La-Haye-du-Puits, Périers and St-Lô. The major objectives of the Americans are those heights controlling the terrain in that area, but to reach them the troops must fight their way hedge by hedge. St-Lô, a town of 15,000 population, is an industrial, agricultural and communications center on the outer bend of the Vire River.

"During the lull on this front," said Major Krznarich, "the enemy had time to dig, string up booby traps, and mine the area. That means slow going to break through the crust of defenses."

In the early morning as the doughboys were getting ready for their attack, the Germans laid down an artillery barrage in the area north of St-Lô and put on a counter-attack under cover of darkness. At the same time they laid forbidding fire on crossroads and bridges along the Vire River.

"They laid a lot of stuff around the Vire where our troops made a river crossing the other day," said Capt. Larry Lane, West Haven, Conn.

In the darkness the enemy infiltrated advance lines north of St-Lô with about a company, but Americans were mopping them up this morning and returning artillery fire tenfold. Most of the enemy encountered in the new drive in the St-Lô area are Germans, with few "ersatz" troops among them. These defenders took one of the worst beatings by artillery in the entire beachhead campaign.   □

Near St-Lô, France, [July 12] (6:18 p.m.) – American infantrymen slugged slowly through German defense outside St-Lô today and tonight were less than two miles from the city on the eastern side. The Germans were making a savage yard-by-yard defense of the city on which they hinged their line to control the St-Lô-Périers-Lessay lateral highway. The doughboys were driving toward that road all along the front.

Fields and hedgerows on the ridges before St-Lô were littered with enemy dead. The Germans took a terrible beating under that mighty artillery barrage which thundered from dawn to dusk yesterday. From a ridgetop could be seen gruesome evidence of the price the enemy paid trying to stem the drive of the Americans who came through the hedgerows behind the crash of shells. Bodies lay in stiff, grotesque positions in ditches and along the thick, green hedges torn by shrapnel and clipped by machine gun bullets.

The Americans had covered the bodies of most of the dead with the enemy's own blankets or with rain shelters. Only their feet stuck out, with the toes of their boots pointing to the sky. Later they will be taken away and buried.

The Americans maintained pressure on the enemy from the east and north of St-Lô but the Germans held on desperately as long as possible. At the same time, the enemy was withdrawing down the western side of the front below La-Haye-du-Puits. The swift drive south from La-Haye today had reached a line south of Angoville-sur-Ay, which is about two miles from the Lessay Road. The troops made a two-mile advance in this sector with the enemy fighting a hard rearguard action.

East of La-Haye, the doughboys cleaned out all of Mont Castre Forest, and then moved on south against the Germans delaying action, in which the enemy developed a new type of defense with 88-millimeter guns. The Germans now are using this high velocity weapon in the front line to fire at point-blank range at the advancing doughboys. The guns fire a few rounds at one place, then move to another where the gun barrels are poked through the hedgerows to cover the advancing line. But in getting their guns this far forward the Germans also take the risk of losing weapons and having the crews wiped out by infantrymen closing in through the hedges.

After weeks without making an appearance, German planes staged a weak raid on La-Haye-du-Puits, and two bombs dropped on the town while other planes strafed roads.

North of St-Lô the enemy put in a counter-attack across the Vire River in an attempt to hit one unit's flank and disrupt the drive southward, but this thrust was smashed by artillery and infantry fire while U.S. troops pushed west of St-Jean-de-Daye to straighten out the line. The infantry passed through the hamlet of St-Georges-d'Elle, and drove on 1,000 yards against comparatively light opposition.   □

With the U.S. Army before St-Lô, July 13 — The fall of St-Lô is drawing near. The savage southern drive of Gen. Bradley's Americans has strained the enemy's defenses almost to the breaking point and the Germans are using rear echelon troops in a desperate effort to prevent a breakthrough, a staff officer declared today.

Moving slowly in on St-Lô, the eastern anchor of the Lessay-St-Lô line, the doughboys are within sight of the city and are battling to sweep the stubborn Nazis from hills overlooking the town from the southeast. Already this important communications hub is untenable for the Germans and is of no value to them except as a rubble-filled fortress from which to fight a delaying action.

American guns can fire point-blank into the town and sweep the roads radiating from it. St-Lô is beaten and battered, with gaunt, shell-wrecked buildings and streets piled high with debris, said civilians who came through our lines. An indication that the German High Command plans to hold it as long as possible is the fact that the most fanatical Nazi troops have been thrown in to defend it.

To the northwest, American troops were little more than a half mile from Les-Champs-de-Losque on the junction of two main roads south of the Bois du Hommet south of Carentan. They also reached the outskirts of Le-Hommet-d'Arthenay, six miles northwest of St-Lô and on the road from St-Jean-de-Daye to Les-Champs-de-Losque.

There is growing confusion in the Germans' entire line. A Nazi officer rode in to the village of La Stelle, near St-Lô, without knowing the place was in American hands. "Their communications are so bad they don't know where the front lines are," an American officer said.   □

With the American Army in France, July 14 — Adolf Hitler is making a strong effort to gain political as well as military control of the German Army with appointment of political commissars whose duties are to indoctrinate troops with his theories of National Socialism and suppress any discontent with the Nazi regime or the course of the war.

Under a plan already operative, every company commander in the army must become not only a military leader of his men in the field but also an instructor responsible to the commissar for the education of his troops in Nazism. This was disclosed today in a remarkable captured enemy document which was distributed to company commanders throughout the German Army upon appointment of the Nazi commissars.

With every battalion there was supposed to be a Führungsoffizier, or guiding officer, to look after the interests of Hitler and the National Socialist party by supervising organization of Nazi "cells" within each company. Not only is military leadership expected of the battalion company commanders and the men they choose to help them but they must also be examples to their men with the proper political attitude.

In effect, the Nazis are building up a Gestapo within the ranks of the German Army to force adherence to National Socialism ideas, strengthen Hitler's hold on Germany's armed might, bolster drooping morale and suppress any actions or talk about Germany losing the war.   □

With American Troops outside St-Lô, July 14 — The fall of St-Lô is drawing near. The savage southern drive of Lt. Gen. Omar N. Bradley's Americans has strained the enemy's defenses almost to the breaking point and the Germans are using rear echelon troops in a desperate effort to prevent a breakthrough overrunning their entire line, a staff officer declared.

Moving slowly in on St-Lô, the eastern anchor of the Lessay-St-Lô line, the doughboys are within sight of the city from heights a mile and a half east of the town and are battling to sweep the stubborn Nazis from hills overlooking the town from the southeast. Already this important communications hub is untenable for the Germans and is of no value to them except as a rubble-filled fortress from which they may fight a delaying action. American guns can fire point-blank into the town or sweep the roads radiating from it. St-Lô is another beaten, battered town, with gaunt, shell-wrecked buildings and streets piled high with debris, said civilians who came through the American lines.

An indication that the German High Command hopes to hold the town as long as possible and make it as costly to the American Army as possible is seen in the fact that the most fanatical Nazi troops have been thrown in to defend it. On the lower slopes of this ridge which points at St-Lô like a dagger, the infantry is fighting slowly forward toward the doomed city lying in the haze a mile and a half away. Half a mile below us is the rapid fire of a German machine gun—a "burp gun" the infantrymen call it because it makes an uncouth noise like a sudden belch.

At the entrance to the command post on the ridgetop—a heavily logged dugout—Capt. Robert E. Walker of Council Bluffs, Ia., pointed out the troop disposition on a map. "It's pretty confused right now," he said. "There are little pockets and gaps in the lines where they are behind our lines and we are behind theirs."

"They are not much to look at, but they fight hard," Walker said of the German parachute troops, many of whom are on this front. "The prisoners we have taken smell like they had been living in the ground at least two weeks without a bath."

We walked down from the ridgetop to a command post of the advance battalion where Walker said we might get a close look at the enemy lines. From another logged dugout crawled Capt. Charles Cawthon of Murfreesboro, Tenn.

"You can't go up to the observation post," he said. "We got only one man there and in the next hedgerow are Jerries."

A tall, lean soldier walked up. He was Lieut. Bernard Boettcher of New York City. "I'm going up and yell over to them to surrender and tell them if they don't we'll blow hell out of them with our artillery," he said.

Boettcher said a group of Germans whose nerve [sic] snapped under the artillery fire started for U.S. lines to surrender last night but a shell crashed into them.

"Two prisoners said another man started to surrender, but an officer shot him in the back," Cawthon added.

"Where's Noonan," asked Lieut. Alvin Uhlfelder, Baltimore, Md., a forward observer.

In a few minutes Noonan—Pfc. Harry H. Noonan, Santa Ana, Calif., came up. Uhlfelder said Noonan climbed a tree yesterday to direct artillery fire when six or seven Nazi tanks were seen moving up to the front, and four of them were believed knocked out.

"I learned to climb trees when I was just a kid," Noonan grinned. "I was sitting up there while they were sniping away at me. The tanks were about 300 yards away behind a hedgerow." □

Outside St-Lô, July 14 — While the French joyously celebrated Bastille Day behind the lines, American doughboys battered the enemy back all along the front today except at St-Lô, where the Germans fought fanatically to stem the tide closing in on them. East of St-Lô the Americans strengthened their positions, while other troops moved slowly toward the city from the north and tightened the nutcracker closing about this communications hub.

With the exception of St-Lô there is one description of the progress on the entire line to the sea—a slow steady advance against bitter rearguard action. The Germans are throwing in more and more reserves piecemeal, in an effort to prevent the Americans from breaking through and enveloping thinning defenses, reinforced somewhat by heavier artillery.

The advance averaged 1,000 yards along the line, even through marshes which have been a hazard since the Americans began the drive to break out of the Cotentin Peninsula. The Germans are putting every available soldier into the front line. Some very young troops who arrived from Germany only eight or ten days ago have been captured. The enemy counter-attacked with infantry and tanks southwest of Carentan, but the doughboys held their ground and inflicted heavy losses.

The contrast between big healthy-looking American troops and under-sized, ill-fed enemy troops has been one of the surprises in this campaign, when it is considered the Germans have been using elite paratroopers and SS men. □

Outside St-Lô, July 15 — The battle for St-Lô, raging through its fifth bitter and bloody day, thundered toward a climax today with big German and American guns dueling in the heaviest shelling of the action for this crossroads town. U.S. infantrymen attacked again at dawn this morning, and edged slowly forward against stubborn Nazi resistance to about 2,000 yards—little more than a mile—of the city's outskirts.

With mobile 758 and 888 ranging the ridge roads southeast of St-Lô, the Germans poured heavy fire on our advancing troops, and threw in long-range fire from south of the city to give support to the parachute-troop defenders. Machine guns, Browning automatic rifles and carbines kept up a continuous clatter all morning as the doughboys swept the hedgerows with heavy fire and dug the enemy out of his hiding places. But it was a yard-by-yard advance, the sternest kind of opposition. "These troops are tougher than those on the beaches," said Maj. William Bratton of Elkton, Md. "There are fewer non-Germans among them and they are real fanatics."

Allied headquarters revealed that between twenty and twenty-five German divisions, 300,000 to 375,000 men, are now in Normandy with eleven or twelve of the crack Nazi divisions facing the American front.

In one sector where our troops advanced about half a mile through shell-torn fields there was not a single dead German found. The enemy was taking every precaution to keep the dead from being left on the battlefield where they would be seen by the Americans. As soon as a man fell he was dragged away by his comrades.

There is little cause for optimism over a possible sudden breakthrough by the Americans in this sector where there are no indications that the enemy is withdrawing. One feature of the day's fighting has been the enemy's increased use of artillery, indicating he at last has been able to get guns up from the rear areas. But the Yanks still have heavy superiority in artillery. □

With American Troops outside St-Lô, July 15 — Along the road to the front, where guns are thundering, there are two villages which will be remembered always by anyone who saw them today—happy little Castilly and sad, ruined St-André-de-L'Epine.

It was Bastille Day in Castilly. In a little gray cemetery in a churchyard villagers gathered to celebrate the independence that came to their nation 155 years ago, and the new independence which the Allies brought to their beloved Normandy. But within Saint-André there was none to celebrate. There was only a hungry goat picking among the rubble, and quiet doughboys looking aged by the terror of explosions which had reduced the village to dusty piles of wreckage.

At Castilly, while passing convoys rumbled by, villagers and country folk gathered in their Sunday best and Curé Jean Julienne, owlish eyes sparkling behind horn-rimmed spectacles, shepherded them into the old church for prayer. We stood outside the cemetery's picket fence just beside a shaft of marble erected to twenty-six sons of Castilly who died for France in the First World War. Someone had tied a small tri-color and an American flag to the fence. Little boys and girls with thick soled shoes, scrubbed and hair plastered down under funny little hats, walked by self-consciously, their heavy shoes kicking up the dust. They were fascinated by the shining instruments of the American band.

The people gathered inside the churches and later came marching out. Small boys led the procession with white surplices over Sunday clothes. One of them carried a crucifix and the padre walked behind them. A Frenchman with a fierce mustache and a row of medals across his worn gray suit carried a tri-color and behind him came the villagers. They gathered around the war memorial with American officers. There were speeches by the mayor, the curé, a French major and an American officer. And then everybody cheered and the band played the "Star Spangled Banner," "God Save the King" and ended with the stirring "La Marseillaise."

We drove from Castilly toward the front and near a ridge overlooking Saint-André-or what was left of the village after the war passed over. On the wall of a wrecked building someone had put a sign: "Off limits to troops." But it wasn't very funny, because Saint-André was a classic picture of all those wrecked towns you remember in pictures of French villages in the First World War.

Even the dead had not been permitted to rest in peace. Shells had blasted great craters in the little cemetery. The steeple of the church was blown away. It once had been a German observation post. Everywhere was destruction and desolation. The villagers had not yet returned to mourn the deaths of their homes.

Pvt. Joe Rhodes, Baltimore, Md., walked through the streets and stopped to look at the ruin around him. He shook his head. "It's the same old story, isn't it?" But he was making a statement, not asking a question.   □

Outside St-Lô, July 17 – Doughboys are fighting in Ste-Croix-de-Lô, one and one-quarter miles from the center of St-Lô. Near this suburb, now a bloody battleground over which American troops have fought for several straight days, was to have been St-Lô's housing project, the city's pride and a model for the future.

The Americans have taken a heavy toll of dead and wounded in storming the most strongly defended positions of their entire forty-eight-mile front and some doughboys have fallen, too. North of St-Lô, the Germans made two counter-attacks today but these failed. "We can handle the situation," was the message from that sector.

It is slow, hard fighting of the bitterest kind. German paratroopers are battling for every field and the attackers are under constant artillery, mortar and small arms fire. This was Troina all over again. It was before Troina in Sicily that the Germans made their great stand to stem the Americans driving for Messina.

In the darkness, just before dawn today the Yanks came out of their foxholes and moved toward St-Lô like wraiths through the swirling fog. There was no artillery preparation to signal the attack to the enemy and every man was under instructions not to shoot, but to dig the enemy out with bayonet and grenade at close quarters.

They moved so silently across the hedgerows that the foe was caught completely by surprise. He was rolled back along the St-Lô-Isigny Road, but reinforcements were rushed up to stem the advance threatening to cut an enemy supply road before the city.

On the east the doughboys were in the extreme outer fringe of the city. They moved down a secondary road toward the village of Martinville, north of the main east road to Bayeux. They cleaned out Martinville with bayonets and grenades in the first hour of attack and then moved on to make a junction with the isolated units on the main road.

The morning sun burned the mists off the low ground and for the first time since they landed in Normandy the Americans fought under a hot cloudless sky reminiscent of a July at home.   □

With American Troops at St-Lô, July 18 – American troops stormed into the outskirts of St-Lô today after German defenses suddenly crumpled on the north and east. The doughboys met only light opposition and there were indications the Germans would not try a house-to-house stand for the city.

The enemy was forced to withdraw from this important middle anchor of their Normandy line, which they fought so savagely to hold in one of the bloodiest and hardest battles of the invasion. The break came dramatically and suddenly, after the doughboys had fallen back last night from the city's outskirts under enemy counter-attacks. But these thrusts were the dying struggles of the Germans, and even as the counter-attacks were made, unengaged troops pulled back. Some units were cut off from communications and were unaware of the orders to withdraw.

At 8 a.m. today, one American unit began attacking along the St-Lô-Isigny Road running northeast of the town. They surged forward with hardly a shot fired at them until they reached the outskirts of the town, where machine guns opened up from some buildings—manned by a few die-hard defenders left behind in the retreat. But this opposition was light, supporting indications that the Germans would not attempt a house-to-house battle to hold the key road hub town.

The enemy's resistance, which had held the U.S. advance to a slow and tortuous hedge-by-hedge move, broke without warning. There were no indications last night that the Germans were beaten—and there then appeared little chance of American entry into St-Lô without more hard fighting.

There was last-minute confusion among German units before St-Lô, and many of them, out of communication with higher echelons, did not know where their supporting troops were. American troops captured a messenger bearing retreat orders to one encircled unit still trying to hold out.

Control of St-Lô will give Lieut. Gen. Omar N. Bradley's forces strategic roadways radiating in all directions, and smash the last anchor point, except for Périers, which the German held along the forty-eight-mile Lessay-St-Lô front. □

With an American Column Entering St-Lô, July 18 – Tired, dusty, battle-stained doughboys moved through the streets of St-Lô tonight in a triumphant entry which still was accompanied by the crash of shells, and the rattle of machine guns.

The column is winching its way forward in pursuit of an enemy whose defenses suddenly crumpled before Lieut. Gen. Omar N. Bradley's infantrymen. As though infuriated at being forced to quit their defenses before this prize city, the enemy's artillery and mortars are shelling St-Lô and hitting at our columns moving along the highway.

The break in the battle came suddenly this morning as the Germans began trying to pull away from the action, the hardest since the Americans landed on the beaches. A column of American troops drove down the St-Lô-Isigny Highway and the first troops entered the outskirts at 10 o'clock this morning.

"The jerries began shooting at us from houses when we reached the edge of town," said Pvt. John Kellas, Rochester, N.Y. "Then we had to go in and dig snipers out one by one."

Behind the first wave of infantry came a special task force, spearheaded by tanks whose mission was to occupy the town and then press on to secure the exits, while wiping out any resistance met along the way.

This was the final bid to crush the German stand around this bastion where the enemy had anchored his line to the west. The western end of the line was smashed when troops broke through at La-Haye-du-Puits several days ago, but St-Lô was an even more vital defense position and the enemy assigned his best paratroopers to hold the doughboy drive. They did it for seven days and just when it looked as though there was a stalemate the break came—and suddenly the Americans surged forward.

I joined a column of the special task force on the dusty road leading to St-Lô. Ahead of us rumbled tanks, churning up dust, and behind the armor came half-tracks, trucks loaded with ammunition and jeeps. The column moved slowly as engineers cleared mines from the road ahead. Columns moving into battle or in pursuit of the enemy don't charge forward in a sweeping rush. Like this column they snake forward cautiously, in halting starts and stops. You wonder what is holding up the advance and there is no one to tell you.

Along the road were evidences of the savage fighting of the last seven days. Hedgerows ripped by mortar fire and machine gun bullets. Tree trunks ripped apart like matchsticks. Ditches and foxholes burrowed into the hedgerows where both Americans and Germans had taken refuge from the flying steel overhead. East of the road the Germans still fought savagely. The doughboys had sideslipped some 200 enemy troops in the region of St-Georges-Montcocq near the outskirts of St-Lô and machine guns clattered.

A sniper opened fire across the field and troops jumped from vehicles for cover. Doughboys unslung carbines from their shoulders and slipped through the hedge. There was the crack of a single shot and the sniper's gun was still.

We moved down the road to a sharp curve at St-Georges-Montcocq just as the enemy opened up with a heavy concentration of mortar and 88 fire hitting at the road. On the ridge above shells were bursting in the air-air bursts which showered the ground with shrapnel.

Pvt. William Wiggins, Greenport, N.Y., shared a ditch with me. The sleeve of his jacket was ripped by shrapnel. "I guess I'm lucky," he said. "Look at that." The shrapnel had cut jagged holes in the sleeve, but merely nicked his arm.

TOP: Official AP photo taken in southern Italy in 1943.

BOTTOM: Press credentials issued in London in preparation for D-Day in Normandy, France. As a journalist, Whitehead was classified as a noncombatant. He was assigned the rank of captain in case of capture by the enemy, so that he would be accorded treatment appropriate to an officer.

Official AP photo taken in southern Italy in 1943.

Official AP photo with soldiers of the First Infantry Division
near Omaha Beach, June 1944.

ABOVE: General Omar Bradley's first briefing of correspondents on the Normandy beachhead, June 1944. His purpose was to reassure the American people that casualties during the invasion had not been as great as many members of the military had expected.

RIGHT: Bill Mauldin sketch originally published in *Life* magazine. The major ETO war correspondents are featured being briefed by General Omar Bradley.

FLASHBACK TO WORLD WAR II—Bill Mauldin recalls some of the noted byliners of 1941-45 at a briefing with General Bradley. Seated right in front are the late Ernie Pyle, and Hal Boyle of AP. A little to the right is A. J. Liebling of the New Yorker and standing in rear are Clark Lee of INS, Don Whitehead of AP and Charles C. Wertenbacker of Time-Life. Over to the left are Maj. C. B. Hansen, the late H. R. Knickerbocker and Will Lang of Life. The Mauldin sketch illustrates the installment of General Bradley's memoirs in Life for April 16 and is reprinted with Life's permission.

Official AP photo taken as Whitehead interviews soldiers
outside of St-Lô fighting in the battle to liberate France.

Official AP photo. Whitehead and good friend and veteran war correspondent
Ernie Pyle prepare breakfast at the Grand Hotel in Paris, August 1944. The
Knoxville News-Sentinel provided the following description of the scene: "With an
air fitting to the solemnity of the occasion, Ernie frys [*sic*] the farewell breakfast on
his desk at the Grand Hotel, Paris, before returning to the United States. Cooked
breakfast was a tradition with Mr. Pyle during his stay in France. A special handmade nickel-plated gasoline stove—a gift of workers at the Coleman Lamp Co., in
Wichita, Kas.—was used for cooking the limited rations."

Official AP photo most likely taken in December 1944, when he was on leave in his hometown of Harlan, Kentucky. The picture captures the serious side of Whitehead, who was described by some who knew him as a bit "reserved" and "standoffish."

Official AP photo of a somewhat younger and less serious man,
perhaps in 1943 before the grueling 1944 campaigns in Northern Europe.

A wireman ran along the road, crouching and unreeling wire leading to the command car of the general who led the task force which drove into St-Lô's Place Gambetta. The general himself was nicked in the arm by a bullet, but was undaunted and kept shouting orders to his troops. Infantry came swinging along the road.

"Keep moving," a lieutenant shouted. "There's a truckload of TNT right behind me and I don't like to be around when this stuff is falling."

Shells whistled in and crashed at a curve in the road. Troops ducked into a ditch.

"Damit, keep moving. Keep moving!" a captain shouted. "Get the hell away from this place. It's zeroed in. Get going."

The troops went forward through smoke, dust and explosion.

Harry Harris, Associated Press photographer, crouched on the road and snapped pictures of a close-up battle scene and then stepped back into the ditch.

"And when people back home see that shot they'll think it's just dust blown up by the exhaust from a tank," he sighed.

The barrage lasted for more than thirty minutes. Shells kept whistling over the ridge right behind which we lay and smashed along the road.

"Who was it said all the Germans had pulled back?" somebody asked sarcastically.

A doughboy slumped down in the ditch beside Harris and me. His jacket and one leg of his trousers were drenched with blood.

"Get me out of here," he moaned. "Get me to a medic."

Each time a shell came he whimpered like a child.

We helped him to his feet and into our jeep. Two other wounded men were brought up by soldiers and we lifted them into the back seat of the jeep. They were so weak from the loss of blood they were unable to sit up. A young lieutenant had a hole in his back from which blood welled in great bubbles.

"Gimme some tablets," one of the men said. "You got any sulfanilamide tablets?" Someone brought out a box of sulfa tablets and the soldiers gulped them down.

The driver wheeled the jeep into the road and we took the men back to a casualty clearing station about two miles behind the lines. A soldier lit cigarettes for the three wounded, but the lieutenant with a hole in his back lay on his stomach quietly, his bloodstained hands hanging limply.

After delivering the wounded to the clearing station we headed the jeep back toward St-Lô. Near the outskirts of the city we were stopped by enemy shelling and mortar fire on the road.

But ahead our troops were pushing on through the city while on our right doughboys were battling the last knot of stubborn resistance before St-Lô. □

St-Lô, France, July 19 — The Germans battered this wrecked city with artillery and mortar shells today as the doughboys dug into the rubble to defend the prize won after eight days of fighting. Explosions are crashing from one end of the city to the other and around three sides the doughboys still are battling Germans caught in the sudden forward surge. St-Lô is the Americans' but the Yanks still are fighting fanatical parachute troops making a last stand.

St-Lô is deserted except for Yanks slipping from building to building, dodging into doorways when shells crash, and for troops manning machine guns, bazookas and defensive positions on the approaches to the town. About 200 Germans were pocketed on the southeastern side of the city, trying to fight their way out, and Capt. Cecil Harvey of Sewickley, Pa., was calling for artillery fire upon them.

In the upper room of a crypt of a cemetery which the Germans had used as a command post was a family altar. There were dried brown bread and a paper bag of stale butter, besides the candles and litter of soldier gear. Doughboys lounged around the wall, trying to get some rest while shells exploded nearby.

"We killed God knows how many Jerries in the draws on the southeastern side of town," Maj. Glover Johns said. Three days' stubble of red beard covered his face, and his eyes looked tired. "We fought our way in and then the Jerries tried to come back and we had to fight them off again. They were trying to escape to the south."

This lean Texan was the leader of the "indestructible clay pigeons," a unit which first fought its way through the entire city. "They call us clay pigeons because we are always out front where everybody can shoot at us," Johns grinned. "We are a little chipped, but we are still flying."

The steel doors of the crypt opened and Capt. Leroy Weddle of Hagerstown, Md., and Lieut. George Grimsehl, Lansdowne, Md., entered the little room. They had led advance units which cleaned out the main part of the city, and then took up defense positions controlling the approaches across the Vire River on the west side of the city.

Once this morning the Germans tried to cross one of these approaches and machine guns killed six driving the rest back.

"We had to clean out the streets house by house with bayonets and grenades," Grimsehl said. "There were a few machine guns, but we took care of them."

A dusty, bearded doughboy poked his head through the doorway and asked for Major Johns. "Major, there's a hell of a lot of Germans in those draws. If we don't get the artillery going they're going to come through," he said.

"We know about 'em," Johns said. "Our artillery should be working on them now."

The soldier smiled. "Thanks, major," he said.

Over against the wall Pvt. Frank R. Avato, Jr., Philadelphia, nodded. Johns noticed how tired the youth looked.

"Kid, why don't you try to get some sleep?"

"I haven't slept for forty-eight hours and I'm too tired to sleep now," Avato said.

Near the door two radiomen kept in contact with the artillery and mortars, passing along fire orders from observers. Soldiers kept crowding into the room to get orders and bring messages from the "front" at the edge of the city.

Pvt. George Wolff of Milwaukee, Wis., passed along the targets for the mortars, and then he listened to a soldier talking in another part of town. "Yeah?" said Wolff. "Well, I'm in a cemetery and there are no ice cream cones here, either."

From the upper room winding steps led down to the lower crypt where Johns had maps spread on the top of a marble vault. Here among the dead was the safest place in all St-Lô as the enemy poured heavy fire into the city.   □

With the American Army in France, July 21 — The U.S. Twenty-ninth Infantry Division, with a proud record behind it of victories in the First World War, was the doughboy division which drove the Germans back and captured St-Lô in the bitterest battle since the invasion of Normandy.

Fighting men from Maryland, Virginia, and Pennsylvania for the most part engineered the major victory which put St-Lô in our hands and won for them the commendation of their corps commander at the end of almost continuous combat.

One unit of the Twenty-ninth came ashore on D-Day alongside a unit of the First Division to spearhead the invasion on this central beachhead and break the Germans' defenses. And from the beaches the division drove on to capture St-Lô.

After the capture of St-Lô, which climaxed eight days of the hardest fighting American troops have yet encountered on the continent, many of these battle-worn doughboys heard the general say, "The capture of St-Lô climaxes an operation which began June 6, 1944, on the Normandy beachhead and carried the Twenty-ninth Division deep into enemy territory in an extended drive which adds a new and brilliant chapter to American military history.

"It was marked by repeated instances of personal and group heroism of the highest order and by unflagging devotion to duty which overcame discomfiture, fatigue, and determined resistance of a resourceful enemy.

"Please convey to your officers and men my pride in their achievements and my sincere congratulations on a job superbly done."

The smashing of the German hold on St-Lô was one of the most important operations since the landing, because the victory gave the Americans a grip on a highway center which was an anchor point of enemy defenses.

The final drive into the city was accomplished by the 115th Infantry Regiment of the Twenty-ninth in a dramatic thrust July 18 which broke through German defenses just as the Twenty-ninth had defeated elements of at least six enemy divisions in its first attack on the Meuse River in the last war.

But other regiments of the division helped make the entry possible by their advances on the flanks.

The division's victory from the beaches to St-Lô was all the more significant because when the Twenty-ninth landed in the assault, its troops were so-called "green" and untried in combat.

The landing was the bloodiest, bitterest fighting on any of the invasion beaches, but the Twenty-ninth fought its way through. It had been trained so long in amphibious operations the men began to gripe that they were suffering from "webbed feet."

Their almost continuous action in the line since D-Day has been one of the longest stretches in the front lines of any of the American troops on the beachhead. The division is commanded by Maj. Gen. Charles Hunter Gerhardt, forty-nine-year-old Tennessean.

Perhaps the greatest hero of the Twenty-ninth is a young major from Virginia, killed when his battalion began assaulting St-Lô. His body was carried in state through the wrecked streets and placed on a great pile of wreckage before the church of Ste-Croix with the folds of a flag draped about him. And there it rested amid the thunder of enemy shelling and the crackle of machine guns as the doughboys wiped out the last defenders of the city.   □

With the American Army in France, July 24 — Gen. Ike Eisenhower has another Kansas farm boy on his team who is helping make a lot of history in France. To his men he's "the old man." Officially he is Maj. Gen. Clarence R. Huebner, commanding general of the First Infantry Division. They were his men who fought their way through the reinforced German division on the beaches of Normandy in the bloodiest battle of the invasion. The battle was not only a test of Huebner as a leader of a division in combat but of all his theories of training and discipline.

Gen. Huebner is not a colorful figure. As one officer said, he had "two and a half strikes on him" when he took over the division from the popular Maj. Gen. Terry Allen who had led it through North Africa and Sicily. But he did not strike out. It is no secret there was some feeling when Huebner came in from African headquarters and took over the division just as it came out of line after the bitter battle of Troina which smashed German resistance on Sicily.

The veteran troops were amazed when they came from the battlefield and were ordered to the range for marksmanship practice. They thought, after a month's combat, they knew all there was to know about shooting— and being shot at. But they were wrong and now they'll admit it. An expert rifleman himself, Huebner says a soldier may do everything else well but if he shoots and doesn't kill the enemy then his whole training isn't worth a couple of empty C-ration cans.

The general learned his theories the hard way in the First World War. He went in as a second lieutenant and came out a lieutenant colonel. He was decorated twice with the Distinguished Service Cross, once with the Silver Star, was wounded twice and the French honored him with the Legion of Honor and the Croix de Guerre with the palm.

The doughboys didn't like it. They groused but now they are realizing what that training did for them on the beaches.

Supply is another of the general's fetishes. He insists that combat troops get everything they need—and that they take care of it.

Huebner enlisted in the Army in January, 1910. He went in as a rifleman in the Eighteenth Infantry regiment and was commissioned a second lieutenant in 1916.

He led a company at Cantigny. When the battalion commander was killed he took over. He led an assault at Soissons, St-Mihiel and the Argonne.

Those battles taught Huebner the value of marksmanship and even now his chief relaxation is shooting at C-ration cans. He is responsible for the pictorial portfolios on rifle marksmanship now used throughout the Army and there is nothing the privates can tell him about shooting that he doesn't already know.   □

With the American Troops in France, July 29 — In a peaceful green Normandy meadow near the sea, white crosses gleam row on row and on a sign which one day will be replaced by stone are these words:

"This cemetery was established on July 11, 1944, by the Twenty-ninth Division of the United States Army as the final resting place for officers and men of the division who made the supreme sacrifice on the battlefields of Normandy. We who carry on the fight salute these comrades and other honored dead of the division who could not be buried here. In command of this valiant legion of Blue and Gray is Lt. Col. William T. Terry, infantry, who was killed in action on July 17, 1944."

Officers and men representing the Twenty-ninth Division marched into the cemetery today to the solemn roll of drums. For a moment they stood at attention and the only sounds were the distant thunder of guns at the front and the roar of fighter planes streaking across the gray skies.

Maj. Gen. Charles Hunter Gerhardt, commanding general, stepped in front of these representatives of his division which originally came from Maryland, Virginia and Pennsylvania.

"The men that lie here I have seen personally on many occasions on the battlefield," he said quietly. "They are comrades in arms in this division and we do honor to their supreme sacrifice for liberty today."

Under the dark skies the men bowed their heads. The chaplain read a burial prayer and then voices were lifted in the old familiar hymns "Abide With Me" and "Nearer My God to Thee."

The divisional adjutant stepped forward and began calling the names of those who had fallen in battle and whose bodies were resting beneath the neat white crosses gleaming against the dark green of the foliage. And as each name was called there came the answer "Here!" by a representative of the dead man's own unit.

A firing squad fired a salvo over the graves. The band played "The Star Spangled Banner." Then General Gerhardt stepped forward again.

"Now let these brave dead hear the battle cry of the division," he ordered.

And from the assemblage came the mighty roar:

"Let's go!"

Drums rolled, boots crunched on the gravel and the men of the Twenty-ninth marched away.   □

Mortain, France, August 4 — There's a strange sense of unreality about the American advance surging across this beautiful green country. American tanks, guns, trucks, jeeps, and troop transports literally are swarming over the roads in an unbelievable mass movement. It flows down the smooth paved highways and washes up the dusty narrow lanes in endless and relentless movement.

Like a tornado which cuts a swath of destruction, and then jumps for miles before striking again, this war has leapfrogged across the country. There are miles of green fields and rolling fertile ridges, untouched by war. And then, suddenly, you come upon a town smashed to crumbling ruins, or fields gashed by shells where the Germans made a stand.

Mortain is one of those little towns crucified on the cross of war. It sits on a hill ridge looking down across the rolling, lovely countryside. Once it was one of the showplaces of all southern Normandy. Now, there's hardly a whole house left standing. The town, captured a week ago by the Americans, was recaptured when the Germans counter-attacked with panzers. Yesterday, our troops retook Mortain or what was left of its smouldering ruins. Bulldozers are clearing the rubble from its streets and a few sad civilians wander about the ruins staring at the awful destruction that made an ugly thing of their once beautiful village.

Troops, walking through the ruins, stare at the wreckage in silence and then look across the valley at the green fields and trees washed in the warm sun, shining from a soft blue sky.

"This sort of thing makes you want to cry, doesn't it," one youth said softly.

But once outside the town and on the road the feeling of sadness gives way to one of exhilaration. It's a stirring sight to watch an army on the move, driving after a withdrawing enemy. And Bradley's troops and armor still are driving hard.

Three weeks ago the front was an almost static line. Today, convoys miles long roar down the roads, hurrying supplies forward to catch up with fast-moving units.

"Where is the division," I asked an M.P. at a crossroads information point.

He shook his head in despair. "Two days ago its command post was here," he said, pointing to a spot on a map. "Yesterday, they moved, and now I hear they are moving again. All I can say is to keep going down that road and keep asking all M.P.'s along the way."

The Germans along this front received orders to withdraw just eight hours before the Americans began to attack, and the drive caught the enemy disorganized.

"They were just as disorganized as fifty youngsters going out on a camping trip all alone," an officer said.

While trying to disengage the main forces, the enemy units, scraped together from odd bits and pieces of various organizations, are providing stubborn resistance, but they are being overrun and the doughboy casualties are extremely light in this phase of the move.

Except for the hard resistance in the Vire Mortain sector, the Germans just haven't had time to get set for the swift moves of the Americans. Often U.S. troops have cut roads or occupied towns before the Germans knew that they were there. And armor has been running wild.

For the first time since the American Army went into combat, armor has been able to break into open maneuverable country and exploit its strength fully. Armor never was able to do much in North Africa. In Sicily and Italy, the infantry did most of the dirty work through the mountains. But now tanks are having their day, and are making the most of it. □

With the American Forces in France, August 15 (7:01 p.m.) — Field Marshal Gen. Günther Von Kluge's Seventh Army is being destroyed today in one of the greatest victories of the war in northern France.

Allied artillery has dropped a curtain of steel across the enemy's narrow corridor between Falaise and Argentan and has slammed shut all the routes of escape for the mass of enemy troops and equipment trapped in the death pocket. Big guns are blasting anything that moves down the few roads left to the Germans struggling to get through the gap.

"Von Kluge's forces have ceased to exist as an army," one American officer declared as troops of his division drove forward in the area of La Ferté-Macé. From the west, south and east the Americans closed in for the kill while the British and Canadians maintained pressure from the north.

A lion's share of the credit goes to Lt. Gen. Omar N. Bradley, American commander in France, who engineered the spectacular maneuvers which closed around the German Army before it could withdraw from the trap. This is one of the greatest military defeats suffered by the Germans in this war and there are some military men who are comparing it to the Russian victory at Stalingrad which wiped out Hitler's Sixth Army.

How many thousands of German troops and how much equipment has been bagged in the pocket nobody knows, but the total is great. It is impossible for much to squeeze through the gap which is not yet occupied physically by our troops.

And our troops are capturing huge stores of ammunition and equipment as they press forward. Hundreds of prisoners are streaming back to the cages. Thousands more are certain to be taken within the next few days.

There are estimates that from 15,000 to 60,000 enemy troops have been trapped, but regardless of the final count, Von Kluge's army has disappeared as a force to be reckoned with in future moves by Bradley's First and Third Armies.

"The Seventh Army has lost the bulk of its equipment and material," said Lt. Col. Robert F. Evans of Davenport, Iowa, "and its organization is gone. Those who got out of the gap can be reorganized to fight again, but there are not enough of them to form an army."

There still is bitter resistance in many places inside the pocket which is being ripped and blasted by big guns and by the Allied air forces, but the Germans are throwing everything they have into the line in a desperate last stand fight.

The best example of the Germans' complete disorganization was in the fact that one American division yesterday took prisoners from eighteen different German divisions. Odds and ends of every available division were tossed to the sacrifice by Von Kluge in his desperation.   □

First U.S. Army Headquarters in France, August 19 – On this seventy-fifth day of the invasion, Germany stands defeated in the Battle of France. American troops can advance on Paris any time Lt. Gen. Omar N. Bradley chooses to throw the weight of his armor and infantry eastward.

There still is fighting ahead for the Allies—hard, bitter fighting against an enemy determined to make the American, Canadian and British troops pay as heavy a price as possible for the progress they make, but victory is inevitable. The Germans have not enough strength left in France to stop this great Allied tide that is pouring in upon them.

Reports from the south are that our troops are driving inland against comparatively light opposition from German forces whose reserves were drained in the futile effort to stem the invasion in Normandy.

Germany lost the Battle of France when the tall, quiet General Bradley outgeneraled the Nazis' best with the spectacular breakthrough west of St-Lô. That was the decisive action. The Germans' only hope of holding France was to keep the Americans bottled up in the Normandy Peninsula, and that hope was quickly smashed.

The breakthrough plans were Bradley's own. He conceived it, planned it and executed it, although the overall strategy of the French campaign was planned by the high command. Through the gap he poured division after division and then turned Lt. Gen. George Patton's Third Army loose on their wild dash to the south virtually unopposed.

The actual battle for Paris was fought out in the Argentan-Falaise-Vire-Mortain pocket when part of Gen. Günther Von Kluge's Seventh Army was trapped by American armor and infantry suddenly swinging north when it appeared they were headed straight for Paris. Actually, Paris is just a military by-product of Bradley's plan to crush the German armies.

There still is no reliable official or unofficial estimate on just how many German troops were caught in the trap. There still are forces of considerable strength holding out in that area fighting bitterly and slowly being crushed. The death toll is running high but there is no doubt Von Kluge managed to get the bulk of his armor out and most of his troops although they took a bad beating and no longer can be considered an army that can be a real threat. They have been reduced to a role of a harassing, delaying force.

The jaws of the trap almost were closed but the Germans managed to keep open a narrow escape corridor through which armor and troops slipped despite the heavy shelling of the roads by Allied artillery. The Americans' hooking drive from the south moved swiftly but the British and Canadians were unable to move as fast from the north to completely bottle up the enemy. Von Kluge's army may make a stand west of the Seine, but their battered ranks can never hold the power which Bradley and Montgomery can loose against them.

Beyond the Seine in the Pas-de-Calais region from which Hitler has been hurling his buzz bombs on England the Germans have more forces. In the past some of these troops have been fed into the Normandy fighting in an effort to support Von Kluge's forces. There is little likelihood the Germans will be able to stalemate the war on a static front in this region unless they are able to bring more divisions into France.

Paris' 3,000,000 population immediately will become a problem for the American Army when the city falls and we must take on the responsibility of the civilians. The Army is ready to accept that responsibility despite the additional burden it places on the transport and supplies. Plans now are to take 3,000 tons of food daily into Paris until the civilian transport system can be restored and farm products can be shipped from the country. The Americans are not likely to put many troops in Paris except for policing purposes.   □

First U.S. Army Headquarters in France, August 22 –
The past eight days have been the blackest of the invasion for war correspondents as the luck of war finally turned. Two are dead, one is near death, two are injured and one is reported a captive of the Germans. All of their names cannot be given until the next of kin have been notified by the War Department.

Tall, dark-haired Tom Treanor of the *Los Angeles Times*, a veteran of four campaigns and one of the most colorful figures among the men who report wars, is dead of multiple injuries received when his jeep was crushed by a tank northwest of Paris. Gault MacGowan, correspondent of the *New York Sun*, is a prisoner of the Germans. A British correspondent who was with MacGowan was shot in the stomach and is near death.

Treanor was returning from the Mantes-Gassicourt area with two companions and a jeep driver when a tank wheeled around and crushed the jeep. The men with Treanor were injured but not critically. Tom was conscious as he was taken to a hospital, but apparently he did not realize the gravity of his injuries. He insisted that the surgeons "hurry up and get this job over so I can file my story."

Most of the correspondents had known and worked with Treanor in the Middle East, Sicily and Italy and then through this campaign. He wrote a column for the *Los Angeles Times* and did broadcasts for the National Broadcasting Company. His D-Day story was one of the finest of the invasion. He returned to London to get out one of the first eyewitness accounts of the landing of American troops.

News of Tom's death spread gloom among the correspondents who knew him as one of the most courageous and enterprising reporters in their ranks. His death came a few hours after another correspondent was killed by a German shell northwest of Chartres. His name can not be given now. He was with Andy Lopez, Acme news photographer, searching for a command post near the front when they saw a burned-out jeep on the roadside.

"We slowed down," Lopez said, "and then there was a terrible explosion. We hadn't even heard a gun fired. I looked around and saw he was hit. He never knew what hit him."

Lopez and the driver, both wounded slightly by shrapnel, jumped into a ditch and crawled on their hands and knees while the German gun shelled them. They hid in a woods for thirty-six hours with nothing to eat or drink while enemy troops moved near them. They were making their way westward in darkness when they ran into a group of French patriots. Mistaking each other for the enemy, the driver and a Frenchman exchanged shots. The jeep driver was fatally wounded. □

Five

THE LIBERATION OF PARIS,
AUGUST 25–28, 1944

Paris, August 25 — Yesterday before I entered Paris, I learned by means of a telephone call that Mrs. Blanchard, housekeeper of the American Embassy at Paris for sixteen years, was excitedly awaiting the arrival of the Americans so that she could raise the Stars and Stripes over the embassy again.

At the town of Longjumeau, Sergeant Adrian Pinsince, of Evanston, Ill., heard a garage man say he had just talked to Paris. We decided to call the embassy. At the Longjumeau telephone exchange a Mrs. Brun said: "Certainly, we can call Paris for you." She put through a call for Anjou 74-60 and Sergeant Pinsince, who speaks French, asked for Mrs. Blanchard, whose name we had learned from a young woman formerly employed at the embassy.

"Who is calling?" she asked in English.

I identified myself, and she exclaimed, "Mon Dieu, where are you?" I explained I was calling from outside Paris. I asked her how things were at the embassy, which has been in the charge of the Swiss government since the United States closed it in June, 1941.

"Everything is going all right now," Mrs. Blanchard said, "but there was an attack against the embassy by German soldiers four days ago. They wounded our guard outside the door and forced their way in after firing on the building. They walked in and went all over the place. Everything is covered with broken glass."

Normally, Mrs. Blanchard lives at her own home in Paris, but when fighting became so general in the streets she decided to stay at the embassy and bring her mother to live with her until the Allies entered the city.

"There is shooting everywhere," she said. "We hear reports that the Americans are already in the city. I was told not to go to the gate, or I might get in trouble. So we stay inside. We have enough food to last for several days.

"Everything in the Embassy is shipshape. You know it is my job to see that it stays that way. Mon Dieu, I hope the Americans move in tomorrow. I am carrying an American flag with me wherever I go. We aren't allowed to fly the flag now, but I hope the Americans will let me help hoist the flag the first time it is flown."

And that concluded the first telephone calls to the American Embassy from outside Paris since it was closed three years ago. ☐

Paris, August 25 — American and French columns fought their way into the heart of Paris today and received a thundering welcome from her citizens as they opened battle with Germans and Vichy militiamen still entrenched in important strongholds. The Allied troops entered the city from the south, and almost immediately—as they reached the beautiful Luxembourg Gardens—the Nazis and their collaborationist militiamen opened fire with machine guns, rifles and pistols.

A column of doughboys streaked for the Île de la Cité in the heart of the capital, to the relief of French patriot forces and police who had been fighting the Germans for nearly a week. On reaching this island in the Seine, the U.S. infantrymen drove to the Cathedral of Notre Dame, reaching there at 11 a.m. and closing in with a mighty ground attack against enemy positions.

Joyous throngs, who greeted the entrance of the tanks with a thundering welcome, fled inside buildings and, within a few minutes, the streets were bare battlegrounds.

As I write this, the Germans still hold out on both sides of the Seine halfway along the Champs-Elysées, Place de la Concorde, Quai d'Orsay, Tuileries, Gardens of the Louvre, the Madeleine, the Chamber of Deputies, the Senate and the Hôtel Crillon. French patriots have a grip on the Île de la Cité, the Palais de Justice, the Préfecture of Police, the Préfecture of the Seine, most of the Mairies [City Halls] and the factory district. But Frenchmen are fighting Frenchmen as well as Germans in liberating this city.

There was much confusion as the French armored column began rolling through a heavy morning fog that made vehicles look like prehistoric monsters. But when the last enemy resistance crumbled at the gate to Paris, this heart of France went mad with happiness.

All the emotions suppressed by four years of German domination burst forth. The streets were like a combined Mardi Gras, Fourth of July celebration, American Legion convention and New Year's Eve in Times Square, all packed into one.

Our column began to roll at 7 a.m. from Longjumeau, six miles south of Paris. A French captain stopped all correspondents one mile from town and insisted no one could enter without a written permit. He told three British correspondents they would be shot if they drove by without a pass. An American colonel heard the story and said the captain was acting without authority. I drove to the blockade and suddenly my jeep lurched forward into the column of troops. It was too late to turn back, so I kept going.

Two miles farther on, the column halted. Forward elements had run into a German strongpoint and mines on the road. French Gen. Leclerc and his staff went into conference. Tanks wheeled to outflank the position, but they returned because they ran into the route of an American infantry advance.

Then the column began to roll again. The strongpoint ahead of us had been knocked out. At 9:57 a.m., my jeep rolled through the gates into Paris. Never did I expect to see such scenes again. There was only a narrow lane through which the armor could roll. Men and women cried with joy. They grabbed the arms of soldiers and cheered until hoarse.

When the column stopped I was smothered, but pleasantly, with soft arms and lips giving the usual French double kiss. They hugged me and my jeep driver, pinned French Tricolors on us, and left us exhausted.

One old man saluted and said with tears in his eyes: "God bless America. You have saved France."

Crowds were banked from the center of the streets to the sidewalks and stretched for miles. Apparently everyone in Paris, except the Germans and collaborationists, was standing there. Our column moved to a point one block from the Luxembourg. Then from all sides burst machine gun fire. From housetops and windows guns rattled. Machine guns of tanks replied. We leaped from the jeep and took cover behind a tank.

Jerry Beatson of Rockford, Ill., was beside me and aimed his carbine at the top of a building. The gun cracked in my ear. "There's one son of a bitch up there," he cried and kept firing.

Bullets glanced off the pavements with ugly whines.

My driver and I leaped into a jeep and raced back down the street, but another burst sent us diving for the curb.

FFI [Forces Françaises de l'Intérieur] resistance leaders ran from door to door, pointing to rooftops and windows.

Up there, shooting down on us, were the Milice (Vichy collaborators). One Frenchman said there were many German snipers in civilian clothes.

Red Cross men in white dashed out of a doorway with a stretcher. A nurse in starched white followed them. They picked up a wounded man and put him on the stretcher while waving a Red Cross flag.

An FFI member ran up to me and cried in English:

"Give us arms and ammunition. That's all we ask. We'll clean out these bastards." □

Paris, August 25 — American and French columns fought their way into and seized the heart of Paris Friday. They received a thundering welcome from her citizens as they opened battle with Germans and Vichy militiamen still entrenched in important strongholds. The Allied troops entered the city from the south. As they reached the beautiful Luxembourg Gardens, the Nazis and their collaborationist militiamen opened fire.

A column of American doughboys streaked for the Île de la Cité in the heart of the capital to the relief of French patriot forces and police who had been fighting the Germans for nearly a week. Latest word at Allied headquarters said that Allied forces joined fighting French on the Île de la Cité after bitter fighting with Germans.

On reaching this island in the Seine, the American infantrymen drove to the cathedral of Notre Dame, reaching against enemy positions. Joyous, happy throngs who greeted the entrance of the tanks and infantry with a thundering welcome fled to the safety of buildings. Within a few minutes the streets that were choked with humanity, laughing and crying over the liberation were bare battlegrounds.

Brig. Gen. Jacques Leclerc, hero of the Fighting French in the North African campaign, was in the forefront of the battle, leading the tanks to the rescue of patriots who had been frantically calling for help as the Germans fought back throughout Thursday night.

The commander of the Paris region for the French Forces of the Interior, Col. Rol, issued this proclamation: "FFI of the Paris region, you have unleashed a rising which has liberated Paris. You have improvised your tactics, animated by the strong desire to win, and you have won."

The Germans were driven from many strategic parts of the city by the combined onslaught of the French military and the fury of citizens fighting for their liberties.

Lt. Gen. Joseph Pierre Koenig, commander in chief of the French Forces of the Interior, announced that all the main official buildings and most of the highways were now under the protection of Leclerc's Second Armored Division.

Speaking to cheering crowds in front of the Préfecture in Paris, Gen. Charles de Gaulle proclaimed Friday night the liberation of Paris and declared, "we will not rest until we march into enemy territory as conquerors."

The president of the French Committee of National Liberation, back in the capital after four years of fighting from exile, told his exultant listeners, "France will take her place among the great nations which will organize the peace."

"France has rights abroad," de Gaulle continued. "France is a great nation and she has rights which she will know how to make heard. Paris is free now—freed by the hands of Frenchmen—the capital of fighting France, of France the great eternal.

"It is not enough that with the aid of our dear and splendid Allies we should drive the enemy from our soil. After what happened to France, we will not rest or be satisfied until we enter—as is only right—upon the enemy's own soil as conquerors. We are going to fight on to the last day—to a day of total and complete victory."

When the last enemy resistance crumbled at the gate to Paris then this heart of France went mad—wildly, violently mad with happiness.

All the emotions suppressed by four years of German domination surged through the people. Never do I expect to see such scenes as I saw on the streets of Paris. There was only a narrow lane through which the armor could roll. Men and women cried with joy. They grabbed the arms and hands of soldiers and cheered until their voices were hoarse.

When the column stopped I was smothered, but pleasantly, with soft arms and lips. Giving not one kiss but the usual French double one. They hugged me and my jeep driver and pinned French Tricolors on us. One old man came up, saluted, and said with tears in his eyes: "God bless America. You have saved France." Crowds were banked from the center of the streets to the sidewalks in a colorful, cheering throng which stretched for miles.

Our column moved to a point one block from the Luxembourg. Then from all sides burst machine gun fire. From housetops and windows guns rattled. Machine guns of tanks opened up in reply. We leaped from the jeep and took cover behind a tank. Bullets rattled on the streets and glanced off with ugly whines.

The crowds, which a few minutes before lined the streets, melted as if a blast from a furnace had hit a snowbank. Then the streets were terribly lonely and barren except for armor with guns clattering.

The drive on Paris began at 7 a.m. Thursday under sullen, drizzling skies. The Germans did not have much in front of us—but enough to make the armor move cautiously, and occasionally artillery would pound gun positions along the way. Our column avoided the main road to Versailles and turned into a secondary road leading to the Grand National Highway running due south of the city to Orléans. Other columns fanned out on other roads. The historic move on Paris was under way.

The column moved in lurches, going forward for short distances, then stopping, either for reconnaissance or to engage strongpoints. In small towns people crowded along the streets, despite the rain, to cheer each vehicle that passed. Never have I seen more joyous faces than those along the road to Paris. It was a triumphal, exciting and colorful march.

From Limours the main column thrust to St-Germain and then turned north for Paris. By this time the sun had broken through the clouds and we raced up the broad Grand National Highway at fifty miles an hour on some stretches. People were wildly excited and almost lined the route all the way. To the French people this symbolized the French Army returning to France and their day of freedom.

With the column moved a weird assortment of private cars, trucks, motorcycles and bicycles carrying Maquis with tommy guns and rifles slung across their shoulders—a civilian army going to battle alongside regulars.

There in the distance was the Eiffel Tower. This was the greatest thrill of the entire drive—but a sign on the roadside said we were six miles from the heart of Paris.

While guns roared and enemy shells fell, nearby a crowd in a café beside the road laughed and chatted as though Paris had already fallen. Jeeps raced up and down the road and tanks lumbered forward.

Pretty girls stood on the roadside and tossed flowers at the vehicles. As the column would stop they would deck the tanks and armored trucks with flowers until they seemed to be camouflaged as mobile flower pots. Farmers tossed fresh tomatoes and apples to the troops.

Suddenly there was an uproar in the streets. Down the road came the French in lightweight summer uniforms which I last saw in Sicily. The Maquis marched down the street with four women whose heads were bald as babies. The crowd jeered and heaped scorn on these women because they had kept company with German soldiers. One of the women glared defiantly at the crowds.

"That woman," someone said, "had a husband in Germany as a prisoner. He escaped and returned to her, but she betrayed him to the Germans and he was shot."

The other women hung their heads and stumbled along with their faces ashen and ugly from fear and embarrassment.

All night the guns dueled, but this was the enemy's last stand before Paris.   □

Paris, August 25 — Street fighting raged through the heart of Paris today as American and French columns drove into the city from the south amid a tumultuous welcome from hundreds of thousands of Parisians.

The first French column to enter the city reached Luxembourg at 10:20 a.m. The Germans, the collaborationist militia and the French Gestapo organization opened fire with machine guns, rifles and pistols and the battle was on. An American infantry column drove to Notre Dame at 11 a.m. in a spectacular ground attack to close in on strongholds still defended by the embattled Germans and the Vichy French militia.

(This dispatch was filed at 12:28 p.m., 6:28 a.m., Eastern War Time.)

The columns fought toward the center of the city where 5,000 French Forces of the Interior and city police have held out for the past week. Machine guns and rifles cracked on all sides as the column I was with drove to within a block of the Luxembourg.

Joyous, happy throngs who greeted the entrance of the tanks and infantry with a thundering welcome fled to the safety of buildings and within a few minutes the streets that had been choked with humanity, laughing and crying over the liberation, were bare battlegrounds.

As I write this story the Germans are still holding out in the area on both sides of the Seine halfway along the Champs-Elysées, Place de la Concorde, Quai d'Orsay, Tuileries, Gardens of the Louvre, the Madeleine, the Chamber of Deputies, the Senate and the Hôtel Crillon.

French patriots have a grip on the Île de la Cité, the Palais de Justice, the Préfecture of Police, the Préfecture of the Seine, most of the Mairies and the factory district. But Frenchmen are fighting Frenchmen as well as Germans in liberating a city wild with happiness over the freedom for which they waited for four years.

There was so much confusion and excitement over the entrance into the city that it is difficult to give a coherent account of the events that moved so swiftly, once the French armored column began rolling through the heavy morning fog that made vehicles look like prehistoric monsters appearing out of the swamps of creation.

But when the last enemy resistance crumbled at the gate to Paris then this heart of France went mad—wildly, violently mad with happiness. All the emotions suppressed by four years of German domination surged through the people. The streets of the city as we entered were like a combined Mardi Gras, Fourth of July celebration, American Legion convention and New Year's Eve in Times Square all packed into one.

Our column began to roll at 7 a.m. from Longjumeau, six miles south of Paris. A French captain stopped all correspondents one mile from town and insisted he had orders that no one without a written permit could enter the city. He told three British correspondents they would be shot if they drove by without a pass.

An American colonel heard the story and said the captain was acting without proper authority. I drove to the blockade and suddenly my jeep lurched forward into the column (of troops). Unfortunately it was too late to turn back, so I kept going.

Two miles farther the column halted. Forward elements had run into a German strongpoint and mines on the road. French Brig. Gen. Jacques Leclerc and his staff went into conference. Tanks wheeled and started to out-flank the position but after a while they returned because they ran into the route of an American infantry advance.

Then the column began to roll again. The strongpoint had been knocked out ahead of us. And at 9:57 a.m. my jeep rolled through the gates into Paris.

Never do I expect to see such scenes as I saw on the streets of Paris. There was only a narrow lane through which the armor could roll. Men and women cried with joy. They grabbed the arms and hands of soldiers and cheered until their voices were hoarse.

When the column stopped I was smothered, but pleasantly, with soft arms and lips giving not one kiss but the usual French double one. They hugged me and my jeep driver and pinned French Tricolors on us, and left us ex-hausted, with our bosoms covered with emblems and ribbons. One old man came up, saluted, and said with tears in his eyes: "God bless America. You have saved France."

Men and women, old and young, and children stormed the jeep every time the column stopped and they were wild with emotion. Crowds were banked from the center of the streets to the sidewalks in a colorful, cheer-ing throng which stretched for miles. There seemed to be no end and ap-parently everyone in Paris except the Germans and collaborationists was standing there to cheer, shout, cry, and leave themselves exhausted with happiness.

Our column moved to a point one block from the Luxembourg. Then from all sides burst machine gun fire. From housetops and windows guns rattled. Machine guns of tanks opened up in reply. We leaped from the jeep and took cover behind a tank.

Jerry Beatson of Rockford, Ill., was beside me and leveled his carbine at the top of the building. The gun cracked in my ear.

"There's one — up there," he cried, and kept firing at the rooftop.

Bullets rattled on the streets and glanced off with ugly whines.

The crowds, which a few minutes before lined the streets, melted as if a blast from a furnace had hit a snowbank. Then the streets were terribly lone-ly and barren except for armor with guns clattering.

My driver and I leaped into a jeep and raced back down the street, but an-other burst of machine gun fire sent us diving for the curb. We felt bare and exposed there in the street. FFI resistance leaders crouched and ran from door to door, pointing to the rooftops and windows.

Up there, shooting down on us were the Milice (Vichy collaborators) who were helping the Germans defend the city. One Frenchman said there were many German snipers in civilian clothes.

Red Cross aid men dressed in white ran out of a doorway with a stretcher. A nurse in starched white followed them. They picked up a wounded man and laid him on a stretcher while waving a Red Cross flag.

An FFI member ran up to me and cried in English: "Give us arms and ammunition. We want guns and bullets. That's all we ask. We'll clean out these—.

"We haven't enough ammunition and most of us have only pistols."

Ahead of us patriots crouched along the buildings and answered the enemy fire. Lying there, I felt lonely and lost in the city which all of us had dreamed of entering as a joyous occasion.

The drive on Paris began at 7 a.m. yesterday under sullen, drizzling skies. The French and American columns had moved into position on Wednesday afternoon facing the enemy's position west of Paris. The Germans did not have much in front of us—but enough to make the armor move cautiously, and occasionally artillery would pound gun positions along the way.

Our column avoided the main road to Versailles and turned into a secondary road leading to the Grand National Highway running due south of the city to Orléans. Other columns of armor, assault guns, half-tracks and supply trains fanned out on other roads. The historic move on Paris was under way.

The column moved in lurches, going forward for short distances, then stopping, either for reconnaissance or for guns to engage strongpoints. Rain glistened on the dark green trees and hedges and gave the countryside a freshly washed appearance.

In small towns people crowded along the streets, despite the rain, to wave Tricolors and to cheer each vehicle that passed. Never have I seen more joyous faces than those along the road to Paris. It was a triumphal, exciting and colorful march.

Pretty girls stood on the roadside and tossed flowers at the vehicles. As the column would stop, they would deck the tanks and armored trucks with flowers until they seemed to be camouflaged as mobile flower pots. Farmers tossed fresh tomatoes and apples to the troops.

Sergt. Bob Farley of Des Moines, Iowa; Private Ray Rooney of Glen Ellyn, Ill., and Pvt. Harry Grant of Hamburg, Ark., sat in a jeep watching this outburst of emotion at the edge of the war. "This is the first real holiday I've had in weeks," Farley said. "We've been doing reconnaissance up where the fighting really was tough. But this is like a circus."

Suddenly there was an uproar in the streets. Down the road came the French in lightweight summer uniforms which I last saw in the desert and

Sicily. Most of them were middle-aged or older, but they looked well fed and in excellent physical condition.

A ripple of excitement ran through the crowds.

The Maquis marched down the street with four women whose heads were bald as babies. The crowd jeered and heaped scorn on these women because they had kept company with German soldiers. One of the women glared defiantly at the crowds.

"That woman," someone said, "had a husband in Germany as a prisoner. He escaped and returned to her, but she betrayed him to the Germans and he was shot."

The other women hung their heads and stumbled along with their faces ashen and ugly from fear and embarrassment.

Late in the day the Germans shelled the town and sent the crowds scurrying to cover. Two shells burst squarely in the main street, but the casualties fortunately were light among the civilians. All night the guns dueled, but this was the enemy's last stand before Paris.   □

Paris, August 26 — Paris is bathed in sunshine and happiness today and below the windows of my hotel in the heart of the city is spread a scene of peace contrasting strangely with the turmoil of battle that raged yesterday.

In the broad crossing of two famous streets Parisians are strolling in the warm sun. Around each parked jeep is a group of men, women and children talking and laughing with American soldiers who are giving them cigarettes and sweets and sharing their hard rations.

Paris is exhausted from that uproarious day of liberation yesterday. It is too much to expect that any people could pour out their emotion in such an overflow of joy as that of yesterday when the American and French forces entered and then keep it going for another day.

Now there is only the sound of tinkling bicycle bells—everyone in Paris seems to have a bicycle—of laughter and occasional cheers. In the distance there is the faint thunder of an occasional gun, but resistance inside the city is virtually at an end.

And this day is just as fantastic as those hours of last evening, when the millions of Paris swarmed through the streets in a carnival of celebration over their long-awaited liberation. Crowds stood in the streets and under the starlight sang the Marseillaise and cheered the American and French troops.

The hotels were palaces of luxury to those of us who managed to get rooms. Electric lights still were on and there was running water. The hotels had no food, but there was wine and champagne and cognac for the celebrators.

Even as the military cleaned out the last resistance French political leaders moved in to reorganize the government of Paris.

Lt. Gen. Omar N. Bradley's forces began the great task of helping feed and administer the city.   □

Paris, August 26 — Parisians paid for liberation of their beloved city in blood—and somewhere in this excited capital is a modern Joan of Arc who was the heroine of the patriots' battle to drive out the Germans. At times the patriots fought tanks with nothing more than rifles, pistols and hand grenades and the boldest of the leaders was a French woman known to the Germans as "The Wildcat." This slender brown-haired woman of forty is a captain in the French forces of liberation. Fighting under her was a group of forty men.

An official at one of the large Paris hospitals told the story today of "The Wildcat," who swore vengeance on the Germans when they killed her brother after he had escaped from a concentration camp. "She swore she would kill as many Germans as she could," this official said. "So she joined the FFI and became one of their most trusted leaders."

The day before Paris fell "The Wildcat" led her band of forty against three Mark IV tanks. Her comrades would not let her fight tanks herself, but she carried their ammunition and brought them grenades and directed the fighting. They destroyed the three tanks.

She is elusive and difficult to find. She moves about the city, staying with friends and rarely in one place very long. Usually she wears a shabby short skirt, a man's shirt and a bandana tied around her hair. "She has a fine face," the official said "except that when I saw her yesterday, her face was drawn with exhaustion. She had gone many hours without sleep or rest. And she talked of her brother and cried."   □

Paris, August 27 — Marshall Henri-Philippe Pétain, Pierre Laval and former Premier Édouard Herriot were arrested by the Gestapo and taken to Germany a few days before American and French forces entered Paris, a reliable informant said today. Before he left, Marshal Pétain sent a clandestine message to the people of France, urging them to unite and stating that all that he had submitted to had been for their welfare.

(Dispatches from Delle, France, dated Thursday, said that Marshal Pétain and Laval were still at Morvillars, near Belfort, France, despite reports that they had been taken to Germany.)

The marshal said in his message that he had known that he would be arrested. On August 20, five days before the Allies entered Paris, he was taken to Belfort, near the Swiss frontier, and then on to Germany. M. Herriot was brought to Paris from Nancy by Laval expressly to attend and join a meeting of the Senate and the Chamber of Deputies to discuss problems arising from the Allies' advance on Paris and the possibility of moving the French Government from Vichy to Belfort. But the meeting never was held.

Many Parisians are whispering that Laval arranged the arrests of Marshal Pétain and M. Herriot and then his own arrest in a deal with his German masters that would prevent the Allies from getting the custody of the others. At the same time, he was said to have tried to make it appear to his countrymen that he had not left Paris voluntarily as the Allies drew near.

Whether these rumors have any basis cannot be determined at this time. Copies of letters reliably reported to have been exchanged between Laval and Otto Abetz, German Ambassador to Paris, make it appear as if Laval had opposed the German determination to move the French Government to Belfort and had been arrested because of his determination and his desire to stay in Paris.

Marshal Pétain was taken into custody by an official of the German Embassy, but he sent this message before leaving:

"Frenchmen: When this message reaches you I shall no longer be free. In the extreme condition in which I now find myself, I have nothing to reveal to you except the simple confirmation of what has motivated my conduct for the past four years.

"Having decided to remain among you, I have tried day by day to find the best way to serve the permanent interests of France loyally and without compromise. I had but one object—to protect you from the worst.

"All that I have done and all that I have accepted, consented to, or submitted to, whether willingly or by force, has been solely for your welfare; because, if I could not be your sword, I wanted to be your shield.

"Under certain circumstances, my words and my acts must have surprised you. You must realize that they have hurt me more than you can possibly imagine.

"I have suffered for you and with you, and I have marshaled all of my forces against what is menacing you. I have shielded you from some certain perils. However, there were some, alas, that I could not prevent.

"My conscience is my witness that no one from any party can contradict me on this point. What the enemy wants today is to take me away from you. I do not have to justify myself in their eyes. I care only for the people of France. For you, as for me, there is only one France—the France of our ancestors.

"Once again, I advise you to unite. It is not difficult to do one's duty, even though it sometimes is hard to recognize it. Yours is simple. Unite with those who will give you a guarantee to lead you along the road of honor and order.

"Order must reign. And, because I represent order legitimately, I remain your chief. Obey me and obey those who will bring you words of social peace without which order cannot be re-established.

"Those who will tell you to follow a policy of reconciliation and renaissance of France through reciprocal forgiveness and love of your fellow countrymen—those are the real French leaders. They continue my work. Be at their side. For myself, I have been separated from you, but I do not leave you and I hope that all of you will give your utmost loyalty to France, which, God willing, will be restored to her grandeur.

"Destiny is taking me away. I undergo the greatest constraint that a man can suffer. It is with joy that I accept this suffering should it be a condition of your deliverance, if, before foreigners, even should they be allies, you remain faithful to the true patriotism that thinks only of the true interests of France, and if my sacrifice enables you to find again the way of sacred union for the renaissance of your fatherland." Henri-Philippe Pétain.

According to my informant, the chronology of events leading up to the situation was this:

M. Herriot, who had been under guard, was brought to Paris on August 15 and stayed at the Hôtel de Ville. On the next day he lunched with Laval and Abetz. At 11 p.m., Laval was told that the chief of the Gestapo had presented himself with an order from the head of the Gestapo, Heinrich Himmler, to bring M. Herriot to Germany.

Laval immediately went to M. Herriot at the Hôtel de Ville. M. Herriot gave the following letter to Laval, dated August 16:

"After having been informed at Nancy by Premier Laval that I was free without any effort to seek freedom on my part, and after having been taken back to Paris, I am again taken to an unknown destination with my wife, who courageously and voluntarily followed me, regardless of the lot that may befall me.

"I have no means to resist the command enforced by arms, especially when this command is a breach of a word of honor. But I want to leave with you, Premier Laval, this solemn protest that I ask you to transmit to the German Ambassador." Herriot.

Laval then sent the following letter to Abetz, dated August 17:

"I was informed by you that I could announce to M. Herriot that he was free. I went to Nancy for this purpose and brought him back to Paris.

"The news of his arrest and his transfer to Nancy or to Germany, which I have just learned, affects me deeply. Should this order be executed, I shall have to construe it as a grave offense to me personally. People will not hesitate to implicate me in this act and you know very well that I have never been a party to this sort of conduct.

"I should ask you to consider me as a prisoner in the same manner as M. Herriot and in any case that you force me to renounce all my powers as head of the State.

"The relations that I have had with Chancellor Hitler authorize me to address myself directly to him through you as intermediary, in order to have him revoke this order." Pierre Laval.

It was reported that Abetz did not reply to this letter, but informed Laval that it was impossible to cancel the order. However, he did send Laval a letter on August 17. It said:

"Considering the situation created by military operations, the German Government begs me to inform you that it believes that, for the welfare of France, the seat of the Government should be transferred from Vichy to Belfort.

"I know that you, as head of the Government, have decided to stay among your people, come what may, and I have so informed my Government of your decision. The German Government well realized the reasons for your wanting to stay but it cannot reconsider.

"This decision will be reconsidered whenever the military situation permits."

To this Laval replied on August 17:

"This is to acknowledge your letter, the contents of which I have made known to the Cabinet.

"The French government does not accept the invitation to change the seat of Government from Vichy to Belfort, regardless of the reasons that you may propose. In this case, after having conferred with all the Ministers present, we cannot consider your invitation to move."

In saying that he had conferred with "all the Ministers present," Laval probably knew that Marcel Déat, Joseph Darnand and Fernand de Brinon had left for Germany two days before.

Abetz' reply to this letter follows:

"M. le Président (of the Cabinet), the communication that I had the honor of sending you this afternoon concerning the transfer of the French Government to Belfort is the irrevocable decision of the German Reich.

"I regret to inform you that, if the French Government refuses to move, forceful means will be employed.

"I trust that you, M. le Président, and the members of the Government will realize that this decision was taken not only to maintain order in the rear of the German Army but to assure the personal security and safety of the French Government."

Laval replied the same day:

"In answer to your letter, I regret to think that the German Government would not hesitate to employ forceful means to effect the transfer of the French Government to Belfort.

"You are very anxious to assure the personal security of the French Government, but allow me to say that my anxiety was of a higher nature—I wanted to accomplish to the very end, regardless of the risks, my duties as head of the Government.

"I am forced to accept. But you understand that under these conditions I can no longer exercise my powers."

Laval was arrested at midnight of August 17 at the Hôtel Matignon and transferred to Belfort. On the same day Marshal Pétain had written to Laval from Vichy, but his letter was dispatched at 8 p.m. and never reached Laval. It said:

"M. le Président, I have just received a visit from M. Rente-Finck (Dr. Cecil Von Rente-Finck, Hitler's personal representative to Marshal Pétain), who informed me orally that the German Government had given its consent to a meeting of the National Assembly.

"In view of the military situation, it is impossible to hold a meeting at Versailles and M. Rente-Finck told me that it would be held at Nancy, where the President would attend in person.

"M. Rente-Finck believes that Vichy is not safe and has asked me to move to another city in the east, the name of which was not divulged and which would eventually become the seat of Government.

"He told me that you yourself would soon leave Paris. Your leaving the city does not agree with what you told me some time ago, which you confirmed by telephone yesterday morning. It was your idea that the Government could not be anywhere else than in Vichy or Paris.

"I told him that I would not make any decision until I had discussed it with you.

"An officer will deliver this letter and I ask you to give him in writing your answer on this question. It is only on the return of this officer that I will decide what is for the welfare of the country."   ☐

Paris, August 28 — The following story of Pierre Laval's last day in Paris was given me by a man who was with Laval most of the day. (Presumably this man was friendly to Laval.) The events took place in Laval's office on August 17 in the Hôtel Matignon which was the seat of the French government in Paris. This is the story:

At 12:30 p.m., on August 17 Former Premier Édouard Herriot and Mrs. Herriot, who had been brought to Paris by Laval, came to the Hôtel Matignon with German Ambassador Otto Abetz. On the previous day Herriot had been informed by the Gestapo that he was to be taken under arrest to either Nancy or Germany.

The Herriots went into an anteroom while Abetz and Laval discussed the German government's order that the seat of the French government be moved, by force if necessary, from Vichy to Belfort.

After Abetz and the Herriots departed Laval was left in a big office with a fireplace. He sat at a desk behind which was a Gobelin tapestry of a seventeenth-century peasant scene. During the afternoon there was an exchange of notes between Laval and Abetz regarding the French government's move to Belfort.

In the notes Laval protested the transfer but Abetz said the action was an order of the Reich government and Laval would be taken forcibly if he refused. Laval stayed at his desk working furiously to finish the duties that lay before him.

At 8 p.m., Laval's last visitors assembled in the big room. They included Jeunier, chief of Laval's private secretaries; Bonnefoy, general secretary for information; Christophe, director of the press; Guérard, Laval's general secretary, and my informant.

Laval was in his shirt sleeves. His white shirt was wilted and open at the neck. His white tie was wrinkled and soiled. His hair [was] disheveled and perspiration stood on his forehead. "He looked like a man in mental torture," said Monsieur M., my informant.

Laval asked Guérard to read aloud his last letter to Abetz in which he said he was forced to accept the German government's demands to move the

French government to Belfort. Then Guérard read a letter written by Laval to M. Taittinger, president of the Paris city council, regarding the transfer of powers.

Guérard was fearful that Laval, by saying he was being "forced to accept" the Germans demands, might create an incident with the Nazis. He wanted to change the word "forced" to "compelled."

"Laval would not agree to the change," said Monsieur M.

By this time dusk of the late evening brought gloom to the big room. The only light in the place was from the fireplace in which Laval was burning his personal papers. Laval wrote a few more letters and talked to the group. Then a Gestapo officer entered the room.

"I have come to conduct you to Belfort," he said to Laval.

Laval said he would be ready when he had signed the letters he had written. The Gestapo officer went outside to wait for him. Laval then began saying farewells to those with him. He shook hands with Christophe and said "Carry on—I will be back with you some day."

Then the group left Laval alone with the Gestapo officer. □

Six

THE DRIVE INTO GERMANY,

FALL 1944

Château-Thierry, France, August 29 — American troops, fighting over the rolling green battlefields where doughboys and marines immortalized themselves in 1918, occupied Château-Thierry and went past Belleau Wood in a smash that swept across the Valley of the Marne to the approaches of Reims today.

Lieut. Gen. George S. Patton's forces encountered only minor resistance from the Germans, whose main body was in headlong flight toward Belgium and the Reich.

Belleau Wood, scene of heavy fighting in the decisive battles in the summer of 1918, is five miles west of Château-Thierry. The magnificent twenty-four-column American Aisne-Marne Memorial, overlooking Château-Thierry and the American Cemetery at Belleau Wood, had not been molested by the Germans. Their grounds have been beautifully kept up throughout the war by French caretakers.

But in the town of Château-Thierry the twin-columned monument to the United States Third Division had been wrecked in fighting between the Germans and French in 1940. The stone memorial church in Chateau-Thierry, built with American funds, had been hit, but damage was slight. A shell struck the tower just above the front entrance during fighting in the town square yesterday.

Residents said the Third Division monument, which stood on the north bank of the Marne, was damaged first when a nearby bridge was blown up in 1940 and then by crossfire of French and German antitank guns. The pyramid-shaped column nearest the river had been toppled and great chunks blasted from the other column.

"Even after it was wrecked we placed flowers there on your Day of Independence and every November 11," a French woman said. "The Germans took them away as fast as we placed them there and we kept putting them back." There was a big bunch of pink gladioli and purple peonies at the monument today, and our troops streaming toward Reims saluted smartly as they passed.

In Belleau Wood at one end of the curving rows of marble crosses are nine fresh graves with wooden crosses. They are for American prisoners of war killed a few months ago when an Allied plane attacked the train on which they were being taken to Germany. Wounded from the same train now are in Château-Thierry Hospital.

Belleau Wood and Château-Thierry are markers in the history of the American troops' part in the Second Battle of the Marne in 1918. The Germans had been fighting back with the desperation of trapped animals. By May 30, 1918, the Associated Press recalled, the tip of a German salient driven into Château-Thierry menaced the road to Paris. On May 31 the Seventh Machine-gun Battalion of the United States Third Division was rushed up to cover the retreat of French colonials in the town. Then it crossed to the south side of the Marne, preventing the enemy from jumping the river.

The American Second and Third Division took up positions to the west and east of Château-Thierry, and the Germans on June 3 attacked the Second Division and French Forty-third Division west of the town. Belleau Wood was a focal point of this fighting.

Early in July the United States Twenty-sixth Division relieved the Second, and the French 167th Division joined their line to Château-Thierry, forming the American First Corps.

The big German offensive to mid-July on a line from Château-Thierry eastward broke down. Without a pause in the fighting, the Allied offensive began July 18, and the American First Corps at Château-Thierry acted as pivot while the west side of the salient was smashed. The Twenty-sixth Division advanced, crossing the Château-Thierry-Soissons road on July 21, and the Third Division east of the town began crossing the Marne, cracking the east side of the enemy salient.   ☐

Reims, France, August 31 — Ghosts of World War [One] memories marched across the battlefields of France as Lt. Gen. Omar N. Bradley's armies rolled forward today across beautiful green fields that were torn by shells and drenched with blood a quarter of a century ago. Behind these victorious troops are such names as the Marne, Belleau Woods, Compiègne, Soissons, Meuse and Reims.

Reims twenty-six years ago was little more than a pile of rubble, its beautiful cathedral shattered. John D. Rockefeller, Jr., restored the cathedral to its former glory and now there is little evidence of war in Reims. There are only occasional reminders that armies have passed up the lush valley of the Marne and through the thriving fields of Epernay's famous Champagne vineyards.

We left Paris in the early morning and sped up the smooth straight road toward Château-Thierry. As we rode along the Marne River through deep shadows of stately trees, we were only occasionally reminded of the war by burned-out tanks and German vehicles caught in the swift advance of our columns. Ahead of us one unit was forming up for an attack in the same ravines where another American unit had made its first attack in the last war.

People waved greetings all along the road and there were the inevitable cries of "bonbon, chewing gum," from the children.

Along our way we saw two marble shafts commemorating the heroism of the Fourth, First and Second Infantry Divisions which fought across this rolling country a generation ago.

At a railway crossing between Chateau-Thierry and Soissons Pvt. Jim Hughes of New Castle, Pa., directed traffic while crowds of civilians gathered to see a German train of nineteen cars which was ambushed by American tanks.

"A Cub plane spotted this train and when it came along tanks were waiting," Hughes said. Four Panther tanks on the flatcars engaged the American tanks in battle and knocked out two of our tanks but the whole train was destroyed. Four passenger cars were loaded with officers, troops and women they were evacuating from Paris. The still smouldering train, ripped by bullets, was black and charred. Some of the tank crews were cremated inside the burning hulks and some Germans never got out of the blazing cars. Two of the cars were loaded with perfume from Paris.

In front of Reims Cathedral was a wall of sandbags at least fifty feet high, erected to protect the edifice. Doughboys with carbines slung on their shoulders walked in awe beneath the vaulted ceiling of the cathedral. Among them were Pfc. Hal Beasley of Sylva, N.C., and Sgt. Marchus Setzer Jr., Hickory, N.C.

Outside was a statue of Joan of Arc astride a charger. An American flag waved from her upraised sword. □

Seloignes, Belgium, September 2 — The American First Army drove twin spearheads into Belgium today. The Americans crossed the French-Belgian border at 11 a.m. They had captured Maubeuge, France, five miles from the border. To the west, an armored column seized Tournai, five miles inside the Belgian border and about forty-five miles from Brussels. (Seloignes is in the Belgian province of Hainaut, of which Mons is the largest city; Maubeuge is on the road to Mons.)

Laughing, cheering and weeping Belgians decked American tanks, trucks and jeeps with garlands of flowers. As I write this I have before me a copy of *The Sun*, of New York, dated May 28, 1940, with the headline, "King of Belgians Surrenders Army" and an Associated Press story datelined Paris which said: "The Belgian Army surrendered today on orders of King Leopold III, leaving the armies of Great Britain and France in an ominously weaker position to resist the Nazi drive toward the English Channel."

But this is 1940 in reverse. The Americans are rolling northward, and this time it is the Nazi legions which are in an "ominously weaker position." The swift push of the American columns has completely disorganized the enemy. In the last eight days Lieutenant General Omar N. Bradley's forces have rolled forward 120 airline miles, and prisoners are being taken at the rate of 2,000 to 3,000 a day. The Germans withdrew last night and this morning from the Belgian border, and our troops met only scattered resistance in the push north. Happy throngs greeted them at every hamlet and crossroads.

I crossed the border with Harry Harris and Pete Carroll, Associated Press photographers, at noon and our jeep looked like a rolling flower garden after the first few miles. At a crossroads hamlet, the Americans were congregated on a side road with the natives crowded about them laughing and cheering and giving the soldiers flowers, eggs, cognac and wine. "This is the greatest welcome I have received since I came across," laughed Corporal Robert Rinehart, of Bradford, Pa., with a garland of flowers dangling from his helmet.

"There isn't much doubt these people are glad to see us," said Sergeant John Marston, of Boston. The last Germans had pulled out just two hours before the Americans came up the road. Then the Belgians broke out their hidden national flags of black, gold and red along with the homemade American emblems and flags of France and Great Britain.

The first column in our sector entered Belgium under the command of Lieutenant Colonel Charles T. Fort, of Winston-Salem, N.C., and was directed by Major Gail Brown, of Sheridan, Wyo. Driving toward the border, we passed long columns of tanks and trucks rolling through the rich, green countryside with no sound of battle ahead. A chill wind swept the fields. The road wound through dark, wet trees in the Forest of Michèle and it was like taking a pleasure drive at home in that quiet, untouched woodland. The birds sang in the thick foliage.

At one town a celebration was under way. All the villagers turned out to give the Americans a welcome, and the troops were showing them their vehicles, guns and equipment. An aged Belgian ran out of a gray stone house and grabbed Harris by one arm while waving a bottle of cognac with the other. His wife leaned from a window waving Belgian and American flags and yelling. At the same time she was screaming at a barking dog.

In Seloignes, Major Albert Bruchac, of Elmhurst, N.Y., Major Keene Wilson, of Selma, Ala., and Private Joseph H. Moore, of Mantic, Ill., were smothered with flowers before they drove forward on a reconnaissance mission to try to get contact with the retreating enemy. None of the villages bore many scars of war. The Germans were too hurried to do any damage except in a few places. In two French villages just below the Belgium border, however, retreating SS (elite guard) troops machine-gunned some civilians and set fire to houses in a rage over their retreat.

"The French people put out their flags in celebration of the arrival of the Americans too soon," one officer said. "When the last column of Germans came through town they were furious. They burned many houses and machine-gunned some of the townspeople, leaving their bodies lying in the street."

Late today the American advance was still progressing and was now being carried into country through which the Germans crossed in 1940 to make their famous breakthrough at Sedan. It was announced officially that since D-Day the First Army had taken 117,908 prisoners.

BELGIANS MET US WITH WINE AND FLOWERS

I crossed the Belgian border yesterday with two photographers. The jeep in which I crossed at noon looked like a flower garden after the first few miles. At a village crossroads American troops congregated on the side of the road, with the locals crowding round them, laughing, cheering, and giving the boys flowers, eggs, chocolate and wine.

"This is the greatest welcome I have received since I came across," declared one soldier, with a garland of flowers hanging from his helmet.

The last Germans had pulled out just two hours before these Americans came up the road.

General Hodge's First American Army drove twin spearheads into Belgium. The first American troops crossed the border at 11 a.m., capturing Maubeuge, while to the west an armored column captured Tournai, forty-three miles from Brussels. The swift drive of the American columns has completely disorganized the Germans. They withdrew from the Belgian border, and our troops met only scattered and light resistance in their push to the north.

Donald Clark, B.U.P. [British United Press] correspondent with the British Forces approaching Belgium, cabled: "Thousands of British troops are roaring across the Somme in what I can only describe as a gigantic avalanche. They are going forward at the rate of forty miles a day toward the frontiers of Belgium and Germany."

There are at least three columns moving northward, with orders from the highest authority to "leave pockets where necessary, but keep moving." One Londoner I spoke to said: "It seems as if the whole blinking British Army is moving. I've been in the Army since '39, but I have never seen anything like this.

The whole Somme line presents the most fantastic spectacle with Allied armor bypassing groups of from four to six hundred Germans who have been left in the woods and copses. Most of these small German units are as dispirited as the fifty I saw give themselves up to a young British lieutenant.

The Maquis have been playing a most important part in the advance, relieving the Allied troops of the job of mopping up. At one point, outside Amiens, they rounded up 400 German cavalry horses and organized their own cavalry troop, whooping off across the countryside with the greatest enthusiasm. The same reports come from all sectors—the Allies are pushing ahead in a vacuum, with a complete lack of organized resistance against them. The villages along the way were filled with the roar of Allied transport which simply staggered the French.

I wish that all British civilians could have traveled with me through the dozens of villages liberated in the past few hours, and others where we appeared to be the first Allied vehicles. This was the harvest of "blood, toil, sweat, and tears"—the full face of victory smashing and complete, and apparently won with casualties slighter than even the most optimistic of us expected.

This is what millions of you dreamed of and that for which thousands worked and died—the end in France. Though there is still likely to be some fighting in France, it is obvious that the enemy is moving out just as quickly as his wrecked transport system will move him.

In the villages and towns through which we move there are the usual rejoicings, but more impressive were the lonely country crossroads where farmers, laborers and their wives and daughters gathered and virtually mobbed any Allied vehicle that stopped. It is impossible to write of a front here, because the front has just ceased to exist.   □

With the American First Army in Belgium, September 5 — Lt. Gen. Courtney H. Hodges' First American Army—after scoring one of the greatest victories of the invasion by trapping thousands of

Germans at the French-Belgian frontier—drove deeply into Belgium yesterday toward the German border and the famed West Wall or Siegfried line.

More than 8,000 prisoners were bagged Sunday and uncounted thousands were streaming into prisoner pens in one of the biggest hauls since the Yanks landed on the beaches of Normandy three months ago. Truckload after truckload of Germans in green-gray field uniforms were rolling down the roads in the vicinity of Mons where Hodges sprang a trap to envelop the confused, panicky enemy which now is utterly without battle form or organized leadership.

It can be disclosed now that the Americans, after the capture of Paris, drove straight toward the German border and the Sedan region through which the Germans made their famous breakthrough four years ago. But before reaching Sedan the column wheeled north just as it did at Le Mans to spring the Falaise-Argentan trap. This time the jaws of the trap closed.

Spearheaded by the armored column, infantry moved ahead fast, riding trucks, tanks, artillery pieces and anything on wheels. Many of them had to make long forced marches afoot because there was not enough transport to carry all. They made a sensational advance, and the hooking movement caught the Germans by surprise.

Three German generals and several other high officers were taken prisoner by the doughboys. Hundreds of prisoners have been walking down the roads without guards as the armor rolls on with no time to stop and put them under guard. White flags of surrender have been fluttering from every forest, town and field.

"Now we're seeing Hitler's V-5 [rocket]," grinned Lt. Col. Clarence Beck, Daytona Beach, Fla. "The V-5 is a very white flag on a very long pole."

In the thrust on Mons, the armored column and the infantry columns were in the peculiar position of being in the line of the enemy's retreat. Germans by the thousands were stampeding back to the German border. For five days they had been without communication and did not know where the American columns were.

In the past thirty-six hours the Germans have been trying desperately to find a way out of the bag. Doughboy engineers, cooks, military police and headquarters companies were battling them in one of the most confused battle pictures of the entire war. Prisoners are being taken all over the rear areas.

These are some of the astonishing things that have been happening:

Two nights ago military policemen were directing artillery into the fields. A German Panther tank came rolling down the road with our column and turned as directed into the fields. The driver thought he was traveling with his own column. The boys knocked it out next morning as the frantic driver tried to escape.

Eighty Germans led by a major tried to get through a division headquarters command post but they were rounded up by the headquarters company. Pvt. Richard Jensen, Homestead, Fla., had been directing traffic at a division headquarters post all day. When a general and his staff officers called for their jeeps, eight Germans popped up from a field fifty yards away, waving a white flag of surrender.

Sgt. Eric J. Metzger, New York, and Pvt. Paul Stein, Kalamazoo, Mich., were going toward Mons last night with a group of doughboys. They entered the town of Maubeuge, through which American armor had passed several hours before. Metzger and the men with him had to stop and clean out 150 Germans still holding houses in one street with five machine guns.

A group of engineers under Lt. Col. William B. Gara, New York, had built a span of one bridge and had equipment laid out for another when a German armored car towing an artillery piece came roaring down the road.

"The armored car hit that equipment on the unfinished side of the span," Gara laughed, "and piled into the Serre River, throwing Germans in all directions. They came crawling out of the river screaming at the lieutenant who had taken the wrong turn in the road. That was the funniest sight of the war."

The Germans broke up into groups of fifty to two hundred men, all attempting retreat to the German border in the general rout. The fighting continuing for two days by the Germans is a desperate, bewildered effort to find some way out of the trap. All along the roads are wrecks of columns of enemy vehicles and black hulks of burned-out tanks.

At a town near the Belgian border American military police under direction of Capt. Raymond L. Regan, Lancaster, N.Y., former New York State Trooper, was putting prisoners in an old French barracks.

"This job is too big for my little group of men to handle," he said.

Through the gate by twos came a long column of Germans. Trucks kept bringing more in every few minutes.

"This looks like the lineup for tickets at the Yankee Stadium," said Pvt. John Kock, of Garret, Ind.

At the gate Lt. William Bradford, of Rutland, Vt., and Sgt. Martin Lewkowicz, New Orleans, La., checked off the prisoners as they entered. Bradford had a ledger marked "score card," in which he was keeping tally. The count for the day had reached 5,000 at this one collecting point.

The prisoners leaned out the windows of the three-story buildings yelling to friends as they entered the gate. Not many seemed dejected over capture.

The guards searched each man and relieved him of knives, mirrors, forks and anything else which might be used as a weapon.

This roundup was the result of a swift and decisive move by troops under Lt. Gen. Courtney H. Hodges. The speed with which the drive was made was illustrated by the move of one infantry division. On August 27 the division had crossed the Seine. The troops moved through Soissons and Sunday had traveled 165 miles, an average of more than twenty-five miles a day for eight days.   ☐

Chimay, Belgium, September 7 — Belgium's "White Army"— patriots who have resisted the Germans during four years of occupation— has come out of hiding to help Allied armies drive the enemy from Belgian soil. They are also dealing out justice to the Rexist Quislings who collaborated with the enemy.

León Degrelle, greatest Belgian Quisling of them all, is reported to have escaped into Germany, but there are many satellites left behind to face the wrath of their own people. When the crisis came they found their Nazi friends would not even bother to give them transportation to the comparative security of Germany.

There were forty persons from nearby villages, accused by the White Army of collaboration, herded into barracks here today under guard of youthful members of the Patriot Army. With these roving bands were many American youths, airmen who joined the White Army after parachuting from planes shot down by the enemy.

Driving through this village with Associated Press photographers Peter Carrol and Harry Harris we noticed excited crowds gathered about gates to a huge barracks. We asked what was going on and Belgians replied, "They have Belgian traitors in there."

In the courtyard young men with assorted weapons stood guard. Everything seemed to be orderly and well-organized and the men were disciplined. They wore civilian clothes, but each wore a black, gold and white armband with the initials "F.I.N.," which means Independence Front of Namur Province.

Inside the barracks the young leader of the White Army group was giving orders to lieutenants. The young leader looked as if he hadn't begun to shave. He was a nice-looking kid with wide direct blue eyes and brown hair. His men called him Stan.

"At last we are getting our revenge against these Rexist Quislings," Stan said. "Before the Americans came we carried out our own executions, but now we will let proper authorities handle these cases."

Stan was a student in Brussels when the hated Germans invaded his country. He was only eighteen then, but with five friends of the same age he organized a band to harass the enemy. Soon there were sixty members.

"We could not stay in the cities," Stan said. "There was too much danger. So for two years we have been living in the woods and moving about the country from place to place. Farm people gave us food and shelter and helped protect us from the Germans."

Stan said seventy per cent of the Gestapo agents were Belgian collaborators who received 500 francs for each Patriot they turned over to the Germans. Then the Germans would torture the youths and try to make them reveal the names of their comrades and their hiding places.

"Many of my friends were tortured or killed by the Germans," Stan said, "but now these Quislings will pay." And then the youth added, as matter-of-factly as though we were talking of mad dogs, "I have killed three Quislings myself. People told us of their oppressions. At night I went to the homes of these Quislings and shot them dead."

Stan led us upstairs and opened the door of a large room where the prisoner Quislings were being held. A nondescript group of men and women lounged on double-deck bunks, their faces expressionless except for eyes which followed every move of their captors with fear and hatred.

And then we saw the cause of this fear. Kneeling beside one of the bunks was a man who was a revolting sight to see.

"That," said Stan contemptuously, "is his excellency, the Mayor of the village of Olly. He turned over forty patriots to the Germans himself. Fourteen of them were killed."

The man kneeled in a stupor. He wore only a pair of blue trousers. His feet were bare. His body from waist to shoulders was livid with welts and bruises. His face was swollen and bloody. His hands hung to the floor like those of an ape. Blood had clotted over a cut near his eye and his thick lower lip hung in a quivering pout. His eyes were glazed and there was an expression of bewilderment on his swollen face as if he were unable to believe things could happen to him that he had caused to happen to others.

"People of his village did that before we got him," Stan said.

A woman came up and plucked at Stan's sleeve and they talked rapidly in French.

"She says there are hundreds of Germans near her farm who want to surrender, but they are afraid of the White Army and they want to surrender to Americans." □

Liège, Belgium, September 9 — Twenty-four hours after their liberation the people of this industrial city on the banks of the Meuse River still were wildly acclaiming the Americans today as infantry and armored columns passed through and closed in on the Siegfried line.

Along the Boulevard Frères Orban and in the Place St-Lambert in the heart of Liège thousands of people stood and cheered the troops. Every time a vehicle stopped, girls rushed to it and kissed the occupants. Grinning, embarrassed doughboys and tankmen in battle-stained uniforms were having a fine time, and so was the city of Liège.

The flags of Belgium, France, Britain and the United States fluttered from every building. Apparently the Belgians had not expected the Americans, for flags of Britain and France predominated, but some Star-Spangled Banners were hastily manufactured, and one enterprising businessman even turned out some printed paper flags for street sales.

The Germans wrecked most of the main bridges across the Meuse but American engineers quickly threw pontoons across the wide stream and the advance continued with little delay.

The sun shone brightly today and the townspeople all wore their most colorful clothes to hail the victorious troops of the First Army. They lined the Meuse banks and stood on the dynamited ruins of the bridges, cheering the Americans crossing on the pontoons in a parade of tanks, guns, trucks and jeeps. Everyone agrees that this Belgian welcome is even more enthusiastic and heartwarming than the great ovation the troops received in France. □

With U.S. Troops in Germany, September 14 (5:53 p.m.) — Doughboys of the First Army, supported by tanks, pierced the first line of the Siegfried defenses today and drove deeper into Germany.

Infantry commanded by Capt. Kimball Richmond of Windsor, Vt., broke the back of the formidable line in the sector where this is written, deep in the Aachen Town Forest. The doughboys are not yet through all the Siegfried line there because the enemy had built a double belt of concrete tank barriers and thick-walled forts, but they have smashed the first and are on their way to the second. Yesterday Richmond studied his maps and said:

"I think I can slip my boys in through here."

He pointed to a trail through the heavily-wooded forest. Today he did just that.

On the crest of a rolling ridge across which tanks could approach, the Germans had built a belt of dragon's teeth tank barriers, made up of concrete piles set deep in the ground and ranging from two to four feet high. Tapering slightly at the top, they were set in rows five deep.

Behind this belt are the fortifications, almost invisible to a casual observer because they blend so well into the green of the forest and the grass. When the Germans built them, they piled dirt on top and during the years the grass has grown thickly there.

Richmond called on his tanks for artillery support when his infantrymen reached the Siegfried line and they blasted the forts into submission. Infantry crossed the belt of dragon's teeth, then engineers cut a path and the tanks rolled on to continue their supporting role.

For some reason—probably lack of manpower—the enemy has not manned all fortifications. This breach was made swiftly. Germans poured out of the forts in surrender, but some of them died inside. Richmond's men knocked out four forts and an observation tower in making the breach.

When his troops were fired on from the main fort in this area, Richmond brought up tanks. Their shells crashed into the target. Six German soldiers, a forty-year-old woman and a three-year-old girl came running out with their hands in the air. Then, in rapid succession, other points collapsed.

The woman and child, it was learned, had fled into the fort when a shell set fire to their nearby home. "She came out and spit at me and called us swine," said Sgt. John Sullivan, 676 E. 238th St., New York.   □

With American Infantry inside Germany, [September 14] — American doughboys dug in Wednesday on heights overlooking the city of Aachen after they had fought into outposts of the Siegfried line against surprisingly weak opposition. There are strong indications that the Germans will not make their big stand on this line but will try to hold the Rhine River, running some thirty-five miles or more to the rear.

The troops, consolidating positions after infantry beat back an enemy counter-attack, dug in solidly in the deep, cool shadows of the Aachen Town Forest. As this is written, they are sitting on heights looking down on the city of Aachen, two miles inside the border. The Germans still are fighting from pillboxes and dugouts in the woods. The rattle of machine guns, the thump of mortars and crash of shells echo sibilantly.

Troops under Lt. Col. Edward Driscoll, of Long Island, N.Y., were the first infantrymen to cross the border in strength in this sector. In some places the Germans quit their positions ten minutes before Driscoll's troops were upon them. Why they pulled back so suddenly with no effort to defend many strongpoints is not explained as yet.

In his command post the division commander pored over his map and shook his head almost in disbelief that this could have happened. "I can't figure it out," said a staff officer. "We expected a heavy battle and were ready for it. Now look what's happened."

Long columns crossed into Germany, moving along all side roads and sometimes cutting cross country through narrow lanes barely wide enough for single vehicles. The troops seemed to take this historic move matter-of-factly. There was no apparent elation or spontaneous outbreak of cheers at the border.

Coming into Germany the troops saw what looked like a concrete fortification on a hillside overlooking the route of the advance. Closer inspection showed it was just a house camouflaged to look like a concrete fortification. It was not manned. The entry into Germany was blocked for a time at one point, so we searched for an open route and finally found a column moving across the border north of a little hamlet.

Occasionally people waved from the windows but most of them stood on the roadside and stared with stolid faces. People in this area are predominately German.

On the crest of the hill, the troops found two enemy positions, both unoccupied. One was a concrete emplacement of some sort but with no apertures for weapons. On the top was an opening for ventilation. They overran a battery of 88-millimeter guns in open emplacements. There were troops in the trenches around the guns but they put up no resistance.

"Most of the prisoners we've taken look like kids of sixteen to eighteen," an American officer said. ☐

With American Infantry in Germany, September 15 — Smashing forward on a wide front east of Aachen in a spectacular twenty-four-hour drive, doughboys of Lt. Gen. Courtney H. Hodges' First United States Army broke through the main Siegfried line today.

This headlong attack, carrying into Germany the same sweep that had won France and Belgium, found the line weakly defended. In some places apparent defensive positions were fakes. The doughboys were well supported by tanks, but essentially it was an infantry victory—one of the greatest of the invasion. The assault on the Siegfried line began yesterday. In this sector there was a double belt of defenses—one before Aachen and the other on the other side.

Troops led by Capt. Kimball Richmond, Windsor, Vt., fought their way through the first line defenses yesterday. The infantry kept right on driving. In twenty-four hours the doughboys pushed forward 6,000 yards and then stood before the second belt of pillboxes, dragon's teeth antitank defenses and trenches.

Then it was time for someone else to carry the ball. And this time the spearhead of the drive was a unit under the command of a young lieutenant, Frank Kolb of Kentucky.

"We thought we'd get hell knocked out of us when we began to move on the last line of defenses," said Maj. John Lawton, Glendale, Calif. "We sent a patrol toward the line and thought we would be lucky to get the boys back. The next thing we knew the boys were sitting right smack in the middle of the defenses."

They not only sat in the middle of the defenses but they kept driving forward to knock out enemy pillboxes one by one until they cleared a wide path by knocking out twenty-one concrete emplacements or by occupying them. Then armor came up the roads. Engineers blasted away some of the concrete dragon's teeth set in wide belts before the fortifications.

At one point engineers found the Germans had dummy tank barriers. They camouflaged trucks and piles of dirt which only had to be shoved aside to open way for the armor.

One of the most amazing things in all the invasion has been the unexpected weakness of German defenses within the Siegfried line. Had they manned all these formidable forts with their six-foot thick walls then our troops would have had a bloody battle to break through.

But for lack of manpower, or because they believed the Rhine River would be a better defense line, the enemy did not make his big fight in the Siegfried defenses. The Germans left only part of the forts occupied by machine gunners and had comparatively light artillery.

In twenty-four hours our crack infantry moved 6,000 yards through the very heart of the potentially strongest defenses ground troops ever assaulted. They did it swiftly and methodically and with extremely few casualties.

And now Hitler's famed wall of defense against attack from the west is broken. Once such defenses are breached, then the entire line has lost its real worth. That is what has happened. Fighting men were heaping praise on twenty-one-year-old Kolb who is a veteran warrior despite the fact that he looks like a lad of eighteen.

"That guy is absolutely fearless," said Major Lawton, "and look what he's done—led the drive to break this line. His men did the job. I remember when he was made a company commander. He worried about him being able to command thirty-five-year-old platoon sergeants, but now they would follow that kid anywhere he wanted to take them."

The Germans were shelling Kolb and his men when they finally broke through and opened the way for others to follow, but the shelling did not stop them.

At the command post in Aachen Forest reports came in from the front on the assault troops. The lines on the map moved forward so fast that command officers were checking back to make sure they were correct.

"I was completely astounded," said Lawton. "Look at those positions with their beautiful fields of fire. If they had put their artillery back here and manned boxes they could give us hell but all our men are getting is machine gun fire and a little artillery." ☐

With American Forces in Germany, September 15 — A former personal bodyguard for Adolf Hitler told today of the surprise and elation with which the Führer greeted the signing of the 1939 non-aggression pact with Russia—the pact that enabled him to attack Poland five days later.

The former batman, captured in the Allied drive on the homeland, said he was stationed at Hitler's quarters on the day the pact was signed. Foreign Minister Von Ribbentrop telephoned the Führer from Moscow to announce the successful conclusion and the batman, hearing a shout and fearing something was wrong, rushed into Hitler's private room.

He found Hitler dancing and gesticulating, he said, meanwhile shouting: "I didn't think it would work! I didn't think it would work!"

The prisoner said he left a job as a waiter to enter the Waffen SS unit in 1935 and later was chosen as one of Hitler's personal bodyguards. He stayed in the service of the Führer until 1940, when he fell into disfavor because of a drunken brawl at Berchtesgaden at the time Hitler was resting after the French campaign.

He described Hitler as a capricious and irascible insomniac who neither drinks, smokes, nor eats meat. He said there was no truth to reports of an affair between Hitler and Leni Riefenstahl, but that the Führer had become enamoured of a stenographer and carried on an affair which as far as he knows still continues.

Hitler, he declared, is guarded by a carefully selected group of forty officers, half Gestapo and half young officers in training. The Führer keeps three batmen who wait on him, but the care of his clothing and cleaning of his rooms is done by a maid.

Another prisoner said that Hitler's headquarters in East Prussia was a huge underground arrangement with walls so thick that no bomb could collapse them and that while he is there Hitler is guarded by a cordon of SS officers.

After looking at pictures this prisoner did not think the attempt on Hitler's life was made at the Führer's headquarters.

The batman said he found Hitler difficult to know even though he served him for three years.

"He was different every day," the batman said, "alternating between kindness and brutal harshness toward his subordinates."

He said Hitler was extremely nervous and, before the war, never went to bed before 3 a.m. and was not awakened until 10 a.m. Now, he said, Hitler is called at 8 a.m. daily when he breakfasts on milk and arrowroot.

Staff officers who come to see Hitler were described as extremely nervous before the conferences. Once, the batman said, when Dr. Emil Hácha, Czech president, came to see Hitler, the Führer told his personal physician to be ready to give Hácha stimulants—and that Hácha did collapse under the strain of the interview and needed two injections. □

With U.S. First Army in Germany, September 16 – In just 102 days of breathtaking battle Lieut. Gen. Omar N. Bradley's infantry and armor have made enough military history to keep historians busy for many years—and they are still on the move.

On June 6 millions of people all over the world wondered with apprehension whether the Allies could successfully invade Europe, where the Germans had spent four years preparing a defense. There were pessimists who thought it could not be done or that the cost in lives would be too great.

But since that time Bradley's troops have stormed the beaches of Normandy, captured Cherbourg, smashed through the enemy's defenses west of St-Lô, captured Paris, swept across Belgium and blasted holes in the Siegfried line.

Germany is beaten-battered into submission by armies which outfought, outgunned and outmaneuvered them with the magnificent support of a mighty air force.

It is an old infantry gag to say, "It is all over but the fighting," but those of us who have followed the armies for many months in the field see that the end is near. Even the most pessimistic wonder what is keeping the Germans on their feet. They are punch groggy and now it is a matter of when the knock-out blow will land.

In the last war the German Army never believed it was whipped on the field of battle. The collapse of 1918 was blamed on the home front. But this time there is no such excuse. They have been beaten on the battlefield— thoroughly, efficiently and decisively.

Not once since American troops landed have the Germans had the initiative. Not once have they won a battle. Not once have they been able to check our armies or even to anticipate their moves.

Only the desperation of Nazis who have nothing to lose and the inbred discipline of German soldiers seem to be holding the battered defenders of ·the Reich together. With the Allies controlling the air, they are unable to mount any large-scale offensive to drive the Allies back, and can depend only on localized attacks to impede and delay.

Obviously the Germans hope to bring about a stalemate. Their stubborn stand along the Siegfried line has checked our advance for the time being, but their counter-attacks have cost them heavily in casualties. And on a man-to-man basis the Germans cannot afford to lose as many men as the Americans.

While the German divisions are watered with teen-age boys, men too old for the strain of prolonged combat, and the physically-unfit, the American units are kept near top strength by a steady flow of replacements, all youths in first-class physical condition who lack only combat experience.

The greatest problem for the American Army has been supplies. For many weeks most of the tonnage came either through Cherbourg or across the beaches, which was a long haul to the front. But with the capture and re-pair of channel ports and of Brest this situation may eventually be eased.

While optimists do not expect the war to last through the winter, the army nevertheless must make its plans for a winter campaign in the event Hitler is able to keep his armies fighting to the last.   ☐

With the United States First Army in Germany, September 16 — Troops of the First United States Army will not be permitted to fraternize with German civilians and are expected to remember that they must treat them as enemies. For the first time, American troops are going into country where the civilian population can be expected to be hostile and the army does not want the men to expose themselves to unnecessary danger, nor permit any leaks in security through the natural friendliness of doughboys.

In the drive across France, Belgium and Holland the troops were among friendly, sympathetic populations which were eager to assist. These conditions change at the border. There is no doubt many of the Germans will be happy to see the arrival of the Americans because it means the end of war for them, and end of the dreaded Gestapo and the finish of Nazi domination. But who will be a friend and who an enemy no soldier can say.

No longer can a doughboy stop along the road and chat even casually with the people and only those on official business will be able to leave bivouac areas to mingle with civilians. Their relations will be business only.

Neither can soldiers wander about the country in small groups or singly on sight-seeing expeditions, for there always is the danger of ambush by some of Hitler's fanatics of SS (elite) troops who have donned civilian clothes.

American soldiers will not be allowed to forget that for four years the Germans have been waging total war against American allies and much of that time against America herself, and that the Germans individually and collectively are soldiers of the enemy.

Troops will be expected to conduct themselves in a reserved, soldierly manner to dispute enemy propaganda which has terrified the average German of the arrival of the American Army. □

With the American First Army, September 19 — Hitler has failed in a crucial test of authority over millions of Nazi-bossed Germans as thousands remain in their Rhineland homes today in defiance of evacuation orders.

As patrols of the First Army stab through the West Wall toward the heart of the Rhineland, many civilians are remaining quietly to receive them as occupying troops, despite the fact their Nazi overlords said such action would brand them as traitors.

The evacuation order for the Cologne-Aachen area was issued by the regional Gauleiter September 12. It urged the people to resist the American advance in every way possible, and laid down regulations for evacuation of those under fifteen and over sixty years old. Others were to remain and help build community defenses until such time as ordered to withdraw.

Included in the edict was a warning that those who refused to obey would be considered traitors and would be in danger of their lives. But these threats have not strengthened the party's hold on the people. Many Germans remember too well the American occupation after the last war and the decent treatment they received from the troops and their officers.

The first evacuation order was directed to approximately 2,000,000 people in the central third of the Rhineland. If disobedience continues on a large scale, then it clearly shows the Nazi Party's lack of power to influence the rank and file.   □

With the U.S. First Army, September 20 — There was little doubt today that the Germans are making a major stand at the Siegfried line. Some troops have entered the line with orders to "hold at all costs," and, while the fighting is growing more bitter at the line, the enemy probably is feverishly building defenses on the eastern bank of the Rhine.

There were indications earlier that the Nazis intended to make their major stand at the Rhine, but more and more troops are being thrown in at the Siegfried line and this is rapidly developing into one of the great battles of the invasion.

Apparently Hitler has given orders to hold the Allies at the borders of the Reich at all costs and this accounts for the stubborn defense and reinforcement of units in the line plus the wheeling up of the heaviest artillery concentration the Germans have been able to muster since the beach landings.

Since Lieut. Gen. Courtney H. Hodges drove his First American Army across Belgium and penetrated the Siegfried defenses, the Germans have been trying to bring some order out of the confusion into which the troops were thrown by the swift advance of our armored and infantry columns.

Now their counter-attacks are well coordinated with heavy artillery preparation. The battle at the Siegfried has mounted in fury with the enemy bringing out his air force for the first time in weeks in any strength.

In Stolberg, troops fought from house to house against a stubborn enemy using every obstacle in an effort to delay the American advance. The town is almost surrounded.

In Aachen, troops heard loud explosions and there were reports the Gestapo and police were forcing the people to evacuate the battered city.

One American unit fought all day today to clean out the inner defenses of the Siegfried where a new breach was developing. Many Germans in pillboxes surrendered when the Americans worked behind the fortifications and called on them to throw down their arms. Others, however, refused, and bulldozers were rolled up and pushed dirt against doors of the pillboxes, sealing the Germans inside.   □

In Germany, September 21 — The Germans have begun dismantling factories west of the Rhine and are shipping the machinery to Eastern Germany to prevent its falling in the hands of American troops.

The Yanks, meanwhile, held firmly onto their breaches in the Siegfried line against continued counter-attacks. Forward observers in the Aachen area saw the Germans dismantling a factory and loading the machinery on a train and trucks. They immediately called for air and artillery missions to blast the transport.

In Stolberg the doughboys still fought house to house, cleaning out stubborn resistance. The Germans had made every house a strongpoint but the town was almost cleared as American troops reached high ground on its eastern side. □

In Germany, September 22 — The Germans are fighting in their Siegfried line with all the stubbornness of the Normandy hedgerow battles and they seem determined to make this the major stand in defense of the fatherland. There is no indication that they intend to pull out for the Rhine even though the morale of some of the prisoners taken by Lt. Gen. Courtney H. Hodges' First Army is extremely low.

The prisoners declare they have been without food or replacements for three days and they have been left with no entrenching tools to dig in against the dreaded American artillery fire. Their comrades, however, are throwing in counter-attacks and are stubbornly refusing to surrender when the bulldozers grind up in front of the Siegfried line pillboxes and shove smothering mounds of earth against the doors. On one sector thirteen pillboxes were smashed today by direct artillery fire.

The doughboys control the major part of Stolberg, six miles east of Aachen, but there still was some house-to-house fighting. East of Stolberg American troops beat off a counter-attack and left one hundred Germans dead in the field. They took fifty prisoners.

The Germans continued to put heavy concentrations of artillery fire and shells from leveled anti-aircraft guns against our ground troops. One shell fell inside a prisoners' cage and killed twenty Germans. At one point two platoons tried to surrender, but before they could arrange it an SS officer arrived and broke off negotiations.

Near Geilenkirchen, twelve miles north of Aachen, the Germans attacked with tanks, infantry and horse-drawn artillery, but a concentration of artillery fire forced them to break it off.

There is no indication that German civilians are obeying Nazi orders to wage war on American troops. As a matter of fact, in many cases the civilians have ignored party orders to evacuate to points back of the firing line and are remaining in their homes. □

With the American First Army in Germany, September 24 — Shells from big 240-millimeter guns of Lt. Gen. Courtney H. Hodges' American First Army were pounding targets only eighteen miles from the Rhine today, while the Germans strengthened their defenses of the Reich. East of the frontier city of Aachen, German civilians were put to work digging trenches and preparing fortifications.

The Germans apparently are pulling together all the odds and ends of the units they can muster and putting them in line to impede the American advance. Most of these "sacrifice" units are composed of elderly men, boys and misfits. "These boys are souped up for the time being," one Allied officer said, "but they are not good for the long pull because they have got a lot of secondary stuff in the ranks. After they are hit a time or two they'll begin to believe the stories of the boys from Normandy that Germany has lost the war."

Heavy guns strung along the First Army's front are hurling shells into Duren and other communications centers in a strategic shelling to cripple railroads and harass the enemy's movements of troops and supplies. In no other campaign have the Americans mustered such a concentration of big guns as now are blasting at the enemy, and when the weather permits, fighter-bombers are hitting hard at the enemy's rear lines.

For the past several days the weather has hampered Hodges' efforts to build up supplies. The fall rains have set in and muddy roads have slowed convoys and multiplied supply problems while at the same time giving the enemy relief from steady pounding from the air. The officer said the First Allied Airborne Army in Holland had been of invaluable aid to the U.S. First Army because it threatened the German Fifteenth Army and disrupted the enemy's overall plan of defense.

The enemy's desperation is shown in the fact that when he cannot reconstruct divisions battered by the Allies he forms brigades and shoots them into the line wherever the threat looks greatest. "Some of these brigades are One-Round Hogan outfits," the officer said, "and are fighting over their weight. When they come in and get a good shellacking they lose a lot of their spirit and are not so ready to come back for another beating."

Fresh enemy troops coming in from the East appear vigorous and strong because they have not suffered the long reverses of units which retreated all the way from Normandy. Because this spirit is spread among the newly arriving troops there is every indication that heavy fighting is ahead before the back of the enemy's defenses can be broken. During the day the Americans beat back two minor counter-attacks and inflicted an estimated forty per cent casualties on the attacking troops. □

With the U.S. First Army in Germany, September 25 — The famous fighting First Infantry Division has done it again. The boys proudly wearing No. 1 on their arm patches who fought through Tunisia and Sicily, whipped an entire German division on the Normandy beaches D-Day, and then helped engineer the great breakthrough west of St-Lô, were among the first ground troops to fight their way across the German border and were the first to breach the Siegfried line.

The battle record of this great combat division is one of the epics of this war, for wherever the fighting has been the heaviest the First Division usually has been in the middle of it. They are still "the Fighting First from hell to victory." It took them just twenty-four hours to breach the Siegfried defenses east of Aachen in a sudden thrust which pierced two belts of antitank ditches, dragon's teeth barriers, and concrete pillboxes. In twenty-four hours they were plunging through those formidable defenses which Hitler had built along the German border to protect the Reich.

An armored division fighting alongside the First was the first to penetrate the Reich in force on September 14. Tanks rolled across the border just a few minutes before doughfoots of the First crossed and Lt. Col. Edward Driscoll of Long Island (no further address available) radioed: "This is Driscoll reporting from Germany." These doughboys penetrated first into the somber shadows of the Aachen Town Forest and the next day began the Siegfried assault. □

Groenstraat, Holland, October 2 — The heavy rain clouds broke early today and then the bombers came in. They streaked overhead in measured, majestic flight by the hundreds, and dumped their deadly cargoes onto the Siegfried line. The attack was on.

For ten days, the entire United States First Army front has been comparatively quiet. In the high echelons, they called this period a lull. But to the infantry in their cold wet foxholes up front, there was no lull. The enemy was counter-attacking and the shells were coming toward them all the time.

For ten days, the Army has been building up supplies and reserves in preparation for this drive. Now Lieut. Gen. Courtney H. Hodges was ready. His troops were in position. Hundreds of big guns were massed along this sector.

The break in the gray skies which had blanketed the fighting front for days was the signal for the attack. A few minutes before 7 a.m. there came a sullen and distinct rumble from the skies where the gray cloud masses still scudded across a brilliant blue background. The low rumble grew into a roar and then you saw them—the silvery toys up there catching the glint of the sun.

Peasants driving along in high-wheeled carts stopped on the roadside to stare open-mouthed. Men and women turned their heads to the sky and children stopped, shouting at passing vehicles to point at the planes overhead. Housewives leaned from windows to watch and troops stood in the fields with faces turned upward. It seemed as if this part of the world stood still and held its breath for what was to come.

Then it came.

There was a drumming, rolling thunder of exploding bombs that made the earth tremble. This was the bombing of St-Lô repeated—not on such a grand scale but an awful spectacle just the same. Great columns of black smoke billowed up. The haze of explosions clung over the bomb zone in the evil gray mist. The bombers were striking at pillboxes, foxholes and entrenchments over the path down which the Americans would attack.

Behind the mediums came the swift fighter-bombers, wave after wave of them. For two hours the planes thundered across and then the artillery—hundreds of guns—started a rolling barrage against the enemy strongpoints.

At 11 a.m. Capt. Ross Simmons of Tulsa, Okla., and Lieut. Ferdinand Bons of Salt Lake City led their units across the green fields to spearhead the attack. They advanced to the Würm River and sloshed through knee-deep icy water. They kept on driving into the mass of pillboxes and emplacements.

Down muddy roads behind these shock troops slogged other infantrymen. Infantrymen always look tired with their slow tread and heavy loads of ammunition, machine guns and mortars. About their mouths were the tight looks of warriors going into battle. Occasionally they shrank involuntarily as a shell moaned in and crashed across the ridge. A column turned from the road into a field and marched to an embankment at the ridgetop. Across that flat ridge they were exposed and in view of the enemy.

"Keep it spread out there," shouted a sergeant.

At the ridgetop the men scrambled up the embankment and ran coughing across the open field like troops in the last war going over the top. They ran heavily with black mud holding their feet in a dogtrot and with their heavy weapons and ammunition boxes making their effort for speed seem ridiculous. You wanted to shout "faster, faster" but they could go no faster.

Another group reached the embankment.

"Spread out and be ready to go on the double," shouted a young officer, and then the men charged up the embankment and ran slowly across the field, disappearing down another slope.

In a village a few hundred yards back, troops stood on the sidewalks on either side of the street waiting to move ahead. Shells crashed into buildings nearby and the men melted into doorways and behind buildings. The street was suddenly deserted.

"When those things are coming it is time to disappear," said Pfc. Vaughn Carmack of Chambersburg, Pa., and Pfc. Eugene Garbarini of 87 Baxter Street, New York, nodded agreement. □

Groenstraat, Holland, October 2 — Because the Germans have prepared positions in depth for some 15,000 yards at the point of today's attack north of Aachen, no one here expects Lt. Gen. Courtney H. Hodges' First Army to make a sudden grand sweep to the Rhine. Indications are that the battle will be a hard, bitter and bloody one all the way, since the Germans are determined to protect the rich industrial region toward which the First Army is pointed.

Hodges waited for forty-eight anxious hours for a break in the weather so that the air force could blast a path for his troops into the Siegfried line. With supplies of ammunition, food and gasoline built up for the push, Hodges was ready to throw the most concentrated attack against the enemy since Lt. Gen. Omar Bradley made the breakthrough near St-Lô last July 27. But the full force of the thrust depended on the weather.

Two days ago the outlook was bad. The forecast indicated at least four more days of heavy overcast. But over the attack zone this morning the clouds broke and the sun shone to give the airmen a chance to hit the enemy.

The bad weather which kept the air force grounded for the last two weeks and the need to pause and build up supplies gave the Nazis a chance to strengthen their positions and bring in fresh reserves. "They are putting cannon fodder into the front lines and keeping their best fresh troops in reserve for counter-attacks," Lt. Col. Stewart L. Hall of Newark, N.J., said. "They've brought new stuff into the line and are definitely committed to making a stand for the Siegfried line. They've got Hitler's orders to hold or else."

In the rear of the hodge-podge manning the Siegfried defenses Hitler has his tough SS troops and mobile armored units to backstop wherever the danger appears greatest. The fact that the doughboys were able to cross the Würm River within forty-five minutes of the beginning of the attack this morning was a remarkable accomplishment. But the way was paved last night when a patrol went out and dynamited several pillboxes commanding the river approaches.

The Germans have been ordered to make a stand for the winter at the Siegfried line and west of the Rhine, but Hodges has other ideas about this although everyone is agreed that the fight to the Rhine will be hard all the way. The rainy season makes it difficult for tanks to maneuver, while at the same time, the Germans are digging in for a determined stand.   □

Groenstraat, Holland, October 3 — German troops holding the Siegfried line have been told by their commanders that any man who retreats will be shot, and if an entire company should fall back, one man in every ten will be shot, American officers said today. "They're doing everything they can to hang onto the defenses, and these threats are necessary to keep many troops in line," said Lieut. Col. Harold Hassenfelt of Oconto, Wis.

Heavy fighting raged for the second day as First Army troops battered deeper into the Siegfried defenses. Under gray skies and in a wintry wind, they battled from house to house in the town of Ubach at Rimberg, just inside the walls of the ancient, moated Rimberger castle, converted into a fortress. Americans hold half the castle and are shooting across the courtyard at Germans in close-range battle.

The first surge of infantry yesterday, behind a heavy air bombardment and a rolling artillery barrage, carried through the heavy crust of German Siegfried defenses which are 15,000 yards in depth at this point. The attack caught the enemy by surprise.

A German prisoner said the Nazis were alerted for a tank and infantry attack expected between 5 and 7 a.m., but when nothing happened the troops relaxed. When the bombers came over at 9 a.m., they were not particularly disturbed, since the bombs were not falling on their positions—but they were not prepared for the heavy artillery fire and sudden infantry assault which followed.

The deepest penetration into the Siegfried defenses in this sector was led by young Capt. Robert Spiker of West Virginia. "Nobody thought about Spiker as the leader because he was a sort of retiring little cuss," said Major Eugene H. Thomas of Nashville, Tenn. "But now they can't hold him." It was Capt. Spiker's unit which drove into Ubach and began a house-to-house fight. His men were among troops under command of Lieut. Col. Ernest Frankland of Jackson, Tenn.

Once through this heaviest crust of defenses in this area, the Americans were able to turn and began a flanking attack on pillboxes from the rear. While the battle for Rimberger Castle was raging Lieut. Col. Daniel Quinn of St. Augustine, Fla., took a special task force with tank support to wheel in behind enemy positions giving the doughboys trouble near Rimberg.

Capt. Spiker and his men led the assault which knocked out eleven enemy pillboxes and opened the way into the Siegfried defenses. Special assault teams armed with machine guns, bazookas, pole charges and flamethrowers, charged the pillboxes, knocked out the defenders, and then blew up the concrete forts.

"The boys did a great job," Col. Hassenfelt said.

One of the finest jobs was done by engineers who came in behind the spearheads and threw bridges across the Würm River within a few hours, permitting jeeps, guns and tanks to roll on in support of the ground troops.

"It was terrible," one German prisoner said after being routed from a pillbox. He was amazed by American marksmanship. "Every time one of our men manned a gun at the embrasure in a pillbox he was drilled with a bullet between the eyes," the prisoner said.

The Germans tried to organize a counter-attack from the north last night to pinch out the salient, but a heavy artillery barrage broke up the formations. The enemy still was meeting the attack with heavy concentrations of small arms, mortar and artillery fire.   □

Polenberg, Germany, October 4 — In the dimly lit, evil-smelling tunnel of an old coal mine near here 300 men, women and children live like caged animals—waiting to see what their American conquerors are going to do with them. They have lived there three weeks. For the past few days a battle has raged around their underground refuge. They thought at first the Americans would behead each of them. When Lt. Glenn Poppe of Mason,

Ohio, and Cpl. William Reifsnyder, East South Bend, Ind., accidentally discovered the shelter while taking cover from enemy artillery, people kneeled, praying to be spared.

I entered the shelter with a civil affairs officer, Maj. J. D. Ackerman of Colorado Springs, Colo. It is approximately 200 feet long, six feet wide and seven feet high, with chambers leading off each side. Along the walls flare tiny jets of light from a carbide gas pipe. Benches line each side of the corridor, and there are double-deck bunks in the chambers. Old men and women lie on the benches or sit in chairs cushioned with blankets and quilts.

Three weeks ago the Germans ordered civilians to evacuate Palenburg, which sits in the middle of the Siegfried line. Most of the 6,000 inhabitants fled, but ninety coal miners and their families were ordered to stay and keep the mine operating as long as possible. Workers ordered to stay gathered up a few belongings and food and came with their families to the community shelter.

Staff Sgt. Roy Cestary, Youngstown, Ohio, was shooting at a pillbox with a machine gun when a woman rushed from a house to his gun. "It was the craziest thing," Cestary said. "She had her four kids in the basement and begged us not to hurt them."

Last Friday artillery fire became so heavy that work at the mine stopped entirely and people just huddled in the tunnel, waiting. Then Poppe and Reifsnyder found the entrance. Yesterday the Germans counter-attacked, but the attack was beaten back, with Tech Sgt. Fred C. Leno of Salem Station, N.C., directing artillery fire. The people will be held in their shelter until it is safe for them to return to their homes. Meanwhile, sentries stand guard at the tunnel entrances.

Pvt. Ludwig Klatt, Detroit, and a young German girl who speaks English have been acting as interpreters, and civilians quickly obey every order given them. And every chance they get, they try to tell Klatt how much they hated the Nazis, and to explain that Rhinelanders never were strong for Hitler, anyway. □

Rimberg, Germany, October 4 — Savage, bitter fighting raged within and beyond the Siegfried line today as doughboys battled to widen their new breach in Nazi defenses which Hitler has ordered held to the death. With chill winds blowing across the fields and woods, American infantry slowly was driving the Germans from pillboxes, foxholes and houses. The enemy was using all the manpower he could scrape together in the attempt to halt the drive of Lieut. Gen. Courtney Hodges' First Army.

From Ubach south to Merkstein and Hofstadt the battle is flaming intensely. The Germans are rushing up 75- and 88-millimeter guns for direct fire, and artillery is thundering all along the bitterly contested front. Three times in the early morning the Germans counter-attacked trying to drive doughboys back from hard-won positions. But each time U.S. infantry and artillery poured fire into the enemy and broke up the forays with no loss of ground. These counter-attacks were in from company to battalion strength.

The Germans are shelling their own towns as they are forced out of them—setting a pattern of what can be expected as the Americans drive farther into Germany. Ubach, which fell to Hodges' men yesterday, was shelled heavily by the enemy during the night.

The Germans also turned their artillery—in the heaviest concentrations the Americans have faced in the invasion—on bridges across the Würm River, trying to stem the flow of troops, guns, and material across the stream. □

With the First U.S. Army, October 5 — American tanks advancing more than a mile captured Beggendorf today. Beggendorf is three miles inside German territory from the nearest tip of the Dutch border, and its capture placed American forces across the Aachen-Geilenkirchen Highway and within a mile of the main highway to Gladbach.

Fierce battles developed as the tank column smashed through what front-line troops described as the heaviest German artillery barrage of the European campaign. After capturing Beggendorf the American tanks fanned out to exploit a breakthrough. Tanks reached the area behind the most permanent fortifications of the West Wall and approached the Nazis' new earthworks, which in themselves are a formidable barrier.

The capture of Beggendorf broke the back of an abortive attempt by the Germans to make the town the southern anchor of a short second defense line back-stopping the ruptured Siegfried line. The northern hinge of this line was at Waurichen, a little over two miles to the north. The Germans had been unable to man it fully.

The new surge came after American tanks and infantry had beaten back three counter thrusts by enemy armor. Sherman tanks knocked off a number of enemy tanks and American artillery polished off three in one clash.

Low gray clouds under cold skies grounded Allied air support. The Germans were battling desperately to prevent their entire line north of Aachen from crumbling.

The First Army attack swept through the fourth day with fighting mounting in bitterness. Never have the Germans concentrated so much artillery in one sector of this front. Guns thunder continuously. The Germans are making a rubble heap of their own town of Ubach.

Tanks, guns, infantry, and supplies are pouring through the gap in the Siegfried line and putting mounting pressure on the enemy. The Germans are frantically rushing up every reserve to be found and trying to check the advance. Enemy troops are being brought from pillboxes north and south of the breakthrough gap and thrown into the battle raging northeast and south of Ubach. The enemy is suffering heavy losses in throwing in numerous small counter-attacks.

Last night, American artillery gave the Germans there "serenades" in awful, thunderous blasts. They turned every gun from 75-millimeters to big 240-millimeters on one area. And when Maj. Dwight McReynolds of Cleveland, Tenn., led his men forward south of Ubach to storm heights just east of Herbach, he radioed back to the command post: "There are so many dead Germans on the road that it is tough going."

Lieut. Col. Samuel McDowell, Rocky Point, N.C., had called McReynolds to ask what was delaying his advance and McReynolds replied promptly: "Not a damned thing but dead Germans on the road. I'll get moving when I get them out of the way."

The toughest fighting centered around a hill east of Herbach—a height looking down on the town and commanding the approaches through the Siegfried line from Rimberg. But McReynolds' men stormed up the hill and smashed three pillboxes. A white flag fluttered from a fourth.   □

With American Infantry at the Siegfried Line, October 6 — From inside Germany has come a story that Adolf Hitler intends to guide the destiny of the Reich through secretly trained, fanatical young Nazis even though he should flee into exile. Hitler Youth and other young Nazis are being trained in secret schools to carry on National Socialism as an underground movement after Allied occupation of the Reich, according to this information. It is said that the most fanatical of the Nazis preach a doctrine that nothing irreparable can happen to Germany as long as Hitler lives to keep the flame of National Socialism from being snuffed out.

Even though Hitler should flee into exile or go into hiding, they say, he will keep in touch with the graduates of his "Junkerschulen" or "Schools for rulers" and through them rule the Reich. Very little is known of this clandestine movement because its activities are closely guarded secrets and each student is sworn to reveal nothing about the schools or his affiliation with them. One informant said there are believed to be eight of these schools operating in Germany to perpetuate the ideology of National Socialism even though Germany should be overrun and present Nazi leaders seized.

During 1936 and 1937 the Nazis established schools under Robert Ley, leader of the German labor front, and Dr. Alfred Rosenberg, so-called Nazi philosopher, which gave indoctrination courses for Kreisleiters, Gauleiters (local and regional leaders) and high SS members who were to take key roles within the Nazi party. Since 1937 this educational program has been extended gradually. Hitler Youth were brought in for training, but none was permitted entrance except those whose background had been examined carefully with regard to racial purity and leadership ability.

They were to be future rulers of Germany, men devoting their lives to seeing that National Socialism as expounded by "Der Führer" should live. And it was to be their responsibility to run the underground movement.

After the United States entered the war and the tide of battle in the east swung against the German armies, schools began to stress a program of keeping National Socialism alive in defeat.

Religious mysticism is mixed into the schooling in true Nazi tradition. Each school is reported to have a secret chamber which only special students are permitted to enter. There at a high Nazi shrine they dedicate themselves to worship of the perfect man.

In addition to technical subjects and languages, each participates in sports and flying. Upon graduation they are urged to continue their studies of the sciences and are given income sufficient to make them financially independent.

According to the story of the informant, the names of students never are revealed and graduates do not disclose any connection with the party. Instead they hold key positions of an inconspicuous and unofficial nature. □

With American Infantry at the Siegfried Line, October 6 — The battle of the Siegfried line spreads to south of Aachen today as doughboys launched a new attack through the Hürtgen Forest and American tanks reached the edge of Geilenkirchen near the Ubach breach to the north. Geilenkirchen is three miles north of Ubach and four miles inside Germany. The new drive southeast of Aachen carried to within six miles of Duren. The new attack was supported by hundreds of fighter bombers while light, medium and heavy artillery laid down a barrage on the Hürtgen Forest. Then at 11:30 the doughboys jumped off in the "Battle of the Forest."

North of Aachen, fighting raged about the breach in the Siegfried defenses and one officer described the battle as "equal to anything in the Anzio Beachhead" below Rome. American troops who entered Beggendorf yesterday had to pull back today from that town east of Ubach under heavy enemy pressure. The new attack was ten miles southeast of Aachen and in its first stage the American infantry advanced more than half a mile deeper into Germany.

Skies were cloudless and this allowed fighter bombers by the hundreds not only to bombard the Hürtgen Forest but to batter at the second belt of Siegfried line strongpoints. Fighting as bloody and fierce as any in the entire invasion blazed around the doughboy's wedge in the main Siegfried line as the Germans threw their first sizable counter-attack, supported by armor against the Americans in an effort to seal off the penetration.

The Germans continued to pour heavy artillery fire upon Ubach, and just to the east of Ubach the "Battle of the Barracks" was developing into a stiff battle. The Germans were defending a cluster of four-story concrete barracks extending for 500 yards along the road southeast of Ubach. They had converted it into a veritable fortress with antitank weapons, mortars, machine guns and infantry.

Doughboys were within rifle range of the gray walls and Allied planes were dive-bombing the buildings. Progress was slow. It was yard by yard fighting for the infantry, just like the doughboys faced through the thick green hedgerows of Normandy—but this time with pillboxes instead of hedgerows.

The Germans, whose superiors have threatened them with death if they retreat or surrender, were backed by the heaviest artillery they had been able to concentrate against Americans since the war began.

The heaviest engagement was on heights overlooking Herbach, which the infantry stormed yesterday, knocking the enemy out of pillboxes. The summit of these heights commands the terrain south of Ubach. The doughboys fought their way to the top late yesterday. At 7 a.m. the Germans counter-attacked in force. Infantry, supported by tanks, came out of the mists to the southeast.

The first Nazi surge drove the doughboys from the heights and gave the Germans control of seven of the pillboxes which they had lost, but on the side of the ridge. Cox and his men held fast.

Then the sun burned off the mists, the first bright clear day in weeks developed and our planes roared in. The first flight arrived at 9 a.m. and lanced out against enemy armor and infantry. This was one of the closest air support missions yet flown. □

With the U.S. First Army, October 9 — The jaws of Lieut. Gen. Courtney H. Hodges' pincers closing on Aachen cut the main road to Jülich and Cologne today and were within a mile and a half of the complete encirclement of Aachen itself. This highway is the main escape road left to an estimated 1,500 enemy troops entrenched in the rubble of industrial Aachen.

The Germans have only a few secondary roads left over which to pull out troops and equipment. The thrust from the north toward Aachen pushed south of Alsdorf, overran Bardenburg and reached the edge of Würselen, but three miles north of Aachen. This was the upper jaw of the pincer.

The lower jaw which hooks around Aachen from the southeast is at Crucifix Hill, near Haaren. The distance between Haaren and Würselen is but a mile and a half, the width of the escape corridor.

The Germans put in counter-attacks today in a desperate bid to hold open the jaws. One of these was toward Alsdorf, with nineteen tanks, a small infantry force and a heavy concentration of artillery. But it was beaten back. A German shell fell in a column of Nazi prisoners and forty of them were killed or wounded.

South of Aachen the American troops fought their way through the Hürtgen Forest yard by yard against the strongly entrenched enemy.

Three times the Germans counter-attacked up Crucifix Hill northeast of Aachen today in a desperate effort to break the pincers slowly throttling Aachen, but each time the doughboys hurled them back. The Germans' losses were heavy.

Big guns thundered on both sides as savage fighting raged where the doughboys attacked before dawn yesterday and seized the high ground near Verluntenheide.

The Germans were making every effort to hold on to the industrial city, which had a population of 155,000 before most civilians were evacuated. Along the southern outskirts of Aachen itself American troops worked methodically from house to house digging out defenders who were obeying Hitler's orders to stand and fight to the death.

However, there has been no main assault on the city. The main thrusts are from the north and toward the north on the east side of the city, with less than four miles separating the two spearheads threatening to surround the city.

Stubbornness of the enemy defense is plainly indicative of the military and political importance the Germans attach to Aachen, an important road center and beginning of the great Adolf Hitler Highway, a multi-lane speedway to Cologne.

There would be political implications too, in the American capture of Aachen. It would be the first large city inside Germany to fall to the Allies, and its capture might have repercussions throughout Germany, for Hitler promised that the Allies would not set foot on German soil. In the house to house fighting, an officer said, "It's a job for bazookas, machine guns, grenades and rifles. We'll just have to winkle them out one by one."

The city, reduced to rubble, no longer is of any value to an army except for the highway which runs through its center.   □

With the First Army in Germany, [October 11] — The Germans bitter stand-or-die defense north of Aachen collapsed suddenly today under growing American First Army pressure, and U.S. tanks and infantry surged forward on a sweeping drive. The defenses which yesterday were so stubborn and appeared to be holding firm under heavy artillery support gave way this morning when the doughboys launched an attack. More than 300 prisoners were taken in the first two hours.

Tanks rumbled east of Beggendorf and infantry fanned out south of Ubach and overran Herbach, Merkstein, Hofstadt, Alsdorf and Baesweiler. The Yanks now are six miles inside of Germany north of Aachen.

The break came with virtually no indication that the enemy had reached the breaking point or was preparing a withdrawal. Last night the Luftwaffe came over and kept up a continuous bombing and strafing from 7 p.m. until 6 a.m., this morning. Two to six planes were over the front-line areas in what appeared to be shuttle bombing. But when the doughboys attacked through a heavy mist from the ground, the German defenses which had been so stubborn for five days fell apart and Lt. Gen. Courtney Hodges' units burst out east of Beggendorf and south of Ubach in swift movement.

Yesterday the First Army was locked in a bitter, bloody struggle with the Nazis east and south of Ubach. The Germans threw in counter-attacks supported by tanks in an effort to drive the Americans back. But this thrust was stopped and then this morning Hodges' infantry and tanks dashed out again. The drive overran the enemy's defenses. The breakthrough came as a spectacular reverse of yesterday's savage fighting with the enemy fighting under orders to stand or die.

This morning the sky was clear for the second successive day giving the air forces another chance to smash at the foe. Forward elements of the advancing columns driving on against comparatively light opposition have penetrated to a depth of about six miles into Germany to the Baesweiler area.

The thrust south to Alsdorf swept the Nazis back giving the Army a gap in the Siegfried defenses about six miles wide.

Roughly now the line extends from the outskirts of Geilenkirchen east to the outskirts of Immendorf to Baesweiler and south to Oidtweiler. The capture of Alsdorf and a road junction a mile and a quarter to the south placed tanks astride important communications lines. And the advance is continuing with tanks, guns and supplies pouring along dusty roads behind combat elements.

At 8 a.m., the doughboys and tanks went into the attack. Heavy artillery roared in support. The Germans had reached the breaking point. They did not withdraw. They stood and fought. But the terrible weight of Hodges' attack was too much. Tanks and infantry overran enemy positions and the sweep to the east and south was swift.

The effect on the troops was electric. News of the break swept back from the front lines and there was almost a jaunty air about the columns moving through.   □

Outside Aachen, October 11 — The fate of Aachen was sealed today when the German commander of the garrison there declined to accept the United States First Army's twenty-four-hour ultimatum to surrender the city. At exactly noon the Yanks began hurling a terrible weight of heavy shells and aerial might against the ancient city of Charlemagne. Eight-inch Long Toms and 105-millimeter howitzers unloosed a thunderous assault. The cacophony signaled that the assault on Aachen had begun, and served as a warning to the rest of Germany that their cities will be destroyed if they are turned into fortresses.

Not all the German troops inside Aachen wanted to stay and fight to the death as their Führer had ordered. Before noon more than one hundred slipped through their own lines. They said many more wanted to accept the ultimatum, but their officers would not let them. At dawn the Yanks saw hundreds of white sheets hanging from Aachen windows—obviously placed by civilians who defied Nazi orders for evacuation of all towns in this area.

If he accepted the ultimatum, the German commander of Aachen was to send a representative under a flag of truce to the railway on the outskirts of the city and arrange the surrender. The enemy was to pass through the line in groups of fifty, leaving weapons behind.

Lookouts kept a watch on the prearranged meeting place. Several times it appeared as though the garrison might be surrendering when German soldiers neared the spot but they were only trying to escape and bore no message.

At 10:50 a.m. no one had appeared. Automatically the plans for battering Aachen by artillery and air began to take shape. Noon was set for the opening of the artillery barrage. Extra ammunition had been issued to the gun crews. They stood in readiness. Dive-bombers were alerted, and within a few minutes were winging toward Aachen.

On a ridgetop before Aachen we waited at a command post for word from the forward unit which was to receive the surrender if the enemy capitulated. No correspondents were permitted to visit that advance unit.

"We do not want anything to happen which might prevent the surrender," an officer explained.

"If there is any unusual movement, the enemy might get suspicious, and there might be a hitch. We want to give them every possible chance—and then what happens after that is their own responsibility."

The hands of an old grandfather clock in one room ticked off the minutes. Artillery kept firing, not into Aachen but northeast of the city against enemy troops forming up for a counter-attack against Crucifix Hill. Planes circled overhead.

The hands of the clock reached 10:50 and moved on.

A high-ranking officer came to the doorway of the command post and shook his head. "Yesterday we told the Germans at Aachen to surrender or we would destroy their city," he said. "This morning they decided to let us do it. The officers refuse to surrender. Now we have to break the will of the officers.

"This ultimatum is not without its mixed blessings. We got a lot of prisoners. Each one of them was carrying a copy of the leaflets we dropped. There were about one hundred in one group who came out of their pillboxes, and that is a lot of men when they are inside pillboxes. It saves us the trouble of digging them out."

In a cage nearby were nineteen prisoners taken out of Aachen. A Nazi lieutenant was sleeping off the effects of a spree which resulted when all troops inside Aachen yesterday were issued whisky and wine rations: one bottle of whisky to three men, and a bottle of wine for each two men.

Many of their comrades wanted to surrender without fighting at Aachen, the captives said, but the officers threatened to shoot any who did not stand and fight. The Aachen garrison has SS officers commanding troops to keep them at their posts.

Near noon the bedsheets hanging from windows began to disappear. Evidently the Nazis were forcing civilians to take them down. □

Outside Aachen, October 12 — Infantrymen of the United States First Army moved against the burning and wrecked city of Aachen today after smashing a desperate enemy effort to reinforce and relieve the Nazi garrison. Lieutenant General Courtney H. Hodges's doughboys attacked this morning while heavy artillery pounded the besieged Germans and dive-bombers screamed out of the heavens to blast them from their hiding places.

Fires burned in the southeastern part of Aachen and gray smoke drifted over the sprawling city.

Under a bright sun, Aachen lay like a festering sore in the path of the First Army, battered and beaten by a terrible weight of explosives but not destroyed. It is too big to be wiped out entirely except by weeks of steady pounding.

From a ridgetop, overlooking the city, however, fires and smoke could be seen boiling up from exploding shells and bombs and from wrecked buildings in which the Germans who declined a surrender ultimatum were hiding.

In a move of utter folly late yesterday, the Germans brought their columns from the east toward Aachen in broad daylight, to attack the Americans' virtual ring of steel about the city. The two-pronged assault force, estimated at division strength, moved into the open under direct observation of the Yanks. More than one hundred big guns, including 240-millimeter rifles, turned on these columns, which moved into action at about dusk. A battle raged for two hours. Then the shattered enemy columns fell back. They had failed either to relieve or reinforce Aachen's defenses.

At 8 a.m. today the American infantry began its move on the ancient city of Charlemagne, driving toward the factory district on the northeast side, known as Schlachthof, and toward Observatory Hill, which looks down on Aachen from the northern edge of the city. "The enemy is hidden in ancient caves, sewers, and basements which are almost impregnable to air and artillery attack, but we'll take it," a high-ranking officer said.

Despite the fires and smoke, in the clear sunlight of noontime I could see the tall, blackened spire of the cathedral in which Charlemagne was buried.

The dive-bombers came over at 10 a.m.

They circled swiftly in the blue sky and then plummeted down. The first bombs fell east of Crucifix Hill on enemy troops who were beaten back in yesterday's counter-attack. Great columns of smoke rolled up, and there was one terrific explosion as though an ammunition truck or dump had received a direct hit.

Private Herbert McCabe of Neodesha, Kans., stared out of the window of our vantage point—an old barracks overlooking Aachen—and said: "Last night at 6 p.m. we couldn't even see across the town at any place, there was so much smoke from the artillery barrage. They really laid it on."

And they were laying it on again. Another flight of Thunderbolts dived in and laid a pattern of explosives on Observatory Hill. There was a fury of sound in diving planes, exploding bombs and the crash of artillery.

Then suddenly it was so quiet in one of those strange lulls in battle that you could hear the birds singing and the wind singing through the trees. There was not even the sound of a single rifle shot. At our feet a black cat with white stockings lay in the straw and purred.

This lull was broken by another flight of planes, this time Lightnings. They made long slanting runs. When the bombs were dropped they climbed back steeply, circled and then came down again and strafed the enemy. They were not even challenged, and I did not see a single burst of ack-ack thrown against them from inside or outside Aachen.

This was in addition to 5,000 rounds of shells poured into the city yesterday along with more than one hundred tons of bombs. The principal targets were Lousberg and Observatory Hills north of Aachen, the Quellenhof Hotel area and the factory area on the northeast side of the city which the enemy has been using as a command post and supply area.

During the day one patrol entered the city. It is believed now there are five battalions in Aachen and that from 5,000 to 25,000 civilians remained in their homes.

Almost 300 prisoners surrendered yesterday just before and after the expiration of the time of the ultimatum which demanded surrender of the city. Most of them carried the leaflets dropped by the Allies, bearing the text of the ultimatum.

"But our artillery and mortar fire still are the deciding factor which make the German soldier at this stage of the campaign say 'Kamerad,'" said Lieut. Col. Roberta Evans of Davenport, Iowa. "The leaflets had a good effect, for the prisoners said they did not want to die for the Führer at this late hour." □

Before Aachen, October 13 — Doughboys of Lieutenant General Courtney H. Hodges's First Army, supported by heavy air and artillery bombardments, fought their way into Aachen street by street today against surprisingly light opposition. But the Germans were rushing up crack reinforcements from the east in a desperate effort to save the city.

At 9:30 a.m. Captain Ozell Smoot of Oklahoma City, Okla., led his troops across the railway tracks on the southeastern side of Aachen and began working through the streets, house by house. Then another unit under Captain Roland Weeks of Long Island moved into the attack while the thunder of battle rolled over the burning, smoking city being punished by screaming dive-bombers and crashing artillery.

By darkness last night American troops had seized all the suburban Schlachthof factory district on the northeastern outskirts. From the vantage point of an old shell-wrecked building near the railway tracks we watched artillery and dive-bombers battering Aachen, which at close range looks like a hulk of ruins. Many buildings are intact, but the city has taken a terrible beating. Fires burned in many parts, cloaking its sprawling length with spirals of gray and black smoke.

Out of the broken clouds roared dive-bombers with machine guns and cannon clattering. Then bombs fell, and great columns of smoke mushroomed upward. Self-propelled guns thundered nearby and made the old building and the windows rattle. Lieutenant Colonel Derill M. Daniel of Geneva, N.Y., pointed out the line of attack. "It's very slow going," he said, "because the boys have to search every room, cellar, outhouse, and well where the enemy might be hiding."

Asked what the guns were shooting at, Daniel said: "They are shooting up everything they can to make the Germans keep their heads down. If there is a housetop which looks like a good observation point they take a crack at it." While Smoot and Weeks led their units into the edge of Aachen proper, Lieutenant Beasor Walker of Tuscaloosa, Ala., waited for the signal to cross the railway tracks. "When you stop those Krauts from shooting from the west," Daniel told Smoot, "I'll send Walker in."

Smoot reported back that the Germans were not resisting as stubbornly as had been anticipated and were surrendering at every chance they got. "We have taken thirteen prisoners who were pretty docile and we are doing all right," he said.

"Well, Walker is champing at the bit, waiting to go: so let me know when you have things under control," the colonel said.

Captain James Libby, Burlington, Vt., said resistance inside Aachen appeared to be disorganized and was by small groups hidden in cellars and strongpoints covering street approaches.

While the fighting carried into Aachen, shells and bombs poured on enemy troops and armor moving along secondary roads in the vicinity of Rohe, five miles northeast of Aachen. The enemy kept his columns off the main roads, and no traffic moved on broad Adolf Hitler Highway from the direction of Cologne. But on the side roads there was a heavy movement of troops toward Aachen.

With the Germans pouring in reserves of their best troops a major battle appeared to be developing in an enemy effort to break the Allied pincers closed around the city. "Those roads near Rohe are alive with people," said Major Wilson McNamara of Northfield, Vt.

Planes smashed two German artillery batteries in that area, and over Aachen an observer reported the telephone and telegraph building still intact. "Do you want it bombed or shelled?" asked Captain Phil Dunley of Manlius, N.Y.

"Shelled," was the answer.

"Okey doke," McNamara said, and immediately gave directions to the artillery.

There was an occasional rattle of small arms fire from across the railroad as the infantry moved forward. Behind the infantry came self-propelled guns, which had found a way to get across the tracks. They were commanded by Lieutenant Smoky Sanders of Texas.

While guns shook the building we were in, Pfc. Marlon Krusienski of Canonsburg, Pa., calmly brewed hot coffee at the entrance where a little knot of soldiers watched the drama unfolding before them. Smoke boiling up from the center of the city enveloped the dome and spire of the Aachen Cathedral, resting place of Charlemagne. We could not tell from where we stood whether the historic monument had been hit, but it will be a wonder if it escapes all the destruction being hurled into the town.

Among the prisoners taken in the factory district was the lieutenant to whom the surrender ultimatum was presented last Tuesday. He had re-marked when he received the ultimatum, to be handed to his commander, that he did not think it would be accepted and that the garrison would fight on. But when his troops met the Americans, he surrendered.

One lieutenant colonel, a veteran soldier of eighteen years who received a decoration for breaking through with his regiment in Russia, was captured. He broke down in tears because his military career was ended in such an un-heroic manner. Before his capture, he told his men: "I have led regiments and I have led battalions, and I will be damned if I cannot lead a squad out of this mess."

During the night, German raiders bombed the village of Brand, two miles southeast of Aachen, with the net result of two German civilians killed and six wounded. □

With the U.S. First Army, October 14 — Early in August, after the great American breakthrough near St-Lô, the Yanks fought one of the most decisive battles of the invasion, won hands down, and the Germans lost the battle of France.

In desperation the enemy threw in seven divisions in an effort to seal off the corridor between Mortain and Avranches through which Gen. Omar Bradley's infantry and armor were pouring around the exposed flank of Field Marshal Günther Von Kluge's German Seventh Army. Doughboys, artillerymen, tank destroyers and tankmen stopped the Nazis cold, and a lean, gray general who had risen from the ranks said with a Georgia drawl:

"We slammed 'em until hell wouldn't have it!"

It was Lieut. Gen. Courtney H. Hodges.

His army continued in the same stride across France, Belgium and into Germany, and stopped only because of the weather and the necessity of reorganizing his supply system.

Just two months ago Hodges was not well known in America, even though he had played a large part in building a fighting force at home. Then Bradley stepped up to command the Twelfth Army group, and Hodges quietly took his place.

His troops and armor "slammed 'em" all the way to the Seine, captured Paris, and drove on to Belgium.

South of Mons, Hodges' men hooked northward once again, squarely into the path of Germans trying desperately to escape. There, in the Maubeuge-Mons pocket, his troops chewed up five German divisions, captured some 27,000 prisoners. Then they continued east, crossed the southern tip of Holland and broke into the Siegfried line.

Hodges had stepped into a very large pair of Bradley shoes and the army had continued to function as though there had been no change.

We began to ask: "Who is this man?"

This is what we found!

On May 1, 1887, a son was born to Mr. and Mrs. John Hodges of Perry, Ga., a well-known peach belt family. The father was editor and publisher of the *Houston Home Journal*, a self-contained, kindly man who reared three sons and five daughters. Courtney's father took him on hunting trips. At ten he had his own rifle, soon was one of the best shots in the area, and wanted to be a soldier.

In 1904 he got an appointment to West Point, but failed in mathematics. Then his determined streak showed itself, and he enlisted at Fort McPherson. By 1917 he was a second lieutenant in the Sixth Infantry of the Fifth Division—one of the divisions now under his command. His climb was steady, but nothing spectacular.

Hodges went to France in 1918 as a captain and fought at St-Mihiel and in the Meuse-Argonne drive, winning the Distinguished Service Cross and

Silver Star. He was Bradley's deputy commander, and visited almost every unit he was later to command. As a result, he knows his army from top to bottom.

Whenever an officer did not measure up, someone more able relieved him. This phase of the army's development in the early invasion was little known. "It was one of the hardest things Bradley and Hodges had to do," one officer said. Often it involved an old friend. But they saw no alternative.

Hodges is a career man, but no martinet. He enjoys democratic relations with his officers and troops. "We aren't like the Germans, and that's as it should be," he says. "We are a democracy, and we have a democratic army. That is one of our great strongpoints." He understands G.I. problems because he once was a G.I. himself.

He served with occupation forces in Germany after World War I, returned home a lieutenant colonel, but reverted to the peacetime rank of captain. In 1920 he was assigned to duty in the department of tactics at the military academy—the first non-graduate to receive such distinction. In 1938 he went to the Philippines. Whenever possible he left his offices to go hunting there and in Indo-China.

His wife, now living in Atlanta, is an excellent shot, too, and teases the general by saying he proposed to her because of it. As she tells it, they were walking near Langley Field, Va., where he was stationed from 1926 to 1929. Hodges handed her a rifle and she hit the bull's-eye with the first shot. "Courtney was so surprised that he proposed to me then and there," she laughs.

As assistant commandant and commandant of Fort Benning's infantry school, and as chief of infantry and commander of the army ground forces replacement and school command, Hodges had an important part in building and equipping the American Army and shaping the policies under which it operates today. Yet, because of his retiring nature, he was not widely known, even after he was promoted to lieutenant general in 1943 and given command of the Third Army and the southern defense command with troops in Texas, Arizona, Oklahoma, Colorado, Arkansas, Mississippi, Louisiana and Florida.

The drive across France was a series of incredible hooking moves in which corps were crossing each other's supply lines and the First Army seemed to be going in all directions at once. But behind these moves which completely befuddled the enemy was a cool, sound Georgian who knew what he was doing.   □

Aachen [October 15] — Soldiers of Lt. Gen. Courtney H. Hodges' First Army worked their way deeper into Aachen in house-to-house battle today against increasingly stubborn resistance. American guns and planes continued to pound Nazi reinforcements east of the city and balk any major enemy counter-attack.

There is a possibility that the Germans have succeeded in strengthening the Aachen garrison by slipping small groups at night through the narrow corridor which they managed to hold open on the northeastern side of the city.

During the last five days this American division which is assaulting Aachen has taken about 1,000 prisoners, but it is estimated that there still are about 2,000 left in the burning and battered city.

"The enemy's escape gap is as good as closed now," said Lt. Col. Robert Evans of Davenport, Ia. "They can get almost nothing in or out of the city. Our boys are taking it slow in cleaning up Aachen for we don't want any more casualties than absolutely necessary."

This morning more than sixty prisoners were taken to add to the more than 300 routed out of cellars and strongpoints yesterday. The fighting inside the city is hard but the doughboys are advancing steadily. They are methodically knocking out pillboxes and driving the Nazis out of the houses and cellars with machine guns, rifles and grenades. Small arms fire crackles through the streets and there is the crump of heavy artillery fire massing on enemy strongpoints. Members of the Aachen police force, who have been used as infantry, reported when taken prisoner that there were about 10,000 civilians remaining in the city.

Combined artillery and aerial bombardments so far have smashed every Nazi effort to mount a heavy counter-attack to save Aachen. More than 200 guns, including eight-inch weapons, were turned on enemy concentrations yesterday in the vicinity of Broichweiden and Wurselen and those points still were being pounded today. The threat of a heavy counter-attack has not passed, but the enemy has taken heavy punishment in trying to rush columns of armor forward under the direct observation of our artillery and air force. □

Aachen, October 15 — American troops and guns smashed the greatest German attack of the battle of Aachen today, turning back strong forces of infantry and armor that for a time overran U.S. positions in touch-and-go conflict. The Nazi attempt to relieve the Aachen garrison sprang from south of Weiden, five miles northeast of the besieged city, but broke under the barrage of massed artillery and antitank guns.

In the city of Aachen—where German defenders were supplied overnight by parachutes from six transport planes—doughboys worked ahead slowly digging Nazis from pillboxes and houses. (A radio correspondent at the front said Americans had won control of about "fifty square blocks" in the industrial city.)

For days the enemy has been massing reserves east of Aachen, with American artillery and planes taking heavy toll of men and materiel. Today the big blow fell shortly after noon. The German tanks broke into American defenses but antitank guns and a thundering artillery barrage raked the Nazis and forced the armor to pull back.

American artillery hurled volleys from more than one hundred big guns to smash the assault. The Germans moved up large reserves under the protective fire of the largest concentration of anti-aircraft guns fliers said they had encountered in the area.

The enemy attack was made by infantry of battalion to regiment strength with thirty to forty tanks supporting the drive. For a time it was "touch and go," an officer said. "The enemy is expected to try to take the breaks in the weather and make a large scale effort under the cover of rain or fog to break the American hold on Aachen," the officer said.

This attack had been anticipated for two days as observers saw men, guns and tanks being concentrated east of Aachen. Dive-bombers and artillery have pounded the area continuously.

"This sector of the front has been extremely sensitive for days," an officer said. "Our men have not been able to move fifty feet during the day without drawing heavy fire and if they moved more than fifty yards at night things began to pop."

The sun shone through broken clouds during the morning, but in the afternoon rain clouds closed in and a cold drizzle set in. The Americans continued to take prisoners from the Aachen garrison, which has been ordered to fight to the death to hold the first major city to be attacked by the Allies on German soil.

Two of the prisoners were fourteen and sixteen years old. They said they came to Aachen ten days ago to collect some of the possessions left in the city by a family which had been evacuated. When they reached the city, they related, German soldiers took them to the commander who accused them of coming to the town to pillage.

"Since you are not able to leave Aachen all that is left for you to do is to get into a uniform," they quoted the commander as saying. The boys said they agreed and were outfitted with uniforms and given rifles which they had learned to use as members of the Hitler Youth.

Another prisoner reported all patients had been removed from the City Hospital. The prisoner said he had worked for two days and nights carrying small arms ammunition into bunkers inside the city. These bunkers, he said, have slots for machine gun emplacements and form the principal defense system together with air-raid shelters and buildings located at strategic intersections.

Since the attack began thirteen days ago in the Aachen area the First Army has captured 9,000 prisoners or the equivalent of a full-sized German division. Since D-Day the First Army prisoner total now stands at 194,374. □

Outside Aachen, October 16 — Balked by steel yesterday in a desperate attempt to smash the American ring about Aachen, the Germans counter-attacked again this morning but after three hours of furious battle were driven back for the second time with heavy losses.

In the mists and rain of dawn, Nazi infantry and tanks thrust south from Weiden to try to knife through the lines of Lieut. Gen. Courtney Hodges' First Army. Inside Aachen, the Americans continued their slow, methodical cleanup of the defenders.

Once again, the Americans turned a thunderous artillery barrage on advancing troops and tank and after three hours the enemy had had enough. His attack waved and broke. Four enemy tanks were disabled.

With rain clouds hanging low over the battlefield, infantry and artillery, with tank support, had to stop the German attack without the support of aircraft. As the bad weather closed in again, the enemy was expected to make use of the lack of Allied air support to mount additional attacks.

There was no question that the Germans were making a major effort to keep Aachen from falling into Hodges' hands, and the First Army intends to make an example of this industrial center as a warning to other German cities that the same destruction will be carried to them if the Nazis use them as fortresses.

North of Aachen, American infantry, supported by tanks and heavy artillery, attacked at 6 a.m. in a drive against the thin corridor which the Germans have fought frantically to maintain. Prisoners taken by the First Army since D-Day total 194,718. In addition, the army has buried 14,789 Germans. □

With the U.S. First Army Near Aachen, October 19 — David Lardner, correspondent for the *New Yorker* magazine, was killed and Russell Hill, correspondent for the *New York Herald Tribune*, was injured today when their jeep was blown up by road mines near Aachen. The jeep driver also was killed.

Lardner, son of the late famed humorist Ring Lardner, and Hill were returning from the smashed German city to a press camp when they ran into a mined area. One report said the jeep touched off a string of seven anti-vehicular mines. Hill suffered a broken arm and cuts and bruises.

Lardner, twenty-five, father of two children, was rejected by the army for poor eyesight. A brother, James P. Lardner, was killed in 1938 during the Spanish Civil War while fighting for the Loyalists as a volunteer in the International Brigade.

David Lardner is survived by his wife, Mrs. Frances Chaney Lardner, a son, Joseph, six months old, and a daughter, Katherine, two; his mother, Mrs. Ellis Lardner, and two brothers, Ring Jr., a motion picture writer, and John, a writer for *Newsweek* magazine.   □

Aachen, Germany, October 20 — The German border city of Aachen, reduced to wreckage by American shells and bombing planes and torn by days of savage street fighting, fell today to American troops who drove the last of its desperately resisting Nazi garrison from their burrows in the city proper.

Tonight the victorious Yanks began mopping up the remnants of Nazis hopelessly trapped in pockets on the outskirts of this mass of wreckage. There were estimated to be between 500 and 1,000 Germans trapped in the vise, in addition to approximately 2,000 already captured.

Troops under the command of Lieut. Col. Merril Daniel of Geneva, N.Y., knocked out the last major German strongpoint in the city at 3:30 p.m. (9:30 a.m. Central War Time) with direct fire from a 155-millimeter rifle blasting at close range. The big gun literally knocked down a building in which SS elite guard troops had made a last desperate stand.

With the strongpoint reduced to smoke and rubble, the doughboys swiftly advanced through the remainder of the ruined city and squeezed the Nazis into a final pocket.

"Aachen is ours," said an American officer, matter-of-factly announcing the capture of the first large German city by Allied invasion armies. "When we knocked out that building we knocked out the guns of their defense."

Lieut. Gen. Courtney H. Hodges' First Army troops have been attacking Aachen, medieval seat of Charlemagne's empire and important bastion of the Siegfried line, since September 15. On October 10 the city's German garrison was ordered to surrender within twenty-four hours or be annihilated by American guns and planes. When the ultimatum was rejected the Yanks launched an all-out assault that quickly settled into house-to-house fighting.

Aachen, whose peacetime population was 165,000, is forty miles from Cologne on the Rhine and 340 miles from Berlin. Its famous cathedral, resting place of Charlemagne, was standing tonight with only relatively minor wounds.

Aachen's fall nails down the right flank of a solid eighty-five-mile front anchored at Arnhem in Holland, behind which the Germans declare Gen. Dwight D. Eisenhower is mounting a great offensive designed to knock Germany out of the war before winter snows set in.

The damage in Aachen is appalling, and if the German people in the cities to the east could see the havoc wrought by the decision of their leaders to fight in every street and every city it would be an object lesson they would never forget.

There was no grand rush to capture Aachen after the surrender ultimatum was ignored and our artillery and bombers lashed at the city in a fury of explosions. The doughboys went about the job slowly and methodically.

"That is why we were able to take the city with so few losses," an officer said tonight. "One look at our casualty figure and it would appear that we had no opposition. As a matter of fact, the enemy fought hard and bitterly, but our boys outsmarted them."

Even yet civilians trudge through the wreckage to the safety of a little colony which has been established for refugees. They come from basements and dank shelters and holes in the ground like a procession of lost souls, pushing their little carts filled with a few belongings. Here was defeated Germany on parade.

Tonight the men who captured Aachen received the plaudits of their commanding general, who praised them for a great job. The ceremony took place in an old building battered by bullets and shells, and toasts were drunk from three bottles of champagne dug up from some German store.

While the troops inside Aachen were slowly squeezing the garrison to death, other Yank forces outside the city on the north and northeast did a job of at least equal and probably greater military importance in beating off five full-scale Nazi counter-attacks. Altogether, two German units have been effectively written off as offensive threats.

No estimate is possible of the number of German civilian casualties in Aachen. Our ultimatum gave them ample warning and time to get out but in one instance sixteen wounded German civilians were found with ninety-one wounded German soldiers.   □

Aachen, [October 20] — Eight hundred Germans, the remnants of the Aachen garrison, surrendered unconditionally today, and all organized resistance ended in the city and its suburbs. The last defenders, who had been ordered by Hitler to fight to the death, laid down their arms at noon after savage doughboy attacks had hammered them into traps from which there was no escape. A dramatic silence suddenly fell over the shell of a city as the guns became quiet for the first time in days.

Capt. Seth Botts, former University of Kentucky engineering student, was preparing to launch an assault on a bunker where the German remnants had a command post when the enemy decided to surrender and hung out a white flag. Botts and his troops had closed in on the bunker last night fighting through houses by flashlight in one of the weirdest combats of the war.

Out of the bunker came a slender dapper colonel at the head of 300 troops. They marched smartly in column under the guns of Botts. The men and officers were all well groomed, with shining black boots. With them was an American lieutenant and thirty-two enlisted men who had been held captive by the Germans for the past week.

The German commander was taken to the command post of Lt. Col. John Corley, Brooklyn, N.Y., in one of Aachen's wrecked buildings. There an American brigadier general waited to receive the commander, who was told he must surrender unconditionally. Reluctantly the officer wrote out the surrender of his troops and ended the document by saying "Aachen is in American hands and therefore everything belongs to the Americans that was German."

But when the silver-haired American general had the surrender translated he was not satisfied because it did not say unconditional. The German officer, a professional soldier for twenty-eight years, asked for five minutes to think it over. He said his reluctance was caused by the fact that if he signed unconditional surrender terms he was afraid for his family in Germany.

There was silence in the little room as the German pondered with the American watching him intently. In the room with the general and Corley were Capt. Edward Crawford of Somersworth, N.H., and Lt. John Reynolds, Winston-Salem, N.C.

Finally the German colonel turned, picked up the pen and hurriedly wrote another document. This time he said: "Aachen—the defending German garrison ran out of food and ammunition. I am forced to give up my command and surrender Aachen unconditionally with all its stores to the commanding officer of the victorious Americans."

The surrender was signed at noon. Then the colonel asked and was granted permission to speak to his troops outside the building. There were eight staff officers with him, all as immaculate as their commander. One of them had been a student at Heidelberg and there were the scars of dueling foils on his face.

The commander climbed onto the hood of a jeep. His men came to attention, and in a voice heavy with emotion he said to them: "Dear German soldiers. I am speaking to you at a painful moment. I was forced to surrender because we ran out of ammunition, food and water. I saw that further fighting was useless. I was acting against orders. I was supposed to fight to the last man. At this time I have to remind you that you are still German soldiers. Please behave as such.

"I also wish you the best of health in your future travels and fast return to the fatherland after hostilities have ended. Return to Germany to help rebuild our country. I was refused by the Americans the authority to give the 'Sieg Heil' and 'Heil Hitler.' But we can still do it in our minds."

Then he saluted smartly and stepped down. He was taken under guard to the prisoner cage in the rear. Other strongpoints, unaware their commanding officer had put up the white flag, fought on.

A party was sent by Botts with a lieutenant under a flag of truce to arrange the capitulation of the others.

Another 300 surrendered en masse when it was explained that their commander had decided to quit fighting and that they were no longer bound to continue the futile struggle. And then the others came out of their hiding places in small groups until 800 were trudging through Aachen's battered streets.

After the surrender was completed a high-ranking officer came to the American command post and congratulated the commander of the operation along with Corley and Lt. Col. Derril Daniel of Geneva, N.Y. He grinned and said, "Well, this war is over, isn't it?"   □

Aachen, October 21 — "That guy has killed more Germans than anyone in my outfit," said the officer pointing to Pvt. William M. Harris of Tellico Plains, Tenn., who was resting against a bomb-wrecked building.

"We were walking along the other day and he picked off two before I saw them," the officer recounted.

Somebody asked Harris just how many Germans he had killed.

"Well, I killed twenty-two and winged three," drawled the thirty-year-old doughboy.   □

With U.S. First Army in Germany, November 8 — With the presidential election decided, the strict Army censorship which has prevented any sort of poll or questioning of the troops on its political aspects was relaxed today.

(A dispatch from Rome said Army public relations officers there notified correspondents that the War Department had ruled soldiers still could not be quoted on political aspects of the election.)

In the areas around Aachen, G.I.s discussed the election, many of them expressing approval of President Roosevelt's reelection. Pfc. Dick Jamieson of Omaha, Neb., listened to radio reports of Roosevelt's victory, and said: "Well, I'm glad to see they left the old boy in office."

Up in the front lines where the doughboys are battling Germans there was not a great deal of interest, because those men are fighting for their lives, and they did not have time to think much of a political fight at home. But one sergeant drawled: "Well, I'm glad the election is over. Maybe now the people will remember we have a little war on over here that we think is important."

In battered Aachen a group of soldiers discussed the election. Lieut. Robert S. Latchaw of Martinez, Calif., grinned and said: "My dad probably will be sore about the results, but I'm glad it came out that way."

In Eupen, Pvt. Charles Lewis, Trenton, N.J., had put up a blackboard six feet long and four feet wide on which he kept a radio report of the results. He stayed up all night getting the returns and had a crowd of G.I.s around the board while civilians looked on curiously.

It wasn't unanimous, however, for there were some who were disappointed that Dewey failed to make the grade.   □

Eifall, Germany, November 13 — Two companies of American soldiers deep in the snow-mantled Hürtgen Forest were safe again today after being cut off for three days by Germans who brought up tanks in an effort to wipe them out.

For three days Lt. Kirby Brigham, Bloomfield, N.J., and Lt. Robert Daspuit, Houma, La., held their men together while ringed by the enemy and beat back every attempt of the Nazis to annihilate the group.

Once the doughboys fought off tanks with machine guns and bazookas. They even called for their own artillery to concentrate fire on their own positions to break up the enemy attacks.

Yesterday Lt. Col. Bill Sibert, Ho Ho Kus, N.J., led his battalion through the dense pine trees and snow-covered mud and rescued the two lost companies. For a time Sibert's men, too, were cut off, but they grouped their forces and fought their way back through the Germans. □

With the U.S. First Army in Germany, November 14 – The Nazis have launched their new secret weapon—V-2, a supersonic rocket—against targets in Belgium, northwest and northeast sectors of France and in Holland.

Very little can be disclosed at this time except that rockets are being used against certain countries now in Allied hands. The Germans also are sending buzz bombs into these areas and troops in certain parts of the First Army area can hear daily the throbbing shudder of the robot weapons thundering overhead from launching sites somewhere in Germany.

Neutral sources report V-2 weighs about fifteen tons when launched. The warhead is believed to contain about a ton of explosives encased in light metal to give a terrific blast effect. When at full speed, the rocket is believed to travel at a stratosphere level. When it strikes the ground, the rate of speed is estimated at about 900 miles per hour. □

With U.S. Forces, Germany, November 16 – The U.S. First Army, conquerors of Aachen, went on the attack again today. Lieut. Gen. Courtney H. Hodges' forces launched an assault at 11 a.m. behind the drumming thunder of a heavy aerial and artillery bombardment.

Big guns crashed and planes roared overhead, heralding the new move by the army, which helped drive the Germans from the Cherbourg Peninsula across France, Belgium and Holland into Germany.

The attack, which followed advances by the Third and Seventh Armies, was loosed with the first break in the weather. General Hodges was waiting only to get aerial support.

For more than a week rain, snow and sleet had been falling from low-hanging clouds which blanketed the battlefields and kept the bombers tied to their bases on the continent. But the break came today and the battle was on.

At bases far in the rear of the front lines the bombers had been waiting. They rose in great flocks this morning with fighters swarming about them and roared to the battlefield, dropping their bombs on enemy positions.

After the bombers had passed, the doughboys came out of their muddy foxholes and assaulted enemy positions.

For days the army had been preparing for this move. Convoys rolled over muddy roads to the front with food and ammunition and other battle supplies. Guns were drawn up in new positions in the snow-covered fields and tanks ploughed in, getting ready to support the infantry. Supply was the big problem—and once he got his supplies, Gen. Hodges was ready for the attack. The break in the weather turned his legions loose.

The attack broke a comparative lull since the fall of Aachen some three weeks ago. One unit of the First Army had made a limited attack in the somber Hürtgen Forest and fought bitterly to improve the position, but this was the only action in the interim. The army's leaders were confident as other outfits made their moves toward the Rhineland, even though winter has turned the battlefield into a mire.   □

With the U.S. First Army in Germany, November 16 – Behind a great aerial bombardment and a thunderous artillery barrage, Lt. Gen. Hodges' First Army plowed deeper into Germany today. Tonight a staff officer said, "This was a day when everything clicked. The attack is going well."

Hodges beat the Germans to the punch and apparently caught them as they were trying to build up forces for an assault against the First Army. "It was a race to see which would hit first," an officer said. "They were building up to take a sock at us and we beat them to the punch."

Hodges waited for five days for a break in the weather so that he could get support from the United States Air Forces and the Royal Air Force for his doughboys, and that break came today. Against patches of blue sky we could see the mighty aerial armada roaring over.

"This is the largest heavy bomber strike in support of ground troops in the war," an air officer said.

The bomb line was so well marked that there were no shorts, as in the St-Lô bombardment, where American bombs fell inside the American lines. When the heavy bombers approached, German civilians in towns at the front ran in terror from their homes to seek safety in caves and shelters. Some women sobbed in fright and when artillery roared nearby they seemed to think it was the noise of bombs falling around them.

At 12:45 p.m. the doughboys rose from their muddy foxholes and went into the attack, which Hodges had been preparing since the fall of Aachen on October 21.

We stood at the edge of Mausbach, seven miles east of Aachen, to watch the attack. Planes dived at enemy positions and down the road a mortar squad was tossing shells at the enemy. A few hundred yards across the valley guns began to roar. A cluster of tanks rolled forward with guns flaming. At the end of a ridge shells exploded and sent columns of dirt and smoke against the sky.

"That's a helluva sight, isn't it?" said Capt. William MacPherson of Hobart, Ind.

Tanks rolling across a field startled a herd of cattle, which fled in confusion.   □

Eschweiler, Germany, November 23 — Under gray, dripping skies on this dismal Thanksgiving Day, doughboys of Lt. Gen. Courtney H. Hodges' First Army inched forward all along the line in some of the bitterest fighting of all the invasion.

The savagery of this plodding battle is told by the dead strewn on the slopes of Hill 232, where the doughboys fought one of the epic defenses of the war. There they had beaten off wave after wave of German attacks as machine gunners performed great acts of heroism.

In two machine gun units totaling fifty men a large number were killed or wounded, but as soon as one machine gunner was a casualty, another would jump in to take his place.

Today 150 German bodies were taken from the hillside, and there are 150 more lying in the rain which is turning the countryside into a vast mudhole.

The American advance southeast of Eschweiler's rain-soaked ruins is through the dark, cruel forested country where every foot of gain exacts its price. Advances are measured in yards of soggy, brown mud, over which many small streams are raging in torrents.

But the boys are almost out of the woods—literally and figuratively. Then the going may be a bit easier. Then they will be able to get support from tanks and self-propelled guns.

The Germans are fighting back with fanatical tenacity, throwing in heavy artillery fire to hold their defenses and keep this veteran hard-hitting army from crashing through to the Rhineland.

Putzlohn, a little village north of Eschweiler, has been one of the hottest battlegrounds of any front. It is just a cluster of about a dozen houses on an intersection of highways, but in forty-eight hours it changed hands five times.

There was tank-to-tank fighting around the hamlet, captured by the doughboys yesterday, and then the Germans counter-attacked with infantry, supported by from ten to fifteen tanks and self-propelled guns. Hodges' men had to fall back to the Germans' own system of entrenchments which are dug west of the city. There a counter thrust developed and five enemy tanks were destroyed.

The doughboys advanced in the early morning mists, retook the village, and lost it again to a counter-attack. Then the Yanks attacked again. ☐

With the U.S. First Army in Germany, November 24 – Doughboys of Lieut. Gen. Courtney H. Hodges's First Army fought into Weisweiler, northeast of Aachen, today a house at a time amid indications that the Nazis were pulling out of the town under cover of a strong rearguard action.

Hard fighting continued all along the First Army front. The infantry slugged forward under dismal, dripping skies in a slow progress which a staff officer described as "tree-to-tree" fighting. The German withdrawal from Weisweiler was indicated by the movement of trucks and horse-drawn vehicles along highways leading to the northeast. Heavy artillery pounded the Germans' escape routes out of Eschweiler, two miles west of Weisweiler, over which more heavy German traffic was seen moving.

Both Allied and German movement was complicated by driving rain which sent small streams flooding from their banks and overflowing onto the highways. The Germans threw in fresh reserves in an effort to stem the army's advance. West of Weisweiler the doughboys encountered storm troops ordered into the attack to try to save a deteriorating position.

"The enemy's resistance is stubborn and the going is slow and difficult," a staff officer said in summing up the day's operations. He said 3,530 Germans had been captured by the First Army since the offensive began November 16 and approximately 5,700 by the Ninth Army. ☐

With U.S. First Army in Germany, November 26 –
The U.S. 104th (Timberwolf) Infantry Division, commanded by Major Gen. Terry Allen, who led the First Infantry Division through North Africa and Sicily, was the first American outfit to enter Eschweiler.

At the same time, censorship permitted disclosure that the First and Fourth infantry divisions were waging the battle of Hürtgen Forest, one of the bitterest of the invasion. When Allen's 104th Division entered the line on the First Army front, his men relieved the First Division, which moved into a new sector. That day was almost like a homecoming for the slender, dark-haired Terry Allen, as he went about the First Division seeking his old friends with whom he had fought in the Mediterranean.

The 104th troops landed in France September 7, the first Americans in this war to land in France directly from the United States.   □

An American Field Hospital in Germany, November 28 –
Medical theories on what the human body can endure are being revised as American doctors perform surgical miracles with men wounded in the battle of Germany. When heavy fighting rages the doctors and nurses often work eighteen to twenty hours daily, sometimes even longer.

This hospital is an old schoolhouse. Four surgical teams, working under improvised lights, operate day and night. In the same room patients lie on stretchers resting on wooden horses. Brought in from the field, the wounded sometimes arrive within two hours after they are injured. At home many of these cases would require the services of two doctors and two private nurses each. Here a small group of doctors and nurses must handle them all.

"We've had to throw out many of the concepts of civilians' surgery" said Maj. D. S. Meyers of Kingston, N.Y., formerly with the Kingston Hospital. "For example, we thought if we had to cut out more than three feet of bowel we might as well give up, because the patient didn't have a chance to recover.

"But there have been (war) cases where I removed six, nine and even ten feet of intestines and a few days later the patients have been begging for something to eat."

As civilians most of these surgeons would have thought it impossible to operate successfully under present conditions, and operations which would have been considered sensational are accepted as everyday work.

"Anything like one of these abdominal operations in civil practice would have brought everybody in the hospital out to watch," Meyers chuckled. "Here a doctor, with an enlisted man who used to be a soda jerker at home as a helper, is doing it alone. There was a time when, if I did two or three major operations a year, I thought I had to go away to recuperate."

Now Meyers does as high as twenty operations a day, most of them on serious abdominal or chest injuries. And he is one of many. Others here include Maj. Robert Sinclair, Wilmington, N.C., Maj. Louis Stoller, Red Hook, N.Y., and Maj. Wilson Weisel, Rochester, Minn.

But the surgeons appreciate the aid of people at home. "Tell them not to quit donating blood," said Sinclair. "We need it badly. As soon as there is good news from the front, people stop donating, but now is no time to quit."

A single patient frequently is given twelve pints of blood to bring him safely through the crisis—and that means blood from twenty-four donors. At one period in the invasion, blood became scarce and immediately the death rate went up. Troops had to be bled to get enough whole blood for the wounded.

The need for blood became great in the Hürtgen Forest battle. There the Germans threw in the full weight of their artillery. The death ratio was high because of the difficulty of getting the wounded out of the forest. Some were not found in the underbrush for two or three days. Winter exposure and early darkness added to their complications. If a man is wounded after dusk, he may not be evacuated until morning. Then speed in getting him to the hospital is a lifesaving factor.

These battles increase the demand for transfusions. Blood spilled in them must be replaced. □

Paris, December 2 — The heaviest fighting of the war is raging along the Western front as the German armies make their last savage stand in an effort to stem the American advance into Germany. The soil of Hitler's Reich is being won slowly. Every yard is contested by Germans fighting as they never have fought before.

The Germans are making the American gains as costly as possible, and they are costly. There is every indication that the fighting throughout the winter will be the same bitter slaughter until a final decision is won. Three months ago hopes ran high that the war would be over before Christmas. But the German armies did not collapse as expected. The German home front, in its straitjacket of Nazi control, did not fold up as so many persons had thought it would. The enemy showed that he intended to fight to the last, and that is what he is doing now.

There always is the probability of a sudden crumbling of German resistance, but there are no signs of it up front, where the fighting is hard and bloody and where the roar of cannon echoes continuously across the cold, sodden forests and plains. A great deal of American blood is being spilled on German soil. No battle in this war—and many veterans say none in the last war—can compare in heartbreaking sacrifice and hardship with the battle for Hürtgen Forest southeast of Aachen.

So far the Germans have been clubbed back slowly under a terrific artillery barrage, armored assault and whenever the skies have cleared, by air power. But these all have been secondary instruments of destruction. Muddy, slogging G.I. Joe, the infantryman, still carries the burden of the battle.

In Normandy the enemy had only a thick crust of defenses. Once a break was achieved, there was nothing behind. On their home grounds, the Germans have defenses in depth, and doughboys must fight their way through all of them to get at defenders who are under orders to fight to the death.

A sudden breakthrough such as that at St-Lô looks virtually impossible to those of us who have been watching the First Army's offensive plowing through the deep mud and thick forests. The consensus is that the American armies face a long, hard winter of fighting which is to cost much in lives and suffering—a price that must be paid for victory over a fanatical enemy. □

Paris, December 4 — Thousands of new Gold Stars will appear in the windows of American homes this winter; the hardest and most savage fighting of all the invasion is under way. Allied Armies are locked with the Germans in the first of great battles of decision—battles which will decide when the war will end. The Nazis have no chance of winning the war but they are not yet defeated.

Those of us who have watched the slow, costly progress of the American First Army against the fanatically stubborn enemy can foresee no early end to the war. A winter campaign seems inevitable. The Germans are showing no indications of cracking up either on the military or home fronts. That is not a cheerful pre-Christmas picture but it is the sober opinion of most of the observers with the fighting troops.

The American High Command has done a magnificent job in driving the Germans back onto their homeland, which is taking a terrible punishment since the first doughboys stormed ashore just short of six months ago. France has been virtually freed. Belgium and Luxembourg have been liberated, Holland has been freed partially and the Americans have a solid hold on the soil of the Reich. Now slow, costly slugging is under way in the Allied drive toward the Rhine.

For a time there was speculation as to whether the Germans would make a stand in the Siegfried line or fall back behind the great water barricade of the Rhine River. It soon became apparent the Germans had decided to fight west of the Rhine to protect the heart of the Reich. In dense forests and behind an incredible maze of fortifications, trenches and wire barricades, the enemy dug in to make the Americans pay for each yard of advance. German commanders exhorted their troops to fight to the last man. Death was the penalty for retreat.

The German still is one of the most skillful and courageous fighters in the world. He does what he is told to do and while more than five years of war have skimmed off the cream of the once great Wehrmacht it still is formidable, hard fighting and well equipped. It still can do a great deal of damage.

Lieut. Gen. Omar Bradley always has worked to gain victory with as little loss of life as possible. He never has hurled troops forward into a hopeless conflict. But always there comes a time when losses must be taken if vital objectives are to be seized. That time has come.

In the savagery of battle, this war almost has reached the stage of a war of attrition as the doughboys' advances are measured in yards against strong positions, numerous counter-attacks and heavy artillery.

The Germans are suffering heavy casualties—losses which they are not able to afford as well as the Allies. But it gives them time to prepare more defenses farther east and to marshal their battered forces so that Allied armies will pay dearly for each kilometer of advance. That is their only hope— to make the Allies pay so dearly in lives that the conquest of Germany will be too costly to continue.   □

New York, December 10 — On December 1 there was no critical shortage of shells on the First Army front—but there was a shortage in shells needed for future operations against the Germans on the soils of the Reich. Even though the shortages are in futures this makes the need no less

---

*Editor's Note: As stated in the introduction, in early December 1944 Whitehead returned to the United States for a well-earned rest and reunion with his family, whom he had not seen in almost nine months. This explains the time lag until his next dispatch dated February 13, 1945. Unfortunately, he missed reporting the Battle of the Bulge, assuming "nothing much was going to happen," which was what he had been told by a trusted military confidant.

urgent, for the winter campaign will be handicapped seriously unless shells pour across the Atlantic in an unbroken flow.

Army commanders are looking ahead to the next moves of their armies, estimating their needs for battles yet to come, planning where to strike the enemy next. That is where the real shell shortage exists. Unless the slump in American production of artillery ammunition is corrected at once, it will lead to inevitable tragedy at the fighting fronts—a rising toll of dead and wounded. American losses in Germany already are heavy, but if our troops fail to get the ammunition they need then they will die just as surely as though their own guns were turned against them.

Artillery support is the greatest protection the infantry has as our guns pound enemy positions, break up counter-attacks, silence the enemy's artillery fire, and halt tank attacks. Without this support the infantry is left to fight alone against uneven odds.

It isn't quite accurate to picture American gun crews sitting idle in Germany for lack of shells to fire at the Germans. Shells are rationed to each battalion of artillery just as food, clothing, cigarettes, chewing gum and other supplies are rationed. Each must stay within certain imposed limits or there would be no check on vital supplies. Even our vast production at home will not permit prodigal and unrationed expenditure.

At the beginning of invasion we had one army in the field—Lt. Gen. Omar Bradley's First Army. Now there are four American armies in action against the Germans. The supply requirements have increased proportionately.

There is no question that supply needs were underestimated, both in large and small calibers. This was apparent in Normandy particularly with small arms ammunition used in the hedgerow fighting. But also in shells. One officer told me at the time we were using four to five times the total requirements anticipated before invasion.

Estimates had been based on fighting in North Africa, Sicily and Italy, but suddenly the army encountered a new type warfare—hedgerow fighting in which the Germans dug themselves into each thick hedge bordering the Normandy fields.

First we would shell the hedgerows and then troops would go in with tanks and automatic weapons to spray every yard of the hedges with steel. In each town where the Germans made a stand we would call up the artillery to pound the stronghold.

Artillery has been one of the American Army's greatest weapons in this war. We use our artillery in support of our ground troops probably more than any other army, laying a blanket of explosives before them each time they make a move. We depend on artillery to break up enemy troop concentrations, to soften up strongpoints, to smash counter-attacks and to harass the enemy at every chance. This requires enormous supplies of shells.

The need for shells has increased tremendously in Germany, where the fighting has been slow, hard and bloody. The Germans are in trenches, fox-holes, bunkers and machine gun nests all the way to the Rhine. They have made each town and crossroads hamlet a stronghold.

Every time the doughboys attack one of these strongpoints they get support from the artillery to make their path easier, but as soon as the infantry captures a hill or a strongpoint the Germans are certain to counter-attack. That calls for more artillery fire.

The Army's demands for more and more shells underline the winter strategy of the high command—to continue pounding the Germans throughout the months of snow and ice and give them no respite. This slow progress against stubborn and skillful enemy resistance is costly, but cheaper in lives than permitting the front to bog down into static warfare.

Seven

ON TO BERLIN,
FEBRUARY–MAY 1945

Paris, February 13 — Doughboys who have been away from home so long they may have forgotten the little social graces no longer need fear embarrassment because of occasional lapses into the rough language and customs of life in the field. All they need to do to prepare for return to civilian life in the United States is to undergo an indoctrination course thought up by some army wit, who has listed instructions such as these:

"1. Belching in company is strictly frowned upon. If you should forget about it, however, and belch in the presence of others, the proper remark is, 'Excuse me.' Do not say, 'It must be that lousy chow we've been eating.'

"2. The typical American breakfast consists of such strange foods as cantaloupes, fresh eggs, milk, ham, etc. These are highly palatable and although strange in appearance are extremely tasty. Butter, made from cream, is often served. If you wish some butter you turn to the person nearest it and say quietly, 'Please pass the butter.' Do not say, 'Throw me that grease.'

"3. Upon leaving a friend's home after a visit one may find one's hat misplaced. Frequently it has been placed in a closet. One should turn to one's host and say, 'I don't seem to have my hat—could you help me find it?' Do not say, 'Don't anybody leave this room. Someone has stolen my hat.'

"4. Traveling in the United States, particularly in a strange city, it is often necessary to spend the night in a hotel. Hotels are provided for this purpose and one can get directions to the nearest hotel from almost anyone. Here for a small sum one can register and be shown a room where he can sleep for the night. The present practice of entering the nearest house, throwing the occupants in the yard and taking over the premises will cease.

"5. Whisky, a common American drink, may be offered to a soldier on social occasions. It is considered a reflection on the uniform to snatch the bottle from the hostess and drain the bottle. All individuals are cautioned to exercise control in these circumstances.

"6. In motion picture theaters seats are provided and helmets are not required. It is not considered good form to whistle every time a female over eight and under thirty crosses the screen. If vision is impaired by the person in the seat in front there are plenty of other seats which can be occupied. Do not hit him or her across the back of the head and say, 'Move your head, jerk, I can't see a thing.'

"7. It is not proper to go around hitting everyone of draft age who happens to be in civilian clothes. He might have been released from the service for medical reasons. Ask for his credentials, and if he can't show any, then go ahead and slug him." □

With the U.S. First Army, [February 24] — Premonition of death or injury clouds the spirits of almost all doughboys going into battle for the first time, but Major Gen. Terry Allen has developed a front-line combat training program for his 104th "Timberwolf" Division which lifts much of this dark fear from green troops.

The reinforcements are learning not only to be confident of themselves and their weapons, but also tricks of combat from veterans which are certain to save many lives.

It is a strange sight to see men practicing the art of warfare, and it is reminiscent of maneuvers back in the states, but these men are in deadly earnest. They know they soon may be in action and the lessons they learn may be the difference between life and death.

The general objectives are to instill discipline into the new troops, improve their physical condition and technical proficiency and, what is tremendously important, give them pride in their unit.

Just because a man wears a uniform doesn't mean that he knows how to fight. Replacements, or what the army prefers to call reinforcements, are being drawn from rear echelon noncombat units. Cooks, clerks, truck drivers, antiaircraft gunners and air corps personnel are donning the doughboy gear.

All had basic training in the states, but it was not serious business then. Actual combat seemed a remote possibility and most of them knew little about weapons or infantry tactics. But once they know they are going into the fight they are deadly serious about learning all they possibly can about the job ahead of them.

Lieut. Col. Edward Rager of Seward, Pa., is in charge of the school. His instructors are Lieut. Roy Williams of Portland, Ore., Lieut. Melvin Pechacek of Temple City, Calif., Lieut. John Kalman of Cudahy, Wis., and Lieut. Stephen Keglovitz of Saginaw, Mich., all combat veterans.

"Many of these men come up thinking their number is up," said Williams. "The first thing they want to know is how long a man lives in combat. They have heard so much of casualties that many of them think a casualty means a dead man.

"We show them that it's not all blood and hell and there is some rest and relaxation even in combat. That makes them feel better."

Pechacek, who won a battlefield commission for leadership, said a surprising number of men arrive for training knowing virtually nothing about their weapons. They were taught in the states but never took the course seriously and hardly know how to fire a rifle.

"Some of these men come to us feeling bitter about changing units and going into the infantry," Kalman said. "But they hang on every word you tell them and their attitude changes fast. They leave with an entirely different attitude."

Each class is given two weeks' training which involves several night problems. There is nothing theoretical about the fieldwork. They operate just as though they were in combat, learning how to patrol, how to place weapons for greatest efficiency, how to take care of themselves and what to do in defense and on attack.

"If we can tell a man how to protect himself, we've done a great deal," Williams said, "and if we save the life of one man then all this work is worthwhile." ☐

With American Infantry on the Roer River, February 24 — The moon was very bright—too bright—for a night attack. But orders had been issued for H-Hour at 3:30 a.m.

"Hell, the Krauts can see us coming a mile away," a soldier growled.

The men in a battalion command post in a basement near the flooded Roer River didn't have much to do now except to wait for the hour of attack, which had been held up for days by the Germans releasing water from the dams to the south. All plans had been made and troops were in position near hidden assault boats in which they were to cross the river.

Capt. Robert Neilsen of Bloomington, Calif., looked at his watch. His face was drawn and his eyes red from lack of sleep. It was midnight.

"It will be a lifetime from now till 3 o'clock," Neilsen commented. Outside guns boomed occasionally. There was an undercurrent of tenseness in the little room. A truck idled by outside and the slight noise made everyone look up.

Maj. Ray Waters of Richfield, Utah, laughed. "When I walked down the road a few minutes ago I tried to tiptoe. Those noises sound awfully loud at night with the Jerries just across the river," he said.

A telephone rang and someone reported figures were moving about on our side of the river. Neilsen began checking units to see who they were.

"We'd feel silly as hell if the Jerries came over and stole our boats," Waters chuckled.

They appeared relaxed and easy, but these men were sweating out those last hours before the attacks. There were Neilsen, Waters, Lt. Allen Dean of Phillips, Tex., Capt. Max Eisner of Pittsfield, Mass., and Capt. Frank Schiele of Staten Island, N.Y.

Lt. Col. Fred Needham of Auburn, Calif., slept in the next room, resting up for the hard grind ahead. Neilsen's check disclosed the men on the riverbank were our troops putting out smudge pots to be used if necessary to throw up a smoke screen.

We decided to go down to the command post of Capt. Jerry Hooker of St. Petersburg, Fla., who was to lead one of the assault companies in the river crossing. The road toward the river was deserted and there was no sign of troops waiting inside the dark ruins of houses along the way.

Hooker looked much too young to be commanding a company. He looked younger even than his twenty-four years as he talked to tall, handsome Lt. Sam Jenkins of Cartersville, Ga., his weapons platoon leader.

"Don't wait for a signal from me," Hooker told Sam. "Three minutes before H-Hour, shove 'em off."

Sam said, "Okay, will do," and he went out into the night.

There wasn't much talk here and what there was usually was brief and to the point. With Hooker were Sgt. Charles Courtney, Fort Worth, Tex., Sgt. Robert Ogilvie, South Pasadena Calif., Lt. Francis Ahrnsbrak of Marshall, Okla., and Sgt. George L. Woods of Riverside, Calif.

Hooker pulled out a bottle of Scotch with a couple of drinks left in it. "I have been saving this," he explained. He took a drink and handed the bottle to Ahrnsbrak, saying, "Have one, Francis."

"Thanks, I wish I had those nine bottles I ordered," the lieutenant replied.

A shell landed nearby and the little house shuddered.

"That one was coming in, Pop," said Hooker. "It belongs to us now."

A lamp on the table cast long shadows on the walls and made the youthful faces look old, at times, as the light played across the lean, serious features of the men.

Hooker slung an automatic weapon across his shoulder, folded a single blanket and tied it on his back by crisscrossing a rope around his chest. He said, "I wish it were darker. It's a lot harder to get shot if they can't see you." Then he hung a grenade on his chest strap.

Suddenly the big guns, which had been firing only occasional rounds, opened up with a mighty roar. The lamp trembled on the table and shadows danced in jitterbug nervousness.

"There the fireworks go," Tufts said.

Punctuating the booming of the artillery was the clatter of machine guns raking the enemy-held shore. The soft moonlit night turned into a hellish roar of guns, the whispering of shells and the sound of the explosions.

At 3:15 Hooker said quickly:

"Okay, boys, let's go."

They stepped into the night. Houses were disgorging troops who moved silently in the moonlight.

We climbed into the attic of a battered house some hundreds of yards from the river to watch the attack go in.

Artillery shells burst in ripples of flame along the German-held banks of the Roer. Bright red chains of tracer bullets streaked the leaden waters. There was a continuous, pulsing roar of guns and angry outbursts of machine guns that grated against the nerves like someone dragging his fingernails across a blackboard.

The dull glow of fire lit the skies and the smoke of explosions drifted upward, forming a fog in the moonlight.

Below us figures materialized from the shadows, lifted assault boats and walked to the river. They slid the craft into the swollen stream and clambered in and began paddling furiously.

The current caught the boats and they seemed to shoot downstream. Most of the boats got across safely with a few German guns challenging them on the crossing, but some swamped in the swift stream and the men plunged into the icy waters—to be dragged under by the weight of their gear.

Once ashore they began clawing their way against mounting German opposition. Fog began to settle over the river, shielding the movements, but then the German guns began bombarding the riverbanks and approaches.

The heavy crump of the shells made the old building tremble and the crash of artillery and explosions became louder. But on the ground floor a youth snored serenely as though it was a quiet spring night. He was Pfc. Allen Clawson, Philadelphia, Pa.

"That guy can sleep through anything," a soldier remarked, and Clawson snored.

Across the river the fighting raged as the doughboys fought deeper into enemy-held positions. □

With the U.S. First Army, February 25 — Long columns
of vehicles, big guns and equipment are streaming across the bridges of the
Roer, and none could watch this great movement without realizing that this
was one of the greatest drives ever put on by the First Army. While convoys
moved forward, German prisoners moved back to rear areas. One division
alone has captured approximately 2,000.

Casualties among assaulting troops have been extremely low, a staff officer said, and the ratio of killed to wounded is less than in any attack ever
made by the First Army. Many men in one battalion of the Eighth Infantry
Division lost their weapons in the river crossing so they went into the attack
with grenades and knives. They armed themselves with the weapons of dead
or captured Germans.

The doughboys foxed the Germans in setting up a new bridgehead south
of Düren. They crossed the river into the established bridgehead and then
struck south clearing the Germans from the east side of the Roer and elimi-
nating the necessity of a hazardous assault boat crossing.   □

Birkesdorf, Germany, February 25 — "The Fighting 45," a
group of men led by a hell-for-leather young man from Texas, were among
the heroes of the U.S. First Army's drive across the Roer River. For fifteen
blurred hours they battled through an area which was supposed to be the
battleground for 200 doughboys. They went into this shell-smashed city
shooting tommy guns from their hips and they routed the Germans in an all-
day fight.

Lt. Ernest Andrewratha of Texas started across the swollen river at 3:30
a.m. Friday with a full company which had been hiding in the moonlight for
hours waiting for the attack.

Swiftly his men launched assault boats. Several boats were lost either by
direct mortar hits or by being swamped in the swift current of the stream.
Two of them plunged over a small dam and sank.

"Nobody knows yet how many of these men were lost," said Lt. Col.
Charles Fernald of Los Angeles, who commanded troops in this sector.
"Many of them may turn up with other units."

But when Andrewratha reached the eastern enemy-held bank he had only
twenty-one infantrymen and twenty-three machine gunners with him. The
machine gunners had lost their heavier weapons but they still had their
tommy guns and light machine guns.

The Texan knew there was only one thing to do and that was to attack. So these forty-five doughboys went into battle.

The Germans were holed up in a factory near the riverbanks and Andrewratha and his men went in after them as the moonlight filtered through the windows. When the fighting was over there were eighteen German prisoners. The others were dead.

Then Andrewratha and his men began cleaning out adjoining strongpoints. Before they had finished their work that day they had cleared seven full blocks and were still going strong when other troops from their company arrived to give them support. □

Cologne Plain, February 26 — Lt. Gen. Courtney H. Hodges' armor and infantry plunged over the "billiard table" flat plains within twelve miles of Cologne today under drizzling skies, and artillerymen wheeled up their big guns. The attack is rolling now, tanks taking over the spearheading role and moving swiftly across the level country. The infantry had done the spearheading up until dark.

The plains are unbroken by the ridges, dense forests and valleys such as the Americans fought across through Belgium. Only one real barrier stands between the army and Cologne—the Erft River and Erft Canal, neither of which are barriers such as the flooded Roer. Except for the mud, the tanks are operating on the best terrain since their dash across France.

Casualties are light. Towns are being captured without a single man being killed. The Germans toss in the towel when they see that a situation is hopeless. There probably are two reasons. One is that the Germans sent a great many troops from this front to meet the Russians, leaving defenses weakened against an attack which they undoubtedly did not expect so soon or in such force.

A staff officer gave the second reason when he said: "I believe the German high command sees the defense of the Cologne plain as a hopeless military task, but political leaders say they must fight."

A tide of guns, armor equipment and supplies is sweeping eastward. It moves along in a roar of motors behind tanks and infantry combat elements. There is a cheerful air among the men, for now they are on the move again after the bitter winter fighting. It shows in their faces, in the briskness of their walk, and in their laughter. When the army is on the move, it's another step toward home for the homesick army.

Germany's entire defense system before the Rhine was threatened by the powerful surges of the U.S. First and Ninth Armies.

"There is a rapid deterioration of the enemy's situation," a staff officer said in assessing the German defenses.

Across the sodden flat plains before Cologne the Americans are rounding up large numbers of prisoners trapped by the swift moves. Long lines of miserable-looking gray-clad Germans are marching to the rear with a look of disbelief as they see tanks, guns and supplies rolling forward.

This is what [Field Marshal Gerd] Von Rundstedt told them couldn't happen when they attacked last December into the Ardennes. □

With the U.S. First Army Near the Erft River, February 28 — Lt. Gen. Courtney H. Hodges' armored spearheads blasted their way through stiffening German resistance yesterday to within less than nine miles of Cologne while the big guns wheeled up behind the combat troops lobbed shells into the great Rhineland city.

Sixteen towns fell to the driving armor and infantry along the First Army's twenty-five-mile battlefront across the Roer River and the armor was fighting in Sindorf, two kilometers from the Erft River.

Last night the Germans brought tanks across the Erft in a desperate effort to halt the forward surge of the First Army. On the flat plains and in the small towns near the river tanks fought tanks, but the enemy was unable to halt the drive which began four days ago when the doughboys crossed the Roer in a moonlight attack.

As the armor and infantry converged on the Erft, the Germans put up a stiff fight with their tanks and they fought hard in Elsdorf, Sindorf and other small villages guarding the approaches to the river barriers which is the only natural obstacle between Hodges' men and Cologne.

Once across the Erft, the 104th and Eighth Infantry Divisions spearheading the attack would have only flat plains before them. The plains west of the Erft are jammed with armor and guns and vehicles. Roads are thick with the traffic of an army on the move. The strength which the Germans have thrown in to stop the offensive has scarcely slowed its forward surge.

One tank column led by a Texas colonel was engaged by seven Tiger tanks near Sindorf while another column driving on the same objective ran into six Tiger tanks and five Mark V's. The American armor won the roaring battle and moved on into Sindorf. There was no official count of the number of enemy tanks destroyed.

Another column moving toward Elsdorf was engaged by tanks and a battery of artillery firing at point-blank range.

This was the first time the Germans had challenged the First Army's advance with tanks in any great strength and there were unmistakable signs that the enemy was trying to slow the advance along the Erft to give their disorganized units time to recover from the beating they have taken in the past four days.   ☐

Kerpen, Germany, March 1 — More than 5,000 German civilians, including a justice of the high court of the Rhine Province, were abandoned by the German Army as it fell back before the swift advance of Lieutenant General Hodges' First Army.

In fields beside traffic-laden roads and in the little towns of Blatzheim and Heppendorf and near this battle-scarred village they jammed into buildings and air raid shelters waiting to see what the Americans were going to do with them.

Maj. Stanley "Pug" Bach of Lexington, Ky., said he found large stores of food in the cellars of Blatzheim—some of which was stacked three tiers deep.

(Bach starred in three sports—football, baseball and track—while attending the University of Kentucky in the early 1930s. He was one of the fastest halfbacks in the South. He played baseball for several years after his graduation and earned a tryout with the Cincinnati Reds.)

Most of the civilians said the military government officer would have preferred to evacuate the homes before the arrival of the Americans but the German Army left them without transport.

About ten per cent of the civilians in Kerpen were Poles, French, Czechoslovaks, Russians and other nationalities who have been forced to work for the Germans. They will be given preferential treatment and returned to their countries.

The Germans were forced to fall back so fast that they were unable to take food stores with them or drive away herds of cattle still grazing in the fields.

A Cologne resident said he did not believe there were more than 5,000 civilians left now in that metropolis, peacetime population of 700,000. He said the city was damaged worse than shattered Düren.   ☐

With the U.S. First Army, March 2 — "The end cannot be long now—for Germany is a madhouse." This is the belief of a German prisoner of war who traveled recently across Germany from the east and saw conditions which, he said, were bordering on panic.

On all trains through the Reich soldiers are traveling singly and in small groups, despite the fact that all except emergency furloughs have been cancelled by the army. Apparently these groups, whom the military police are unable to control, or do not try to control, are merely "marking time" until the war ends, and have no intention of rejoining their units.

Trains, too, are crowded with civilian refugees fleeing from the advancing Russians in the east and the British and Americans in the west, trying to find homes. Theoretically, civilians are supposed to pay fares, but all trains usually stop two or three hours outside of stations, and any control virtually is impossible.

"When refugees arrive from the east, panic spreads, because these people saw the cruelty of their own troops," the war prisoner said.   □

With the U.S. First Army at the Erft River in Germany, March 2 — A staff officer said today the "Germans show no signs of strengthening their defenses west of the Rhine—the bulk of their traffic movement is eastward across the river." He said the great American offensive was developing as planned.

Under gray, dripping skies tanks and infantry poured across the Erft into a bridgehead now approximately two to three miles deep and drove for the high ground just east of the river, from which the Germans have observation points directing accurate artillery and mortar fire onto the bridge sites.

The doughboys "buttoned up" on the bridgehead during the day and prepared for the next move. In the past twenty-four hours the First Army has captured twenty-seven towns. The Ninth and First Armies together since the start of the offensive have captured 20,000 prisoners.

Our troops cleared most of Bergheim and are only about a mile from Oberaussem. Among the towns captured were Quadrath, Ichendorf, Pingsheim and Rath. The doughboys are fighting in Wissersheim.

There were no advances today on a direct line toward Cologne as the bridgehead was being secured, but all along the line the doughboys strengthened their positions, while Lt. Gen. Courtney H. Hodges gathered the power of his First Army for the next move eastward.

Quadrath and Ichendorf were captured by the 104th Infantry Division in another of its famous night attacks. It is the second river crossing for this division since the offensive began February 23; and really the third since they also had to cross the twelve-foot-wide Grosse Erft.

By daybreak the doughboys had secured the crossing of the main Erft channel and tanks had followed. Both towns had been cleared by mid-morning. □

On the Outskirts of Cologne, March 5 — The surge of First Army infantry and tanks into battered Cologne today proved the American soldiers' ability to take a lot of punishment and come back slugging.

And the triumphal American march to the Rhine likewise underlined the fact that Field Marshal Von Rundstedt's great counter-offensive failed completely to wreck Gen. Eisenhower's plans for a winter offensive. The amazing recuperative power of the American Armies which were so sorely pounded in the Battle of the Bulge is one of the highlights of the invasion.

Sixty days ago the First Army was locked in a bitter struggle with powerful enemy forces trying to smash their way to Liège and north to Brussels and Antwerp. Today American doughboys are on the Rhine.

After driving Von Rundstedt's offensive back, the Americans went on the offensive themselves. Their push was the greatest drive yet mounted by Eisenhower.

Even while Von Rundstedt's push was being halted, supplies were pouring onto the continent for the present American drive. Many believed that the German commander had thrown Eisenhower's plans awry at least until next spring—that our Armies could not recover quickly from such hard blows. But the Americans came back strong with plenty of spirit.

The abundance of supplies and material for the American drive was evident in many ways, even in little luxury items for front-line troops such as candy and cigarettes. Recently at a front-line command post soldiers were distributing cigarettes, toilet articles, candy and post exchange items.

Once they were set the Ninth and First Armies made their moves and the Germans did not have enough men and guns to halt the advance. In just ten days the First Army reached the Rhine and wiped out the Germans' defenses before Cologne. Today is the eleventh day of the offensive.

The First Army's drive to the Rhine was spearheaded by Maj. Gen. Terry Allen's 104th "Timberwolf" Infantry Division and Maj. Gen. Maurice Rose's Third Armored Division, which was the first into Belgium and the first into Germany.

Men of the 104th crossed the flooded Roer River and beat back the Germans until the engineers could get bridges over the stream. Behind them came Rose's armored columns. Working as a team the two divisions then pushed to the Erft River. There Rose's columns accomplished an unusual feat for armor—they grabbed bridgeheads across the Erft before the infantry.

Rose's orders did not call for that. However, he saw a chance while the enemy was disorganized and spurred his tank leaders with the offer of a case of scotch for the first task force commander to establish a bridgehead. It was a race between Lt. Col. Samuel Hogan of Pharr, Tex., and Lt. Col. Walter Richardson of Beaumont, Tex. Hogan won.

Once they had bridges across the Erft and a canal these two divisions gathered their strength and began the dash for Cologne, battering their way through a series of mining communities which were enemy strongpoints.

The Third Armored Division crushed resistance in Stommeln and Pulheim which formed the enemy's last line of resistance, and reconnaissance troops under Lt. Col. Prentice "Iron Mike" Yeomans of Syracuse, N.Y., pushed on to the edge of the Rhine north of Cologne.

Armored columns followed, sealing off the north side of the city, and Rose was in position to send his tanks toward Cologne at 4 a.m. today while Allen's men were pushing in from the west. □

Niederaussem, Germany, March 5 — In deep brown mud along the roads outside Cologne trudged straggling lines of men, women and children today, bearing their little bundles of food and clothing—and the misery of defeat.

They were returning to their homes; in most cases to piles of rubble and debris that once had been home. They could not get on the roads, for the roads were jammed with tanks, trucks, jeeps and guns moving forward. So they walked in the fields and ditches soaked by a cold dismal rain.

These were the people who such a little while ago listened to and believed the tales of world power the Nazis told them. Now they were paying the price of defeat. Their bubble had burst. Now they were merely trying to exist until some order came out of chaos.

Looking into their faces it was difficult to tell what these people were thinking. There was no fear apparent. In most stolid countenances there seemed to be a worried resignation and acceptance of catastrophe which had come so swiftly.

Along the road, too, were horses wandering aimlessly or running frantically from the thunder of many motors. Cows with milk-swollen udders walked painfully across the fields. No one had taken the trouble to milk them as the battle passed this way. Chickens and geese fluttered foolishly about deserted farmhouses and the Americans looked at them with interest.

In a weather-stained old church in this village were crowded 500 civilians. It was a foolish place to take refuge in war, for churches are not exempt from shelling—their steeples almost always make excellent observation posts for the enemy.

The church would seat perhaps 150 people comfortably, but these refugees jammed into every nook of it, and their voices make a harsh hum that rose and fell like the sound of swarming bees. They had lived there for days and there was the strong stench of sweating and unwashed bodies, of straw and the odor of food.

A few candles burned in the church to illuminate the weird scene, and high in the wavering shadows above the altar hung the crucifix.

Out in the muddy courtyard some people stood in the rain to get a breath of fresh air. Children baked potatoes in the hot ashes of an open fire, and an elderly woman doled out preserved fruits and vegetables from a collection of jars salvaged from a shelled house.

Major Charles Kapes of Hazelton, Pa., provost marshal for the Third Armored Division, walked into the churchyard, and a babble of voices rose. A doctor wanted to know if there was medicine for sick people in the church. A woman wanted permission to go to her home and get food from her basement. Another wanted to open up a kitchen to feed her family.

Major Kapes said wearily: "The Military Government will take care of all these things. My job is to see that these people stay off the roads, and do not interfere with the war."

But he granted as many requests as he could, and said that others would have to wait until the Military Government took over.

The interpreter was a middle-aged woman who said she had two brothers and two sisters living in New York and a brother-in-law who owned a fox ranch in Wyoming. She said her husband had taught French and English in Düsseldorf until two years ago when he entered the army. He is now fighting in Italy, she added.

Then the woman leaned forward and whispered: "Many people were forced to go into the party who did not want to join. If you didn't join, you couldn't get bread. My husband was forced to join, and he always said that Germany could not win the war. Five years ago he said it was hopeless because the Americans would come in on the side of England, and we could not fight against such masses of material as you could produce."

The woman said that people had been living in basements and in the church for the past week, afraid to go out because of the shelling and fighting which came nearer and nearer, passed through the town, and moved on to the east. ☐

Cologne, March 6 — American First Army infantry and tanks cleared out last vestiges of resistance within shattered Cologne last night. The great industrial and communications center was conquered much more easily and speedily than anticipated. The garrison, which elected not to stand and fight, fell back toward Bonn to the south through a narrowing corridor along the river.

Cologne's capture was more spectacular because it was accomplished by an army which only a few weeks ago was fighting for its life in the Belgian bulge. From the doorstep of defeat, Lt. Gen. Hodges rallied his army for this steamroller drive, which began in the predawn moonlight of February 23 when his troops crossed the Roer River.

The Third Armored Division and the 104th Infantry Division closed relentlessly on the last known resistance inside Cologne. The troops were amazed to see civilians amid the wreckage displaying friendliness and relief. The fighting was not the last stand, do or die defense expected.

Cologne is no Aachen. It was not manned by a garrison prepared to fight house to house and street to street. Instead of making a fortress of each house, the Germans manned key defense points. After knocking out one key point the tanks and troops frequently moved a block or more before being engaged from another strongpoint.

Cologne is estimated to be eighty-five per cent in ruins, with more than ninety-five per cent of the older part a rubble heap. "Cologne looks like Stalingrad," said an R.A.F. officer. There are some 2,000 acres of devastation in the city. Cologne's industry, like Detroit's, was spread through the city. The only way to attack the industry was to destroy the city." ☐

With U.S. First Army, Cologne, March 6 — Lieut. Gen. Courtney H. Hodges' troops, moving in from the north and west, drove an iron fist deep into Cologne today and reached the Ringstrasse, which circles the ancient heart of the city, against surprisingly light resistance.

Infantry and tanks rolled through the great industrial area in the north and west and shelled the freight yards.

The deepest thrust was made by a task force commanded by a lieutenant-colonel who was the first to lead American troops past Cologne's city limits. This column at dawn had pushed through the city to a point where a net of railroad tracks makes an arc about the city along the Ringstrasse, which was the site of the ancient wall guarding Cologne.

Maj. Gen. Terry Allen's 104th Infantry Division, moving in from the west, cleared suburban Müngersdorf and moved through Braunsfeld, a distance of 4,000 yards, with little opposition from the enemy, who was reported to have drawn his defense forces back into the old city for a last-ditch fight.

The fall of bomb-battered Cologne is merely a matter of hours—the time it will take for the infantrymen and the tanks to work their way through a maze of streets, for there is no doubt that the Germans lack sufficient forces inside the city to halt the Third Armored and 104th Infantry Divisions.

North of Cologne the drive to the Rhine continued. Infantrymen reached the river at another place four miles south of Düsseldorf, cleared Rheinkassel and were at the outskirts of Langel.

On the southwestern outskirts of Cologne the 104th pushed up to the southern suburbs without opposition. Outside the city troops captured the great Goldenberg power station which provided electricity for a large mining and industrial area.

The infantry division drove forward another 5,000 yards and stood within three miles of the Rhine just south of Cologne. Armored and infantry elements pushed ahead 9,000 yards to within seven miles of Bonn.

Infantrymen in the town of Müggenhausen battled to drive back a Nazi counter-attack by twenty foot soldiers and eight tanks, which had pushed back into the town. Fighting still was in progress there. □

Cologne, March 6 — Doughboys and armor of the U.S. First Army captured Cologne today, rolling through this fourth largest of German cities with astonishing speed against light resistance.

The Germans gave up the fight and made no effort to hold Cologne as they had Aachen, and the fall of the city, announced by First Army headquarters officially tonight, came much sooner than anyone had anticipated.

It had been the consensus that Cologne, a city normally of 168,000 population, would be a hard nut to crack, with the Germans dug into the rubble and contesting every house and every street.

Cologne fell on the twelfth day of Lt. Gen. Hodges' powerful offensive, and it climaxed one of the most sensational drives since the First Army broke through at St-Lô and smashed across France into Germany last summer.

Tonight there was resistance only in the southeastern part of the shell-shattered city, standing at the head of a corridor down which the enemy had fled southward toward Bonn before the blasting drive of the Third Armored Division and the 104th Infantry Division, which spearheaded the offensive and crossed into Cologne.

Capture of the city was made the more spectacular because it was accomplished by an army which only a few weeks ago was fighting for its very life in stopping the powerful December offensive launched by Nazi Field Marshal Von Rundstedt. From the doorstep of defeat Gen. Hodges rallied his army for this steamroller drive, which began in moonlight on the morning of February 23 with the crossing of the Roer River.

The great Rhineland industrial metropolis was an appalling mass of wreckage from 42,000 tons of bombs dropped by the American and British air forces since May, 1942, when the R.A.F. made its first great raid on the city.

Cologne is estimated to be eighty-five per cent in ruins, with more than ninety-five per cent of the old inner city a rubble heap.   □

Cologne, March 7 — Doughboys walking through the streets of Cologne looked up today from the awful wreckage of the ruined city to see the miracle of Cologne Cathedral with its slender, graceful spires rising above the devastation wrought by Allied air raids.

Those fragile, beautiful spires, blackened by the weather of seven centuries, rose straight into the heavens out of the most terrible destruction yet witnessed by the American troops who have seen the rubble of many blasted cities.

All around the ancient edifice the heart of Cologne lay in waste. For block upon block there was nothing but the gutted skeletons of buildings and debris piled many feet high. Tons of bombs had ripped out the heart of Cologne. Great chunks of concrete had been tossed about like pebbles and huge steel girders lay twisted like hairpins.

And yet in this devastation was the miracle of the cathedral. Seven times in two years the famous cathedral had been hit by bombs and yet it stood with remarkably little serious damage to its Gothic beauty. How it survived, while everything around it was laid waste, no one can say.

But there it was like a promise of hope amid the shambles of despair, and in and out of its doors wandered doughboys while shells from American guns rustled over and crashed into the city on the east side of the Rhine.

The cathedral had its scars, but it was as though some power had saved it from destruction which reached to its very doors. Across the street were blackened and still burning Panther tanks which had been knocked out by a Sherman tank in one of the last fights inside the city.

Inside the cathedral, whose floor was littered with debris, doughboys walked in silence, their helmets in their hands as they gazed at the vaulted ceiling and towering columns. □

With the First Army on the Rhine, March 8 — Veteran doughboys of Lt. Gen. Courtney H. Hodges' First U.S. Army poured across the Rhine south of Cologne today and deepened their one-day old bridgehead, established with dramatic speed and extremely light casualties after the fall of Cologne.

The first infantryman across reached the eastern shore at 4:30 p.m. yesterday—a pathfinder for others who have raced across since and seized a good hold on the east bank.

This sudden crossing of the most formidable natural barrier on the Western front gave the First Army a firm toehold on enemy territory, which most military experts did not think could be reached for days.

The Germans were in such confusion after their frantic retreat before Hodges' men across the Cologne plain that they never were able to make a real stand.

There was little artillery or mortar fire on the crossing site during those first twenty-four hours and that in itself was proof of the enemy's disorganization and unpreparedness for the assault.

The Germans did not even have prepared positions on the far side of the stream and the spearheading units of doughboys quickly fanned out and began deepening this unexpected bridgehead while the High Command moved with speed to take advantage of the situation which developed far swifter than was anticipated.

As a result of the bridgehead being secured—and it is no military secret that we are over the river in strength—troops rushed up to strategic positions so that the bridgehead can be exploited in full.

For months, military experts have been planning the crossing of the Rhine. Elaborate plans had been made for large-scale amphibious operation much on the same basis as the experts planned the amphibious assault on the beaches of Normandy. It was generally accepted that once our armies got to the Rhine there would be a pause for regrouping and reshuffling to get set for the giant effort to bridge the stream. The most optimistic thought it would be at least months before the crossing could be made.

But the doughboys who got across thought otherwise and the result is that spirits are soaring tonight all through the army. Hodges has no intention of losing this valuable hold on the eastern bank and is strengthening it as fast as men and material can be moved up.

First Army censorship clamped a strict blackout for the time on the place of crossing. The means by which the bridgehead was secured is one of the dramatic stories of the war and one of the most important, for there is not the slightest doubt that the swiftness with which the bridgehead was obtained was the means of saving untold lives and possibly speeding the end of the war by months.

This was the feeling which swept through the First Army today as news of the river crossing filtered down from army to divisions to bewhiskered, begrimed doughboys out in the front lines. They had been dreading that crossing, for spanning a river the size of the Rhine is a dangerous, costly task and they knew it.

"This means we've got 'em licked months sooner than we might have otherwise," one officer said.

Lt. Col. Robert Evans of Davenport, Ia., said: "If we can hold that bridgehead it means the war is months nearer the end."

And that's the way the doughboys felt about it, too.

The crossing of the Rhine had become more a symbol of coming victory than most of them had realized, for the men felt that once across the river they would be on the highroad to the heart of Germany. □

Bonn, Germany, March 8 — Doughboys fought their way through the streets of Bonn tonight while this birthplace of Beethoven, one of Germany's cultural centers, was raked by shells from both German and American guns.

The famous fighting First Infantry Division was plowing through stiff opposition here while a few miles to the south the Ninth Infantry Division was cleaning out the resort town of Bad Godesberg, the scene of the second Hitler-Chamberlain conference which ended with the disagreement over Czechoslovakia. American troops tonight had cleaned out resistance in about half of both towns.

For the first time American troops were meeting some resistance from civilians and the battle for Bonn was much more bitter than that for Cologne.

Although there were thousands of civilians still in the city the Germans were pouring rockets and artillery fire into the town and many Germans were being killed by their own shells.

A prisoner of war said the Germans had a guard at the western end of the Rhine bridge with orders to shoot any civilians trying to flee to the eastern bank and that the defenders received orders from Hitler last night to fight to the last.

City police were trying to force civilians to fight alongside the troops, this German said, and there were frequent clashes between police and the population, which had no stomach for the fight.

The First Division attacked the outskirts at 5 a.m. today.

I entered the city in an armored car with Lt. Col. Edward Driscoll of Long Island, and Capt. Charles R. Clark of Corbin, N.J. The Germans still held flak gun positions on each side of the corridor leading into the city and frequently swept the road with shell fire.

As the car rolled down the Dorotheenstrasse toward the waterfront, German civilians gazed stolidly from the doorways and windows.

There was too much shelling and too much of the city in enemy hands to go on a sight-seeing tour and check on the damage to historical places such as the University of Bonn and the famous library, Beethoven's birthplace and Münster Cathedral.

But judging from the sections on the northwestern side, Bonn has escaped destruction such as that at Cologne. There were rows upon rows of houses virtually undamaged and even with the window glass intact.

Two blocks from Saint Johannes hospital near the riverfront a group of doughboys was in a little needle and thread shop, and behind the counter sat Pvt. Winifred Collins of New Hope, Ark., looking as though he was ready to do business with any customers. There was a machine gun across the top of the counter.

Lt. Wayne Hoffman, 2453 Spalding Ave., Chicago, Ill., walked in with a tommy gun.

"Dammit, we can't get at those tanks," he said. "I took my platoon up to try to knock them out and one of my men had a leg blown off. We got him back to the medics fast."

The two tanks were four blocks down the street, standing back to back, with their guns covering the approaches in all directions.

Two civilians inside the shop munched hunks of bread. Nobody seemed to know just why they were there.

Capt. John Stan Winter of Dresden, Kan., whose company was first into the town, suddenly noticed them. He waved his pistol.

"Tell 'em to get the hell out of here and stay out and to get inside a building before somebody shoots 'em," he said.

The Germans understood the tone if not the words and they went into the street dangling handkerchiefs in their hands. Nearly all civilians carried handkerchiefs or white cloths to show their passive acceptance of the Americans' arrival.

"When we came in they were waving bedsheets and petticoats and anything white," said Lt. George Boving of Winchester, Ohio.

A cluster of big rockets passed overhead.

"There'll be another bunch in a minute," said Pfc. Curtis Sweigart of Lancaster, Pa. "They always shoot those rockets in two bunches."

He was right. In the middle of the street was a wrecked German car with two headless Nazi soldiers.

"A German tank did that," Sweigart said. "Just blew hell out of their own men."   □

On the Rhine Bridgehead, March 9 — A gangling embarrassed butcher boy from Holland, Ohio, received the praise today of his commanding general for leading the heroic charge across Remagen Bridge and completing the capture of the span which gave the U.S. First Army the first Allied bridgehead across the Rhine.

A careful check disclosed that Sgt. Alexander A. Drabik actually was the first American to step on the east bank of the Rhine. And behind him came ten riflemen shooting as they ran in a wild dash which surprised the Germans before they could blow this vital link which right now is perhaps the most valuable bridge in the world.

This takes none of the glory from Lt. Emmet Burrows, Jersey City officer whose platoon was in the fight also and helped capture Remagen Bridge.

Brig. Gen. William M. Hoge, of Lexington, Mo., praised Drabik's heroism as the greatest single factor in establishing the bridgehead and singled him out as the man who deserved the most individual credit. It was Hoge's combat "Command B" which took the bridge.

Drabik was called from his platoon to come to Hoge's command post to be interviewed. He stooped as he entered the doorway, bending his six-foot frame, and then stood fidgeting in embarrassment. He had never been interviewed before and he didn't quite know what to make of this sudden attention.

It was obvious that Drabik never thought about the job he did as being one of the most dramatic heroic actions of the war. And there were no flourishes to the simple story he told. ☐

On the Rhine Bridgehead, March 10 — A thirty-four-year-old Ohio sergeant has been singled out as the man first across the Rhine in the daring establishment of the U.S. First Army's bridgehead.

Without detracting glory from other soldiers in the history-making coup, Brig. Gen. William H. Hoge, of Lexington, Mo., whose armored forces took the Remagen Bridge, named Sgt. Alexander A. Drabik, butcher boy of Holland, Ohio, as the outstanding hero of the day.

Hoge said yesterday a careful check disclosed Drabik actually was the first American to step on the east bank of the river, in the forefront of ten riflemen shooting as they ran in a wild dash which so astounded the Germans they failed to blow up the vital structure.

Also in the vanguard of the first Americans over the river was Lt. Emmet Burrows, Jersey City officer whose platoon was in the initial fighting. And today it was disclosed that the first tank to roll into the now solidly held bridgehead carried sons of four states.

Hitting the shore Wednesday, the tank was manned by Sgt. William B. Goodson, Rushville, Ind.; Cpl. William E. Richard, of Shrewsbury, W.Va.; Pvt. Berthold Fried, of Shade Hill, S.D., and T-4 Robert A. Jones, of McKee, Ky.

Goodson was in command as the iron war horse crashed through the murky night. Fried, the cannoneer, Richard, the gunner, and Jones, at the controls.

Drabik was called to Hoge's command post yesterday to be interviewed.

Still grimy from combat and cradling an M-1 gun in his arm the raw-boned Ohioan spoke in simple, matter-of-fact phrases of one of the war's most dramatic moments.

"It was like this," he said. "Lt. Timmerman told us to go across the bridge, with the first platoon leading. I've got the third platoon of a rifle company. We had fought through Remagen to the river and our company was at the edge of the town about 200 yards from the bridge. I waited until the first platoon got out on the bridge, but they were held up by machine gun and sniper fire from those big stone towers at the eastern end.

"When I brought up my men the first platoon was keeping the Germans in the tower busy. So I went by them and yelled to my men to go across—firing into the tunnels in the hill on the other side."

Drabik said the first platoon had the Germans "pretty well down" with their fire.

"We ran down the middle of the bridge, shooting as we went. I didn't stop because I knew if I kept moving they couldn't hit me. My men were in squad column and not one of them was hit."

A machine gun squad came up behind as Drabik's riflemen ran forward 200 yards on the German side of the bridge and formed a skirmish line to "hold the enemy if they did come."

"We took cover in some bomb craters," Drabik said. "Then we just sat and waited for the others to come in. That's the way it was."

It was disclosed today that the American engineers who moved in and repaired the bridge after the brilliant stroke by the infantrymen were under the command of Lt. John Mitchell, Brentwood, Pa.   □

On the Rhine Bridgehead, [March 10] — The first major battle of the Rhine bridgehead appeared shaping up today as German reinforcements drove toward the American-held territory on the east bank of the river.

Enemy artillery already is pumping heavy caliber shells at the 1,200-foot span at Remagen across which American infantry and armor are pouring in a steady flow.

The German columns were seen approaching last night with all lights on—evidence of a violent reaction to this growing threat to inner Germany. There is no doubt the Germans are making a supreme effort to bring up available strength for a counter-attack designed to drive the Americans back across the Rhine.

It is a race now between the Germans and Lt. Gen. Courtney Hodges' First Army to get infantry, tanks, guns and supplies to the scene. But after seeing the flow of men and fighting tools which are moving up to the bridgehead there can only be one reaction—the Germans already have lost the race.

The bridgehead is growing stronger by the hour, and the Remagen Bridge has become the most important stretch of highway on any fighting front. All roads seem to lead to Remagen and all those roads are literally jammed with convoys moving toward the bridgehead in an awesome display of power.

The First Army High Command is losing no time in exploiting this dramatic success engineered by the Ninth Armored Division under the command of Maj. Gen. John Leonard, Toledo, Ohio, who issued the order for the troops to seize the span.

The bridgehead has the highest priority for all fighting tools and manpower, and they are pouring forward. As soon as a unit gets across the span it goes into the line.

"We put them into action as soon as they come over," said Maj. Ben Cothran of Rome, Ga., former city editor of the *Knoxville, Tenn. Journal.* "There's no time to fool around. As soon as a man steps on this bridgehead he's got to start fighting."

The Germans are trying desperately to knock out the bridge with heavy guns and suicide air raids. Four planes made passes at the bridge Thursday night and all four were shot down by ack-ack. Three more dived in yesterday from low-hanging clouds and dumped their bombs.

The Remagen Bridge is the hot spot of the entire Western front as the Germans pour shells in increasing numbers. They are lobbing in 155- and 210-millimeter shells trying to knock out this span, which is the lifeline for our troops and armor in the bridgehead.

As the doughboys make the run across the bridge, shells whiz over viciously and the time it takes to cross the 400 yards of concrete and steel is packed with the suspense and drama of war. The tempo of the shelling increased yesterday and no one tarries on the span unless he is forced to.

The doughboys go onto the bridge on a trot and no one slows down to a walk until he is safely across.

In the center of the bridge is a dead German—his head pointed to the west as though he were running forward to halt the doughboys when their fire cut him down. No one has been able to take time out yet to remove the body.

Priority of travel is toward the east, and once a vehicle gets on the bridgehead it may stay for hours before there is a break in traffic for westbound travel.

Most of the wounded are collected in a hillside tunnel at the eastern end of the bridge and are carried across by litter bearers who brave shell fire to get the wounded to ambulances on the west bank. "It's a pretty tough job carrying the wounded over," said T-4 James P. Butler, London Mills, Ill., "but we are getting along all right. So far we have had surprisingly few casualties."

Evacuation is being directed by Capt. William Gibble, Henryetta, Okla., who accepted surrender of a German hospital in the little town of Erpel. There he found three American patients who had been wounded in the Battle of the Bulge and were taken prisoner by the Germans. They are now on their way to an American hospital.   □

With the First Army on the Rhine, March 12 — Staff Sgt. Eugene Dorland, who once delivered butter and eggs in Chicago, is known around the Remagen bridgehead these days as "Horatio" after the job he did on the great Ludendorff Bridge the day it was seized by the U.S. First Army.

Dorland and men from B Company combat engineers of the Ninth Armored Division had the dangerous job of cutting wires and removing TNT charges which were supposed to explode at 4 p.m. on March 7 and dump the span into the Rhine.

Ten minutes before the time the Germans had set for the demolition Dorland, Lt. Hugh B. Moft of Nashville, and three doughboys went onto the bridge under German machine gun fire. They found the conduit carrying the wires leading to the demolition charges but the conduit was too tough to cut.

"I'll fix it," Dorland said, and placed his carbine against the conduit and split it with two shots. Then it was simple to cut the wires before the Germans could throw the switches.

The Germans did succeed in setting off one small charge that blew a hole in the bridge decking but there was another of 1,400 pounds which failed to go off.   □

With the First Army on the Rhine, [March 12] — American engineers today attributed the failure of the Germans to blow the Remagen Bridge across the Rhine to a faulty fuse cap which prevented hundreds of pounds of TNT from exploding.

This is the story of the nineteen most fateful days since the Allied invasion of Europe. These nineteen days have seen the entire course of the war changed on the Western front and the end of the conflict brought unquestionably nearer by the daring and initiative of American arms.

The climax of that span of time came when lanky Sgt. Alexander Drabik of Holland, Ohio, led the charge across the Ludendorff Bridge at Remagen on the afternoon of March 7. The mighty Rhine had been crossed. Behind

Drabik—a butcher in private life—streamed powerful forces of Lt. Gen. Courtney H. Hodges' First Army to establish the first bridgehead on the eastern bank of the river barrier.

The Rhine crossing was not a knockout punch to end the war. Only a super-optimist could fail to see that there is much bloody fighting ahead before Germany is beaten into total defeat. But there is every reason for jubilation over the combination of luck and courage which gave the First Army a bridge intact over the Rhine.

The drive across the Rhine did place the Allies in position for the knockout blow and left the enemy vulnerable and with weakened defenses for future Allied smashes which might come at any time and any point.

Whether the Remagen bridgehead will develop into the main Allied threat to central Germany or whether there will be another massed crossing of the Rhine, only the Allied High Command can say. But for the time being, the Remagen bridgehead is being exploited as a steel pointed spear pressing into the vitals of the Reich.

Ironically, the Rhine proved the easiest stream to cross in the entire drive into the Rhineland.

The Roer River was a stumbling block for three months. Even the little Erft River, which anyone could spit across on a windy day, held up a division for twenty-four hours. The Rhine was crossed in the time it took Sgt. Drabik and his ten riflemen to dash the length of the 1,200-foot span.

The story of this spectacular campaign began in the dark hours before dawn on February 23. Lt. Gen. William H. Simpson's Ninth Army and Hodges' First Army had built up strength for the drive in a surprisingly short time. Only a few weeks before, these armies were battling for their lives to stop Field Marshal Von Rundstedt's offensive in the Ardennes.

In the initial phases, the Ninth Army started the attack with the First Army's Seventh Corps, under Maj. Gen. J. Lawton (Joe Lightning) Collins of New Orleans, providing flanking protection on the south. Once the drive was under way, Hodges gradually was to step up the power of his attack until the whole front was blazing.

At 4:30 a.m., the Ninth and First Armies launched coordinated attacks across the flooded Roer behind the crash of thousands of shells supporting the crossing. Red tracers ripped into enemy positions on the eastern bank.

Maj. Gen. Terry De La Mesa Allen's 104th (Timberwolf) Division spearheaded the First Army crossing alongside the Eighth Division, commanded by Maj. Gen. William Weaver. Jülich fell to the Ninth Army. Düren toppled to Hodges' men in the first day of fighting. The attacks surged across the plains before Cologne.

The Ninth Army's powerful offensive overran München-Gladbach and carried to the Rhine while the First Army closed in on Cologne, fourth largest city of Germany.

Once these two armies began the steamroller offensive, it was evident that the Germans would be unable to halt them. The enemy started retreating eastward and pouring across whatever Rhine bridges there were left for escape. Thousands of prisoners flowed into prisoner cages and in each little town, soldiers found civilians by the thousands. They were unable to get away before the sweep of the doughboys overrunning villages.

But even if the civilians had left, there was no place for them to go for central Germany already was jammed with civilians fleeing from the Russians. Rhineland defenses had crumbled before American power. At 7:10 a.m. on March 6 Maj. Gen. Maurice Rose sent the leading elements of his Third Armored Division into Cologne while Allen's 104th closed in from the West.

Everyone had anticipated that the Germans would make a house to house defense of the battered shell of Cologne. But they were so disorganized there was no coordinated defense. Cologne was a pushover and those Germans who could escaped to the south toward Bonn and left only feeble parties in the city's ruins. The day after entering the city the Americans had wiped out all resistance. Cologne had fallen. But on that same day great events were taking place farther south.

At dawn on March 7 the Ninth Armored Division of Maj. Gen. John W. Leonard of Toledo, Ohio, attacked toward the Rhine with two combat teams. Combat Command B under Brig. Gen. William Hoge, had the mission of capturing Remagen, on the west bank of the Rhine, and if possible of seizing the great Ludendorff Bridge should it prove to be intact.

It was a dramatic moment when the leading elements of Combat Command B about midday stood on the hills looking down into the beautiful Rhine Valley. And there above the river was the Ludendorff Bridge intact, a sight which none had expected to see. German vehicles still were streaming across it.

Pouring into the valley, Combat Command B captured Remagen and then Lt. Col. Leonard Engeman of Redwood Falls, Minn., directed a company commanded by Lt. Carl Timmerman of West Point, Neb., to capture the bridge.

The men who stormed the Remagen Bridge made the biggest gamble of their lives that afternoon. The Germans had mined the bridge with hundreds of pounds of TNT and had set the demolition hour at 4 p.m. It virtually was a death warrant for anyone who ventured on the span, but the try had to be made.

Timmerman sent his first platoon on the bridge and they were engaged by Germans shooting from the railway tunnel and from the great stone towers on the far side of the bridge. While the first platoon pinned down the enemy defenders with intense fire, Sgt. Drabik led his platoon through it and made the dash across the bridge.

Once again luck played a major role. The Germans tried to blow the bridge. A small booster charge of explosives blew a section of the bridge but the main charge of TNT did not go off. Engineers attributed the failure to a faulty fuse cap.

Behind the armored infantry came engineers commanded by Lt. John Mitchell, Brentwood, Pa., who slashed all the wires on the bridge and dumped the explosives into the river while German machine gun and rifle bullets splattered about them.

The engineers quickly threw planking across the damaged section of the bridge and tanks rolled in behind the first wave of armored infantry who had seized the span. The first medium tank across was commanded by Sgt. William B. Goodson of Rushville, Ind.

At dawn on March 8 there were two battalions of infantry and a tank company over the river and other troops and tanks were pouring across. The Germans tried desperately to knock the bridge out with shelling and air raids. But while several shells hit the span and caused temporary damage, the enemy never was able to knock it out and most of the shells fell harmlessly into the water. Then the engineers threw a pontoon bridge across the river, giving a double lifeline to the troops on the east bank.

Since then men, tanks, guns and material have poured into the bridgehead and it has developed into the major threat to central Germany. ☐

With the U.S. First Army on the Rhine, March 13 – The Americans now have a tank in action on the Western front which can stack up with the German Mark V Panther and Mark VI Tiger. The new battle behemoth is the 45-ton General Pershing, mounting a 90-millimeter gun of high velocity.

For three years German tanks have outgunned the Americans' Sherman, with its 75- or 76-millimeter weapon, but at last some of the Yank tankmen are going into battle on more even terms.

The Pershings were used for the first time by our armored divisions in the drive from the Roer River to the Rhine which opened February 23. It still is too early in the fighting here to call the Pershing the best on the Western front, but the men who handle it are enthusiastic. They believe it to be the equal at least of the Panther, if not of the Tiger.

In the Rhine drive the Pershings knocked out several enemy tanks, including Mark V's and VI's. Only one of the new tanks was hit, and that one will be back in action in a few weeks.

There were only a few Pershings available to the First Army for the initial battle test. Those sent over were divided between two armored divisions so that opinions and reactions could be obtained from different groups.

The Pershing has thicker armor than the Sherman, weighs some twenty tons more, carries a more powerful gun, has tracks six inches broader and still equals the Sherman in speed and maneuverability.

The Pershing is known technically as the T-26.

Maj. Gen. J. Lawton Collins, commanding the Seventh Corps, said it was as easy to drive as an automobile and its gears were just as easy to shift.

Tankmen have seen enough of the Pershings in action to want more of them—and want them fast. □

Bonn, Germany, March 13 — The Germans fled in such confusion that they forgot a little matter of eight million marks—all the funds in the banks and city treasury of this Rhine city. They also abandoned large food stores in warehouses. Many homeowners had stocked their shelves with bountiful supplies.

Ninety per cent of the great University of Bonn, where members of the Hohenzollern family and other German aristocrats were schooled, has been demolished by Allied air raids.

Losses to the university's celebrated library of some 500,000 volumes have not been assessed, but presumably the Germans removed the more valuable books and manuscripts to a safe hiding place. The university was founded in 1717.

The birthplace of Beethoven escaped a direct hit, although the building has been damaged and the surrounding area has been blasted.

The house has been closed to keep out trespassers, and Maj. Edwin Boney of Fresno, Cal., said no assessment yet had been taken of interior damage.

The city in general had been about fifty per cent damaged by raids.

The twelfth-century cathedral is repairable, although damaged by near misses. Services are being held in the crypt.

The food situation is such that normal rationing still is being carried on. Only a few days before arrival of the Americans, 52,000 ration cards were issued to Bonn residents. They still are being honored.

The city is packed with civilians who elected to stay rather than flee to central Germany. But that fact does not deter German artillerymen. Twenty civilians were killed or wounded as they walked the streets yesterday. Only 1,000 inhabitants took advantage of offers of transportation to the east with the German Army.

Allied military government officers who moved in behind the combat troops of the First Infantry Division found Bonn in much better condition than expected and far better than in Aachen. Civil administration still was functioning.

"We told the city officials for the time being to carry on as they had been," said Maj. Everett J. S. Cofran, Washington, D.C., deputy administrator to Maj. Edwin W. Boney, Fresno, Cal. "As fast as possible we will screen the top officials to weed out the rabid Nazis and dangerous characters."

Virtually all the police remained when the United States troops arrived. The first thing Cofran did was to tell them to take off their uniforms, which are almost exact copies of the German Army garb. Now they are wearing civilian coats and hats with an armband to show they are police.

Bonn civilians have been docile for the most part. Cofran said he had no trouble except from a few drunks who were attempting to drown the sorrow of defeat in the ample wine stocks left behind.

American troops found the city jail empty. The Germans had turned loose all the small-fry inmates. They had evacuated the long-term criminals to the east bank of the Rhine.   □

With the U.S. First Army on the Rhine, March 16 – American infantry tramped tonight on Hitler's super military highway, an event which the rulers of Nazi Germany never anticipated when they built it as an avenue of European conquest.

The first doughboys to fight out onto this six-lane highway connecting the Ruhr with Frankfurt on the Rhine were from the Seventy-eighth Infantry Division, which fought astride the autobahn at 11:14 a.m.

Then in the afternoon, another unit of Americans less than a mile south reached the broad highway. The Seventy-ninth reached it near Brünsberg, eight miles northeast of the Remagen Bridge. The others came by way of the village of Hövel, which they had to fight through house by house.

The Germans were desperately building up forces for a major counter-attack and today they hit back in force with tanks for the first time.

The brunt of the attack fell to the south on the Ninth Infantry Division, which was engaged in the heaviest fighting of the bridgehead while assaulting the enemy's key defense point at Strodt. There also was hard fighting in Kalenborn and nearby Vettelschoss, a mile or so farther north.

In this area the Germans have built up their major defenses on the east edge of the bridgehead, and they are putting up a bitter fight to hold on to key terrain and prevent the Americans from surging eastward.

The Germans threw in twenty-four tanks against the Ninth Infantry, trying to keep Lt. Gen. Courtney H. Hodges' troops from closing in on their key points east of Remagen.

With blazing guns and bazookas, the Americans knocked out five of the attacking tanks, including three Tigers, and blasted one self-propelled weapon. The strong defense knocked the assault back and the remaining tanks withdrew from action.

The enemy made another attack from wooded country northeast of Rottbitze at 10:50 a.m., near where the doughboys cut the highway.

There was a sharp and furious melee before the Yanks drove the Germans back.

Indications are that the Germans are working hard to reorganize their supply system for the bridgehead line, and are trying to get set to meet this surprise threat.

Excellent weather for the last three days has given the Americans a chance to put their air force out in strength and slash at the enemy's supply lines.

While the Germans make an effort to build up their forces and take the initiative, the First Army is still pouring forces across the Ludendorff Bridge and an auxiliary pontoon bridge which the Germans have been unable to destroy.

Should the enemy get a run of bad flying weather, it is possible he will be able to assemble a formidable panzer and infantry force to meet this threat.

The advances during the day expanded the bridgehead to thirteen miles wide and seven miles deep.

On the north flank, the Seventy-eighth Division sent units through Koenigswinter along the Rhine and to Ittenbach, three miles east.

In the south, troops began the job of clearing Hönningen after seizing high ground dominating the town.

White flags were flying from the houses of civilians, but the Germans left a fighting force behind to contest the final occupation.

The Americans have taken fifty towns and villages east of the Rhine since seizing the bridgehead, and in almost all towns in the path of the advance, villagers have hung out white flags and are pleading with the German Army not to make their towns a battleground to be destroyed by American artillery.   □

With U.S. First Army East of the Rhine, March 17 – Georgia's Hodges is the man of the hour on the Western front as his army battles deeper into Germany east of the Rhine.

General Hodges, who got his yearning to be a soldier by watching the Perry Rifles march down the dusty street of Perry, Ga., when he was a boy, has his veteran troops right in the middle of another spectacular offensive phase.

Like his army, this man who worked his way up through the ranks from buck private to lieutenant general is tough and resilient.

He gives the impression of being retiring; he seldom speaks unless spoken to, or there is something important to say. A good many people are fooled by his quiet manner.

He likes to be up forward as much as possible to see for himself how all is going, and he generally operates from his trailer at the tactical command post in advance of the regular army headquarters.

An ardent hunter and outdoor man, Hodges prefers life in the field to the more comfortable life in the rear area, or in an office job. He's a sharpshooter with a rifle like his superior, General Bradley. His father, who publishes a weekly newspaper in Perry, gave him a rifle on his tenth birthday.

Hodges' drive with the First Army through France, Belgium and into Germany was one of the most dramatic campaigns in American military history, and one of the most unorthodox as he juggled corps and divisions while chasing the enemy into the Reich.

When Field Marshal Von Rundstedt's offensive smashed into the First Army in December, Hodges' troops were cut in two but he quickly reshuffled his divisions to meet the main threat to the northern flank of the bulge while the Third Army of General Patton battered up from the south.

Quickly rebuilding his army's strength, Hodges loosed his offensive across the Roer and his divisions rolled through the Cologne plain to the Rhine. Before anyone could be aware of what was happening, vanguards had captured the Remagen Bridge and were consolidating a beachhead on the east bank of the river.

Hodges moved quickly to exploit this development, which was not in the books of the high command because nobody had anticipated a bridgehead across the Rhine being seized so quickly, and with such ease. Today the First Army is dug in so firmly on the east bank that the Germans' chance to drive them back is gone.   □

With the First Army, [**March 19**] — Officers and men of the First Infantry Division hope that some day they will get a look at the terrible-tempered Nazi, Col. Becker.

The colonel is sort of a division pet and if anybody but the First Division captures the terrible-tempered Col. Becker, everybody in this veteran outfit is going to be sore. They feel he belongs to them personally.

The Division has built up quite a history on Col. Becker, who is one of the toughest, meanest, roughest officers who ever sent his troops into a counter-attack. Day by day the file grows.

The First Division encountered the colonel and his Fifth Paratroop Regiment back in Normandy beachhead days and he was formidable opposition. In fact, he is so ornery and tough his own men admire him. Prisoners of war taken from the Fifth Paratroop Regiment always are willing to talk and tell stories about their colonel, and he always is showing up opposite the First.

It seems that on one sub-zero day a German soldier with frozen feet was being taken back to the hospital for treatment but had the misfortune of running into Col. Becker.

"What's the matter with you?" asked the colonel with ire.

"My feet are frozen," the soldier said.

"What color are they?" queried the colonel.

"White," the soldier said.

"Then go back to your foxhole until they turn blue," Becker ordered.

On another occasion the colonel heard complaints that his troops' feet were freezing as they stood in foxholes with no relief.

"If their feet are freezing," the colonel was quoted as saying, "they can kick each other to keep them warm."

It is the colonel's contention, his men say, that there is no such thing as frostbite and for everyone just to ignore it. And once when his troops were cold, wet and hungry he sent word that if he heard any more complaints he'd cut off their rations for a week.

The terrible-tempered Becker always is sending out orders to his men to "fight to death" and "do or die"—but he rarely gets any nearer to the front than twelve kilometers.

There is one story on the colonel that during the American breakthrough in Normandy he ordered his men to "hold to the end." Then he took his regiment's only usable vehicle and scrammed.

"He's a tough one, though," said Lt. Col. Robert Evans of Davenport, Iowa. "He puts on the toughest counter-attacks of anybody we fought against and you can always bet his ground is well organized."

"That's right," agreed Major Johnny Lawton of Berkeley, Calif. "If he's got ten men he'll send five of them in to make a counter-attack and use the other five as reserves."

Once the terrible-tempered Becker roughed up one battalion of the First Division in the Hürtgen Forest and he received personal praise from Hitler. But the First has kicked Becker's Fifth Paratroop Regiment around so much they always are surprised when he shows up again with a reformed outfit.

Capt. Carl Oelze of Cleveland, Ohio, said, "If the terrible-tempered Becker turns out to be just a little pot-bellied guy then . . ." He shook his head. □

With U.S. First Army East of the Rhine, March 19 – The battle of the bridgehead has developed virtually into man for man combat. The enemy has thrown in reinforcements to whittle down the initial superiority in numbers gained by the First Army in its surprise crossing of the Rhine.

Military textbooks say attacking forces should enjoy a three to one superiority over enemy defenders but Lieut. Gen. Courtney Hodges' men slugging their way forward through rough terrain have no such advantage in manpower.

"We are having the hardest and slowest going since the fighting through the hedgerows in Normandy," an officer of the Ninth Infantry Division said today. "When a doughboy advances fifty yards on the map it means he actually fought his way forward 1,500 yards up and down these hills."

After the Rhine crossing the bridgehead forces had to fight for elbow room in which to maneuver. They just now are reaching that stage, with the bridgehead eight miles in depth.

The tough core of German resistance has been in the east where the enemy concentrated tanks and self-propelled weapons to prevent the Americans from breaking out toward Berlin.

Loss of the Ludendorff Bridge at Remagen was a blow to the First Army and no one attempts to minimize it, but it did not go until the army had thrown across a pontoon bridge.

To say the bridge had "served its purpose" would not be quite accurate, for there were many future uses for the span had it been saved. It could have been used later for rail traffic to carry supplies and for the speedy evacuation of the wounded from deeper in Germany.   □

With the United States First Army East of the Rhine, March 21 – Negro infantrymen who left their jobs in rear echelons and volunteered for combat duty are fighting on the First Army's bridgehead east of the Rhine.

Early reports made by white officers say that the Negro troops have given a good account of themselves in their initial action alongside white troops.

The army is keeping close check on the Negro platoons, since this is the first time they have been placed in the same divisions with white soldiers on the fighting front. Weekly reports are to be made on their morale, fighting ability, casualties and the number of Germans they capture.

"All our reports so far have been good," said Capt. Edward Finnegan of New York.

The army has moved cautiously in breaking its long-established tradition of keeping white and Negro units separated, and the Negro rifle platoons are being fed into divisions gradually, with one platoon to each regiment now in action.

These Negro doughboys asked for the chance to fight. Many of them voluntarily gave up their stripes as staff sergeants and technical sergeants to get into the fighting.

They are fighting as platoons under white officers who have had combat experience.

When the Negro platoons arrived recently at one veteran division's location, each member got a personal letter from the commanding general along with the divisional shoulder patches. They then were greeted personally by regimental commanders. This is the identical welcome given all white reinforcements.

As yet the army has set up no replacement pool for the Negro platoons. When their fighting strength is reduced to such a level that they are unable to function as units, then remnants of two or more units will be reorganized into a full-strength platoon.

Praise for the Negroes came from Tech. Sergt. Casper F. Koch of Beaver Dam, Wis., who helped lead a Negro platoon into action four days ago against the town of Berghausen.

"We didn't want to give them too tough a job in their first fight," Koch said, "so our platoon went down a street where there were only about nine houses. We didn't think there would be many Germans in them.

"In the first house the Negro boys captured eleven Jerries and killed two. By the time they'd gotten to the end of the street they had captured fifty-three prisoners and killed I don't know how many.

"They worked perfectly. They are eager to learn and ask a lot of questions. When you tell 'em to take an objective they want to know what to do after they get there." ☐

Somewhere in Germany, March 22 — A low-flying troop carrier plane towed a casualty-filled glider from the First Army's Remagen bridgehead today, inaugurating a spectacular new shuttle service for evacuating wounded from areas near the cross-Rhine battlefront.

It was a dramatic moment on the little landing strip in a cabbage patch east of the Rhine when the transport swooped low, caught a towrope and swept the glider off the ground.

At noon, a Douglas C-47 flew over the Rhine and disengaged a glider piloted by Maj. H. H. Cloud, Jr., Louisville. The glider slipped down on the landing strip, marked by colored cloth.

(Major Cloud, twenty-five, is a son of Mrs. Pearl B. Cloud, 1110 Eastern Parkway. A group glider commander for the 440th Troop Carrier Group, he participated in the landings in Normandy, Southern France and Holland. In England with the Eighth Air Force is his brother, Second Lt. Lewis K., twenty-two, while their father, Col. H. H. Cloud, Sr. serves with the Quartermaster Corps in the South Pacific.)

The front of the glider opened and wounded men were carried from parked ambulances—men injured only a few hours earlier. All knew they were to be evacuated by glider. None objected. Most were conscious.

Pretty brown-haired Lt. Suella Barnard, twenty-six, Waynesville, Ohio, an air evacuation nurse, volunteered to be the first nurse to ride on a glider snatched from the ground on this front.

"I was a little nervous about it at first," she smiled, "but I am all right now."

Glider evacuation of wounded men has been carried out in India and Burma, but this was the first time in Europe.

Capt. Donald Haug, Wenatchee, Wash., of the Troop Carrier Command, said plans were to shuttle ten large gliders to the bridgehead daily, each making three trips to carry out twelve litter cases or nineteen walking wounded a trip. □

U.S. First Army across the Rhine, March 24 (6:46 p.m.) – Powerful Allied assaults on the Western front have wiped out Rhine River defenses and General Eisenhower's armies now stand on the threshold of complete victory over Germany.

This is the feeling along this army front tonight.

Not in two and a half years of war has such optimism prevailed among troops and officers as that which is cheering soldiers hearing news of new crossings on the Rhine against light enemy resistance.

There is a growing feeling that "this is it."

Everywhere there is that sense of an impending finish to a long conflict— that this time the Germans cannot muster enough strength to stop the powerhouse drives of the Allies.

It is becoming more evident day by day the battle of the west has been won west of the Rhine.

The Germans lost more than 200,000 troops as prisoners of war alone during the past thirty days—more than three full-strength armies. With the Russians threatening the Reich from the east, the Germans cannot stand such losses as these.

There was great optimism about the end of the war during the drive across France. But even that expectancy did not reach the heights of the present outlook, which envisages within a short time the complete collapse of organized effective opposition.

Even the more rabid pessimists admit the situation is brighter than it ever has been. German strength which was massed before the Allies west of the Rhine has been shredded under terrific onslaughts.

Prisoners have flowed into prison cages by the tens of thousands. Millions of dollars worth of equipment and supplies have been captured.

And that formidable barrier—the Rhine—has been crossed with such ease that even the Allied High Command can hardly believe it has happened.

Great sections of Germany's industrial might have been seized by the Allies or are under shell fire or have been wiped out by massed air raids.

The Germans are dipping into the bottom of the barrel for manpower because of the terrific losses they have incurred in recent weeks.

There is no doubt that the Wehrmacht is on the ropes and that the Allies are wading in for the knockout punch.

The enemy is trying desperately to muster and juggle reserves to meet the threats which are growing daily all along the line from Lieut. Gen. Alexander M. Patch's Seventh Army in the Palatinate to the British and Canadians in the north. □

With the United States First Army, March 26 — Smiling and in excellent spirits, Gen. Eisenhower visited the First Army east of the Rhine today, and declared he expected the First Army "to lick everybody they come up against."

"They did it all the way across France, and I see no reason why they should stop on the road to Berlin," the supreme commander said.

There was a feel of victory in the air as Gen. Eisenhower rode in a jeep across a pontoon bridge, and for the first time inspected this bridgehead seized by the First Army.

Gen. Eisenhower obviously was jubilant over developments all along the line. He looked much younger and less careworn than the last time I saw him just before the invasion of Normandy, and he laughed and joked with his generals as they met at the sprawling Petersberg Hotel which overlooks the Rhine from atop the 1,086-foot-high Petersberg Mountain. It is the same hotel where Prime Minister Chamberlain stayed during his conferences with Hitler at Bad Godesberg in 1938.

With Gen. Eisenhower were Lieut. Gens. Omar N. Bradley and Courtney Hodges. In the hotel's red plush-carpeted terrace restaurant staff officers had set up maps at one end, while a cheerful wood fire burned in an open fireplace at the other. Gen. Bradley chatted with his old friends of the First Army, while Gens. Eisenhower and Hodges huddled at one of the maps showing the progress of the First Army's breakout drive from the bridgehead since the attack started before dawn Sunday.

From windows of the long room Gen. Eisenhower could look across the beautiful mountains and down into the valley where the Rhine stretched like a broad silver ribbon under gray skies. It was the Valley of Decision, for down there Gen. Hodges's men had fought in from the river, built up a strong force, and then struck out eastward. □

With the U.S. First Army, March 26 — Unleashing the most powerful tank force ever assembled on the Western front, Lt. Gen. Courtney Hodges drove an armored spearhead of the First Army twenty-two miles eastward today into historic Limburg, and tonight this city on the Lahr River was being cleared of enemy troops.

The armored column burst into Limburg at 3:45 p.m. to climax a whirl-wind attack that started at dawn five miles northeast of Coblenz.

Tanks rolled forward in the gray dawn and hit the Cologne-Frankfurt superhighway north of Montabaur, eleven miles northwest of Limburg, and then drove down the broad military route to knock out what opposition remained in the way.

For hours this was a "mystery column," its movements cloaked in secrecy on grounds the enemy did not know where the leading elements of the First Army were in their surprise dash to the east.

Tonight the security blanket was lifted to pinpoint this great advance by the First, whose hard-riding tankmen and doughboys gripped one of the most picturesque towns in western Germany.

It is a town of some 12,000 population, with its big cathedral standing on the summit of a cliff overlooking Limburg, which sits on the left bank of the Lahr.

The only thing that slowed the tanks were demolished bridges and debris piled on roads. Engineers quickly cleared paths with bulldozers and the armor kept driving on.

An officer who flew over the line of advance from Montabaur to Limburg said that as U.S. tanks approached a factory on the outskirts of town, enemy machine guns opened up.

"Then I saw a spout of flame and a cloud of dust and guns in the factory stopped firing," he said. "A little farther on, machine guns fired on the tanks again and the Yanks blasted houses from which the fire came," the officer said.

South of Limburg, vehicles were racing to get away from the advancing Shermans. The towns of Openrod and Nentershausen, which straddle the road to Limburg, were left in flames. And in Obererbach north of Nentershausen, civilians were in the streets waving white flags.

This was a day much like the Normandy breakthrough, with tanks plowing forward hell-for-leather and infantry closing behind to mop up bypassed opposition.

There was no solid line in front of the First Army now. Drives on north and south of the Remagen bridgehead have chopped up the opposition into isolated pockets and the principal trouble comes from self-propelled weapons, artillery, and small units of disorganized infantry.

The attack is rolling forward with tremendous power and Hodges is pouring his massed might into the breaches. Roads, dampened by cool spring showers, are heavy with traffic rolling east.

To the north, probing fingers of armor plowed forward against their toughest resistance to a point east of Altenkirchen and to Herpteroth, two and one-half miles southeast of Altenkirchen, and to the vicinity of Hasselbach.

On this line of advance, the Nazis tried desperately to stem the tide with mortars, artillery and self-propelled weapons, but they lacked a fixed position on which to stand and fluid armored drives backed by fast-closing infantry gave them no chance to get set.

The First Infantry Division, which had beaten back strong enemy counter-attacks for two days, finally smashed forward for gains of 4,000 yards and had elements in the outskirts of Eitorf on the Sieg River.

Ahead of the First Division, German troops pulled back to disengage troops and armor before being swept up by this tide, which was now grinding out steady gains and rounding up hundreds of prisoners. A total of 3,147 prisoners was captured yesterday.

The First Army is on the move all along the line and the Germans have been able to muster only spotty resistance. In some sectors, there was very little opposition and tanks just rolled down the roads.

In the center of the attacking line, the Ninth Infantry Division ran into heavy small-arms fire and shoved in to clean out the dug-in Germans.

The Ninety-ninth Division closed in behind the speeding spearhead to consolidate gains, while other units reached Hohr, Grenzhausen and Mallendar, north of Coblenz.

Limburg is a town of considerable antiquarian interest. From 1420 to 1803 it belonged to the electors of Trier.

Many ancient dwellings are preserved in the old quarter, their picturesque gables surmounted by the spires of the well-known German cathedral built in the thirteenth century. Architects regard it as one of the best examples of Rhenish transitional style.

Tourists formerly visited the great castle near Limburg until its destruction by fire in 1929. □

With the U.S. First Infantry Division across the Rhine, March 26 — If a lot of people at home could see themselves as they appear to battle veterans after two and a half years of combat they would not be proud of the picture.

But that's how it is. The men told their stories as they waited in a little room near the front for an officer to escort them back to the Twenty-sixth Regiment, which they left January 12 for home leave.

There were nineteen of them. Their leave was ended and they were going back into battle.

All had been overseas with the First Division from the time it landed in North Africa. Most wore the Purple Heart and many had decorations for bravery. They were going back into the line with vivid memories of home, but not all of them were happy.

Sure, it was good to be home again and just sit around and do nothing but listen to the radio and eat home cooking, they agreed. The girls were wonderful and more sympathetic than most of the boys thought they would be. Home was just like it always was, but still:

"Things have changed," said Staff Sgt. Howard Ashby, Martinsburg, W.Va. "Sometimes I didn't think the people thought much of a soldier or the way we acted. Maybe it was just me.

"There were not many of my friends left at home. Most of them are in the army and there were just a few guys left. Somehow you were disappointed in seeing you didn't really mean anything to a lot of people, even if you had been fighting for more than two years. Your family's not that way of course, but other people are."

"Yeah," said Sgt. Michael Halko of Stockton, Pa. "Some people feel the war, but others don't give a damn. They are making a lot of money and doing all right.

"Why, there was one woman who is making a lot of money in war work who said she hoped the war lasted ten more years. Can you figure that one out? I had a notion to slap her face, but I didn't.

"Then some people who had sons overseas seemed to resent the fact that I was at home and their boys were not. They would ask me why was I allowed to come home when their boys weren't. All I could say was that I didn't have anything to do about anybody getting home. It wasn't my fault."

Staff Sgt. John Duda, Adah, Pa., said:

"When you tell 'em a story they won't believe it. They say it couldn't be that bad and then most people start talking about their own troubles and how tough it is at home with rationing.

"Old veterans knew what we were talking about. They understand what the score is and don't ask too many questions."

Capt. Linwood Billings, Dover, N.H., said that was the way most of the men felt.

"Most people don't know what is going on," he said. "I would say seventy-five per cent of the people at home are behind the war efforts and the other twenty-five per cent don't give a damn.

"It is different in smaller towns because they feel closer to the war. In Dover, people know just about all the boys who are overseas and they are glad to see them when they get home. Most everybody there is doing war work too, or trying to do something to help."

Lt. Steve Phillips Jr., of Greenville, S.C., said:

"I felt lost at times with most of my old friends gone. All I wanted to do was stay at home with my wife. I told her I guess she thought I was crazy just sitting and listening to the radio and reading the papers, but she said she was happy and that was all that mattered. That was enough for me." □

With the U.S. First Army Driving East, March 27 – The victory-flushed First Army continued its sweep toward Berlin today with armored and infantry columns running wild in another twenty-four hours of spectacular gains.

Except for stubborn enemy resistance in front of the First Infantry Division just south of the Sieg River at the southern boundary of the Ruhr industrial region enemy opposition has fallen apart before the hammering from Lieut. Gen. Courtney H. Hodges' mighty tank forces.

The armored columns are followed closely by infantry, and are flowing eastward over roads like water churning down streambeds.

The rout is under way and hundreds of prisoners overrun by the swift armored dash are pouring back, sometimes without even a guard.

The advances are so swift that even divisional headquarters maps most of the time are far behind the actual gains of the columns, and corps headquarters officers just shake their heads and point vaguely to the east, saying: "They are somewhere out there."

The priority on bridges and roads is to the east, and supplies are pouring behind the rampaging armor and motorized infantry.

At one Rhine bridge, an almost endless convoy was rolling across and military police shuttled back and forth on the road to break up any possible traffic jam. On the eastern bank, trucks waited for a break in traffic. They were jammed with German prisoners who stared at the truck columns as though they couldn't believe such action was taking place before them. Most of these prisoners looked very young.

There is heavy traffic on all Rhine bridges, and from the looks of the roads, General Eisenhower had build up tremendous stockpiles in anticipation of this drive on Berlin.

In the thick of the fight were the Ninth, Ninety-ninth and Seventy-eighth Infantry Divisions. But there were other divisions, including powerful armored divisions, whose identities still are covered by security censorship.

At one command post Maj. Walter Hillenmeyer, of Lexington, Ky., watched as maps were marked showing new locations of the armored spearheads.

"The trouble is," he said, "we can't keep enough maps on the wall to keep up with the advances."

The attack boiled on east of Altenkirchen and ancient Limburg. It spilled across the Lahn River to engulf Limburg. It rolled to the east, mile after mile falling behind the roaring tanks.

Areas which only a few days ago were battle zones now are quiet sectors being taken over by rear echelon units moving up across the Rhine. The whole front is ablaze with the fire of victory. An infectious spirit of competition is spurring one division to outdo another in the race.

I tried to catch up with the forward spearheads today but it was impossible. They were moving too fast and the roads were jammed with miles-long convoys thundering forward with food, gasoline, ammunition, ordnance equipment and material to keep the attack rolling undiminished.   □

With the U.S. First Army, March 27 — Franz Oppenhof, forty-one-year-old Burgermeister (mayor) of Aachen and first mayor appointed by the Allied military government in a major German city was assassinated Sunday night, it was announced today.

Oppenhof was shot through the temple at 11:30 p.m. as he stood on the back porch of his home on the outskirts of the city.

Military intelligence officers investigating the case said the motive had not yet been established, and that it had not yet been established officially whether the mayor was killed by Nazis because he had assumed the post of Burgermeister under the Americans. It was possible he may have been the victim of a personal enemy.

This was the story that was given by Oppenhof's neighbor to the army:

Oppenhof and his wife were at a neighbor's home when the Burgermeister's maid called and said three men were waiting to see him.

The neighbor accompanied the official to his home. A uniformed trio met the mayor on the back porch and told him they were German air force officers whose planes had crashed. They said they wanted food and shelter, and protection from the Americans.

The mayor was quoted by his neighbor as replying that he would be obliged to turn the group over to American Army authorities.

The neighbor returned to his own home and informed Oppenhof's wife the mayor would be delayed. Shortly afterward, Oppenhof was shot.

A German patrolman who heard the shot, fired at the three fleeing figures but they escaped, apparently without injury, the army was told.

Prior to the capture of Aachen last October by the First Army, Oppenhof was an attorney for the Archdiocese of the Catholic church in Aachen and Düsseldorf.

It was known at the time that his appointment by the military government was opposed by trade unionists who had suspected him of Nazi sympathies, and the opposition was expressed openly at the first meeting of the trade unions to be held in Aachen—and possibly the first such meeting to be held in Germany—since the Nazis clamped restrictions on unions.

But inasmuch as Oppenhof had chosen to accept the American appointment, many civilian community leaders in Aachen have adopted the view that the assassination was the work of Nazis, and that this might have been a Nazi method of intimidating others who might dare to cooperate with the Allies.   □

With the American First Army, March 28 — The war has just run off and left the "front-line" correspondents.

In the first place, nobody knows just where the front is, and trying to get up forward to get news from spearhead elements of Lt. Gen. Courtney H. Hodges' fast-traveling First Army is giving newsmen a beating worse than they took during the dash across France last summer.

The surging attack has left the press camp far in the rear, and as a base of operations it now is almost useless—except for daily briefings by a staff officer in the morning and late afternoon, meals, and a place to sleep.

But no correspondent can get too far away from the censorship and communications center, so the daily problem is to get as much news as possible, and then to get back and get it sent.

Correspondents returning from the field with stories late in the day and sometimes after dark look like dirt-track race drivers, their faces are so blackened by the dust thrown up by endless convoys.

Hal Boyle of the Associated Press, for example, set out for the front yesterday morning and, after six hours of jeep-riding, bucking convoys, waiting at bridges, taking detours and pursuing a tank column he managed to reach a division command post which was ready to move for the fourth time during the day.

With the front moving at such speed, correspondents are trying to get a mobile press camp which can keep at least within reasonable driving distance of the forward elements, and at the same time maintain reliable communications, because there are no indications of any immediate halt to the attack. □

At an American Evacuation Hospital near the Rhine, March 28 — Two gaunt American soldiers who almost died of starvation in a German prison camp near Limburg told today of brutal treatment in Stalag XII—the first such camp for Allied prisoners to be seized east of the Rhine.

They are safe now in this Rhine Valley hospital and before long they will be on their way home—as soon as they recover a little more from the effects of prison life. They said the men were so hungry they would fight for food— food which a sick man could hardly eat. The guards sold small-sized potatoes for one hundred Belgian francs each and a cigarette brought 250 francs.

The tag at the foot of the bed occupied by Staff Sgt. Francis Holley of Rome, N.Y., read, "Malnutrition due to starvation. Dysentery."

The farm youth's arms were thin and his tired blue eyes had a look of suffering which was put there since the morning in February when he was captured near Hollerath in a waist-deep snow as he went forward with a mortar observation squad from H Company of the First Division's Eighteenth Infantry Regiment.

Sgt. Holley and his men were pinned down by machine gun and mortar fire and there was nothing left to do but surrender after two of the five men were wounded.

His captors at the front treated him pretty well, he said—treated him like a soldier should be treated. But it was different the further he went back. He said that by the time he reached Flamerscheid there was not much to choose between the way the Germans were treating prisoners and what he had heard about the Japanese.

It took just twenty days at Flamerscheid to make a hospital case out of Sgt. Holley. He was marched thirty-six miles to a hospital—a march which he said killed one man. At the hospital he did get a special diet of thick soup, jam and cheese.

After eight days he was released from the hospital and sent to Limburg prison.

"Maybe they couldn't help it because the hospital was overcrowded," Sgt. Holley said. "They didn't have enough medicine and if anybody had a bad leg it meant amputation. Badly wounded men were lucky if they got their bandages changed every five days. They washed out the bandages and used them over and over again. They always were wet."

At 1 a.m. two days before the Americans entered Limburg the guards waked up the prisoners and loaded them into boxcars. Sgt. Holley slipped away in the fog and hid until tanks of the United States Ninth Armored Division rumbled into town.

In the bed next to Sgt. Holley was Sgt. Edgar D. Garwood of Troy, Ohio, who was captured last December near Marche when Field Marshal von Rundstedt made his bid to smash the Allied armies in the west. Sgt. Garwood was with the Thirty-fifth Regiment of the Eighty-fourth Division.

He was taken to the same train with Sgt. Holley. The prisoners were loaded into cars which sat on a siding from Friday morning until the next Monday and each day they had only a small square of bread and a little cheese.

American planes came over and bombed and strafed the train and the guards fled, leaving the men locked inside. They broke out and identified themselves as prisoners by forming a large P-W. But fourteen were killed and twenty-six wounded in an air raid before the planes went away.

Sgt. Garwood was marched to a labor camp at Gerolstein. There his job was digging bodies from bomb wreckage or filling road craters from 7:30 a.m. to 5:30 p.m. daily. He said the prisoners were treated brutally.

"Five or six men died there every day," he said. "One of my buddies was in a bad shape and couldn't stand digging. He started to sink to the ground, but we knew if he fell he'd be clubbed by a guard. Another soldier and I tried to hold him up and we all went down.

"Then the guard kicked us and kept us there four more hours. We were cold and wet through when we got back to the camp and had to sleep without even a blanket. One of the men got frostbitten feet and they were so swollen he had trouble getting his shoes on. A guard got mad because he was delaying the working party and shot him through the neck and eyes."

A jeep picked Sgt. Garwood up and took him to a medical station after the Americans arrived.

"They were eating raisin bread," he said, "and I never saw anything more beautiful in my life."

More than 2,000 prisoners from Stalag XII were taken back into Germany, he said. ☐

With the U.S. First Army, March 29 — Suddenly wheeling north, Lieut. Gen. Courtney H. Hodges' armored divisions burst through Westphalia and hammered on toward the northern plains of Germany in another day of sensational gains against feeble opposition.

Jumping off in the gray dawn of a chill and cloudy day, the tanks drove from sixteen to thirty-nine miles ahead in the first seven hours and were reported officially tonight to have reached the vicinity of Langewiese, forty miles north of Giessen, in the deepest penetration in this new direction.

Other columns reached Hallenberg and Frankenberg in the same area.

This wheeling movement to the north—if the direction of the attack is maintained—will drive the powerful First Army in behind the Ruhr as the southern jaw of a pincers with Field Marshal Montgomery's forces. ☐

With the First Army, March 29 — Quick-thinking American and British captives being herded from a German prisoner of war camp at Limburg saved themselves from a deadly attack by United States planes through a human alphabet maneuver reminiscent of between-halves formations by football cheering sections.

With Ninth Armored Division tanks roaring toward the ancient cathedral city, the routed Germans tried to cram some 2,000 of the Allied prisoners into six cars for a rush to the east. American fighter-bombers, seeking out any moving rail stock, swooped in to bomb and strafe the train.

The Nazi guards fled. The prisoners broke open the doors spilled into the fields nearby and, as the American planes dived for the kill, hastily formed lines spelling out the letters PW, for prisoners of war.

The pilots veered away, but not before fourteen men had been killed and twenty-seven wounded.

When the Ninth Division moved out they discovered the Germans were packing even seriously wounded prisoners into boxcars and evacuating them from hospitals in the path of the First Army.

Officers said the Germans apparently had no hospital trains available to move the casualties, many of whom are in serious condition from lack of proper medical treatment and malnutrition. The enemy has neither ambulances nor gasoline to evacuate hospitals.

At Wetzlar, northeast of Limburg, the Ninth Infantry found 277 American prisoners of war locked in boxcars on a railway siding. They immediately lifted them from the cars and took them to evacuation hospitals for treatment.

Some of the prisoners at Limburg's Stalag XII escaped before the Germans tried the evacuation move. These also were suffering from malnutrition and improper medical care. ☐

With the United States First Army, March 30 — Rolling at the rate of more than twenty-five miles a day, the American First Army's armor swung almost without hindrance tonight toward a juncture east of the Ruhr with the United States Ninth Army.

His defenses crumbled from the Lahn to Sieg Rivers, wily Field Marshal Kesselring was reported striving desperately to reform his shattered remnants into some semblance of an army and put them on the line to check the tide of defeat sweeping in on what remains of the Wehrmacht.

Lieut. Gen. Courtney H. Hodges's spearheads reached Paderborn, 185 miles from Berlin, during the day, chalking up gains of more than 125 miles in five days. Reports from the advance elements, however, were at least eight and one-half hours behind actual advances.

The gap between vanguards of the American and British forces had been narrowed to sixty-five miles.

Expert opinion was that Kesselring had neither the means nor the time in which to make any formidable stand and that he can only reconstitute his broken divisions and merge commands of miscellaneous units while trying to bring up whatever reserves are left in Central Germany, Norway and Denmark.

Some troops being brought to the front, it was reported, are being told to find arms on the battlefield, but they have neither the training nor the weapons with which to halt the greatest tank force ever assembled on the Western front.

This mighty tide of armor, it was revealed today, is led by Maj. Gen. Maurice Rose's Third Armored Division which also paced the drive from the Roer River to the Rhine. Following the Third rolled Maj. Gen. Terry Allen's 104th infantry and Maj. Gen. Robert Hasbrouck's Seventh Armored.

The pace-setting task force in the forefront of the drive is commanded by Lieut. Col. Prentice Yeomans of Syracuse, N.Y., with almost parallel columns under command of Lieut. Col. Walter Richardson, Beaumont, Tex., and Lieut. Col. John Welborn of Southern Pines, N.C.

On the right flank of the Seventh, Maj. Gen. John W. Leonard's Ninth Armored Division wheeled around the "elbow" of the First Army's turn to the north to reach Fritzlar on the Eder and Alt Wildungen on the Wilde River, a gain for the day of twenty miles and a total advance of one hundred miles in five days.

Tanks of the Ninth Armored, which established the Remagen bridgehead by capturing the Ludendorff Bridge, also reached Barken and Tresta and the main Frankfurt-Kassel railroad.

At the bend of the elbow, the First Infantry advanced to a point two miles south of Siegen to clean out comparatively light opposition.

Observers, noting the continued absence of any appreciable opposition, said that Kesselring, whose troops made such a stubborn defense of Italy, was a past master at the art of taking whatever troops were available and putting up a stout defense. These observers said the German leader might be able to constitute some sort of line in front of the Allied drive—but he simply does not have enough reserves available to throw up a defense strong enough to stop the power unleashed by the Allies.   □

With the U.S. First Army, March 31 — German guards voluntarily surrendered their arms and captive American airmen manned the machine guns of the transient prisoner of war camp at Wetzlar when the American First Army approached and freed them.

Those airmen did not intend for any of the enemy to come and take them away when liberation was so near, and the German guards were prepared to help prevent their removal.

Another group of American soldiers, most of them captured in Belgium during the Battle of the Bulge last December, were freed at Giessen after the Germans had taken them from a camp at Limburg. But American armor fortunately moved faster than the prisoners were able to walk, so they were free today and soon will be on their way home.

Both American and British airmen were kept at the Wetzlar camp. They lived in big barracks just outside the town and received excellent treatment, with plenty of food and clothing. There were hot water, showers and electric lights until the power from Giessen failed as the American forces approached.   □

With the U.S. First Army, [April 2] – The Germans launched their first coordinated attack today to break an escape corridor through the Allies' steel ring circling the Ruhr. Hard fighting still was in progress early tonight.

German infantry supported by tanks hit the First Army's Ninth Division near Winterberg about halfway between Paderborn and Siegen, trying to smash a lane through Lt. Gen. Courtney H. Hodges' lines to the east.

But at last reports the doughboys were holding firm and beating back this desperate attempt of Marshal Kesselring to save some of his troops trapped in the Ruhr.

Tens of thousands of German troops were caught in a steel vise formed by the juncture of the First and Ninth Armies, who had cut all major escape routes.

Swift American infantry, following quickly in the wake of the Third Armored Division, mounted guard over all possible escape avenues as disorganized enemy troops and tanks stabbed to the east and northeast, trying frantically to uncover an escape gap.

The trap, which is throttling all northwestern Germany, was sprung when Lt. Col. Matthew Kane of Des Moines, Iowa, sent a task force east from Paderborn yesterday to meet the Ninth Army's Second Armored Division at Lippstadt, fifteen miles to the west. The Third Armored had wiped out the last enemy resistance in Paderborn by yesterday afternoon, clamping an iron grip on that important road junction.

Field Marshal Albert Kesselring moved too slowly to get his troops back on another line before Berlin. The rapid moves of Hodges' mighty tank force which swung north outflanked the Ruhr and the advances by Lt. Gen. William H. Simpson's Ninth Army from the Rhine had swept around the Ruhr before the enemy could fall back.

Approximately 1,000 German infantry and twenty tanks were bypassed by the U.S. armored columns in the woods near Niedermarsburg. They attacked late yesterday to the south and southeast, trying to crack the First Army line. For two hours fighting raged between these Nazis and the Ninth Armored Division's tanks and troops. The American armor drove them back and knocked the fight out of eight tanks in the slam-bang battle inside First Army lines.

The Ninth Army drive had carried from the Rhine east to Essen and then along the Lippe Canal, bypassing Hamm and continuing east through to the juncture with Hodges' troops which were cleaning out the enemy forces desperately trying to hold Paderborn center on a main road to Berlin. The spectacular moves by the two American armies sealed off a Ruhr box roughly fifty-five miles wide from Hamm to Siegen and seventy-five miles deep from Düsseldorf to the First Army lines south of Paderborn.

There is hard fighting ahead and anyone who thinks the war will be over in the next few days is likely to be badly fooled. Even though disorganized, the enemy still is putting up a fight and there are no indications of mass surrender. ☐

With the U.S. First Army, April 3 — Maj. Gen. Maurice Rose, brilliant commander of the Third Armored Division which spearheaded the First Army's great drive from the Rhine River deep into Germany, was shot to death near Paderborn March 30 by a German tankman as the general started to surrender his arms after being captured.

Companions said the tall, handsome general was shot through the head as he lifted his pistol holster from his shoulder to hand it over to the German covering him and his aide with a machine-pistol from the turret of a tank which infiltrated into American lines south of Paderborn.

Rose, who was always forward with advance elements giving personal directions to his combat and task force commanders, had gone to the area to direct the Third Armored Division's fight to capture an important road junction.

He started back in a jeep with his aide, Maj. Robert Bellinger of White Plains, N.Y., trying to find another of his task force commanders, when he turned a curve and ran head on into Tiger tanks on the road which a short while before had been carrying First Army traffic. An armored car was following with other members of his staff.

The general's driver wheeled the jeep across a field through woods, but ran head on into another German tank and the general got out of his jeep to surrender.

As he stood with hands over his head the German holding a machine pistol in the tank turret unloosed a torrent of words.

"I don't understand," the general kept saying, according to Bellinger.

Then apparently the general thought his captor meant for him to surrender his arms and he took his hands down to lift the holster from his shoulder. That was when the German fired.

Bellinger and other officers and men in the armored car made a dash for freedom and escaped. The general's body was found where he was shot. ☐

With U.S. First Army, April 3 — One German prisoner of a panzer outfit, still cocky, was asked if he had known his unit was surrounded and there was no escape.

"We knew we were surrounded," he replied, "but we have been surrounded before and fought our way out."

Hundreds of German soldiers are taking off their uniforms and donning civilian clothing, and are trying to make their way out of the trap to an assembly point. Each carries a civilian pass. They mingle with hundreds of German civilians and liberated slave laborers wandering about.

Intelligence officers are screening every male from fifteen to sixty, and in one division about fifty per cent of those checked were disclosed to have been soldiers in civilian clothes.

Among the prisoners was one who belonged to an SS (elite guard) company which had assassinated captured Americans in a snow-covered field near Malmédy, Belgium, during the German Ardennes counter-offensive last December.

When an intelligence officer discovered he had belonged to that unit, the German hastily produced a certificate purporting to show he was in a training school during that battle. He protested he had nothing to do with those murders and on the contrary, was shocked.   □

With the United States First Army, April 4 — Valuable art treasures from Germany and France have been found in a dank tunnel used by German civilians near the front as an air raid shelter. Works of Rembrandt, Rubens, Van Gogh and Van Dyke; the famous jeweled and gold sarcophagus from the cathedral at Cologne, sculptures and other treasures from museums, cathedrals and private collections were found.

They had been moved from one hiding place to another by the Germans until First Army soldiers in the Siegen area overran an enemy position and discovered the cache. An inventory will be made to determine the value of the collection and to find out how much was German and how much from occupied countries.

In the dank, fetid air of the cavern, civilians slept next to a painting by the great Rembrandt, or curled up beside a magnificent carved door from the Cologne Cathedral. Russian and French slave laborers made their homes hard by the bones of Charlemagne, brought to the cave from their resting place in Aachen's cathedral.

There were 500 original scores in the handwriting of Ludwig van Beethoven, taken from the composer's birthplace at Bonn. There were paintings by Holbein; Rembrandt's celebrated self-portrait, and Rubens's self-portrait and his famous Madonna were there.

The sarcophagus from the Cologne Cathedral probably was the most valuable item of all. Virtually all the treasures of that cathedral were moved two years ago when Allied air forces began pounding Rhineland industrial cities.

The cache in the cave was under the care of an aged man who once was curator of the Aachen Museum, but even his care could not save the paintings from being somewhat affected in the damp underground passage.

The sarcophagus referred to presumably is the Reliquary of the Magi, or Shrine of the Three Kings. It is regarded as the most magnificent specimen of reliquaries which has been preserved. After the storming of Milan, in 1162, the supposed relics of the Magi were carried off and taken to Cologne, where a magnificent casket of precious metal, nearly six feet long and four and one-half feet wide, was constructed for them. This costly specimen of Romanesque workmanship, adorned with fine antique gems, was injured seriously in 1794, when it was carried away for concealment from the French, and it was unskillfully restored in 1807. It was kept in the treasury of the Cologne Cathedral.   □

With the United States First Army, April 5 — The first of Europe's scrambled millions to be liberated from the Nazi yoke have become a major problem for the advancing Americans.

The problem is growing daily as men, women and children who had been taken prisoner or forced from their homes in Russia, Poland, Czechoslovakia and other overrun lands and made to work as slaves begin the long road back.

Somewhere along the line they are taken into camps for displaced persons and processed for the return to their homelands. It is a strange and tragic procession along these roads winding through the hills of Westphalia, of wanderers trying to make their way back to families and friends and familiar scenes which they may never know again as they once knew them.

They sleep in barns or haystacks along the roads. Often doughboys toss them cans of C rations from passing trucks.

On the surface there is little evidence of hatred for the Germans but stories are beginning to be told of old hatreds flaring into violence. In one village which had several factories an owner lived in baronial splendor in an abode overlooking the town. He had more than 200 slave laborers working under him.

"They lived like pigs in little huts around the village," said Lieut. Ervin Hanse of Lincoln, Neb. "It reminded you of stories of medieval times."

Finally came the day when Americans entered the village and seized these factories producing war materiel for the Wehrmacht. The slave laborers were freed.

Next morning the factory owner was found with his throat slashed from ear to ear. Some say that a Russian finally got his revenge.

The first-hand observations of slave laborers living unwillingly behind the enemy lines can sometimes be turned to good account.

There was Maria from the Ukraine, with her straight, stringy light brown hair and molded features. She came to the American command post with Nicolai, who had been taken prisoner by the Germans in Latvia. Nicolai bared his shoulder to show an ugly scar where he had been hit by a piece of shrapnel. It almost had torn off his shoulder.

Maria was taken from Kiev by the Germans three years ago and sent back into Germany where she became a maid for a farm family in a place south of Paderborn. She worked hard for them but never forgot that she was a slave to these people who gave her food and a place to sleep in return for long hours of labor in the house and in the fields.

Maria never learned to speak German but she was observant, and as the Americans drew near the farm she noticed that fifteen or twenty soldiers would come to the farmhouse each day, stay overnight and then leave wearing civilian clothes.

The farm wife told her that when the Americans came and asked if there had been any German soldiers there she must say "no." But Maria, at the first opportunity, escaped with Nicolai and came straight to the Americans to tell them what was happening at this farmhouse. ☐

Fürstenberg, Germany, April 7 — Triumphant foreign laborers liberated from the Nazi yoke by the eastward sweep of First Army Infantry and Armor have seized the broad, fertile acres of Count Metternich, Hitler's curator of arts, and set up the first little Communist community in western Germany.

The Poles, Russians and Czechs finally rebelled against years of repression and took over the running of the rich feudal estate with the white-haired Count and Countess Metternich virtual prisoners in their own great castle.

It is another strange story out of many strange stories among these people who came to work for the "master race" and suddenly found themselves free again with no fear of the Gestapo hanging over them.

When war came, Metternich, professor of history and arts at the famed University of Bonn where the sons of German aristocracy automatically enrolled in former years, needed laborers to till the soil and carry on the work at his four huge estates near here.

Through the Nazi labor office he obtained approximately 1,000 men and women who were under the charge of overseers.

The count himself had little time to oversee his sprawling farms because of his duties as curator of all art treasures in German-occupied territory. One of these duties was superintending the moving of art treasures from the Louvre, such as the Mona Lisa and Venus de Milo.

If any worker became unruly all Metternich had to do was to call in the Gestapo and have him removed to a concentration camp. If the workers didn't like their filthy quarters in the barns or became sullen because the food they ate was not the rich fare enjoyed by the German overseers and workers, then that was too bad.

Those Russians and Poles and Czechs never forgot any brutality by the overseers and they remembered the pregnant woman who was beaten because she dared to steal milk.

Then the Americans came and 250 slaves on one 250-acre farm decided their lives should be changed and that they should enjoy some of the fruits of their labor.

The Russians' officer assumed the title of commissar and with his good friend, the Polish officer with one eye, they established a Communist center and demanded all keys from the bewildered and frightened overseer. The overseer managed to escape from the farm and came rushing in to Captain Erhard Dabringhaus, of Roseville, Mich.

"The Poles and Russians are going to kill us all," he cried.

Dabringhaus investigated and this is what he found:

Count Metternich's Westphalian estate had become a Communist center.

"For five years we watched them eat eggs," one Russian growled. "Now we eat eggs."

They were having steaks three times a day or as many times as they wished. There was plenty of milk to drink and the farm's stores of food had become community property.

"It was like a movie," Dabringhaus said. "There were steaks broiling all day long. Workers released from other farms have joined this community and the doors are not barred to anyone who wants food and shelter."

The Russian and the Pole now were running the show—but the major difficulty was that no one wanted to go back to work. The overseer no longer had authority and the workers no longer feared the stick he carried. So the Russian and Dabringhaus sought to make them see the wisdom of returning to their jobs until such time as they could be returned to their homes.

The Russians confided to Dabringhaus, "I'm no more a commissar than you are, but they will listen to me if I call myself the commissar."   □

Paderborn, Germany, April 9 — Adolf Hitler has collected his toughest Nazi-indoctrinated youths of fourteen to eighteen and thrown them into battle against the U.S. First Army with the now familiar "do or die" orders to halt the Americans.

Although these German youths are not sufficiently trained to match the skill and stamina of Lt. Gen. Courtney Hodges' tankmen, they are fighting hard and desperately. "These youngsters are little city toughs—Dead End Kids," said Lt. Col. Andrew Barr of Urbana, Ill. They are better than the average run of German soldiers and still are enthusiastic over Nazi ideas."

Only a short time before the Americans hammered their way from the Rhine with the Third Armored Division spearheading Hodges' drive, these Nazi youths were brought into the great tank training center in Paderborn and trained to fight with the big Tigers.

They are from the tough SS (elite guard) outfit which killed Maj. Gen. Maurice Rose, who commanded the Third Armored Division. After being taken prisoner the general was shot through the head by a young enemy tankman.

These teen-age German boys had only ten days to two weeks training before they rushed out to meet the First Army's advance.

Even after these fanatical youths are captured they must be watched. Sgt. Edward L. Ellsworth, a veteran medical aid man from Wyoming, was almost killed by a wounded young SS trooper he was attending.

As the American turned to adjust a bottle of plasma the German grabbed a knife from a scabbard on the sergeant's belt. Capt. Edgar Crowe of Mechanicsville, Va., blocked the blow which would have plunged the knife into Ellsworth's back.

There were approximately 1,000 of these tough kids in the tank training school now in the hands of the First Army. The school is providing the Allies with valuable information of German tank training methods.

The school consisted of ten large three-storied barracks and an administration building over which flew a huge flag now being sent to the commandant at Fort Knox, Ky., the American tank training center, as a souvenir.

The German tankmen lived in comfort at the center even though the furnishings were cheap and crude. The rooms now are littered with clothing, torn mattresses, broken pictures, letters and all the odds and ends that soldiers carry.

"These people must have run out damned fast or they would never have left the things they did," said a British major with the Royal Armored Corps who is studying equipment and the layout at the school. "The place is filled with Tiger parts, engine cylinder blocks; tank tracks and bogies and electrical equipment."

The major said he was not able to find anything unusual in the enemy's tank training methods which were not as up to date as British and American methods.   □

With the U.S. First Army, April 9 — For the first time since the great Allied drives opened, Russian and American armies tonight are in a position for tactical field co-operation in cutting up what remains of the German Army.

Marshal Konev's First Ukrainian Army and the armies of Generals Patton and Hodges are only some 150 miles apart and it is possible for them to coordinate their moves in slashing Germany apart at the waist.

Whether there is close coordination at this stage is known only to the high command, but a study of the map shows that with the distances whittled down the Allies are easily able to mesh their operations.

The shortest line between the Americans and Russians stretches from the spearhead of the Third Army near Weimar to Görlitz east of Dresden.

Should simultaneous drives be opened down this line through Leipzig and Dresden the Allies probably would slice Germany in half in relatively short order and a corridor would be opened between the Russian and American fronts.

Some veteran military men foresee capitulation of all enemy forces left in the half of the country that is cut off from Hitler by such a bisecting.

"Once they are away from Hitler's influence and control," one officer said, "I believe we will be in the geographical half of Germany cut off from Hitler. He is the only influence that keeps them going."

This viewpoint coincides with that of General George C. Marshall, who reportedly told the Senate military committee that the quickest way to end the war with Germany would be to kill or capture Hitler because of his influence over the armed forces.

Drawing a line between the two fronts shows that either Leipzig or Dresden would be the most favorable meeting place.

From Leipzig to Berlin there is a corridor of solid ground leading through many lakes and low ground and it is traversed by one of Hitler's superhighways.

One officer declared there was less enemy strength in front of the First Army than at any time since General Omar N. Bradley sent his troops ashore in Normandy.

"We've carved the heart out of Germany's industry by the Russians' capture of Silesia and by pocketing the Ruhr," the officer said. "When Germany is cut in two then it is the finish. Disintegration already has begun. If Hitler retreats to the national redoubt in Southern Bavaria then in my opinion it is highly likely the forces trapped in the northern half will capitulate."

Tactical reconnaissance pilots returning from flights over enemy territory make such reports as "150 plus people in Holzminden," or "thirty plus people walking northeast" or "200 scattered people walking northeast from Göttingen."

There are no reports of any considerable enemy concentrations of troops, tanks or guns—which would be spotted if the enemy was making a stand in any great force. □

Duderstadt, Germany, April 12 — Happy Allied prisoners of war, liberated by troops of Lieut. Gen. Courtney Hodges's First Army from an unbelievable filthy and evil Nazi camp, today described a mid-winter "death march" from eastern Germany in which scores of men died of illness, exhaustion, hunger and clubbing by Nazi guards.

When the Russian drive neared the borders of eastern Germany 60,000 prisoners, including a large percentage of Americans, were taken from their prison camps and marched toward central Germany under appalling conditions.

Men fell from the ranks and died by the roadside, with snow drifting over their bodies. Those who stayed alive stole turnips and potatoes to keep their strength and if they were caught they were punished. They slept in the open in the bitter cold, without cover, huddling their shaking bodies together for warmth.

This was the story told by prisoners awaiting transportation from the prison where they were held until three jeeploads of Americans rolled up to the gate three days ago, bringing freedom.

"The first American I saw," said one New Zealander who was captured at El Alamein, "was Pfc. Earle Howard, Portland, Me. That was a day of days. We rushed out to get around the Yanks and mobbed 'em."

There were only 400 prisoners left in this camp when the doughboys arrived. More than 2,000 prisoners had been marched away to the east—leaving only those who were too weak or too ill to walk.

"This is our Hotel Splendid," the New Zealander remarked.

"Hotel Splendid" was a three-story brick kiln with a single doorway and a single staircase leading to the upper floors. Once it was used only as a transient camp, but after the death march it was flooded with prisoners and often held as many as 3,500 men. There were never less than 2,000 in the filthy kiln, which had no sanitation facilities. The usual meal was a pot of so-called soup, a piece of bread and a stick of stinking cheese.

"Men were dying every day," one man said. "I saw eight bodies in one day in an alleged hospital which was a room with a dirt floor covered with straw. The hospital would accommodate forty patients until death made room for others. It was a pigsty."

Most prisoners had made the march from western Poland and eastern Germany. Some came from a camp near Breslau and others from a camp near Görlitz in Silesia. The death march began on February 15 and lasted for twenty-six days.   □

U.S. First Army HQ, Germany, April 17 — A First Army tank force yesterday stormed through a Mulde River village and captured a stone prison housing "special enemies of Germany," but it was forty-eight hours too late to liberate some prominent captives.

The Germans had rushed many Americans and British by night from this evil-smelling camp, where they had been held as hostages. Yesterday the Germans tried to evacuate 1,000 other Allied prisoners, but these refused to leave, because they could hear American guns and knew that freedom was near.

Lieut. Col. Leo Shaughnessey of Woburn, Mass., led the task force, made up of men from the Ninth Armored Division and the Sixty-ninth Division.

From the windows of their massive prison on a hilltop cheering prisoners watched the battle below.

Liberation was a reprieve for stocky Lieut. Col. William H. Schaefer, who had been sentenced to die because he objected to posting of Nazi propaganda leaflets on the prison bulletin board.

This was the camp for men who were suspected as special cases or who had tried time and time again to escape. They told of cruel Gestapo treatment.□

Leipzig, Germany, April 19 — Doughboys of the Second and Sixty-ninth Infantry Division cracked the last three enemy strongholds in Leipzig today. The soldiers then began ferreting out snipers.

Nearly all the city south of the railroad station already has been mopped up and the remainder is being cleared rapidly.

The prisoner total from Leipzig already has climbed to above 20,000 and the First Army has captured more than 1,000 88-millimeter guns which were used in defense of the city.

The Germans made their last desperate stand at the city hall, at the railroad station and from underground shelters near Napoleon's statue in the southeastern part of the city.

The Second and Sixty-ninth Divisions met in the center of the city late yesterday after clearing out all resistance except around the railroad station and city hall, where the Nazi commander took refuge and refused to surrender.

At dawn today the doughboys attacked a group of 200 Germans holding out at the railroad station and then stormed the city hall against 250 of the enemy.

The Americans began a strong drive at dawn and during the day swept through this fifth largest city of Germany with crushing power. The drive developed some of the weirdest situations of the war—with the German civilians cheering the entry of the Americans and an American general demanding the city's surrender by telephone.

From the west, south and east the troops of the First Army closed on the city after breaking through a belt of more than 1,200 guns. They moved down roads washed by a warm sun and sprinkled with blossoms from blooming fruit trees.

Thousands of German civilians crawled out of their hiding places as the battle passed and clustered on the streets to watch the Americans go by and sometimes to wave and cheer with gratitude that the war was over for them. White flags waved from each building.   □

Colditz, Germany, April 19 — Gay, debonair Wing Comdr. Douglas Bader, famed legless pilot of the R.A.F. who was shot down over France three and a half years ago, wants most of all to "get another squirt at the bloody Hun," now that he is free from German internment.

"Just give me one more shot at those goons," begged the thirty-five-year-old fighter pilot who became one of Britain's great aces with two artificial legs. "I'll never be satisfied until I do."

The laughing, dark-haired hero built up during his prison life an abiding hatred of the Germans and a burning thirst for revenge for indignities heaped on him since he was captured in August, 1941, after his plane collided with another.

He was one of a thousand or so liberated Monday from the great, gray Colditz prison where the Nazis sent Allied captives who would not submit to imprisonment elsewhere. These prisoners had been classed as special enemies of the fatherland, and most attempted to escape from time to time.

Bader had twenty-five planes to his credit when his plane was damaged over Lille.

"I had to jettison one of my legs," he said, laughing as if it were a great joke on himself. "I felt like a bloody fool parachuting down with only one leg."

The Germans found his leg and it was fixed so that he could wear it. None of the Nazis thought the legless flier would try to escape from the French hospital in which he was confined. But one night he tried, sliding down a rope of tied bedsheets. He was caught. For punishment, "those goons" for two weeks wouldn't give him the new leg the R.A.F. had dropped for him when his colleagues learned of his loss.

"It was a magnificent example of how the German mind works," he chuckled. "They wouldn't give me my legs. Two goons carried me while another carried my legs and an officer marched along in front."

Four more times Bader tried to escape. He failed.

Annoyed, the Germans sent him to Colditz prison two years ago. Even there Bader had a try at escaping. Friends tried to construct a glider to be launched from the roof. But the Germans stumbled on to it.   □

Buchenwald Prison, Germany, April 22 — Eight American congressmen walked among the horrors of Buchenwald prison today and got shocked eyewitness proof of a Nazi world in which human life was not worth that of an animal.

They came at the personal invitation of Gen. Dwight D. Eisenhower, who wanted them to see for themselves this village where decency was torn aside and men died like beasts in one of Germany's worst butcher shops.

"This is barbarism at its worst," said Representative Gordon Canfield (Rep.), New Jersey, "and it is a bad commentary on civilization. General Eisenhower has presented proof of the atrocities. This bears out everything he or anyone else has said."

With Canfield were Representatives Manasco (Dem.), Alabama; Henry Jackson (Dem.), Washington; Earl Wilson (Rep.), Indiana; Albert Rains (Dem.), Alabama; Eugene Worley (Dem.), Texas; Marion T. Bennett (Rep.), Missouri, and Frances E. Walter (Dem.), Pennsylvania. They were in England on various missions when they received the invitation from Eisenhower to make a special trip to Buchenwald.

Each said he was shocked almost beyond belief at what he saw and was told by the prisoners.

The Americans liberated 21,000 prisoners in Buchenwald eleven days ago and conditions have improved considerably since then, but there is no way to erase this tragedy as long as the shambles of humanity who were the prisoners wander about the place waiting until somebody takes them home.

Hundreds of Americans, British—and German civilians from the nearby town of Weimar—visit the camp daily to see the living dead and be convinced that the report of Nazi atrocities is not just propaganda.

Behind one building was the most gruesome sight I have ever seen, bodies piled up on each other, like hogs, ready for mass burial. They were pitifully thin and wasted, with the skin tight over bones and purple faces contorted into expressions of suffering. They simply starved to death.

Beside this stack of forty bodies was a truck with some sixty naked dead. Their bodies with names and prison numbers tattooed on the arms were like something out of a nightmare.

In the courtyard nearby was a pile of ashes and bits of bone, the remains of the dead burned in the twelve-furnace crematory. In the furnace grates lay blackened portions of skulls, and in one was a body which the fire had not entirely consumed.

Below the furnaces was a room from which the prisoners said none of their number ever emerged alive. Along the walls were hooks like those in a butcher shop. Bodies, and the prisoners said some that still had life, were hung there until the furnaces were ready.

Yet, somehow, the dead were not as pitiful as those hulks of men and boys walking about the place. There was death in their eyes, but they still moved and talked—zombies created by the Nazis.

Whenever a vehicle stopped these people crowded around it, staring with vacant eyes.

In one barracks which had housed Nazi SS troops, the American camp commandant, Maj. L. C. Schmuhl of Michigan City, Ind., had put 800 children, most of whom had been evacuated from the dread Oswiecim camp in Poland by the Germans.

The youngest of them was a boy who had spent four of his eight years as a prisoner of the Nazis.

He remembers nothing but prison life. He has no recollection of his father or mother or any life except that within Buchenwald.

There was another nine-year-old who had been a prisoner for three years. He has the face of a sixteen-year-old. One of the boys was bald and gray; his eyes were those of an old man.

Most of them are Polish Jews who were brought to Buchenwald to work. None of them knew what had become of their families. Some had a faint remembrance of their mothers and fathers.

For months their daily diet had been a piece of bread, a small bit of margarine and a liter (about thirty-four ounces) of thin soup.

Their arms were thin and emaciated and there was the look of starvation in all their faces.

But now they are getting milk, bread, soup, butter, jam, honey, sugar, eggs, chocolate, peas, food captured from the German Army and now being used to feed Buchenwald's thousands.

The Americans are caring for some 5,000 patients suffering from typhoid, typhus, dysentery, tuberculosis and malnutrition.

The biggest job of the American authorities is feeding and sanitation. Of the 5,000 ill, Williams estimated that ninety per cent can be saved by proper diet, blood transfusions, glucose and saline injections. Since January 1, an estimated 15,000 prisoners died in Buchenwald, principally from starvation.

When the Americans took over the camp the death rate was about one hundred a day, but now it has dropped to less than thirty a day. □

Kössern, Germany, April 25 — Thousands of terrified German civilians frantically tried to get through the American lines on the Mulde River today to escape the advancing Russians, who are nearing a junction with the U.S. First Army.

The Germans are trudging along the roads in straggling groups, carrying bundles of food and clothing or riding bicycles and covered wagons.

There is no escape for them, however, as orders have come down the line that German civilians are not to be permitted to pass through the American front.

"We cannot permit these people to clutter up the roads and impede our operations," one officer said.

The Americans did accept a column of several hundred wounded German soldiers who were brought into the lines in ambulances, trucks and other vehicles along with five German nurses and ten other women.

The exact locations of the Russians are not known, but rumors sweep the American front that they are very near, and American cub reconnaissance planes have spotted columns of troops moving west of the Elbe River.

Not even the tears of a blonde, blue-eyed woman refugee who said she was a princess, cousin of the Prince of Hesse and a distant relative of the British royal family, moved the doughboy guards.

The princess, with a heavy pack on her back, stood with a group of civilians near the bridge. Her husband, Otto Vossler, who said he was a former Rockefeller fellow and professor of American history at the University of Leipzig, sent word to Lt. Col. William A. Smith of Wyoming, asking to "exchange a few words with you."

Smith went across the bridge and talked to the couple. Vossler told him he had studied at Harvard and the University of Wisconsin and was at the Brookings Institute in Washington, D.C., from 1925 to 1927. He said he married the princess last August and that they lived in Leipzig until recently, when they were bombed out and had to move to Grimma, east of the Mulde.

Given a brief fill-in on the horrors of the camp, and the maltreatment and slaughter of many nationalities, she said, "We had nothing to do with that; we know nothing about it."

But she and her husband were not permitted to cross. ☐

With the U.S. Sixty-ninth Division, April 25 (12 midnight) — An American infantry officer and a Russian private squirmed across a girder of a blown bridge in the Elbe River today, pounded each other on the back and shook hands to seal a historic meeting of Gen. Hodges' First Army with Marshal Ivan S. Konev's First Ukrainian Army group.

"Put it there," were the first words Second Lt. William D. Robertson, Los Angeles, called to his Red Army friend in the bizarre meeting at 4:40

p.m. over the waters of the Elbe at Torgau, twenty-eight miles northeast of Leipzig.

It was one of at least three contacts with the Russians made by men of the Sixty-ninth Division.

The union of the two great armies climaxed sensational drives from the west and east and ended intense suspense along the front over which unit would be the first to make the junction.

The Sixty-ninth Division is commanded by Maj. Gen. Emil F. Reinhardt, Detroit, Mich. It won the historic honor of making the first contact with patrols.

Just who was the first individual to meet the Russians was not entirely clear at this writing, but Robertson got a big share of the credit because he was the first to bring back proof to his division headquarters. The proof was a Russian major, captain, lieutenant and private.

One of the first to meet the Russians—if not the first—was Lt. Albert L. Kotzebue of Houston, Texas. (A.P. Correspondent Hal Boyle said Kotzebue was the first.)

The happy Russians, beaming at everyone, were brought into the crowded command post of the division for a celebration of the event.

Each of them made a speech which was interpreted for the throng.

"This is a great day on the meeting of two nations," said Maj. Anaphim Larionov of Konev's Fifty-eighth Guards Division. "We extend warmest greetings and congratulations on the destruction of Nazism. We hope this meeting will be the basis for peace in the world to come."

Capt. Vassili Petrov Nedov added:

"We have wanted to meet you for a long time. This is a great holiday for the whole world."

This linkup with the Russians was one of the strangest stories of the entire war and was not even anticipated when a group of Americans set out in a jeep at 10 a.m.

Among the Americans in the jeep were Cpl. James J. McDonnell of Peabody, Miss., Pfc. Frank P. Huff, Washington, Va., and Pfc. Paul Staub of the Bronx, New York.

This was the story as told by Lt. William Robertson of Los Angeles, Calif.:

"Our company commander sent us out this morning to chase civilians off the roads. They were piling into Wurtzen in droves, running away from the Russians.

"You have no idea of the number of people on the roads. There were thousands of them and among them were many Allied prisoners of war who escaped from prison camps.

"German troops had thrown their weapons into ditches and were standing waiting to be taken prisoner.

"We kept on the move, now and then getting off the congested roads. We met about thirty British boys who were headed for Wurtzen. We told them where they could get food.

"The British told us they had seen some wounded Americans up the road at Torgau.

"We went on east to Torgau and found these Americans who had been held by the Germans to be shot, because they were accused of espionage. They had been in Bavaria quite a while. We got some German guns for them and they guarded German prisoners who had thrown down their arms.

"We could hear small arms fire very close and they told us the Russians were just across the river.

"We left our jeep and went down on foot toward the river. We rigged up a big white flag so they wouldn't shoot at us.

"We didn't know what the Russian uniform looked like and I wasn't sure the Russians would recognize our uniform.

"Near the Elbe was a very large castle with a high tower. "We broke into a drugstore and got some paint. I painted four red stripes on our white flag and a field of blue, because I figured the Russians would recognize the American flag better than anything else.

"I climbed into the tower and stuck my head out and waved the flag. They stopped firing for a while.

"I yelled, 'American, Tovarish, Kamerad.'

"They were yelling at me from across the river and fired two flares but I didn't see any flares to fire back.

"I left the flag flying and went down and found a Russian who had been a prisoner of the Germans. He shouted at the Russians to stop firing and I saw one Russian start across the bridge which was partly blown." ☐

With the United States Sixty-ninth Division, April 26 — There was singing and dancing and music on the banks of the Elbe today as doughboys of Gen. Hodges's First Army and jubilant troops of Marshal Ivan Konev's First Ukrainian Army celebrated their historic junction symbolizing the defeat of Nazi Germany.

Americans and Russians slapped each other on the back, gave each other bear hugs and sat in the warm sunshine drinking champagne from beer mugs and toasting the great occasion of the meeting of the two armies yesterday.

It was an American infantry officer and a Russian private who met on that occasion. They squirmed across a girder of a blown-up bridge above the Elbe. "Put it there," said Second Lieut. William D. Robertson of Los Angeles. It was 4:40 p.m., April 25, 1945, at midstream over the Elbe at Torgau, twenty-eight miles northeast of Leipzig. It was one of at least three contacts made with the Russians by men of the Sixty-ninth Division, commanded by Maj. Gen. Emil F. Reinhardt of Detroit.

Not in all this long war have there been scenes such as those enacted today in the town of Torgau, on the west bank of the Elbe, and across the river in the Red Army encampment where Russian and American troops saw each other for the first time and began to get acquainted despite the handicaps of language. It was enough that they were allies and had whipped the enemy to open the way for this joining of armies in weird Torgau. Parts of the city are deserted and ghostly. In other sections Russian and American troops whooped, sang and formed friendships within a few minutes of meeting.

The whole day was almost too fantastic to believe from the time a column set out in the morning to meet the Russians until dusk settled over the Elbe—and there was nothing more to be wrung from hours crammed with emotional outbursts.

Yesterday, before the junction was effected, the road from the Mulde River to the Elbe was a vivid picture of defeated Germany etched in the pain, misery and fear of people fleeing along the roads by thousands before the Russians, and hoping vainly to find safety within the American lines. Never before had American troops looked on scenes that showed so clearly Germany's defeat. But this darkness faced by the German people only accentuated the joyful meeting of the Allied troops.

On the east bank of the Mulde, thousands of civilians were gathered, hoping that perhaps the Americans would let them into their lines before the arrival of the Russians. They had stacked their belongings into little carts which seemed as though they would crumple under the weight. Bedding, goods, clothing, pots, pans and huge bundles burdened the carts hauled along the highway.

There were incongruous lines of wagons with their tops covered by rich Oriental rugs and wagons pulled by tractors or automobiles or anything that would make them mobile. Mothers hauled their children along in carts, and aged people rode in resignation staring at the passing American vehicles. Women stumbled along with huge bundles on their backs in the choking dust, just as the frightened people of Belgium and France fled before the Germans five years ago. Fatigue and fear lined their faces. There was a frantic urgency in their attitudes.

At one point a bridge was being repaired, and hundreds stood in the fields beside the road waiting for a chance to start moving again. There were old and young, ill and crippled with personal belongings hurriedly packed as the Russians drew near. The roadside was littered with the debris of this army of misery—scattered clothing and trash and boxes and household goods. The burden was too great for many, so they tossed aside the excess weight.

One of the strangest sights consisted of columns of German soldiers marching along the road to the west without anyone to guard them. Some of them were still carrying their arms. Nobody had taken the trouble to disarm them, but they made no pretense of resistance. They were marching voluntarily into captivity.

Here on the road was a picture of things to come, with the German Army in complete disintegration. These men had had enough and they were quitting the fight. I saw one walking along with two concussion grenades swinging on his belt. Many men still carried their sidearms.

These scenes were comical at times. It was not unusual to see liberated British prisoners of war walking in long columns alongside of German soldiers and Hitler Youth whose Nazi indoctrination melted in their fear of the Russians. It was a league of nations on the march, with every country of Europe represented and urged forward by differing reasons.

"Where do you think they are going?" asked Lieut. William Gist of North Platte, Neb. "There isn't enough room for all these people in our lines."   □

With U.S. and Russian Troops on the Elbe, April 27 — Pfc. Leo Kasinsky hitch-hiked to the Elbe today, just to be sure Brooklyn was represented at the meeting of the Americans and Russians—and the Russians gave him "the best time I ever had in my life."

Anyone living who has seen a Kasinsky beam will know just how Leo looked as he hitched another ride back to his unit. He was tired, stuffed with food and drink, and carried memories which he and his pals will never forget.

"It was like this," Kasinsky said. "A bunch of us wanted to go up and see the Russians, so we hitched a ride to Torgau and we got across the river. We were standing right there on the bank when Major General Huebner and the Russian corps commander met.

"We were just a bunch of G.I.'s who had come up for the ride, and there wasn't any higher rank in our crowd than a staff sergeant, but that didn't matter to those Russians. Their officers treated us just like we had their rank.

"It didn't seem to make any difference to them whether an American was an officer or a plain G.I. They gave us a wonderful meal and we had about sixty toasts. Boy, they don't even drink like that in Brooklyn.

"They are about the friendliest people I ever met, and it is hard to tell an officer from an enlisted man when they get together socially. But believe me they are disciplined troops. They are fine troops."

S/Sgt. May Afanesko, Bairdford, Pa., who speaks excellent Russian, felt the same way about the Russian troops.

"All those Russians want to do is fight and kill Germans," he said. "They are regular guys, and their officers are just like G.I.'s."

Lt. Col. Robert E. O'Brien, Washington, D.C., was impressed by the Red troops.

"They look like wonderful soldiers," he said. "They are tough, but they are not mean. They are just good soldiers."

"They really are a rugged bunch of boys," said Pvt. Thomas J. Barnes, Richmond Hill, N.Y., after an afternoon with the Red troops.

It was the consensus, the boys are glad these barrel-chested, thick-legged, tough-looking fighters are on our side. □

Soviet First Ukrainian Army Group Headquarters, May 5 — General Omar N. Bradley smilingly presented the U.S. Legion of Merit to Marshal Ivan S. Konev today at a gay meeting of the two army group commanders who played major roles in the defeat of Germany.

At this headquarters of the Soviet commander, Bradley hung the cerise-ribboned medal around Konev's neck as a token of appreciation of Konev's work.

Konev said he accepted the award not as a personal honor but as a symbol of the achievements of the Russian and American armies together, and exclaimed, "Long live the American Army!"

Bradley and Konev met in a German country home some fifty miles from Berlin. Bradley and his staff and a group of correspondents were wined, dined and lavishly entertained.

Although they had to use interpreters, the two commanders hit it off well from the first. The affair was strictly social, with no discussion of military matters.

Konev, a smooth-shaven man, is gray and balding like Bradley but stockier and half a head shorter.

Konev had set the stage for his meeting with Bradley and it was an impressive drive to his headquarters east of the Elbe.

Russian and American troops were intermingled along the road. Columns of Soviet horse-drawn vehicles were mixed in with American trucks, tanks and armored cars. Most of the Russian vehicles had Red banners and flags on them, carryovers from the May Day celebration.

The villages through which the column passed seemed deserted. Obviously the German citizens had orders to get off the streets and stay inside. There was no sign of civilians during the entire drive—except for droves of liberated Russians, French, Poles and Czechs walking along the roads on the long march home.

Oven the entrance to Konev's headquarters was a Red banner with the words in English and Russian: "Long Live the Victory of the British-Soviet-American Military Alliances."

As soon as Bradley and his party arrived they were seated at tables piled with food. The dinner continued for three hours with Konev, Bradley and others offering a series of toasts.

The banquet was something out of old Russia. The Americans stuffed themselves until they could not eat another bite. This is what they had— white, black and toasted bread, red and black caviar, cheese, smoked salmon, sardines, two kinds of salami, potato salad with cream sauce, lettuce in sour cream dressing, smoked white fish, smoked sturgeon, jellied chicken, herring, hard-boiled eggs, fresh butter, four kinds of wine, vodka, peas, onions, baked chicken with cream sauce, fried chicken, potatoes, baked pigeons, partridge, pork, beef, frozen custard, cakes and chocolate candy.   □

With U.S. First Army, Germany, May 7 — The announcement of complete victory over the Germans comes as an anti-climax to American doughboys who have seen the German Army disintegrate.

They are now asking themselves: "Where do we go from here?"

It is a strange ending to a strange war, an ending nobody could have quite visualized and without the dramatic conclusion most of us had pictured. Suddenly the war just melted away into nothingness and the guns were still.

The war came to an end for this army some weeks ago. That is why V-E Day will be little more than a symbol to troops who had seen victory in the making for days. It took no official announcement for them to realize it was all over.

There is no enemy across no-man's land to come forward with upraised hands in final surrender. Across the Mulde River are the Russians. There is no desolate battlefield and the doughboys are not in foxholes. They sat in the warm sun cleaning their battle-worn gear and weapons.

There are no wild celebrations among the troops. These men have seen too much death and suffering. They have seen this Nazi world come apart at the seams and its miserable people straggling along the roads of defeat, marked more plainly with signs of a fallen nation than any proclamation ever could.□

With the U.S. First Army, [May 8] — Among the men who won the victory in Europe there was a strange apathy today to the official announcement that the war had ended.

It was warm, the sun shone and no guns thundered the sullen rumble of death, pain and destruction. It seemed unreal, and the men who had been in combat could hardly realize it was over even though the fighting for them had been ended for several days and they knew that Germany had collapsed.

"This is the day we looked forward to for a long time," said Cpl. Julian Emig of Brooklyn, N.Y. "Now that it's here we don't want to do any of the things we planned. A year ago we were all planning how we would get drunk on V-E Day. Now look at us, doing the same things we did before."

There was only a simple ceremony at U.S. First Army Headquarters. The American flag was raised over the headquarters for the first time on the continent by military police, who then lowered it to half staff in accordance with regulations on the thirty-day period of mourning for the late President Roosevelt.

Doughboys sat along the west bank of the Mulde River discussing their chances of getting home before going to the Pacific, for most soldiers feel their next move will be to fight the Japanese.

Across the river the Russians were moving in to occupy German territory up to the boundaries set in agreements reached between the Soviet Union, the United States and Britain.

Moving along with the Russian columns are many liberated American prisoners of war whose V-E Day came when the Russians freed them from German prison camps.

"Liberty was so near I couldn't wait to be released and just took off from Luckenwald," said Cpl. Fred W. Miller of Tillamook, Ore. He was captured in Italy when the Forty-fifth Infantry Division crossed the Volturno River. With him was Cpl. Cicero H. Falls of Kings Mountain, N.C., who was captured at Faid Pass. □

Eight

___

RETURN TO NORMANDY,
MAY–JUNE 1945

Carentan, Normandy, May 26 — The final clean-up of the old battlefields of Normandy is disclosing the appalling waste of war as salvage crews uncover everything from jeeps to bulldozers in the green fields and hedgerows where the Yanks won their toe-hold in Western Europe almost a year ago.

There are few troops left now in the "Omaha" and "Utah" beach areas which once swarmed with soldiers. The little Normandy towns look almost deserted and only an occasional G.I. is seen on the streets. Normandy once more belongs to the Normans.

About the only troops left are prison camp personnel, hospital workers and crews whose job is to salvage as much ammunition and equipment as possible from the fields.

The clean-up job has fallen to the Seventeenth Ordnance Battalion commanded by Lieut. Col. Lloyd Littlefield, Springfield, Mass.

"We're pretty much of a oddity" Littlefield said. "We did a clean-up job in England, gathering up all the ammunition and leftover equipment and now we are doing the same job in Normandy."

He estimated some 47,000 tons of ammunition were left on the beaches and his battalion is shipping about 1,200 tons daily to the Unites States and Pacific. Much of the ammunition has to be reboxed.

Right now Littlefield and his men are sweating out removal of 400 tons of nitroglycerine which is staked in one field—enough explosive to blow out a large chunk of Normandy if anything goes haywire.

In cleaning up ammunition dumps Littlefield's men have discovered an amazing amount of equipment worth many thousands of dollars which was abandoned in the hedgerows as the units pulled out to other areas.

Besides jeeps, trucks and trailers the crews have found forty-two pieces of heavy equipment including big D-4 tractor crawlers, D-7 tractor crawlers with hydraulic brakes, tractor cranes and tank dozers.

The battalion is helped in the clean-up work by German and Italian prisoners and by Czechs, Poles, Russians and other nationals who are concentrated in civilian labor camps.

Littlefield estimated the job of cleaning up the Normandy dumps will be finished in another three months. □

Paris, May 30 — Events which thrill the world and change the course of history sometimes are as comical as they are dramatic when the full story becomes known.

Such was the case when the U.S. First Army's Ninth Armored Division seized the Remagen Bridge and established an unexpected bridgehead across the Rhine.

All the story of that spectacular development in the last drive to defeat the German Army was not told at the time, simply because all the facts did not become known until days after the gallant charge led by Sgt. Alexander A. Drabik of Holland, Ohio, which captured the span.

The capture was not in the plans. Nobody expected it and Major Gen. John W. Leonard, commander of the Ninth Armored Division, found himself standing right in the middle of a history-making military operation which grew up like Topsy [in Harriet Beecher Stowe's *Uncle Tom's Cabin*].

For months, the high command had been making plans on how and where to cross the Rhine. In brief, the First Army had begun to attack across the Roer River merely to protect the right flank of Lieut. Gen. William H. Simpson's Ninth Army. Once on the Rhine, the First Army of Gen. Courtney H. Hodges was to stop while the Canadian, British and Ninth Armies massed their power for a grand crossing of the lower Rhine.

But Drabik's charge threw the Army into turmoil, all the way up to Supreme headquarters. And the Army would have been in even greater turmoil had it known that for the first twelve hours, the First Army was holding the bridgehead with one company of infantry.

Luckily the Germans were more confused than the Americans. Three companies of infantry went across the Remagen Bridge that night of March 7, but for some unexplained reason two companies returned to the west bank.

The situation began to sort itself out the next day and troops and armor flowed across despite the fact that columns were snarled in one of the biggest traffic jams of the invasion.

When the order came down to exploit the bridgehead, everybody took to the roads at once. The confusion was magnificent to see. Columns were piled up for mile upon mile. An ordinary three-hour jeep ride stretched into seven or eight hours. As units were fed across the bridge, they were sent directly into action.

The situation reminded one of signs on the road near Major Gen. Terry Allen's 104th Division: "Front line 500 yards ahead. Dismount and begin fighting."

A few weeks after the Remagen bridgehead was seized, this correspondent sat with General Leonard in his command post hearing him discuss the progress of the campaign and the fine work done by his Ninth Armored Division. He recalled the capture of the bridge and gave this version:

"That morning I sent out my combat teams toward the river, which was our objective. Late in the afternoon, one of my commanders called and said, 'General, we've got that bridge.'

"I said, 'What bridge?'

"He said, 'Why that big Ludendorff railroad bridge. We've got men across and we're holding a bridgehead across the Rhine.'

"And I said, 'Gosh, why did you do that! Now we'll all get in trouble.'"

One will always like the general for that story because his was such a normal reaction. But after that first uncertainty and when the high command gave the green light to exploit the bridgehead, Leonard's Ninth Armored Division distinguished itself many more times in daring exploits.　　□

Omaha Beach, Normandy, France, June 2 — Time and the endless tides mercifully have wiped out most of the signs of death and destruction along this invasion beach hallowed by the deaths of so many American youths.

A strange peace has come at last to Omaha Beach, which a year ago was a hellish inferno.

One year ago, on June 6, a mighty armada stood off shore disgorging invading troops. Cruisers and destroyers were racing in with guns blazing to smash at the enemy entrenched on the ridge overlooking the beach—to smash blockhouses and pillboxes from which Germans were raking the beach with a murderous fire.

Men were dying by the scores or their bodies were being torn by flying chunks of steel. Boats were sinking before they could get their human cargoes to the water's edge. Tanks, trucks and guns were being knocked out by enemy fire before they could get into action. Doughboys hugged their bodies against the shallow cover of a gravel embankment in a common misery of fear.

Along with this heartbreaking human wreckage, the sands were strewn with a vast litter of clothing, bedding, helmets, life preservers, rifles, shoes and personal belongings carried ashore by soldiers or washed up by the surf. There was the sight and smell of death on the beach and the air was heavy with the fumes of cordite and curses of fighting men.

But waves and shifting sands have covered most of the signs of the great invasion battle. Rusting skeletons of ships still are clutched in the brown sand as gaunt monuments to a monumental victory. They lie with broken backs or with gaping holes in their sides just as they died in battle.

High on the beaches are LCVP's, some of them with ramps lowered as they were when a shell hit them. They stand in an orderly row as though they just had raced in to put troops ashore.

Ships and boats have the beach to themselves except for a few French wandering about and a group of working German prisoners.

A sturdy, peasant girl walked along the hard-packed sands clinging to the arms of two grinning country youths. They hardly seemed to notice the broken ships. She waved gaily, "Aloo, Babee! Okay, Babee!" and the three laughed merrily at this demonstration of English learned since D-Day.

At the gravel bank which gave cover to assault troops a year ago, German prisoners shoveled stone into trucks. There were no guards, only Negro drivers lolling in the truck cabs. The stone was to be crushed and spread along the walkways winding through Saint Laurent Cemetery on the ridgetop where crosses stand like ghostly sentries looking out across the gray, green channel.

The only sounds were the rustling of the waves, the high-pitched laughter of the Norman girl, the scrape of shovels in the gravel and the singing of birds on the ridge. Occasionally, the Germans paused in their work and looked out into the water at the row of sunken ships which once formed a breakwater for beach loading.

There was a curious sense of unreality to the scene for anyone who remembered that D-Day carnage. Yet many old landmarks remain—blockhouses, pillboxes, a shelled building, dugouts and crumbling trenches on the ridge.

Against the ridge above that part of the beach which ironically was called "Easy Red" still stands a concrete blockhouse with the snout of an 88 sticking from the embrasure. Here was the First Infantry Division's first beachhead command post from which Maj. Gen. Clarence R. Huebner directed the spearheading drive of his men.

Now the blockhouse is being made into a monument to the victory on Omaha Beach. German prisoners have terraced the slopes of the ridge and sodded it, covering foxholes where so many troops dug in to escape the shells screaming into the beach.

A half-mile below the blockhouse is a ten-foot square enclosed by ropes strung from sturdy white posts. The sign says:

"This marks the site of the first American cemetery in France.

"World War Two.

"Since moved to American cemetery number one."

The bodies of men buried a few minutes after landing have been taken up on the windswept ridge to Saint Laurent Cemetery. German prisoners are landscaping the cemetery and building gravel pits. Some perhaps were defenders of the beach.

The French have not forgotten the memorable day when the Americans arrived to liberate them. Every day groups visit the beaches and cemeteries where the first American dead were buried in France.

At La Cambe Cemetery, a brown-haired French girl, Hélène Chapelle, wandered through rows of crosses until she found the cross bearing the name of James Simonian of New York State. There with her mother and brother she knelt and read a letter which the youth's mother had sent to her to be read at the grave. Hélène had been a friend to James' brother, Adam, and each Sunday she comes to place flowers on the grave.

Madame Chapelle bowed her head and tears coursed down her cheeks as the girl spoke in a low voice, reading the letter from an American mother to her dead son:

"Dear Son James:

"You've been away from me since November 18, 1942. Day and night continuously for two years I waited for your letters that gave me hope and faith and cause to live. You always wrote—'My Dearest Mother, my faith and hope are you.'

"My dearest and unfortunate son, on June 16, 1944, like a lamb you died and left me alone without hope. Day and night I weep and grieve and miss you and still you are gone.

"Dearest James, your one thought was always for me so that I might have good health and so that I would live well. Dearest son, I am living, yes, with the blood you gave me so that I might live and as long as I live I will keep your memories alive; and when I die the memories you left will always live on and never be forgotten.

"These few lines I write you humbly with unsteady hands and with blurring eyes, remembering, my dearest James, that your last words to me were, 'Mother, like the wind I came and like the wind I shall go.'

"My unlucky son, I hope and know that your brothers, Adam at the German front and Jerry in the Pacific, will take revenge on the enemy for what you suffered. Your brothers, like men, will always suffer your loss because, my son, your loss was great. In our hearts it has left a painful ache.

"Many friends tell me that you enter into their dreams and say 'I am not dead. When the war is over, I will come home.' And I still live with that hope.

"Dearest son, now you lie in a foreign land and may you rest peacefully until I come, and I will come kneeling with prayers to kiss you."

And when she had finished Hélène placed the flowers on the grave and Madame Chapelle lit two candles which burned with bright teardrop flames.

□

Index

Openrod, 326
Operation Overlord, xxiii
Oppenhof, Franz, 330–31
Oran, 53
O'Reilly, John, 119
O'Reilly, Tex, xxiii
Orglandes, 138, 151
Orléans, 211, 215
Ortman, Earl, 12
O'Sullivan, J. Reilly, 6
Oswiecim concentration camp, 350
Otto, N. E., 173
Oujda, 16
Overseas visa, 119

P-38 Lightning, 48, 263
P-47 Thunderbolt, 263
Pacific Theater, 358, 361
Packard, Reynolds, xviii, 55
Packman, John L., 21
Packwood, Burleigh, 23, 105
Paderborn, 337, 338, 341, 343–44
Paestum, 53
Palais de Justice, 208, 213
Palatinate, 325
Palazzo Venezia, 40, 46
Palermo, x, 29
Pangborn, Clyde, 12
Panzer Grenadier, 37
Paratroops, 128, 134, 135, 138, 143, 167–68
Paris, x, 5, 201, 202, 203, 207, 208–23, 228,
    229, 233, 242, 266, 281, 289–90, 362–63
  advance on, 211–12, 215–16, 218
  Allied entry into, 208–12, 213–15
  battle for, 212–13
  Chamber of Deputies, 208, 213
  Champs-Elysées, 208, 213
  Eiffel Tower, 212
  Hôtel Crillon, 208, 213
  Hôtel Matignon, 221, 222
  Île de la Cité, 208, 210, 213
  liberation of, xix, xxi, 210–12, 216–17
  Louvre, 208, 213, 342
  The Luxembourg, 209, 210, 211, 212,
    213, 214
  The Madeleine, 208, 213
  Notre Dame Cathedral, 208, 210, 212
  Palais de Justice, 208, 213
  Place de la Concorde, 208, 213
  Préfecture of Police, 208, 213
  Préfecture of the Seine, 208, 213
  Quai d'Orsay, 208, 213
  Tuileries, 208, 213
Pas-de-Calais, 202

Pasternik, Chester, 172
Patch, Alexander M., 325
Patterson, George, 47
Patton, George S., x, xxii, 202, 227, 319, 344
Pearl Harbor, xvii
Pechacek, Melvin, 290–91
Peresich, Giles, 47
Périers, 191
Périers Road, 182
Perkins, John C., 63
Perry Rifles, 319
Persano, 73, 74
Pershing tank, 315–16
Pétain, Henri-Philippe, 217–19
Pete (Blenheim pilot), 14–15
Peters, Leonard, 122
Petersberg Hotel, 325
Petersberg Mountain, 325
Pfeiffer, Ken, 60
USS Philadelphia, 50, 51
Philippine Islands, 7, 267
Phillips, Steve, Jr., 329
Phony War, 4–5
Pickens, J. W., 43
Piehler, Kurt, xiv
Pielads, Armand, 31
Pietravariano, 55
Pingsheim, 298
Pinsince, Adrian, 207
Pioneer troops, 48
Piper Cub, 125, 229, 351
Place de la Concorde, 208, 213
Plumlee, Glenn, 160
Plunket, 50
Poland, 14, 176, 340
Polenberg, 252–53
Poles, 297, 341, 357, 361
Political commissars, 185
Poll, Francis, 95
Pontine marshes, 57
Ponza, 45, 46
Poppe, Glenn, 252–53
Porchia, Mount, 95–96
Port Lyautey, 138
Porter, Mackenzie, 62
Pouska, Alexander, Jr., 131
Préfecture of Police, 208, 213
Préfecture of the Seine, 208, 213
Presidential election, 275
Prison camp, 346–47, 348
Prisoners of war, 227–28, 273, 312, 332–34,
    334–35, 336, 345–47, 348, 352, 355, 358
Production of war material, 284–85
Profiteering, 54